Run Run Run

by Fred Wilt

RUN RUN RUN
by Fred Wilt

SBN 911520-08-2

First Printing, Dec. 1974
Second Printing, Dec. 1965
Third Printing, Feb. 1968
Fourth Printing, Jan. 1970
Fifth Printing, Sept. 1971
Sixth Printing, Jan. 1974
Seventh Printing, Feb. 1976

Also by Fred Wilt:
How They Train, 2nd edition, 1973:
- Vol. I: Middle Distances
- Vol. II: Long Distances
- Vol. III: Sprinting and Hurdling

Illustrated Guide to Olympic Track and Field Techniques (with Tom Ecker), 1969
Mechanics without Tears, 1970
International Track and Field Coaching Encyclopedia (with Tom Ecker), 1970
Motivation and Coaching Psychology (with Ken Bosen), 1971
The Jumps: Contemporary Theory, Technique and Training, 1972
The Throws: Contemporary Theory, Technique and Training, 1973

Book Division of Track & Field News

Contents

Author's Note

This volume was originally intended to include only training trends and an overview of cross-country and middle-distance running in various parts of the world. In examining the chapters submitted by the contributing authors, I realized the contents as planned would be heavily weighted in favor of "how" to train; with little comment being made in regard to "why" training should be done in the manner suggested.

Due to an attitude of "athletics maturity" acquired in recent years, coaches and athletes are no longer content to know only "how" training should be done. Today they want to know the "why" of training as well.

For a solution to this problem, I turned to the backlog of material accumulated for eventual publication in "Track Technique", the quarterly journal of technical track and field athletics, of which I have served as Honorary Editor for the past four years. This material included translations of results of recent Russian and German research in training. A number of these translations have been synthesized and included in this book in attempting to identify some of the answers as to "why" training should be done as it is recommended.

I should like to express thanks to each of the authors who have contributed chapters. Special acknowledgement and appreciation is extended to Editor Toni Nett of "Die Lehre der Leichtathletik", published in Berlin, for permission to reprint translations from that periodical. I am exceedingly grateful to Bernhard A. Schettkoe, Phil Diamond, Ernie Westerhove, Gar Williams, Brother G. Luke, Robert Z. Opiola, Dr. Nolan Fowler, Glenn B. Hoidale, and Charles Sullivan for the translations reprinted herein - a labor of love in each instance. I should like to acknowledge the assistance provided by Professor Elliott Plese of Colorado State University, Coach Bill Welch of Terre Haute Gerstmeyer High School in Indiana, New Trier High School Coach Benjamin Almaguer of Evanston, Illinois, Ron Wallingford of McMaster University, and Coach Bill Huyck of Carleton College in reviewing the manuscript of this volume.

To my way of thinking, knowledge which is kept secret is useless. Future progress in terms of performance in running depends in part upon wide dissemination of philosophical, empirical, and scientific training knowledge. It is my hope that this book will be justified upon that basis.

Introduction

Running is the most primitive form of athletic endeavor regarded as a sport, and has been a popular form of competition from the earliest times. It occupied a prominent place in the ancient Olympic games, and continues to grow in popularity and numbers of competitors throughout the world with the passage of time.

Cross-country racing had its inception with the founding of the Crick run at Rugby School (England) in 1837, after which other famous institutions of learning also sponsored annual cross-country races. The Thames Hare and Hounds club held winter cross-country races about 30 years later, and soon thereafter many other clubs throughout England took up the sport. Cross-country racing today undoubtedly enjoys its greatest popularity in England.

English cross-country races are limited in distance for youths (over 16 and under 18 years) to 3 miles, and to 6 miles for juniors (18 to under 21 years). English championships were first helf in 1876 over the 10 miles senior distance.

The first international cross-country race was held between England and France in 1898. A cross-country race was included on the program at the 1912 Olympic Games and won by Hannes Kolehmainen (Finland), but was discontinued after Paavo Nurmi won this event again for Finland in the 1924 Olympics.

In the United States the first National Amateur Athletic Union (AAU) cross-country championship was held in 1890 and won by the New Jersey A.C. This National AAU championship is now standardized at 10,000 meters (6 miles, 376.1 yards), and is held in November or early December annually. The Intercollegiate Association of Amateur Athletes of America (IC4A) has held an annual varsity cross-country championship since 1908. These IC4A title runs have been held over the 5-mile Van Cortlandt Park course in New York City each November since 1916. The National Collegiate Athletic Association (NCAA) cross-country championship is contested annually over 4-miles at Michigan State University, East Lansing, Michigan. High Schools in the USA generally contest cross-country races over 2-miles.

The competitive cross-country season in the USA generally extends from September through November each year. The ages of high school and university cross-country competitors usually fall between 14 to 18 years, and 19 to 23 years respectively, while AAU competition is open to all athletes.

Cross-country is perhaps the most pleasant and interesting form of running training, while harrier competition over hill and dale is among the more joyfull forms of footracing. Most track competitors, including sprinters, and many field event performers include cross-country running as part of their autumn training program in preparation for the American indoor track season (December or January through mid-March annually) and the following outdoor track season (April through mid-June). There are very few cross-country runners today who are not also track competitors. Cross-country racing provides a much needed incentive and stimulus for rigorous training during the autumn preparatory period prior to track competition, during which time actual racing over the country is approached with a serious competitive attitude. The great benefit of cross-country running and racing to the conditioning process of the track performer is beyond question, and as a result the track runner in the USA who does not put in an autumn of intensive cross-country racing and training annually is indeed rare today.

While it is common knowledge that autumn cross-country running is a necessity for the track performer, the number and distance of races over the country is a matter for careful consideration. By contrast with the USA, this problem is more acute in England, where the season is much longer, and the competitive courses are often over greater distances, frequently through heavy mud and over rough terrain. In the case of American track runners, except for sprinters, this problem is usually resolved by a full season of cross-country racing, since the distances are not really excessive, the competitive season is comparatively short, and the courses are generally over relatively fast surfaces, through woods, over golf courses, and even through streets and on roads. Thus our cross-country races over fast surfaces in the USA are in reality "speed races" off the track. Neither rain, snow, sleet, or blow is permitted to cause cancellation of cross-country races, this being one of the few sports almost impregnable by adverse weather conditions.

Cross-country racing today involves the element of speed to such an extent that training for hill and dale competition bears an amazing resemblence to orthodox training for middle-distance track racing. Slow, laborious, long-distance running is regarded with skepticism by knowledgable coaches and athletes today, and indeed the value of this type slow-speed running to the conditioning process of the athlete who wants to race really fast, whether over the country or on the track, is subject to grave question, except possibly in the case of the beginner or in the early stages of training. However, slow running for one athlete may well be fast for another, depending upon individual differences, thus posing a problem worthy of careful attention.

Sprint races are those within the realm of pure speed, and include distances from 100 yards (100 meters) through 440 yards (400 meters). Those races outside the domain of pure sprinting, yet short enough for speed to occupy a decisive role, are known as the middle-distances. They range from 880 yards (800 meters) through 6-miles (10,000 meters). Short middle-distances lie between 880 yards and 2-miles (3,000 meters), while long middle-distances cover 3-miles through 6-miles. Long-distances lie between 6-miles and the marathon (26 miles, 385 yards, or 42,195 meters).

In the case of those who indulge in cross-country running for the physical and mental benefits of the exercise involved rather than competitive preparation, little instruction is necessary. Those who run cross-country as preparation for track and/or cross-country competition should plan and execute their training with care and precision. It is for the benefit of the latter group that this book has been compiled.

A Crash Program for Training Schoolboys

by Fred Wilt

This training is designed for 15-18 year old schoolboys who attend classes Monday through Friday weekly. Since this represents but one example of training, little consideration is given to such important issues as individual differences of athletes, psychology, diet, athletic injuries, and administrative efficiency in coaching. Many of the points covered in this chapter are mentioned in more detail elsewhere in this book.

In suggesting this training, the assumption is made that the athletes are healthy, well-fed, vigorous, strong, disease and disability free, robust, and entirely normal 15-18 year old lads.

When should training begin? Immediately. Don't miss a day. Ideally, runners should train the year round. World-class runners train twice daily in many instances. Even top-class high school athletes today frequently train twice daily.

Where should runners train? Wherever they can. On concrete and gravel roads during foul weather, golf courses, woods, beaches, open fields, gymnasiums, and of course on the track when weather permits. When training in bad weather with strong wind, run on a road accurately marked at 110 yard intervals which extends in the same direction as the wind. Run the fast repetitions with (in the same direction as) the wind, and recover while returning against the wind to the starting point.

The runner needs flat soled warmup shoes (cheap light-weight low-cut tennis sneakers are highly sufficient), spike-shoes, athletic supporter, socks, shorts or trunks, shirt, sweat-pants with elastic around the ankles, and sweat shirt which can be pinned, buttoned, or zippered tightly high up around the neck. In cold weather a cap which pulls down over the ears and gloves (or socks) for the hands are necessary.

Ideally an athlete should train six full months before his first race. However, custom unfortunately does not follow such extensive preliminary conditioning for runners. Four weeks or less is usually available for preliminary conditioning prior to the first competition for schoolboys in this age group. Therefore, the training suggested is made on that basis. In view of the limited four weeks preliminary conditioning period available, I regard these suggestions as a "crash" program of training.

What degree of conditioning may be expected from this 4 weeks "crash" training program? Dr. Woldeman Gerschler, famous German coach, is said to have carried out over 3,000 experiments with untrained individuals. Each of these were trained 21 days. As a result of these experiments it was determined that the heart volume can be increased one-fifth during this 21 days period of training.

Jokl and associates (American Heart Journal, Vol. 54, No. 4, pages 556-560, October, 1957) trained a normal 40 year old man for 30 days, 90 minutes per day, on calisthenics, apparatus gymnastics, weight lifting, and swimming. In the beginning, the calisthenics had to be interrupted every 2 minutes to give the subject time to recapture his breath. On the high horizontal bar he could perform one pull-up. He lifted only 20 lbs., repeating the effort up to 10 times. He swam not more than 3 lengths in the standard-size pool. After 30 days training, he went through an uninterrupted sequence of calisthenic exercises of 10 minutes duration, did 8 pull-ups on the horizontal bar, and performed a number of movements on the parallel bars and the side horse which he was unable to do 4 weeks earlier, lifted 80 lbs. 20 times in succession, and swam 12 full lengths of the pool.

These routines are simple to the extreme, and much too dogmatic.

They represent only one train of thought for a "crash" situation. There are many, many variations in workout programs, none of which are necessarily perfect for all athletes. So long as we have individual differences among athletes there will probably never be one perfect method of training for all. Most good athletes probably would have been equally successful under numerous different workout programs. Nevertheless, the training used by successful coaches and athletes do have many features in common.

Warmup.

Use the same warmup before racing or training. The following warmup is recommended for the half-miler, miler, and 2-mile cross-country runner. While fully clothed in sweat-clothes and wearing flat soled shoes, run one mile continuously in this manner: First 440 y in 3 minutes, second 440 y in 2½ minutes, third 440 y in 2 minutes. The fourth 440 y should be run alternately 50 y fast and 50 y slow until the entire full 440 y is completed. Each of the fast 50 y runs should be a bit faster than the preceding one, with the final 50 y at full speed. Then take 10 minutes for calisthenics (of the stretching variety) and changing to spike shoes before going directly into the workout. Prior to a race, lie down for 10 minutes in a warm, dry place before appearing at the starting line at least 5 minutes before the starting gun. The warmup should be taken in flat-soled shoes if at all possible. For training, especially on grass or cross-country, it is neither necessary nor always desirable to train in spiked shoes.

Warmdown.

Jog one mile in 10 minutes after each workout or race.

"Crash" Training For 2-Mile Cross-Country Racing (Age 15-18).

This is a four weeks training schedule, starting with the first day. Each workout is preceded by the above described mile warmup. Times are quoted for the purpose of illustration only. This training may be done on any suitable running surface. Ideally both the cross-country area and track may be utilized. It may be done entirely on the track when necessary. When training over unmarked surfaces, the training distances may be stepped-off for approximate measurement. End each workout with one mile of jogging in 10 minutes.

First Week.

Monday: 10 x 110 y in 20 seconds each. Walk 110 y after each.

Tuesday: 5 x 110 y in 20 seconds each. Walk 110 y after each. 2 x 880 y in 3:00 minutes each. Walk 5 minutes after each. 5 x 110 y in 20 seconds each. Walk 110 y after each.

Wednesday: 5 x 110 y in 20 seconds each. Walk 110 y after each. 5 x 220 y in 40 seconds each. Walk 110 y after each. 5 x 110 y in 20 seconds each. Walk 110 y after each.

Thursday: 5 x 110 y in 20 seconds. Walk 110 y after each. 1 mile in 7-8 minutes. Walk 5 minutes. 5 x 110 y in 20 seconds each. Walk 110 y after each.

Friday: 5 x 110 y in 20 seconds each. Walk 110 y after each. 5 x 440y in 80-85 seconds each. Walk 2 minutes after each. 5 x 110 y in 20 seconds each. Walk 110y after each.

Saturday: Warmup. Run 2 miles in 15:00 minutes or less. 5 x 150 y acceleration runs. This means jog 50 y, stride 50 y, and sprint 50 y. Then walk 50 y before starting the next.

Sunday: Rest or makeup day.

Second Week.

Monday: 2 x 1 mile in 7-8 minutes each. Walk 5 minutes after each. 10 x 150 y acceleration runs.

Tuesday: 10 x 110 y in 20 seconds each. Walk 110 y after each. 5 x 220 y in 40 seconds each. Walk 110 y after each. 10 x 110 y in 20 seconds each. Walk 110 y after each.

Wednesday: 4 x 880 y in 2:40-3:00. Walk 5 minutes after each. 10 x 150 y acceleration runs.

Thursday: 10 x 440 y in 80 seconds each. Walk 2 minutes after each.

Friday: 3 x 1 mile in 7-8 minutes each. Walk 5 minutes after each. 10 x 150 y acceleration runs.

Saturday: Warmup. $2\frac{1}{2}$ miles cross-country run at speed of 7-8 minutes per mile. Walk 10 minutes. 10 x 150 y acceleration runs.

Sunday: Rest or Makeup.

Third Week.

Monday: 3 miles cross-country run, preferably over hilly course, at speed of 7-8 minutes per mile. Walk 10 minutes. 10 x 110y in 20 seconds each. Walk 110 y after each.

Tuesday: 10 x 440 y in 80 seconds each. Walk 2 minutes after each. 10 x fast striding up a short hill. Walk back to starting point after each.

Wednesday: 5 x 880 y in 2:40 to 3:00, preferably over hilly cross-country course. Walk 5 minutes after each. 10 x 150 y acceleration runs.

Thursday: 10 x 220 y in 40 seconds each. Walk 110 y after each. 10 x 110 y in 18 seconds each. Walk 110 y after each. 10 x fast striding up a short hill. Walk back to starting point after each.

Friday: 6-10 x 660 y in 2:00 each. Walk 220 y after each.

Saturday: Warmup. 2 x 2 miles in 13-14 minutes each, preferably over hilly cross-country course. Walk 10 minutes after each. 5 x 150 y acceleration runs.

Sunday: Rest or makeup.

Fourth Week.

Monday: 5 x 880 y in 2:30-2:40 each. Walk 5 minutes after each. 10 x 150 y acceleration runs.

Tuesday: 10 x 110 y in 16-18 seconds each. Walk 110 y after each. 5 x 220 y in 35 seconds each. Jog 220 y after each. 10 x fast striding up a long hill (no longer than 110 y). Walk back to starting point after each.

Wednesday: 2 x $1\frac{1}{2}$ miles in 9:00 minutes or less. Walk 10 minutes after each. 10 x 150 y acceleration runs.

Thursday: 15 x 440 y in 75 seconds each. Walk 2-3 minutes after each.

Friday: 3 x 1 mile in 6:00-7:00 minutes each. Walk 10 minutes after each. 10 x 150 y acceleration runs.

Saturday: Warmup. 3 miles in 18:00-21:00 minutes, preferably over hilly cross-country course. Walk 10 minutes. 10 x 150 y acceleration runs.

Sunday: Rest or makeup.

Early Competitive Season Cross-Country Training With Two Races Each Week.

Monday: 10-15 x 440y in 70-75 seconds each. Walk 2-3 minutes after each.

Tuesday: Race. Then walk 10-15 minutes. Finally, 10-15 x 150 y acceleration runs.

Wednesday: 10 x 110 y in 16-18 seconds. Jog 110 y after each. Walk 5 minutes. 10 x 220 y in 32-36 seconds. Walk 110 y after each. 10 x 110 y in 16-18 seconds. Jog 110 y after each.

Thursday: 10-15 x 440 y in 70-75 seconds each. Walk 2-3 minutes after each.

Friday: Race. Then walk 10-15 minutes. Finally, 10-15 x 150 y acceleration runs.

Saturday: Warmup. 3-4 miles over hilly cross-country course at speed of 6:00-7:00 minutes per mile.

Sunday: Rest.

Late Competitive Season Cross-Country Training With One Race Each Week.

Monday: 3 miles in 18-21 minutes, preferably over hilly cross country course. 2 x 220 y in 30-35 seconds each. Walk 110 y after each. 2 x 150 y acceleration sprints.

Tuesday: 5 x 220 y in 30-35 seconds each. Jog 220 y after each. Walk 5 minutes. 5 x 440 y in 65-70 seconds each, according to ability. Jog 440 y after each. 5 x 110 y acceleration runs.

Wednesday: 4 x 880 y in 2:20-2:30 each. Walk 5 minutes after each. 10 x 150 y acceleration runs.

Thursday: Rest.

Friday: Race.

Saturday: Warmup. 3-4 miles at speed of 6:00-7:00 minutes per mile, preferably over hilly cross-country course. Walk 10 minutes. 10 sprints up short hill. Walk back to starting point after each.

Sunday: Rest.

Much could be said about tactics in cross-country racing, although for the 15-18 year old runner it is well to remember that the best tactics for any race include (1) indomitable willpower, (2) the highest level of physical condition and racing fitness in accordance with one's personal potential, and (3) even-pace running. Little is to be gained by a fast runner deliberately slowing his pace for the purpose of urging a slower team-mate to a faster performance. In so doing the faster runner loses the benefit of extending himself under the pressure of competition. This experience is highly important in terms of future development. The energy requirement to run uphill is much greater than running downhill on a level surface. In actual competition, runners of all abilities might therefore consider running at a moderate speed uphill, and increasing the speed downhill. It is well to remember that any runner who is with or near the leader at the half-way point in a cross-country race is a dangerous competitor and potential winner.

In cross-country races involving great numbers of competitors, the runners often quickly divide into clusters as the race progresses. There is often a small "primary" cluster of 5-10 strong runners leading the pack. The primary cluster is followed by a few competitors who have lost contact with the leaders but who still remain in contention and are well ahead of the "secondary" cluster. The secondary cluster is usually a large group running strongly, none of whom will win, but most of whom may count heavily in team scoring. This group is followed by a number of individuals who have lost contact with the secondary cluster, but who nevertheless may well "come to life" and figure prominently in team scoring. The third cluster is invariably large, most of the runners in this cluster will finish. The remainder of the competitors behind the third cluster run with varying degrees of determination, some of whom will not finish, and some apparently expending only slightly more energy than those enthusiastic spectators who rush from point to point as the race progresses to see the entire affair.

"Crash" Training For Half-Mile and Mile Racing (Age 15-18).

The following is a four weeks workout schedule, starting with the first day, for normal 15-18 year old schoolboys training for the mile and half-mile races. It should be possible to complete each of these workouts in 90 minutes or less. If the track is wet and soggy, merely mark off distances accurately on a road and run the recommended repetitions in flat-soled shoes with (in the same direction as) the wind, returning against the wind for recovery. The above described mile warmup and warmdown should be utilized. Times are quoted hereafter for the purpose of illustration. Generally speaking, 110 y repetitions need not be timed.

First Week

Monday: 10 x 110 yds. in 20 seconds each. Walk 110 yds. after each.

Tuesday: 12 x 110 yds. in 20 seconds. Walk 110 yds. after each.

Wednesday: 14 x 110 yds. in 20 seconds. Walk 110 yds. after each.

Thursday: 16 x 110 yds. in 20 seconds. Walk 110 yds. after each.

Friday: 20 x 110 yds in 20 seconds. Walk 110 yds. after each.

Saturday: Warmup. Run 2 miles in 15 min. or less. Walk 10 min. 5 x 150 yds. acceleration runs. (An acceleration run means jog 50 yds., stride 50 yds., and sprint 50 yds. Then walk 50 yds. before starting the next.

Sunday: Rest or makeup day.

Second Week

Monday: 20 x 110 yds. in 20 seconds. Jog and walk alternately for 110 yds. after each.

Tuesday: 10 x 440 yds. in 80 seconds. Walk 3 min. after each.

Wednesday: 10 x 220 yds. in 35 seconds. Walk 220 yds. in 3 min. or less after each.

Thursday: 10 x 440 in 80 seconds. Walk 2 min. after each.

Friday: 25 x 110 in 20 seconds. Walk and jog 110 after each.

Saturday; 2 miles in 15 min. or less. Walk 10 min. 10 x 150 yds. acceleration runs.

Sunday: Rest or makeup day.

Third Week

Monday: 30 x 110 in 18-20 seconds. Walk and jog 110 after each.

Tuesday: 10 x 440 in 75 seconds. Walk 2 min. after each.

Wednesday: 10 x 220 in 32-34 seconds. Walk and jog 220 in 3 min. or less after each.

Thursday: 6-10 x 660 in 2:00 each (80 seconds per 440 pace). Walk 220 in 3 min. after each.

Friday: 30 x 110 in 16-18. Walk 110 after each.

Saturday: 2 miles in 15 min. or less. Walk 10 min. 15 x 150 yds. acceleration runs.

Sunday: Rest or makeup day.

Fourth Week

Monday: Milers - 3 x 880 yds. in 2:40 each (80 sec. per 440). Walk 5 min. after each. Half-milers - 4 x 440 yds. in 65. Walk 4 min. after each. Both milers and half-milers finish with 10 x 150 yds. acceleration runs.

Tuesday: Half-milers - 20-30 x 110 in 16-17. Walk 110 after each. Milers - 30-40 x 110 in 17-18. Walk and jog 110 after each.

Wednesday: Milers - 2 x 3/4 mile in 80 per 440 or 4:00 each. Walk 10 min. after each. Half-milers - 2 x 660 in 1:45-1:50. Walk 10 min. after each. Both milers and half-milers finish with 10 x 150 yd. acceleration runs.

Thursday: Milers - 10 x 440 in 72-74. Walk 2 min. after each. Half-milers - 6-10 x 220 in 30-32. Walk 220 after each.

Friday: Milers - Mile in 5:20-5:30. Walk 10 min. Half-milers - 880 yds. in 2:20-2:25. Walk 10 min. Both milers and half-milers finish with 20 x 150 yd. acceleration sprints.

Saturday: 2 miles in 15 min. or less. Walk 10 min. 20 x 150 yds. acceleration sprints.

Sunday: Rest or makeup day.

During the competitive racing season there are frequently two races each week, usually on Tuesday and Friday. I suggest that the athlete not rest the day prior to competition in the early part of the season. They should rest a day prior to competition in the latter one-fourth of the season, or prior to major competition. Prior to major competition, two days rest is often in order, depending upon the individual. The athlete who runs both the 880 and mile in competition should use the miler's workouts.

Early Competitive Season Training with Two Races Per Week

Monday: Milers - 10 x 440 yds., each in 2 sec. faster than mile racing pace. Walk and jog 2 min. after each. Example: 73 sec. for the 5:00 min. miler. Half-milers - 6-8 x 220 at racing speed or one second faster than racing speed. Walk and jog 2 min. after each. Example: 34-35 sec. for the 2:20 half-miler.

Tuesday: Race.

Wednesday: Milers - 30-40 x 110 in 16-17 sec. each. Jog and walk 110 after each. Half-milers - 20-30 x 110 in 14-16 sec. each, depending upon ability. Jog and walk 110 after each.

Thursday: Repeat Monday's training.

Friday: Race.

Saturday: Both milers and half-milers, 2 miles cross-country. Walk 10 min. - 10 x 150 yds. acceleration runs.

Sunday: Rest.

Late Competitive Season Training

Monday: Milers - 10 x 440 in 2-3 sec. faster than mile racing speed. Walk and jog 2 min. after each. Walk 10 min. 6-10 x 150 yds. acceleration runs. Half-milers - 10 x 220 in 1-2 sec. faster than racing speed. Walk and jog 2 min. after each. Walk 10 min. 6-10 x 150 yds. acceleration runs.

Tuesday: Milers - 15 x 220 in 3-4 sec. slower than top speed for this distance. Walk and jog 220 after each. Half-milers - 10-15 x 110 yds. sprints from starting position. Walk 110 yds. after each.

Wednesday: Milers - 2-4 x 880 yds. at racing speed. Walk 5 min. after each. Half-milers - 3-4 x 440 yds. in 2 sec. faster than racing speed. Walk 2 min. after each.

Thursday: Rest.

Friday: Race.

Saturday: 2-3 miles in 6-7 min. per mile speed. Walk 10 min. 10 x 150 yds. acceleration runs.

Sunday: Rest.

It is emphasized that adapting training to individual differences of athletes is one of the coach's primary duties. By necessity this involves good judgement. Caution should be used in applying the above suggested training to all athletes. Some athletes will be unable to cope with this intensity and volume of work, while others may well thrive on considerably more. Furthermore, there are many paths to Rome. There are almost as many training plans and workout programs as there are runners and coaches. Under no circumstance should athletes be bent and twisted to fit a preconceived workout plan. It is much better to fit the training to the athlete than the athlete to the training.

Training volume. The total training volume in general for each workout may be two or three times the actual racing distance, exclusive of recovery or slow running. The half-miler may consider 16-24 x 110, 8-12 x 220, 4-6 x 440, 3-4 x 660, and 2 x 3/4 mile. The miler may consider 32-48 x 110, 8-12 x 440, 4-6 x 880, and 3-4 x 3/4 mile.

Training speeds. After the athlete is in reasonable good condition, the 110 and 220 yd. repetitions can be near full speed; certainly considerably faster than racing speed for the half-miler and the miler. The 440 yards repetitions should be 1-3 seconds faster than average racing speed. (Average racing speed for a five min. miler would be 75 seconds for each 440 yards, for example, or 70 seconds each 440 in the case of the 4:40 miler). The 380 yards repetitions should be from racing speed to 2 seconds slower than racing speed. The 3/4 mile repetitions should be 3-5 seconds per 440y slower than average racing speed, up to 80 seconds per 440 as the slowest within reason.

In the event twice daily training is attempted, I suggest at the morning workout be merely 2-3 miles of continuous track or cross-country running at approximately 7 min. per mile pace. Evening workouts may continue similar to those suggested above.

The criterion by which to determine whether the training is too severe is accurate observation of recovery from one workout to the next. There must be full recovery from one workout to the next. This again demands good judgement on the part of the coach.

How does one train when injuries, weather, studies, employment, personal inclinations, facilities, etc. prevent training specifically when and in the manner preferred? The answer is simple. Train as best you can. Swim, weight-train, run up and down bleachers in the gym, run in place on a thick rubber mat, or engage in any form of training available. But do not give up, fail to train, and waste valuable. But do not give up, fail to train, and waste valuable and all too limited time. Any training is better than none at all.

Time-trials. I oppose time-trials for psychological reasons. Most athletes submit to the indignity of time-trials only to bolster the confidence of the coach. If an athlete runs a fast time-trial, why leave it on the training track? If he runs a poor time-trial, it has a devastating psychological effect on his confidence.

The heart of a healthy athlete will seldom beat more than 180 beats per minute as a result of severe exercise. Through empirical (trial and error) study, it has been determined that after an interval of exercise the athlete should be permitted to recover until his heart-beat drops to 120 beats per minute before continuing with the next repetition. While it is not practical to test this after every repetition, it can nevertheless be used when in doubt about whether an athlete is sufficiently recovered from one training assignment before starting the next repetition. Athletes can be taught to use this test themselves, checking their heartbeat after exercise by placing one hand directly over the heart, and counting the beat for 10 seconds. If the count is 20 or less beats in 10 seconds, recovery may be sufficient to continue. In the case of 110 yds. and 220 yds. repetitions, 1½ minutes or less recovery should be sufficient after each. In the case of 440 repetitions at near racing speed for the half-miler and miler, 2 minutes or less should be sufficient. Recovery after 880 yard and 3/4 mile runs will be much longer. However, recovery will vary with the individual, and when in doubt the above heart-rate test may be used.

Weight-training. This excellent form of training does not seem to offer such high potential for immediate improvement in results in the case of the runner as the field events performer. It was once recommended that athletes who specialize in endurance events should use a program of weight-training involving high repetitions and low poundage. This may well still be best for the 15-18 year old runner. However, recent opinion suggests runners should use low repetition, high poundage weight-training for best results. Light weights may be used daily. Heavy weights are seldom used in excess of three times weekly. Curls, leg lunges, pull-overs, bench presses, toe-raises, two-hand snatches, and lateral raises are among weight training exercises used by runners.

I like to think of sprints as anything up to and including 440 yards. Middle distances include 880 yards to 6 miles, or 800 meters to 10,000 meters. Short middle distance races are 880 yards to two miles. Long middle distance are three to six miles. Perhaps it would help runners psychologically if they regarded the half-mile and mile as merely "short middle-distances." Describing the half-mile and mile as "long distance" races is enough to frighten the novice at the outset.

Runners should be taught to carry a stop-watch correctly, so as to be able to time themselves accurately. Never carry a stop-watch in the hand while running, as the motion of the arm interferes with the movement of the balance wheel of the watch, and usually causes a most inaccurate timing. Have a long shoestring through the handle and suspend the watch around the runner's neck. Hold the watch in the athletic supporter or a pocket in the shirt or trunks in front. Start and stop the watch as it remains held securely to the body in a position at the front where it will be subjected to the least motion. The shoestring by which the watch is suspended around the runner's neck will prevent dropping and damaging the stopwatch.

It is easy to acquire a sense of pace judgement. It is not easy to develop strength to use this knowledge of pace judgement when fatigue sets in and will power starts receding. Briefly, run a series of 440's aiming at a pre-determined speed, such as 75 sec. Each time the runner finishes, ask him how fast he thinks he ran. Do not tell him before he commits himself to a positive answer (or guess). After the first he will come closer to the correct time. At the end of the 10th quarter, you will be amazed at the accuracy with which he is judging his pace. It is not at all uncommon for runners to judge their pace within one to three tenths of a second for 440 yards.

Milers usually use a standing start. Half-milers may use either a standing or crouch start.

One of the most common injuries among runners is the fallen metatarsal arch. This is relieved almost immediately by taping a metatarsal pad $\frac{1}{4}$ inch in thickness just behind (toward the heel) the metatarsal joints. Tape on a metatarsal pad prior to each workout. It will soon heal and the pad will no longer be necessary. Rubber metatarsal pads are available through commercial athletic trainer supply firms.

Racing tactics. Even pace running is most economical. This is especially true in the mile. Ideally, the miler should run his second 880 approximately 2-4 seconds faster than the first 880. The half-miler usually runs the first 440 two seconds faster than the second. Certain information should be considered in deciding upon tactics. These include track conditions (fast, slow, heavy, dry, wet, cut up, curves), number of competitors, weather (hot, cold, humid, rain, wind), ability of competitors, personal ability, minimum speed of leading and following, maximum speed of leading and following, etc. A runner takes the lead for the purpose of increasing the pace, decreasing the pace, gaining tactical position, and sprinting for the finish. The third one-fourth of any race is apt to be the slowest. A tactical increase in pace during the third one-fourth of a race often proves of great advantage in securing a commanding lead over the opposition. In passing an opponent, the runner should make certain he does it fast and decisively, so the opponent won't have a chance to fight him off. Runners should not be afraid to take the pace and lead throughout, or to take the pace from the leader and set their own pace if the opponent does not set a suitable pace. The runner should never lose contact during a race, contact meaning keeping the opponent within effective striking distance wherein he may be caught and passed. This may vary from a few feet to many yards. It is psychologically more difficult to lead than to follow. However, a really good "front runner" has no intention of acting as a pace setter for the rest of the field. His intention is to open a gap, break contact with the field, and settle down to fast even-pace running to make certain the opposition does not get within striking distance. A runner should not pass on the turn unless he is sure he will meet no great resistance.

The empirical philosophy behind training has undergone certain changes over the years. Perhaps one of the first was the notion that by running very long, slow distances, much longer than racing distance, at much slower than racing speed, one could race much faster over a short distance. Thus a man hoping to run a mile in 4:30 might run 6 to 8 miles continuously at a speed of 7 to 8 minutes per mile. This method proved generally false, although there is still merit to the occasional long slow run. For the purpose of a "crash" program of conditioning, this method is next to worthless, and certainly will not produce good results. Basically, it is the speed that hurts in a race, not the distance.

A second notion which has been proven highly successful is the running of repeated repetitions of fast runs over short distances at a pace faster than racing speed. According to this concept, if the runner prepares himself to tolerate the stresses involved in running at a speed much faster than required in a race (even though he trains over distances much shorter than racing distance), then when he runs the full racing distance (which is at a speed slower than that to which he has become accustomed) he can negotiate the full race at a relatively fast pace.

In both speed-play and interval training this second notion is utilized, although another factor has been introduced. This factor is known as "gradual adaptation to stress."

The human body has amazing powers of adaptation and overcompensation if given an opportunity to exercise them. Vaccinate a man for smallpox with a small dose of appropriate strength vaccine. The body adapts itself to this small infection, and overcompensates by producing antibodies of sufficient quantity to ward off and withstand exposure to the disease at a future date. Break an arm, set it properly, and nature overcompensates by healing the break so thoroughly that it is relatively impossible to break the same spot again. Vaccinate the runner with a small dose of running, such as 80 seconds per 440 yards type training, the body adapts to this low grade stress, and overcompensates in the resistance it produces to this intensity of training. Then, on the basis of this adaptation and overcompensation, the body can (during the excitement of competition) race at a much faster pace (perhaps 70 to 75 seconds per 440 yds. speed, for example). Vaccinate the runner with very short repetitions of high-speed running, the body adapts and overcompensates to the stresses involved, and is thus enabled to race over far greater distances at a relatively high rate of speed, although by necessity not so fast as the high training speed. After giving the body an opportunity to adapt to the stress of one training speed and overcompensate in producing resistance to that particular stress, move gradually and moderately to a slightly more intense training speed. For example, after 4-6 weeks at 70 seconds per 440 yds.

speed, the runner under ideal circumstances might try repetitions of 440's at 68 seconds. After adapting the body to running 10 x 110 yds. in 15 seconds, the runner might try 15 x 110 yds. in 15 seconds. Gradual adaptation to stress can and should be a part of the general philosophy of training, regardless of what training distances and speeds are used.

If a gasoline engine in operation is suddenly deprived of oxygen, it stops immediately. This is because the burning (oxidation) of fuel which releases energy is an aerobic (with oxygen) reaction. Without oxygen, the gasoline engine will not function.

In the human body, the oxidation of fuel which releases energy takes place both with oxygen (aerobic reaction) and without oxygen (anaerobic reaction). At very low rates of exercise such as walking or slow running, oxygen is supplied at the same rate the fuel of muscular contraction is oxidized, thus demonstrating an aerobic reaction, (with oxygen). If an athlete runs at a rate which requires 4 liters of oxygen per min., but is able to take in only 3 liters for each minute of exercise, he incurs an "oxygen debt" of 1 liter for each minute of exercise. Then, during the recovery period, his oxygen intake will remain above the resting level until the "oxygen debt" is repaid. Even though the athlete in this example was using oxygen at the rate of 1 liter per minute faster than he could supply it, he did not have to stop as would have been the case with the gasoline engine. This demonstrates the use of nonoxidative (anaerobic) metabolism in the human body.

The effort which can be exerted over a given period of time is limited by the maximum amount of oxygen which the runner can absorb per minute, and by the maximum oxygen debt which he is able to contract. A well trained athlete may be able to absorb 4 liters of oxygen per minute and to acquire an oxygen debt of 15 liters. When maximum oxygen debt is reached, the runner stops. In running the oxygen requirement increases as the square or cube of the speed. The oxygen requirement for a given task is diminished as a result of more efficient use of muscles and elimination of extraneous movements, plus greater mechanical efficiency of the muscles. The maximal oxygen intake is increased through improved capacity of the heart to pump blood through circulatory and respiratory adjustments. We know that training increases the amount of oxygen debt which can be reached, and produces greater cardio-vascular and muscular efficiency. With these preliminary remarks, the problem then is to decide upon what training to use to produce these improvements.

If an athlete were to run 10 miles, he would encounter many stresses, one of which is the oxygen debt, but during this 10 mile run only one high oxygen debt would be created. Theoretically speaking, each time an athlete runs fast enough or far enough to create a high oxygen debt, and thereafter recovers, he is capable the next time he attempts the effort of creating and tolerating a slightly higher oxygen debt (plus tolerance to the other stresses associated with running). Again, each time the runner incurs a high oxygen debt and recovers, it results in improvement which permits him to go slightly (only very slightly) more into (oxygen) debt the next time. We know that a runner who sprints as fast as possible for 100 yds. creates an oxygen debt somewhat comparable to that of the runner who has just finished a 10 mile run. Theoretically, then, the runner who sprints 10 x 100 yds. in one workout gets ten times more benefit from his workout than the runner who takes one long, 10 mile run. This is not the entire story, and it ignors many factors. Yet there is an element of truth to this example, and we must accept as valid the theory that one should strive to create a high oxygen debt on many occasions each workout for best results. In my opinion this will produce better results in a "crash" program of training where time is limited.

Basically modern training falls into two general categories, termed "speed-play" (popularly known by the Swedish word "fartlek"), and "interval-training". Speed-play means running informally over unmarked areas at alternately fast and slow speeds Interval training involves formal fast-slow training over accurately marked distances, with pre-determined recovery periods between the fast runs at pre-determined speeds.

An example of speed-play (fartlek) training might be this: Run in the woods, on a golf course, beach, road, or even on the track, without the benefit of stop-watch, starting with 10-15 minutes jogging at a speed of 8-10 minutes per mile (covering $1\frac{1}{2}$-2 miles) as a warmup. Take 5-10 minutes calisthenics. Run at a fast, steady speed for 4-6 minutes, covering 3/4 to $1\frac{1}{4}$ miles. Walk 5 minutes. Jog about one mile, at a speed of 8 minutes per mile, taking 4-6 x 75-110 yds. sprints enroute. Walk briefly. Sprint 150-200 yds., preferably uphill. Walk briefly, and run about 660 yds. at a fast, steady speed. Finally, jog one mile in 8-10 minutes.

An example of interval training might be one mile of jogging in 8-10 minutes as a warmup. 10 x 440 yds. on the track in 70 seconds each. Jog 440 yds. in $2\frac{1}{2}$ to 3 minutes after each. Finally, jog one mile in 8-10 minutes as a warmdown.

Interval training involves four variables: (1) Distance of the fast run. (2) Speed of the fast run. (3) Number of repetitions of the fast run. (4) Duration of recovery after each fast run. The duration of recovery after each fast run involves an additional problem. This is the action or activity during recovery. Should it be walking, jogging, sitting, or lying on the ground? The answer is that it should be either jogging or walking, with jogging usually considered better because this movement forces the body to break contact with the ground and thus requires more energy. I have found through trial and error that one minute of walking produces as much if not more recovery than two minutes of jogging. The speed of jogging is usually 2-3 minutes per 440 yds.

Regardless of what training method is used it absolutely cannot guarantee success in racing. Training merely makes successful racing possible. A runner must also have the will to win, a subconscious desire for victory, courage, tenacity, and a competitive "killer instinct" to transform the racing potential resulting from good training into reality.

Training for Experienced Runners

by Fred Wilt

These training suggestions are for high school and collegiate runners who have had previous successful racing experience, are strong, healthy, normal, and willing to train hard to improve.

Individual differences must always to taken into account in adjusting training to suit athletes. Workout routines must be tailored to fit the athlete, rather than the athlete being changed to fit a training program. The unimaginative use of written training schedules is always unwise. There is no perfect system of training, and no one fixed training schedule suitable for everyone. It is doubtful if any two athletes should ever use exactly the same training. There is no magic or secret method of training which can guarantee success. Due consideration must be given to body build, physical maturity, diet, sleep, studies, work, interest, temperament, health, weather, motivation, and a multitude of personal and environmental factors in applying training routines in an effort to best serve the individual. The reader is cautioned that the workout routines which appear herein should not be followed blindly. Rather they should serve merely as ideas, guides, and examples from which to construct training plans to best serve the needs of the athlete on the basis of his individual characteristics.

If the runner is not already in active training and good condition for running, then he should carry out the following 4 week pre-conditioning program before proceeding to a regular training plan.

Week I

Monday: Jog 1 mile in 10-12 minutes.

Tuesday: Jog $1\frac{1}{2}$ miles at a speed of $2\frac{1}{2}$-3 minutes per 440y.

Wednesday: Jog 2 miles at a speed of $2\frac{1}{2}$-3 minutes per 440y.

Thursday: Jog $2\frac{1}{2}$ miles at a speed of $2\frac{1}{2}$-3 minutes per 440y.

Friday: Jog 3 miles at a speed of $2\frac{1}{2}$-3 minutes per 440y.

Saturday: Jog $3\frac{1}{2}$ miles at a speed of $2\frac{1}{2}$-3 minutes per 440y.

Sunday: Rest of makeup day.

Week II

Monday: Jog 3 miles at a speed of $2\frac{1}{2}$-3 minutes per 440y. Walk 5 minutes. 4 x 150y acceleration runs. (An acceleration run means jog 50y, stride 50y, and sprint 50y. Then walk 50y before starting the next.)

Tuesday: Jog 3 miles at a speed of $2\frac{1}{2}$-3 minutes per 440y. Walk 5 minutes. 6 x 150y acceleration runs.

Wednesday: Jog 3 miles at a speed of $2\frac{1}{2}$ minutes per 440y. Walk 5 minutes. 8 x 150y acceleration runs.

Thursday: Jog 3 miles at a speed of $2\frac{1}{2}$ minutes per 440y (30 minutes total). Walk 5 minutes. 10 x 150y acceleration runs.

Friday: Jog 1 mile in 10 minutes. Walk 5 minutes. Run 3 miles at a speed of 2 minutes per 440y (24 minutes total). Walk 5 minutes. 10 x 150y acceleration runs.

Saturday: Jog 1 mile in 10 minutes. Walk 5 minutes. 10 x 440y in 80 seconds each. Walk 2 minutes after each.

Sunday: Rest or makeup day.

Week III

Monday: Jog 1 mile in 10 minutes. 5 minutes stretching calisthenics. Run 4 miles at a speed of 2 minutes per 440y (32 minutes). Walk 5 minutes. 5 x 150y acceleration runs.

Tuesday: Jog 1 mile in 10 minutes. 5 minutes stretching calisthenics.

10 x 440y in 80 seconds each. Walk 2 minutes after each.
10 x 150y acceleration runs.

Wednesday: Jog 1 mile in 10 minutes. 5 minutes stretching calisthenics. Run 4 miles at a speed of 2 minutes per 440y (32 minutes). Walk 5 minutes. 10 x 150y acceleration runs.

Thursday: Jog 1 mile in 10 minutes. 5 minutes stretching calisthenics. 5 x 440y in 80 seconds each. Walk 1-2 minutes after each. 10 x 150y acceleration runs. 5 x 440y in 80 seconds each. Walk 1-2 minutes after each.

Friday: Jog 1 mile in 10 minutes. 5 minutes stretching calisthenics. Run 5 miles at a speed of 2 minutes per 440y, or 40 minutes total. Walk 10 minutes. 10 x 150y acceleration runs.

Saturday: Jog 1 mile in 10 minutes. 5 minutes stretching calisthenics. 5 x 220y in 35 seconds each. Walk 1 minute after each. 10 x 150y acceleration runs. 5 x 220y in 35 seconds each. Walk 1 minute after each.

Sunday: Rest or makeup day.

Week IV

Monday: Jog 1 mile in 10 minutes. 5 minutes stretching calisthenics. Run 5 miles at a speed of 7-8 minutes per mile. Walk 10 minutes. 5-10 x 150y acceleration runs.

Tuesday: Jog 1 mile in 10 minutes. 5 minutes stretching calisthenics. 10 x 440y in 75 seconds each. Jog 440y in $2\frac{1}{2}$-3 minutes after each.

Wednesday: Jog 1 mile in 10 minutes. 5 minutes stretching calisthenics. 3 x 2 miles in 6:00-6:30 per mile. Walk 5 minutes after each.

Thursday: Jog 1 mile in 10 minutes. 5 minutes stretching calisthenics. 5 x 220y in 35 seconds each. Jog 220y after each. 10 x 150y acceleration runs. 5 x 220y in 35 seconds each. Jog 220y after each.

Friday: Jog 1 mile in 10 minutes. 5 minutes stretching calisthenics. 2 x 3 miles in 6:00-6:30 per mile. Walk 10 minutes after each.

Saturday: Jog 1 mile in 10 minutes. 5 minutes stretching calisthenics. 10 x 440y in 75 seconds each. Jog 440y in $2\frac{1}{2}$-3 minutes after each. Walk 5 minutes. 10 x 150y acceleration runs.

Sunday: Rest or makeup day.

After having completed the above 4 weeks pre-conditioning program or one similar, or in the event the runner is already in active training and in good condition for running, he is now ready to move directly into the training recommended hereafter. Unless otherwise specified, each of these workouts should be preceded by a warmup.

One specific warmup should be established for use prior to both training and racing. Much valuable training time can be wasted under the guise of warming-up. Briefly, the warmup should consume about 15 minutes, and should include approximately one mile of running, followed by stretching calistenics.

One highly efficient and thorough warmup is this: Run one mile, the first 440y in 3 minutes, the second 440y in $2\frac{1}{2}$ minutes, and the third 440y in 2 minutes. The fourth 440y should be alternately 50y fast and 50y slow until the entire final 440y is completed. Each fast 50y should be faster than the preceding one, and the final 50y should be full speed. This should be followed by 5-10 minutes of stretching calisthenics, possibly changing shoes, and then go directly into the workout.

Another useful warmup involves jogging one mile in approximately 10 minutes, followed by 4-6 x 110y runs, each faster than the preceding one, with the last being at or near full speed. Walk 110y after each of these 110 runs. Finally, do 5-10 minutes stretching calisthenics, possibly change shoes, and proceed directly into the workout.

Unless the weather is quite hot, the warmup should be done in full track-suit (warmup-suit or sweat-suit) and flat soft-soled shoes.

After the warmup prior to competition, an athlete should go to the dressing room, remove his sweat-suit and other clothing, quickly dry the perspiration with a towel, and put on dry racing togs and warmup-suit. Then lie down to rest for 10 minutes before rising, visiting the toilet a final time, putting on spiked shoes, and reporting to the starting line 5-10 minutes prior to the start of the race.

Each workout and race should be followed by a warmdown of at least 880y and preferably 1 mile of gentle jogging.

The specific workouts listed hereafter are described with instructions for progressively increasing their intensity where applicable in attempting to gradually adapt the body to the stress of running. Any particular workout which seems especially difficult should be repeated in prescribed rotation until it can be completed with a reasonable degree of ease before progressing to the next more intensive step in that specific workout. The speed recommended for the various distances are suggested merely as a guide. In actual practice, these workouts will often be run without stopwatch timing. When no track is available, the recommended distances may be estimated and run on road, golf course, or in woods or park.

Morning training should be done early enough in the day to permit complete recovery before the daily evening workout. For most students, this will mean training before breakfast. In this case, it is wise to drink a half-cup of liquid containing sugar before the workout. However, under no circumstance should training be done immediately following breakfast. Running should not be done until about three hours have elapsed since the last meal. It often happens that personal inclination and/or circumstances beyond control of the athlete precludes morning training as recommended below. In such a case, merely forget the morning workouts and proceed with the recommended evening training.

It is seldom wise to train during the heat of the day in summer months unless one is preparing for competition which will take place at that time of day. Training should therefore be done in the cool of the morning and the late evening to avoid the undesirable and uncomfortable effects of the hot weather.

Workout I

I(a) Morning training. No warmup. Run 2 miles in 15 minutes or less. 5-10 minutes hopping, jogging, and squat-jumping with sandbag on shoulders.

I(b) Morning training. No warmup. Start running easily and continue 3 miles in a time of 20 minutes or less. 5-10 minutes hopping, jogging, and squat-jumping with sandbag on shoulders.

I(c) Morning training. Jog 1 mile in 10 minutes. 5 x 110y at a speed of $1\frac{1}{2}$-$2\frac{1}{2}$ seconds slower than best on each 110y, with the following recovery after each: 110y fast (jog 440y); 110y fast (jog 330y); 110y fast (jog 220y); 110y fast (jog 110y); 110y fast. Now jog 1 mile in 10 minutes. 5-10 minutes hopping, jogging, and squat-jumping with sandbag on shoulders.

I(d) Morning training. Jog 1 mile in 10 minutes. 5-15 x 150y acceleration runs. Jog 1 mile in 10 minutes. 5-10 minutes hopping, jogging, and squat-jumping with sandbag on shoulders.

I(e) Morning training. Jog 1 mile in 10 minutes. 2 x 110y., 2 x 220y., and 2 x 110y. Walk 110y after each. Speed of 110's is $1\frac{1}{2}$-$2\frac{1}{2}$ seconds slower than best 110. Speed of 220's is 3-5 seconds slower than best 220. 5-10 minutes hopping, jogging, and squat-jumping with sandbag on shoulders.

I(f) Morning training. No warmup. Alternately run 110y slow and 220y fast until 2¼ miles have been covered. The slow 110y should be about 50 seconds each, and the relatively fast 220y should be in 40 seconds each, or possibly slightly faster in the latter stages of the 2¼ miles. 5-10 minutes hopping, jogging, and squat jumps with sandbag on shoulders.

I(g) Morning training. Jog 1 mile in 10 minutes. 10 "stride-stretchers." This means from a running start use the longest possible running, bounding stride and see how far you can go in 15 such strides. Walk a few seconds after each. Then go to a soft surface such as the landing area for the high-jump or broad-jump, and do 10 x 50 steps running in place, (running on the spot), lifting the knees as high to the chest as possible while pumping the arms in high, exaggerated arm action. Rest 1 minute after each series of 50 steps.

I(h) Weight training. Jog 1 mile in 10 minutes. Then do isotonic weight lifting, using 2/3 to 3/4 your maximum possible for each lift, or a weight sufficiently heavy that you cannot do more than 4-6 repetitions of any particular lift before resting. Rest 1-2 minutes between each set of repetitions. 1-3 x (4-6 curls), 1-3 x (4-6 half-squats), 1-3 x (4-6 military presses), and 1-3 x (4-6 bench-presses). It is best to have competent instruction and the assistance of team-mates while weight-training. To avoid back-injury when lifting a weight from the floor, keep the spine as near to perpendicular as possible, and lift with the legs. If no weights and/or assistance are available, the runner can still get much benefit from weight-training by using a sandbag as heavy as can be handled without great difficulty, lifted in this manner: Place it on the shoulders, keeping the back relatively erect or perpendicular at all times. Do the following sets of repetitions:

2-10 x (10 x squat jumps).
1-6 x (hop 50y on right leg. Hop 50y on left leg).
1-6 x (hop 50y on both legs).
2-6 x (110y jogging. Walk 1-2 minutes after each).

Workout II

This workout involves repetitions of 110y in various series and combinations. The speed of 110y repetitions should usually be from 1½ to 2½ seconds slower than the runner's fastest 110y. For example, if the runner's best 110y is 12.5 seconds, then his training speed for 110y repetitions would be 14-15 seconds each. During workouts these repetitions are taken with a running start. After the athlete has completed a reasonable period of pre-conditioning type training such as listed above, he is advised to progress quite rapidly to the above times for 110y repetitions.

II(a) 4-8 x (110y fast, jog 440y; 110y fast, jog 330y; 110y fast, jog 220y; 110y fast, jog 110y; 110y fast, walk 2-3 minutes).

II(b) 2-6 x (10 x 110y. Jog 220y after each). Walk 5 minutes after each series of 10 x 110y.

II(c) 2-6 x (10 x 110y. Jog 110y after each). Walk 5 minutes after each series of 10 x 110y.

II(d) 2-4 (15 x 110y. Jog 110y after each). Walk 5 minutes after each series of 15 x 110y.

II(e) 2-6 (10 x 110y. Jog 110y after the 1st, 3rd, 5th, and 9th fast 110y. Jog 220y after the 2nd, 4th, 6th, 8th, and 10th fast 110y. Walk 5 minutes after each series of 10 x 110y.

II(f) 1-3 x (20 x 110y. Jog 110y after each). Walk 5 minutes after each series of 20 x 110y.

II(g) 1-4 x (20 x 110y. Jog 110y after each). Walk 5 minutes after each series of 20 x 110y. The speed should be 20, 18, 16, and 14 seconds successively. Thus the 1st, 5th, 9th, 13th, and 17th 110's will be in 20 seconds each. The 2nd, 6th, 10th, 14th, and 18th 110's will be in 18 seconds each. The 3rd, 7th, 11th, 15th, and 19th 110's will be in 16 seconds each. The 4th, 8th, 12th, 16th, and 20th 110's will be run in 14 seconds each.

II(h) 20-40 x 110y. Walk 110y in 90 seconds or less after each.

II(i) 10-15 x 110y all-out sprints. Walk 3-5 minutes after each. Half-milers should run these from starting blocks if available.

II(j) 2-4 x (10 x 110y. Jog 330y after each). Walk 5 minutes after each series of 10 x 110y.

Workout III

This workout involves repetitions of 220y in various series and combinations. The speed of these should usually be 3 to 5 seconds slower than the runner's fastest 220y. For example, if the runner's best 220y is 25 seconds, his training speed for 220y repetitions should be 28-30 seconds. These repetitions are taken with a running start during training. The athlete should, of course, gradually approach the above recommended training times, but after undergoing a reasonable period of pre-conditioning running he should be able to progress rapidly to a speed of 3-5 seconds slower than his best for the 220y training distance.

III(a) 1-2 x (10 x 220y. Jog 440y after each). Walk 5 minutes after each series of 10 x 220y.

III(b) 3-4 x (5 x 220y. Jog 220y after each). Walk 5 minutes after each series of 5 x 220y.

III(c) 4-6 x (4 x 220y. Jog 220y after each). Walk 5 minutes after each series of 4 x 220y.

III(d) 15-25 x 220y. Walk 110y after each.

III(e) 3-4 x (220y fast, jog 440y; 220y fast, jog 330y; 220y fast, jog 220y; 220y fast, jog 110y; 220y fast, walk 5 minutes).

III(f) 2-3 x (10 x 220y. Jog 110-220y after each). The speed should be 8-10 seconds slower than the runner's best 220y. Thus a runner's whose best 220y is 25 sec. would run these 220's in 33-35 seconds.

III(g) 6-10 x 220y all-out sprints. Walk 3-5 minutes after each.

Workout IV

This workout involves repetitions of 330y in various series and combinations. Unless otherwise specified, the speed should be gradually reduced until it is 2 to 4 seconds faster than anticipated average racing pace. Thus for a 4:32 miler, average racing speed would be 34 seconds for each 220y, 51 seconds each 330y, 68 seconds each 440y, etc. Therefore, the 4:32 miler would run 330's in training at 2-4 seconds faster than 51 seconds, or 47-49 seconds each.

IV(a) 10 x 330y. Walk 110y in 2 minutes after each.

IV(b) 10 x 330y. Jog 550y after each.

IV(c) 2-5 x (4 x 330y. Jog 110y after each). Walk 5 minutes after each series of 4 x 330y.

IV(d) 4-6 x 330y at near as possible best effort (sprints). Walk 5 minutes after each.

Workout V

This workout involves repetitions of 440y in various series and combinations. Unless otherwise specified, the speed should be 1 to 4 seconds faster than anticipated average racing speed. Thus a 28:00 minute 6-miler, whose average racing pace is 70 seconds per 440y, would train at a speed of 66-69 seconds per 440y. The 4:00 minute miler, whose average racing pace is 60 seconds per 440y, would train at a speed of 56-

59 seconds per 440y. To ascertain the speed at which to begin running 440's at the beginning of training season, take the best ever 440y time, and add 20 seconds. For example, a 4:32 miler whose best 440y is 54 seconds would add 20 to 54 and start training at 74 seconds per 440y. This time may be reduced by 2-3 seconds per 440y each month until he reaches the recommended training speed of 65-67 in his case. There will, of course, be exceptional athletes who need not adhere to such a gradual and cautious reduction in time of training speed.

V(a) 2-3 x (2 x 440y. Jog 440y after each). Walk 5 minutes after each series of 2 x 440y.

V(b) 1-3 x (3 x 440y. Jog 440y after each). Walk 5 minutes after each series of 3 x 440y.

V(c) 3-5 (4 x 440y. Jog 440y after each). Walk 5 minutes after each series of 4 x 440y.

V(d) 2-6 x (5 x 440y. Jog 440y after each). Walk 5 minutes after each series of 5 x 440y.

V(e) 1-6 x (10 x 440y. Jog 440y after each). Walk 5 minutes after each series of 10 x 440y.

V(f) 1-4 x (10 x 440y. Jog 220y after each). Walk 5 minutes after each series of 10 x 440y.

V(g) 2-3 x (10 x 440y. Jog 110y after each). Walk 5 minutes after each series of 10 x 440y.

V(h) 2-3 x (15 x 440y. Jog 220y after each). Walk 5 minutes after each series of 15 x 440y.

V(i) 20-30 x 440y. Walk 110y after each.

V(j) 1-4 x (440y fast, jog 440y; 440y fast, jog 330y; 440y fast, jog 220y; 440y fast, jog 110y; 440y fast, walk 5 minutes).

Workout VI

This involves repetitions of 660y in various series and combinations. Unless otherwise specified, the pace should be at anticipated average racing speed. For example, the 4:00 minute miler would run 660's in 1:30. The 28:00 minute 6-miler would run 660's in 1:45.

VI(a) 1-3 x 660y at full effort, preferably without being timed. Then walk 5-10 minutes prior to continuing with other assignments.

VI(b) 1-2 x 660y in 1-2 seconds per 220y faster than anticipated racing speed. For example, the 2:00 minute half-miler would run 660's in 1:24-1:27 during this particular workout.

VI(c) 2-6 x 660y. Walk 5 minutes after each.

VI(d) 6-10 x 660y. Walk 220y after each.

VI(e) 6-10 x 660y in 2:00 minutes each. Jog 220y after each.

Workout VII

This workout involves repetitions of 880 yards. Some coaches and athletes may prefer jogging to walking for recovery between these repetitions, but walking will provide a quicker and more thorough recovery after these longer runs.

VII(a) 1-4 x 880y at average racing speed. Walk 5 minutes after each. For example, the 4:00 minute miler would run these in 2:00.

VII(b) 4-8 x 880y at 2-4 seconds faster than average racing speed. Walk 2-4 minutes after each. For example, the 9:20 2-miler would run these in 2:16-2:18.

VII(c) 4-10 x 880y at average racing speed. Walk 2-3 minutes after each. For example, the 14:00 minute 3-miler would run these in 2:20.

Workout VIII

This workout involves repetitions of $\frac{3}{4}$ mile.

VIII(a) 1-8 x $\frac{3}{4}$ mile at racing speed. Walk 4-8 minutes after each. A 4:00 minute miler might run 1 x $\frac{3}{4}$ mile in 3:00. A 10:00 minute 2-

miler might run 3-4 x $\frac{3}{4}$ mile in 3:45. A 28:00 minute 6-miler might run 6-8 x $\frac{3}{4}$ mile in 3:30.

VIII(b) 2-10 x $\frac{3}{4}$ mile in 3-4 seconds per 440y slower than average racing pace. Walk 4-6 minutes after each. A 4:08 miler might run 2-4 x $\frac{3}{4}$ mile in 3:15-3:19. A 28:00 minute 6-miler might run 10 x $\frac{3}{4}$ mile in 3:39-3:42.

VIII(c) 1-4 x $\frac{3}{4}$ mile in 5-6 seconds slower per 440y than average racing pace. Walk 3-5 minutes after each. A 2:00 minute half-miler might run 1 x $\frac{3}{4}$ mile in 3:15-3:18. A 4:12 miler might run 4 x $\frac{3}{4}$ mile in 3:24-3:27 each.

Workout IX

This involves repetitions of 1 mile.

IX(a) 2-6 x 1 mile at racing speed. Walk 4-6 minutes after each. A 9:00 minute 2-miler might run 2-3 x 1 mile in 4:30 each. A 14:00 minute 3-miler might run 3-5 x 1 mile in 4:40 each. A 30:00 minute 6-miler might run 6 x 1 mile in 5:00 each.

IX(b) 3-8 x 1 mile in 3-5 seconds per 440y slower than average racing speed. Walk 3-4 minutes after each. A 28:00 minute 6-miler might run 6-8 x 1 mile in 4:52-5:00 each.

Workout X

This workout involves repetitions of $1\frac{1}{4}$ miles.

X(a) 2-6 x $1\frac{1}{4}$ miles in 3-5 seconds per 440y slower than average racing speed. Walk 3-5 minutes after each. The 30:00 minute 6-miler might run 6 x $1\frac{1}{4}$ miles in 6:30-6:40 each.

X(b) 4-8 x $1\frac{1}{4}$ mile in 80 seconds per 440y, or 6:40 each. Walk 3-4 minutes after each.

X(c) 2-6 x $1\frac{1}{4}$ miles at racing speed. Walk 5-8 minutes after each.

Workout XI

This workout involved repetitions of $1\frac{1}{2}$ miles.

XI(a) 1-5 x $1\frac{1}{2}$ miles at average racing speed. Walk 6-8 minutes after each.

XI(b) 3-5 x $1\frac{1}{2}$ miles at 80 seconds per 440y, or 8:00 minutes each. Walk 4-6 minutes after each.

XI(c) 3-5 x $1\frac{1}{2}$ miles at 5 seconds per 440y slower than average racing speed. Walk 4-6 minutes after each.

Workout XII

This workout involves repetitions of 2 miles.

XII(a) 2-4 x 2 miles in 6:00-6:30 per mile. Walk 5 minutes after each.

XII(b) 3-5 x 2 miles in 80 seconds per 440y, or 10:40 each. Walk 5 minutes after each.

XII(c) 2-3 x 2 miles at average racing speed. Walk 6-8 minutes after each.

Workout XIII

This workout involves repetitions of 3 miles.

XIII(a) 1-3 x 3 miles in 6:00-6:30 per mile. Walk 10 minutes after each.

XIII(b) 1-3 x 3 miles in 80 seconds per 440y, or 16:00 each. Walk 8-10 minutes after each.

XIII(c) 1-2 x 3 miles at 4-6 seconds per 440y slower than average racing speed. Walk 6-8 minutes after each.

Workout XIV

This workout involves continuous running at relatively slow speeds, preferably over cross-country or on roads in winter.

XIV(a) 3-5 miles in 6:30-7:00 minutes per mile. Walk 5 minutes, and run 10-15 x 150y acceleration runs.

XIV(b) 6-10 miles in 6:30-7:00 minutes per mile.

XIV(c) 10-15 miles in 6:30-7:00 minutes per mile.

Workout XV

This workout involves various combinations and series of short, fast runs. The speed of these 110y and 220y repetitions should be identical to those described in Workout II and III.

XV(a) 10-15 x 150y acceleration runs. This means jog 50y, stride 50y, and sprint 50y. Then walk 50y before starting the next 150y acceleration run.

XV(b) 10 x 110y. Jog 110y after each. Walk 2-3 minutes. 5-10 x 220y. Jog 220y after each. Walk 5 minutes. 10 x 110y. Jog 110y after each.

XV(c) 5 x 220y. Walk 110y after each. 1-2 x (10 x 110y. Jog 110y after each). Walk 5 minutes. 5 x 220y. Walk 110 y after each.

XV(d) 5 x 150y acceleration runs. 10 x 110y. Jog 110y after each. Walk 5 minutes. 5 x 220y. Walk 110y after each. 10 x 110y. Jog 220y after each. Walk 5 minutes. 5 x 150y acceleration runs.

XV(e) 6 x 110y. Jog 110y after each. Walk 1-2 minutes. 6 x 150y acceleration runs. 6 x 220y. Walk 110y after each. 6 x 110y. Jog 110y after each. 6 x 150 acceleration runs.

Workout XVI

This workout involves speed-play (fartlek) training, or informal fast-slow running. It should preferably be done over unmarked areas in parks, meadows, woods, or grassland, but it may be done on road or track when necessary. No stopwatch is needed. Run in flat-soled shoes and keep the emphasis on sheer speed, bearing in mind that the purpose of training is to learn to run faster, not slower.

Jog 10-15 minutes. 5 minutes stretching calisthenics.
2 x 3 minutes running (about 1100 yards) at best speed. Walk 5 minutes after each.
2-4 x 150y acceleration runs. Walk 50y after each.
2-4 short uphill sprints, or sprints up stadium steps. Walk back to starting point after each. If no hill or steps are available, then run 2-4 x 75y sprints. Walk 1 minute after each.
Run 880y easily in about 3:00 minutes. Walk 2-3 minutes.
2 x 330y at full speed. Walk 2-4 minutes after each.
Run 880y in 3:00 minutes.
220y at full speed. Walk 2-3 minutes.
2-4 x 150y acceleration runs. Walk 50y after each.
Jog 1 mile in 8-10 minutes.
Full session of weight training described in I(h).

Workout XVII

This workout involves 1-2 x full racing distance on a downhill road run in the same direction as the prevailing wind. Walk 10 minutes after each. The half-miler, miler, and 2-miler might run the full racing distance twice, while the 3 and 6 miler might run it only once. If the road is downhill, and the direction of the run is with the wind, the full racing distance may well be covered in faster time than would be the case in actual competition.

Specific details of individual workouts suggested on the following charts may be reviewed by referring to the foregoing instructions.

Cross-Country Training for Experienced High School Runners Competing at 2-Miles Distance.

This plan is designed for runners whose competitive track season ended about June 1st. They are assumed to have maintained reasonable fitness during the month of June, and are preparing for competition during the months of September, October, and November.

	July First Week	July Second Week	July Third Week	July Fourth Week
Mon.	A.M. Rest	A.M. I (h) Wt.trng.	A.M. I (h) Wt. trng.	A.M. I (h) Wt. trng.
	P.M. XIV (a) 3-5 mi. CC.	P.M. XIV (a) 3-5 mi. CC	P.M. Rest	P.M. XIV (a) 3-5 mi. CC.
Tues.	A.M. I (d) 150 yd. acc.	A.M. Rest	A.M. Rest	A.M. I (a) 2 mi.
	P.M. Rest	P.M. II (h) 110's	P.M. XIV (a) 3-5 mi. CC	P.M. V (c) 440's
Wed.	A.M. Rest	A.M. Rest	A.M. I (d) 150's	A.M. Rest
	P.M. II (j) 110's	P.M. Rest	P.M. V (b) 440's	P.M. Rest
Thurs.	A.M. I (h) Wt. trng.	A.M. I (h) Wt. trng.	A.M. Rest	A.M. I (h) Wt. trng.
	P.M. Rest	P.M. XIV (a) 3-5 mi. CC.	P.M. XIII (a) 3 miles	P.M. XIV (a) 3-5 mi. CC.
Fri.	A.M. Rest	A.M. Rest	A.M. I (h) Wt. trng.	A.M. I (b) 3 mi.
	P.M. XII (a) 2 mi.	P.M. V (a) 440's	P.M. XV (a) 150's	P.M. II (a) 110's
Sat.	Rest or makeup	Rest or makeup	Rest or makeup	Rest or makeup
Sun.	Rest or makeup	Rest or makeup	Rest or makeup	Rest or makeup

Training for Experienced High School Cross-Country Runners During August.

	August First Week	August Second Week	August Third Week	August Fourth Week
Mon.	A.M. I (h) Wt. trng.	A.M. I (h) Wt. trng.	A.M. I (d) 150's	A.M. I (h) Wt. trng.
	P.M. II (b) 110's	P.M. XIV (a) 3-5 mi. CC.	P.M. XIV (a) 3-5 mi. CC.	P.M. V (a) 440's
Tues.	A.M. Rest	A.M. Rest	A.M. Rest	A.M. I (e) 110's & 220's
	P.M. XIV (a) 3-5 mi. CC.	P.M. II (e) 110's	P.M. V (e) 440's	P.M. XIV (a) 3-5 mi. CC.
Wed.	A.M. Rest	A.M. I (f) $2\frac{1}{4}$ mi.	A.M. I (h) Wt. trng.	A.M. Rest
	P.M. V (d) 440's	P.M. VI (e) 660's	P.M. VII (c) 880's	P.M. VIII (c) $\frac{3}{4}$ mi.
Thurs.	A.M. Rest	A.M. Rest	A.M. Rest	A.M. I (h) Wt. trng.
	P.M. VIV (a) 3-5 mi. CC.	P.M. III (c) 220's	P.M. XV (b) 110's & 220's	P.M. XIV (a) 3-5 mi. CC.
Fri.	A.M. I (h) Wt. trng.	A.M. I (d) 150's	A.M. I (h) Wt. trng.	A.M. I (a) 2 mi.
	P.M. III (a) 220's	P.M. XVI Speed-Play	P.M. XVI Speed-Play	P.M. III (b) 220's
Sat.	Rest or makeup	Rest or makeup	Rest or makeup	Rest or makeup
Sun.	Rest or makeup	Rest or makeup	Rest or makeup	Rest or makeup

Training for Experienced High School Cross-Country Runners During September.

	September First Week	September Second Week	September Third Week	September Fourth Week
Mon.	A.M. I (h) Wt. trng. P.M. IX (b) 3 x 1 mi.	A.M. I (h) Wt. trng. P.M. X (a) $1\frac{1}{4}$ mi.	A.M. I (h) Wt. trng. P.M. XIV (a) 3-5 mi. CC.	A.M. I (h) Wt. trng. P.M. XIV (a) 3-5 mi. CC.
Tues.	A.M. I (d) 150's P.M. XIV (a) 3-5 mi. CC	A.M. Rest P.M. V (e) 440's	A.M. I (a) 2 mi P.M. II (c) 110's	A.M. I (d) 150's P.M. III (b) 220's
Wed.	A.M. Rest P.M. V (e) 440's	A.M. I (d) 150's P.M. XIV (a) 3-5 mi. CC.	A.M. I (b) 3 mi. P.M. V (d) 440's	A.M. I (b) 3 mi. P.M. VI (c) 660's
Thurs.	A.M. I (d) 150's P.M. XIV (a) 3-5 mi. CC	A.M. I (h) Wt. trng. P.M. II (e) 110's	A.M. Rest P.M. Rest	A.M. Rest P.M. Rest
Fri.	A.M. I (h) Wt. trng. P.M. III (b) 220's	A.M. I (b) 3 mi. P.M. VII (c) 880's	A.M. Rest P.M. Competition	A.M. Rest P.M. Competition
Sat.	Rest or makeup	Rest or makeup	I (h) Wt. trng.	I (h) Wt. trng.
Sun.	Rest or makeup	Rest or makeup	P.M. XV (a) 150's	P.M. XII (a) 2 mi.

Training for Experienced High School Cross-Country Runners During October.

	October First Week	October Second Week	October Third Week	October Fourth Week
Mon.	A.M. I (h) Wt. trng. P.M. XIV (a) 3-5 mi. CC.	A.M. I (h) Wt. trng. P.M. XIV (a) 3-5 mi. CC.	A.M. Rest P.M. IV (b) 330's	A.M. Rest P.M. IV (b) 330's
Tues.	A.M. I (f) $2\frac{1}{4}$ mi. P.M. II(c) 110's	A.M. I (d) 150's P.M. IV(e) 440's	A.M. Rest P.M. Competition	A.M. Rest P.M. Competition
Wed.	A.M. I (h) Wt. trng. P.M. IV (e) 440's	A.M. I (b) 3 mi. P.M. IX (a) 3 x 1 mi.	A.M. I (h) Wt. trng. P.M. III (f) 220's	A.M. I (h) Wt. trng. P.M. XV (e) 110, 150, 220
Thurs.	A.M. Rest P.M. Rest	A.M. Rest P.M. Rest	A.M. Rest P.M. Rest	A.M. Rest P.M. Rest
Fri.	A.M. Rest P.M. Competition	A.M. Rest P.M. Competition	A.M. Rest P.M. Competition	A.M. Rest P.M. Competition
Sat.	Rest or makeup	Rest or makeup	I (h) Wt. trng.	I (h) Wt. trng.
Sun.	Rest or makeup	XIV (a) 3-5 mi. CC.	XIV (a) 3-5 mi. CC.	XIV (a) 3-5 mi. CC.

Training for Experienced High School Cross-Country Runners During November.

	November First Week	November Second Week	November Third Week	November Fourth Week
Mon.	A.M. I (h) Wt. trng. P.M. III (e) 220's	A.M. I (h) Wt. trng. P.M. IV (a) 330's	A.M. I (h) Wt. trng. P.M. II (h) 110's	A.M. I (h) Wt. trng. P.M. XIV (a) 3-5 mi. CC.
Tues.	A.M. I (a) 2 mi P.M. VIII (a) $\frac{3}{4}$ mile	A.M. Rest Competition	A.M. I (f) $2\frac{1}{4}$ mi. P.M. XIV (a) 3-5 mi. CC.	A.M. Rest P.M. V (d) 440's
Wed.	A.M. I (d) 150's P.M. V (d) 440's	A.M. I (d) 150's P.M. VI (e) 660's	A.M. I (d) 150's P.M. V (e) 440's	A.M. Rest P.M. X (c) $1\frac{1}{4}$ mi.
Thurs.	A.M. Rest P.M. Rest	A.M. Rest P.M. Rest	A.M. Rest P.M. Rest	A.M. Rest P.M. Rest
Fri.	A.M. Rest P.M. Competition	A.M. Rest P.M. Competition	A.M. Rest P.M. Competition	A.M. Rest P.M. Rest
Sat.	I (b) Wt. trng.	I (h) Wt. trng.	I (h) Wt. trng.	Major Competition
Sun.	XIV (a) 3-5 mi. CC.	XIV (a) 3-5 mi.CC.	Rest	Rest

Winter Training for Experienced High School Half-Milers and Milers.

This plan is designed for runners who have participated in the preceding cross-country season, may or may not race competitively indoors, and will race outdoors starting in late March or April.

	December First Week	December Second Week	December Third Week	December Fourth Week
Mon.	A.M. I (h) Wt. trng. P.M. XII (a) 2 miles	A.M. I (h) Wt. trng. P.M. V (b) 440's	A.M. I (h) Wt. trng. P. M. II (b) 110's	A.M. I (h) Wt. trng. P.M.Half milers V (b) Milers V (d) 440's
Tues.	A.M. I (f) $2\frac{1}{4}$ mi. P.M. II (h) 110's	A.M. I (b) 3 mi. P.M. XV (a) 150's	A.M. I (g) P.M. IV (a) 330's	A.M. I (b) 3 mi. P.M. IV (b) 330's
Wed.	A.M. Rest P.M. Rest	A.M. Rest P.M. Rest	A.M. Rest P.M. Rest	A.M. Rest P.M. Rest
Thurs.	A.M. I (h) Wt. trng. P.M. XVII 880 or mi.	A.M. I (h) Wt. Trng. P.M. V (c) 440's	A.M. I (h) Wt. trng. P.M. XVII 880 or mi.	A.M. I (h) Wt. trng. P.M. Half Milers V (b) Milers V (d) 440's
Fri.	A.M. I (a) 2 mi. P.M. III (d) 220's	A.M. I (d) 150's P.M. VI (c) 660's	A.M. I (a) 2 mi P.M. III (b) 220's	A.M. I (d) 150's P.M. $\frac{1}{2}$mi VI (c), 660's Milers VII (a), 880's

Sat.	XV (e) 110, 150,220	XIV (a) 3-5 mi. CC.	XIV (a) 3-5 mi. CC.	XIV (a) 3-5 mi. CC.
Sun.	Rest	Rest	Rest	Rest

Winter Training for Experienced High School Half-Milers and Milers During January.

	January First Week	January Second Week	January Third Week	January Fourth Week
Mon.	A.M. I (h) Wt. trng. P.M. $\frac{1}{2}$ milers V (b) Milers V (d) 440's	A.M. I (h) Wt. trng. P.M. $\frac{1}{2}$ milers V (b) Milers V (e) 440's	A.M. I (h) Wt. trng. P.M. XV (e) 110, 150, 220.	A.M. I (h) Wt. trng. P.M. II (c) 110's
Tues.	A.M. I (b) 3 mi P.M. II (c) 110's	A.M. I (f) $2\frac{1}{4}$ mi. P.M. XV (b) 110's and 220's	A.M. I (a) 2 mi. P.M.Half milers V (b) Milers V (d) 440's	A.M. I (b) 3 mi. P.M. $\frac{1}{2}$ milers V (b) Milers V (e) 440's
Wed.	A.M. Rest P.M. Rest	A.M. Rest P.M. Rest	A.M. I (h) Wt. trng. P.M. $\frac{1}{2}$ mil. VI (c) 660's Milers VIII (a) $\frac{3}{4}$ mile.	A.M. I (h) Wt. trng. P.M.$\frac{1}{2}$ mil.IV (d) 330's Milers VII(a) 880's
Thurs.	A.M. I (h) Wt. trng. P.M. XVII 880 or mile	A.M. I (h) Wt. trng. $\frac{1}{2}$ mil. VIII (c) Milers VIII (b) $\frac{3}{4}$ mi.	A.M. Rest P.M. Rest	A.M. Rest P.M. Rest
Fri.	A.M. XV (a) 150's P.M. III (b) 220's	A.M. XV (a) 150's $\frac{1}{2}$ mil V (b) Milers V (e), 440's	A.M. Rest P.M. Compet- ition or XVII	A.M. Rest P.M. Compet- ition or XVII
Sat.	XIV (a) 3-5 mi. CC.	XIV 3-5 mi. CC.	XIV 3-5 mi. CC.	XIV 3-5 mi. CC.
Sun.	Rest	Rest	Rest	Rest

Winter Training for Experienced High School Half-Milers and Milers During February.

	February First Week	February Second Week	February Third Week	February Fourth Week
Mon.	A.M. I (b) 3 mi. P.M. III (b) 220's	A.M. I (h) Wt. trng. P.M. XV (d) 110, 150, 220	A.M. I (b) 3 mi. P.M. II (c) 110's	A.M. I (f) $2\frac{1}{4}$ mi. P.M. III (b) 220's
Tues.	A.M. I (f) $2\frac{1}{4}$ mi. P.M. XVI Speed-play	A.M. I (b) 3 mi. P.M.$\frac{1}{2}$ mil.VI (a) 660's Milers VII(a) 880's	A.M. I (f) $2\frac{1}{4}$ mi. P.M. XVI Speed-play	A.M. I (b) 3 mi. P.M. XVI Speed-play
Wed.	A.M. I (a) 2 mi. P.M.$\frac{1}{2}$ mil.V(b)	A.M. I (h) Wt. trng. P.M.$\frac{1}{2}$mil.V (b)	A.M. I (d) 150's P.M.$\frac{1}{2}$mil.III(a) 220	A.M. I (d) 150's P.M.$\frac{1}{2}$mil.IV (d), 330

	Milers V(d)440's	Milers V(e)440's	Milers V(d)440's	MilersV(d)440
Thurs.	A.M. Rest P.M. Rest	A.M. Rest P.M. Rest	A.M. Rest P.M. Rest	A.M. Rest P.M. Rest
Fri.	A.M. Rest P.M. Compet-ition or XVII.	A.M. Rest P.M. Compet-ition or XVII.	A.M. Rest P.M .Compet-ition or XVII	A.M. Rest P.M.Compet-ition or XVII
Sat.	XIV. 3-5 mi. CC.	XIV. 3-5 mi. CC.	XIV. 3-5 mi. CC.	XIV. 3-5 mi. CC.
Sun.	Rest	Rest	Rest	Rest

Winter Training for Experienced High School Half-Milers and Milers During March.

	March First Week	March Second Week	March Third Week	March Fourth Week
Mon.	A.M. I (f) $2\frac{1}{4}$ mi. P.M. XV (e) 110, 150, 220	A.M. I (h) Wt. trng. P.M. $\frac{1}{2}$mil.III(g) Milers III(b)220's	A.M. I(d) 150's P.M. XVI Speed-play	A.M. I(c) 110's P.M. III (d) 220's
Tues.	A.M. I (b) 3 mi. P.M. XVI Speed-play	A.M. I (b) 3 mi. P.M. $\frac{1}{2}$mil.VI(a) Milers VI(c)660's	A.M. I (f) $2\frac{1}{4}$ mi. P.M.XIII (b) $\frac{3}{4}$ mi.	A.M. I (b) 3 mi. P.M. $\frac{1}{2}$mil.V(b) Mil.V(d)440's
Wed.	A.M. I(a) 2 mi. P.M. $\frac{1}{2}$ mi.IV(d) 330 Milers V(d)440's	A.M. Rest P.M. Rest	A.M. I (d) 150's P.M. $\frac{1}{2}$mi.V(b) MilersV(e)440's	A.M. I (h) Wt. trng. P.M. II (h) 110's
Thurs.	A.M. Rest P.M. Rest	A.M. Rest P.M. Rest	A.M. I(b) 3 mi. P.M. XVI Speed-play	A.M. I(g) P.M. $\frac{1}{2}$mi.V(b) mi.V(d)440's
Fri.	A.M. Rest P.M.Competit-ion or XVII	A.M. Rest P.M. Compet-ition or XVII	A.M. I(g) P.M. XV(d) 110, 150, 220	A.M. I(f) $2\frac{1}{4}$ mi. P.M.XV(d) 110, 150, 220
Sat.	Rest	Rest	Rest	Rest
Sun.	Rest	Rest	Rest	Rest

Spring Training for Experienced High School Half-Milers and Milers During April.

	April First Week	April Second Week	April Third Week	April Fourth Week
Mon.	A.M. I (b) 3 mi. P.M. $\frac{1}{2}$mil.II(i) MilersII(d) 110's	A.M. I (b) 3 mi. P.M. $\frac{1}{2}$ mil.V(b) Milers V(d)440's	A.M. I (h) Wt. trng. P.M. $\frac{1}{2}$mil.IV(d) Milers IV (a) 330's	A.M. I (h) Wt. trng. P.M. $\frac{1}{2}$mil.V(b) Milers V (d) 440's
Tues.	A.M. I (a) 2 mi P.M. XV(d) 110, 150, 220	A.M. I (a) 2 mi. P.M. XVI Speed-play	A.M. Rest P.M.Competit-ion or XVI (Speed-play)	A.M. Rest P.M. Competit-ion or XVI (Speed-play) no. wt.trng.
Wed.	A.M. I (h) Wt. trng. P.M. VIII (a) $\frac{3}{4}$ mi.	A.M. I (d) 150's P.M. $\frac{1}{2}$mil.III(g) 220 Milers V(d) 440's	A.M. I (f) $2\frac{1}{4}$ mi. P.M. $\frac{1}{2}$mil II(I) 110 Milers V(d)440's	A.M. I (b) 3 mi. P.M. XV(d) 110, 150, 220

Thurs.	A.M. I (f) $2\frac{1}{4}$ mi. P.M. III (b) 220's	A.M. Rest P.M. Rest	A.M. Rest P.M. Rest	A.M. Rest P.M. Rest
Fri.	A.M I (b) 3 mi. P.M. XV (e) 110, 150, 220	A.M. Rest P.M. Competition or XVII.	A.M. Rest P.M.Competition or XVII.	A.M. Rest P.M.Competition.
Sat.	Rest	Rest	XIV 3-5 mi. CC.	XIV 3-5 Mi. CC.
Sun.	Rest	Rest	Rest	Rest

Spring Training for Experienced High School Half-Milers and Milers During May.

	May First Week	May Second Week	May Third Week	May Fourth Week
Mon.	A.M. I (f) $2\frac{1}{4}$ mi. P.M. $\frac{1}{2}$ mil. III (g) Milers III (b) 220's	A.M. I (h) Wt. Trng. P.M. $\frac{1}{2}$ Mil. IV (d) Milers IV (c) 330's	A.M. I (h) Wt. trng. P.M. $\frac{1}{2}$ mil. III (g) 220, Milers V(d), 440	A.M. Rest P.M. $\frac{1}{2}$ mil. II(i) 110 Milers V (d) 440's
Tues.	A.M. I (b) 3 mi P.M. XVI Speed-play	A.M. Rest P.M. XV (e) 110, 150, 220	A.M. Rest P.M. XV (d) 110, 150, 220	A.M. Rest P.M. XV (c) 110 & 220
Wed.	A.M. Rest P.M. $\frac{1}{2}$ mil. V (a) Milers V (d) 440's	A.M. I (b) 3 mi. P.M. $\frac{1}{2}$ mil. V (b) Milers V (d) 440's	A.M. Rest P.M. $\frac{1}{2}$ mil. VI (a) Milers VI (c) 660's	A.M. Rest P.M. $\frac{1}{2}$ mil. V (a) 440 Milers XII (a) 880's
Thurs.	A.M. Rest P.M. Rest	A.M. Rest P.M. Rest	A.M. Rest P.M. Rest	A.M. Rest P.M. Rest
Fri.	A.M. Rest P.M. Competition	A.M. Rest P.M. Rest	A.M. Rest P.M. Competition	A.M. Rest P.M. Rest
Sat.	XIV 3-5 mi. CC.	Major Competition	Rest	Major Competition
Sun.	Rest	Rest	Rest	Rest

Cross-Country Training for Experienced College Runners Competing at 3-5 Miles Distance.

This plan is designed for runners whose competitive track season ended about June 15. They are assumed to have maintained reasonable fitness during the remainder of June and July by swimming, basketball and other ball games, golf and running. Their competitive cross-country season will start about the last week of September, and continue into November.

	August First Week	August Second Week	August Third Week	August Fourth Week
Mon.	A.M. Rest P.M XII (a) 3-5 mi. CC.	A.M. I (h) Wt. trng. P.M. XIV (a) 3-5 mi. CC.	A.M. I (h) Wt. trng. P.M. XIV (a) 3-5 mi. CC.	A.M. I (h) Wt. trng. P.M. XIV (a) 3-5 mi. CC.
Tues.	A.M. I (h) Wt. trng. P.M. Rest	A.M. Rest P.M. XV (a) 150's	A.M. I (f) $2\frac{1}{4}$ mi. P.M. V (a) 440's	A.M. I (b) 3 mi. P.M V (b) 440's

Wed.	A.M. Rest P.M XII (a) 2 mi.	A.M. I (e) 110's and 220's P.M. XII (a) 2 mi.	A.M. Rest P.M. XIV (a) 3-5 mi. CC.	A.M. Rest P.M. XIII(a) 3 mi.
Thurs.	A.M. I (h) Wt. trng. P.M. Rest	A.M. Rest P.M. II (h) 110's	A.M. I (h) Wt. trng. P.M. IV (a) 330's	A.M. I (d) 150's P.M. III(c) 220's
Fri.	A.M. Rest P.M. XIV (a) 3-5 mi. CC.	A.M. I (h) Wt. trng. P.M. XIV (a) 3-5 mi. CC.	A.M. I (d) 150's P.M. XIV (a) 3-5 mi. CC.	A.M. I (h) Wt. trng. P.M. XIV (a) 3-5 mi. CC
Sat.	Rest or makeup	Rest or makeup	Rest or makeup	Rest or makeup
Sun.	Rest or makeup	Rest or makeup	Rest or makeup	Rest or makeup

Training for Experienced College Cross-Country Runners During September.

	September First Week	September Second Week	September Third Week	September Fourth Week
Mon.	A.M. I (c) 110's P.M. XIV (b) 6 mi. CC.	A.M. I (d) 150's P.M. XIV (b) 6-10 mi. CC.	A.M. I (c) 110's P.M. XIV (b) 6-10 mi.CC.	A.M. I (h) Wt. trng. P.M.XIV(b) 6-10 mi. CC
Tues.	A.M. I(h) Wt. trng. P.M. V (c) 440's	A.M. I(h) Wt. trng. P.M. V (d) 440's	A.M. I (h) Wt. trng. P.M. V (e) 440's	A.M. I (d) 150's P.M. V(e) 440's
Wed.	A.M. Rest P.M. XVI Speed-play	A.M. I (b) 3 mi. P.M.XVII (c) 880's	A.M. I (d) 150's P.M. IX (b) 1 mile	A.M. I (h) Wt. trng. P.M. III (a) 220's
Thurs.	A.M. I (h) Wt. trng. P.M. II (b) 110's	A.M. I (h) Wt. trng. P.M. III (b) 220's	A.M. I (h) Wt. trng. P.M. XV (d) 110, 150, 220	Rest P.M. X(c) $1\frac{1}{4}$ mi.
Fri.	A.M. I (g) P.M. XIV 6 mi. CC/	A.M. I (f) $2\frac{1}{4}$ miles P.M. VIII (c) 4 x $\frac{3}{4}$ mi.	A.M. Rest P.M. Rest	A.M. Rest P.M. Rest
Sat.	Rest or makeup	Rest or makeup	XVII 3-5 miles CC.	Compet- ition or XVII
Sun.	Rest or makeup	Rest or makeup	Rest	Rest

Training for Experienced College Cross-Country Runners During October.

	October First Week	October Second Week	October Third Week	October Fourth Week
Mon.	A.M. I (g) P.M. XIV (b) 6-10 mi. CC.	A.M. I (h) Wt. trng. P.M XIV (b) 6-10 mi. CC.	A.M. I (h) Wt. trng. P.M.XIV (b) 6-10 mi. CC.	A.M. I (e) 110's &220's P.M.XIV (b) 6-10 mi. CC.
Tues.	A.M. I (h) Wt. trng. P.M. V (e) 440's	A.M. I (f) $2\frac{1}{4}$ mi. P.M. V (e) 440's	A.M. I (d) 150's P.M. V (e) 440's	A.M. I (h) Wt. trng. P.M. V (e) 440's
Wed.	A.M. I (d) 150's P.M. II (c)	A.M. I(h) Wt. trng. P.M. III (a)	A.M. I (b) 3 mi. P.M. XVI	A.M. I (b) 3 mi. P.M.XV (e)

	110's	220's	Speed-play	110, 150, 220.
Thurs.	A.M. I (h) Wt. trng. P.M. XI (c) $1\frac{1}{2}$ mi.	A.M. I (b) 3 mi. P.M.XII (c) 2 mi.	A.M. I (g) P.M. VI (d) 660 yd.	A.M. I (h) Wt. trng. P.M.VIII(a) $\frac{3}{4}$ mile
Fri.	A.M. Rest P.M. Rest	A.M. Rest P.M. Rest	A.M. Rest P.M. Rest	A.M. Rest P.M. Rest
Sat.	Competit-ion or XVII	Competit-ion or XVII	Competit-ion or XVII	Competit-ion or XVII
Sun.	Rest	Rest	Rest	Rest

Training for Experienced College Cross-Country Runners During November.

	November First Week	November Second Week	November Third Week	November Fourth Week
Mon.	A.M. I (h) Wt. trng. P.M. XIV (b) 6-10 mi. CC.	A.M. I (d) 150's P.M. XIV (b) 6-10 mi. CC.	A.M. I (h) Wt. trng. P.M. XIV (b) 6-10 mi. CC.	A.M. I (d) 150's P.M. V (e) 440's
Tues.	A.M. I (d) 150's P.M. V (i) 440's	A.M. I (h) Wt. trng. P.M. V (j) 440's	A.M. I (d) 150's P.M. V (d) 440's	A.M.I (c) 110's P.M. X (c) $1\frac{1}{4}$ mi.
Wed.	A.M. I (h) Wt. trng. P.M. XV (d) 110, 150, 220	A.M. I (b) 3 mi. P.M. XV (b) 110's & 220's	A.M. I (c) 110's P.M.VIII (a) $\frac{3}{4}$ mi.	A.M. Rest P.M.XVI Speed-play
Thurs.	A.M. I (b) 3 mi. P.M. IX (a) 1 mile	A.M. Rest P.M. Rest	A.M. Rest P.M. Rest	A.M. Rest P.M. Rest
Fri.	A.M. Rest P.M. Rest	A.M. Rest P.M. Rest	A.M. Rest P.M. Rest	A.M. Rest P.M. Rest
Sat.	Competition or XVII	Major Compet-ition	Competition or XVII	Major Com-petition
Sun.	Rest	Rest	Rest	Rest

Winter Training for Experienced College Half-Milers and Milers.

This plan is designed for runners who have participated in the preceding cross-country season, may or may not race competitively indoors, and will race outdoors starting sometime in March. It is suggested that runners who have participated in the preceding cross-country season will benefit from 1-4 weeks of "active rest" prior to the beginning of winter training.

	December First Week	December Second Week	December Third Week	December Fourth Week
Mon.	A.M. Rest P.M. Rest	A.M. Rest P.M. Rest	A.M. Rest P.M. Rest	A.M. Rest P.M. Rest
Tues.	A.M. I (h) Wt. trng. P.M. $\frac{1}{2}$ mil. XIV (a) 3-5 mi. Milers XIV (b)6-10mi.	A.M. I (h) Wt. trng. P.M. IV (a) 330's	A.M. I (h) Wt. trng. P.M. V (c) 440's	A.M. I (h) Wt. trng. P.M. $\frac{1}{2}$ mil. V (b) Milers V(d), 440's
Wed.	A.M. I (d) 150's P.M. IV (c) 330's	A.M. I (b) 3 mi. P.M. XV (e) 110, 150, 220	A.M. I (b) 3 mi. P.M. II (a) 110's	A.M. I (b) 3 mi. P.M. III(g) 220's
Thurs.	A.M. Rest P.M Rest	A.M. Rest P.M. Rest	A.M. Rest P.M. Rest	A.M Rest P.M. Rest

Fri.	A.M. I (h) Wt. trng. P.M. ½ mil. XIV (a), 3-5 mi. Milers XIV (b) 6-10 mi.	A.M. I (h) Wt. trng. P.M. V(b) 440's	A.M. I (h) Wt. trng. P.M. III (b) 220's	A.M. I (h) Wt. trng. P.M.XVII ½ milers -880, Milers -1 mi.
Sat.	II (h) 110's	III (c) 220's	½ milers, IV (b) 330's Milers -VI(c), 660's	XV (d) 110, 150, 220
Sun.	½ milers - XIV(a)3-5 mi. Milers - XIV (b) 6-10 mi.	½ mil.XIV(a) 3-5 mi. Milers XIV (b), 6-10 mi.	XV (e) 110, 150, 220	XV (a) 15 x 150

Winter Training for Experienced College Half-Milers and Milers During January.

	January First Week	January Second Week	January Third Week	January Fourth Week
Mon.	A.M. I (b) 3 mi. P.M. ½ mil. III(c) 220 Milers V(c) 440's	A.M. I (b) 3 mi. P.M. III (c) 220's	A.M. I (b) 3 mi. P.M. ½ mil. III (g) 220. Milers V(e)440	A.M. I (b) 3 mi. P.M.III (b) 220's
Tues.	A.M. I (h) Wt. trng. P.M. ½ mil. VI(c) 660. Milers VIII(b) ¾ mi.	A.M. I (h) Wt. trng. P.M. II (c) 110's	A.M. I (h) Wt. trng. P.M. ½ Mil.VI(c) 660. Milers VIII(b) ¾ mile.	A.M. I (h) Wt. trng. P.M.XV(e) 110, 150, 220's
Wed.	A.M. I (f) 2¼ mi. P.M. ½ mil.II(b) 110 Milers V(d)440's	A.M. I (b) 3 mi. P.M. ½ mil.IV(d) 330 Milers V(e)440's	A.M. I (f) 2¼ mi. P.M. ½ mil.II(c) 110 Milers V(d) 440's	A.M. I (f) 2¼ mi. P.M. ½ mil. V(b) Milers V(e) 440's
Thurs.	A.M. I (h) Wt. trng. P.M. ½ mil. V(b) 440 Milers VII(a) 880	A.M. I (h) Wt. trng. P.M. XV (e) 110, 150, 220	A.M. I (h) Wt. trng. P.M. ½ mil.V(b) 440, Milers VII(c)880	A.M. Rest P.M. Rest
Fri.	A.M. I (b) 3 mi. P.M. ½ mil. II(i) 110 Milers V(e) 440's	A.M. I (b) 3 mi. P.M. III (e) 220's	A.M. I (b) 3 mi. P.M. ½ mil. III (e) 220. Milers V(d)440's	A.M. Rest P.M. Rest
Sat.	Rest or makeup	Rest or makeup	Rest or makeup	Competition or XVII
Sun.	Rest	Rest	Rest	Rest

Winter Training for Experienced College Half-Milers and Milers During February.

	February First Week	February Second Week	February Third Week	February Fourth Week
Mon.	A.M. I (b) 3 miles P.M. ½ mil.III	A.M. Rest P.M. II (c)	A.M. I (b) 3 miles P.M. ½ mil.	A.M. I (h) Wt. trng. P.M. ½ mil.

	(b) 220's Milers V (e) 440's	110's	IV (b) 330. Milers V(j) 440	II(i) 110 Milers III(b) 220's
Tues.	A.M. I (h) Wt. trng. P.M. $\frac{1}{2}$ mil. V(b) 440's Milers VIII (b) $\frac{3}{4}$ mi.	Rest P.M .III (b) 220's	A.M. I (h) Wt. trng. P.M. $\frac{1}{2}$ mil. VI(c) 660 Milers VII(c) 880	A.M. I (b) 3 miles P.M. $\frac{1}{2}$ mil. V(b) Milers V(e) 440's
Wed.	A.M. I (b) 3 mi. P.M. XV (d) 110, 150, 220	A.M I (h) Wt. trng. P.M. $\frac{1}{2}$ mil. V(b) Milers V(e)440's	A.M I (b) 3 mi. P.M. XV (e) 110, 150, 220	A.M. I (h) Wt. trng. P.M.XV(d) 110, 150, 220
Thurs.	A.M. I (a) 2 mi P.M. $\frac{1}{2}$ mil.IV(d) 330 Milers V(d)440's	A.M. Rest P.M. Rest	A.M. Rest P.M. $\frac{1}{2}$ mil.II(b) 110. Milers V(d) 440's	A.M. Rest P.M. Rest
Fri.	A.M. Rest P.M. Rest	A.M. Rest P.M. Rest	A.M. Rest P.M. Rest	A.M. Rest P.M. Rest
Sat.	Competition or XVII	Competition or XVII	Competition or XVII	Competition or XVII
Sun.	Rest	Rest	Rest	Rest

Winter Training for Experienced College Half-Milers and Milers During March.

	March First Week	March Second Week	March Third Week	March Fourth Week
Mon.	A.M. I (b) 3 mi. P.M. $\frac{1}{2}$mil. III (g) 220 Milers V(j) 440's	A.M. I (b) 3 mi. P.M. XVI Speed-play	A.M. Rest P.M. Rest	A.M. I (a) 2 mi. P.M. XIV (a) 3-5 mi. CC.
Tues.	A.M. I (d) 150's P.M. XVI Speed-play	A.M. I (b) 3 mi. P.M. XV (e) 110, 150, 220	A.M. Rest P.M. Rest	A.M. I (d) 150's P.M. XVI Speed-play
Wed.	A.M. I (b) 3 mi. P.M. $\frac{1}{2}$ mil. IV(b) 330 Milers V(f) 440's	A.M. I (h) Wt. trng. P.M. $\frac{1}{2}$ mil. V (b) Milers V(d) 440's	A.M. Rest P.M. Rest	A.M. I(d) 150's P.M.XIV(a) 3-5 mi. CC.
Thurs.	A.M. Rest P.M. Rest	A.M. Rest P.M. Rest	A.M. Rest P.M. Rest	A.M. I (f) $2\frac{1}{4}$ mi. P.M. XVI Speed-play
Fri.	A.M. Rest P.M. Rest	A.M. Rest P.M. Rest	A.M. Rest P.M. Rest	A.M. I(c) 110's P.M. $\frac{1}{2}$ mil. XIV(a) 3-5 mi. cc. Milers XIV(b) 6-10 mi.

Sat.	Competition or XVII	Competition or XVII	Rest	Rest
Sun.	Rest	Rest	Rest	Rest

Spring Training for Experienced College Half-Milers and Milers During April.

	April First Week	April Second Week	April Third Week	April Fourth Week
Mon.	A.M. I (b) 3 mi. P.M. $\frac{1}{2}$ mil. III(c) 220 Milers V(e)440	A.M. I (b) 3 mi. P.M.$\frac{1}{2}$ mil. II(i) 110. Milers XV (d)110, 150, 220.	A.M. I (b) 3 mi. P.M. $\frac{1}{2}$ mil.III(g) 220. Milers V(j) 440's	A.M. I (b) 3 mi. P.M. XV(b), 110's &220's
Tues.	A.M I (h) Wt. trng. P.M. $\frac{1}{2}$ mil. VI(a) 660. Milers. VIII(b) $\frac{3}{4}$ mi.	A.M. I (h) Wt. trng. P.M. $\frac{1}{2}$ mil. III(c) 220 Milers, V(e) 440's	A.M.I (d) 150's P.M. XVI Speed-play	A.M. I (b) 3 mi. P.M. XVI Speed-play
Wed.	A.M. I (b) 3 mi. P.M. XV (d) 110, 150, 220	A.M. I (b) 3 mi. P.M. $\frac{1}{2}$ mil. V(b)440's Milers, III(b) 220's	A.M I (b) 3 mi. P.M. $\frac{1}{2}$ mil.IV (d) 330's Milers V(f)440's	A.M. I (f) $2\frac{1}{4}$ mi. P.M. $\frac{1}{2}$ mil. IV (d) 330. Milers, V(j) 440's
Thurs.	A.M. Rest P.M. $\frac{1}{2}$ mil. II(c) 110 Milers, V(f) 440's	A.M. Rest P.M. Rest	A.M. Rest P.M. $\frac{1}{2}$ mil. VI (b) Milers, VI(c)660's	A.M. Rest P.M. Rest
Fri.	A.M. Rest P.M. Rest	A.M. Rest P.M. Rest	A.M. Rest P.M. Rest	A.M. Rest P.M. Rest
Sat.	Competition or XVII	Competition or XVII	Competition or XVII	Competition or XVII
Sun.	Rest	Rest	Rest	Rest

Spring Training for Experienced College Half-Milers and Milers During May.

	May First Week	May Second Week	May Third Week	May Fourth Week
Mon.	A.M. I (b) 3 mi. P.M. XVI Speed-play	A.M. I (b) 3 mi. P.M.$\frac{1}{2}$ mil.III(c) 220 Milers. V(f) 440's	A.M. I (b) 3 mi. P.M. XV (d) 110, 150, 220	A.M. I (b) 3 mi. P.M.$\frac{1}{2}$ mi. III(b) 220 Milers.V(j) 440's
Tues.	A.M. I (g) P.M.XIV (a) 3-5 mi. cc.&XV(a)150's	A.M. I (h) Wt. trng. P.M.$\frac{1}{2}$ mi. II(i) 110's Milers, VII(c), 880's	A.M. I (b) 3 mi. P.M.XVI Speed-play	A.M. I (h) Wt. trng. P.M.$\frac{1}{2}$ mil. IV(d) 330's Milers III(b) 220's
Wed.	A.M. I(e) 110's & 220's P.M. XV (e) 110, 150, 220's	A.M.I(d) 150's P.M.$\frac{1}{2}$ mil.V(b) Milers, V(j)440's	A.M. I (d) 150's P.M.$\frac{1}{2}$ mil.II(i) 110's Milers, III(b) 220	A.M. I (b) 3 miles P.M.$\frac{1}{2}$ mi.II(c) 110's.Milers VI(c) 660's
Thurs.	A.M. Rest P.M.$\frac{1}{2}$ milV(b)	A.M. Rest P.M. Rest	A.M. Rest P.M.$\frac{1}{2}$ mi.V(a)	A.M. Rest P.M. Rest

	Milers V(e) 440's		Milers V(e) 440's	
Fri.	A.M. Rest P.M. Rest	A.M. Rest P.M. Rest	A.M. Rest P.M. Rest	A.M. Rest P.M. Rest
Sat.	Competition	Competition	Competition	Competition
Sun.	Rest	Rest	Rest	Rest

Summer Training for Experienced College Half-Milers and Milers During June.

	June First Week	June Second Week	June Third Week	June Fourth Week
Mon.	A.M. I (b) 3 mi. P.M. XV (e) 110, 150, 220	A.M I (b) 3 mi. P.M.$\frac{1}{2}$mi.II(i) 110's.Milers V(j) 440's	A.M. I (b) 3 mi. P.M. XVI Speed-play	
Tues.	A.M. I (f) $2\frac{1}{4}$ mi. P.M. XVI Speed-play	A.M. I (d) 150's P.M. $\frac{1}{2}$ mi.III(c) Milers, III(b)220's	A.M. I (f) $2\frac{1}{4}$ mi. P.M. $\frac{1}{2}$ mi.III(c) 220 Milers, V(f) 440's	
Wed.	A.M. I (b) 3 mi. P.M.$\frac{1}{2}$mi.II(i) 110's Milers, III(b) 220's	A.M. I (b) 3 mi. P.M. $\frac{1}{2}$ mi. V(b) Milers V(j), 440's	A.M. Rest P.M.$\frac{1}{2}$ mi.VI(a) Milers,VI(c)660's	
Thurs.	A.M. Rest P.M. $\frac{1}{2}$ mi. V(a) Milers, V(d)440's	A.M. Rest P.M. Rest	A.M. Rest P.M. Rest	
Fri.	A.M. Rest P.M. Rest	A.M. Rest P.M. Rest	A.M. Rest P.M. Rest	
Sat.	Competition	Competition	Final Competition	
Sun.	Rest	Rest		

Winter Training for Experienced College Runners Who Will Race at 3 and/ or 6 Miles in Collegiate Championship Competition During June, But Will Otherwise Race Mostly, Over 2-Miles During Winter Indoor and/or Spring Outdoor Competition.

This plan is designed for runners who have participated in the preceding cross-country season. It is suggested they may benefit from 1-4 weeks of "active rest" prior to the beginning of winter training.

	December First Week	December Second Week	December Third Week	December Fourth Week
Mon.	A.M. I(a) 2 mi. P.M. III (f) 220's	A.M. Rest P.M. Rest	A.M. Rest P.M. Rest	A.M. Rest P.M. Rest
Tues.	A.M. I (h) Wt. trng. P.M.XIV(a) 3-5 mi. CC.	A.M. I (h) Wt. trng. P.M. VI (e) 10 x 660	A.M. I (h) Wt. trng. P.M.VIII (b) $\frac{3}{4}$ mi.	A.M. I (h) Wt. trng. P.M. X (a) $1\frac{1}{4}$ mi.
Wed.	A.M. I (d) 150's P.M. IV (a) 330's	A.M. I (b) 3 mi. P.M. II (h) 110's	A.M. I (b) 3 mi. P.M. III(d) 220's	A.M. I (b) 3 mi. P.M.XV (e) 110, 150, 220.
Thurs.	A.M. Rest P.M. Rest	A.M. Rest P.M. Rest	A.M. Rest P.M. Rest	A.M. Rest P.M. Rest

Fri.	A.M. I (h) Wt. trng. P.M. XIV(a) 3-5 mi. CC.	A.M. I (h) Wt. trng. P.M. VII (c) 880's	A.M. I (h) Wt. trng. P.M.IX(b) 1 mile	A.M. I(h) Wt. trng. P.M.VII(c) 880's
Sat.	V (c) 440's	V (d) 440's	V (d) 440's	V (e) 440's
Sun.	XIV (b) 6-10 mi.CC	XIV (c) 10-15 mi.	XIV (c) 10-15 mi.	XIV (c) 10-15 mi.

Winter Training for Experienced College 3-6 Milers During January.

	January First Week	January Second Week	January Third Week	January Fourth Week
Mon.	A.M. I (a) 2 mi. P.M. XIV (b) 6-10 mi.CC	A.M. I (b) 3 mi. P.M. V (e) 440's	A.M. I (h) Wt. trng. P.M.XV (d) 110, 150, 220	A.M. Rest P.M. Rest
Tues.	A.M I (h) Wt. trng. P.M. II(h) 110's	A.M. I (h) Wt. trng. P.M. XI (c) $1\frac{1}{2}$ mi.	A.M. I (b) 3 mi. P.M. XII (a) 2 mi.	A.M. I(h) Wt. trng. P.M.X (b) $1\frac{1}{4}$ mi.
Wed.	A.M.I (b) 3 mi. P.M. V (e) 440's	A.M. I (d) 150's P.M. III (b) 220's	A.M. I (h) Wt. trng. P.M. V (d) 440's	A.M. I (b) 3 mi. P.M.XV(c) 110, 220.
Thurs.	A.M. Rest P.M. Rest	A.M. Rest P.M. Rest	A.M. Rest P.M.XVI Speed-play no wt. trng.	A.M I (h) Wt. trng. P.M. V (i) 440's
Fri.	A.M. I (h) Wt. trng. P.M. VIII (a) $\frac{3}{4}$ mi.	A.M. Rest P.M. Rest	A.M. Rest P.M. Rest	A.M. Rest P.M. Rest
Sat.	XIV (c) 10-15 mi.	Competition or XVII	Competition or XVII	Competition or XVII
Sun.	Rest	XIV (c) 10-15 mi.	XIV (c) 10-15 mi.	XIV (c) 10-15 mi.

Winter Training for Experienced College 3-6 Milers During February.

	February First Week	February Second Week	February Third Week	February Fourth Week
Mon.	A.M. Rest P.M. Rest	A.M. Rest P.M. Rest	A.M. Rest P.M. Rest	A.M. Rest P.M. Rest
Tues.	A.M. I (h) Wt. trng. P.M. II (g) 110's	A.M. I (h) Wt. trng. P.M.XIII(a) or XIII(b), 3 mi.	A.M.I (h) Wt. trng. P.M. VIII (a) $\frac{3}{4}$ mi.	A.M. I(h) Wt. trng. P.M. XII(a) or XII(b), 2mi.
Wed.	A.M. I (b) 3 mi. P.M. V (f) 440's	A.M. I (b) 3 mi. P.M. III(e) 220's	A.M. I (c) 110's P.M. XV (d) 110, 150, 220	A.M. I (c) 150's P.M V (f) 440's
Thurs.	A.M. I (d) 150's P.M. XII(b) or XVI 2 mi. or speed-play	A.M. I (d) 150's P.M. V (i) 440's	A.M I(b) 3 mi. P.M. V(j) 440's	A.M.I (b) 3 mi. P.M.III(a) 220's
Fri.	A.M. Rest P.M Rest	A.M. Rest P.M. Rest	A.M. Rest P.M. Rest	A.M. Rest P.M. Rest

Sat.	Competition or XVII	Competition or XVII	Competition or XVII	Competition or XVII
Sun.	XIV 10-15 mi.	XIV 10-15 mi.	XIV 10-15 mi.	XIV 10-15 mi.

Winter Training for Experienced College 3-6 Milers During March.

	March First Week	March Second Week	March Third Week	March Fourth Week
Mon.	A.M. Rest P.M. Rest	A.M. Rest P.M. Rest	A.M. I (h) Wt. trng. P.M. II(g) 110's	A.M. I (h) Wt. trng. P.M. XV(d) 110, 150, 220
Tues.	A.M. I (h) Wt. trng. P.M. VII(c) 880's	A.M. I (e) 110, 220 P.M. IX (a) 1 mi.	A.M. Rest P.M. Rest	A.M. Rest P.M. Rest
Wed.	A.M. I (b) 3 miles P.M. II(e) 110's	A.M. I (h) Wt. trng. P.M. III (e) 220's	A.M. I (d) 150's P.M. X (c) $1\frac{1}{4}$ mi.	A.M. I (b) 3 miles P.M. XII(b)or XII (c), 2 mi.
Thurs.	A.M. I (g) P.M. XVI Speed-play	A.M. I (b) 3 mi. P.M. V (f) 440's	A.M. I (d) 150's P.M. VI (d) 660's	A.M. I (d) 150's P.M. V (i) 440's
Fri.	A.M. Rest P.M. Rest	A.M. Rest P.M. Rest	A.M. Rest P.M. Rest	A.M. Rest P.M. Rest
Sat.	Competition or XVII	Competition or XVII	Competition or XVII	Competition or XVII
Sun.	XIV 10-15 miles	XIV 10-15 miles	XIV 10-15 miles	XIV 10-15 miles

Spring Training for Experienced College 3-6 Milers During April.

	April First Week	April Second Week	April Third Week	April Fourth Week
Mon.	A.M. I (d) 150's P.M. II (h) 110's	A.M. I (h) Wt. trng. P.M. XIII(b) or XIII(c) 3 mi.	A.M. I (h) Wt. trng. P.M. XII(b) or XII (c) 2 mi.	A.M. I (h) Wt. trng. P.M. II(h) 110's
Tues.	A.M. I (c) 110's P.M. XVI Speed-play	A.M. I (d) 150's P.M. III (e) 220's	A.M. I (d) 150's P.M. XV (d) 110, 150, 220	A.M. Rest P.M. Rest
Wed.	A.M. I (e) 110, 220. P.M. VIII (a) $\frac{3}{4}$ mi.	A.M I (b) 3 mi. P.M. XVI Speed-play	A.M. I (b) 3 mi. P.M. V (j) 440's	A.M I (b) 3 mi. P.M.XI (a) $1\frac{1}{2}$ mi.
Thurs.	A.M. I (d) 150's P.M. V (d) 440's	A.M. I (d) 150's P.M. V (i) 440's	A.M. Rest P.M. Rest	A.M. I (d) 150's P.M. V (f) 440's
Fri.	A.M. Rest P.M. Rest	A.M. Rest P.M. Rest	A.M. Rest P.M. Rest	A.M. Rest P.M. Rest
Sat.	Competition or XVII	Competition or XVII	Competition or XVII	Competition or XVII
Sun.	Rest	Rest	XIV 10-15 miles	XV (a) 150's

Spring Training for Experienced College 3-6 Milers During May.

	May First Week	May Second Week	May Third Week	May Fourth Week
Mon.	A.M. I (h) Wt. trng. P.M. XII(b) or XII(c), 2 mi.	A.M. I (d) 150's P.M. X (c) $1\frac{1}{4}$ mi.	A.M. Rest P.M. Rest	A.M. I (h) Wt. trng. P.M. XV(d) 110, 150, 220
Tues.	A.M. I (d) 150's P.M. XV (d) 110, 150, 220	A.M. I (h) Wt. trng. P.M. II(g) 110's	A.M. I (h) Wt. trng. P.M. XII(c) 2 mi.	A.M. I (b) 3 mi. P.M. XVI Speed-play
Wed.	A.M. I (b) 3 mi. P.M. V (j) 440's	A.M. I (b) 3 mi. P.M. V (g) 440's	A.M. I (d) 150's P.M. XV(d) 110, 150, 220	A.M. I (d) 150's P.M. V(d) 440's
Thurs.	A.M. I (f) $2\frac{1}{4}$ mi. P.M. VII (b) 880's	A.M. Rest P.M. XVI Speed-play, no wt. trng.	A.M. I (b) 3 mi. P.M. VII (c) 880's	A.M. Rest P.M. Rest
Fri.	A.M. Rest P.M. Rest	A.M. Rest P.M. Rest	A.M. Rest P.M. Rest	A.M. Rest P.M. Rest
Sat.	Competition or XVII	Competition or XVII	Competition or XVII	Competition or XVII
Sun.	Rest	XIV (b) 6-10 mi.	Rest	XIV 6-10mi.

Summer Training for Experienced College 3-6 Milers During June.

	June First Week	June Second Week	June Third Week	June Fourth Week
Mon.	A.M. I (h) Wt. trng. P.M. XV (e) 110, 150, 220	A.M. I (h) Wt. trng. P.M. VIII (a) $\frac{3}{4}$ mi.	A.M I (b) 3 mi. P.M. X (c) $1\frac{1}{4}$ mi.	
Tues.	A.M. Rest P.M. Rest	A.M. I (d) 150's P.M. V(j) 440's	A.M. I (d) 150's P.M. XVI Speed-play	
Wed.	A.M. I (b) 3 mi. P.M. XII (b) or XII(c), 2 mi.	A.M. I (f) $2\frac{1}{4}$ mi. P.M. XVI (Speed- play) no.wt.trng.	A.M. I (b) 3 mi. P.M. V (d) 440's	
Thurs.	A.M. I (d) 150's P.M. V (i) 440's	A.M. Rest P.M. Rest	A.M. Rest P.M. Rest	
Fri.	A.M. Rest P.M. Rest	A.M. Rest P.M. Rest	A.M. Rest P.M. Rest	
Sat.	Competition or XVII	Competition	Major Com- petition	
Sun.	Rest	XV (a) 150's		

Training Tips and Points to Ponder

by Fred Wilt

Most runners who wish to improve are continually looking for solutions to the many problems concerned with running a given distance in a faster time. Although the issues confronting different athletes are seldom identical, many of them are common to the majority. Some of these issues are discussed hereafter in suggesting a basis on which to formulate a systematized approach to training.

When should one start training?

If you want to achieve the maximum of your potential, then start immediately. Don't wait until tomorrow, next week, or next month. Don't wait for warm weather, or until the snow melts. Start today!

Can training harm the normal heart?

No. There is too much medical evidence available to bother arguing this point. Training will benefit the "normal" heart, not harm it!

At what age should boys start regular training?

Normal, healthy boys age 12-13 years may start regular training with a beneficial effect providing that they do so voluntarily, that they maintain continuous interest and enthusiasm, and that they follow widely varied training programs carefully graduated in intensity to produce gradual adaptation to the stress of running. There is no reason why children 8-12 years of age cannot also benefit from training, although this age group seldom has the interest for regular training. For this reason a program of running is seldom advocated for the 8-12 year old age group on a daily basis. Training for both the 12-13 and 8-12 year age groups must be carefully planned on an individual basis if a good, rather than adverse effect, is to be achieved. In the U.S.A. there is very little competition for the 8-12 year age group, while some competition is provided in junior high school for the 12-13 year age group. High school competition often starts with the 14 year old athlete. Regular training among high school athletes (age 14-18) is not only recommended, but it is a necessity in terms of health and the possibility of achieving desirable results.

How many days each week should one train?

Mature athletes should plan on workouts each day, and make every effort to maintain daily training, with the exceptions listed elsewhere. High school athletes (age 14-18) should train at least five days weekly, except during the competitive season. Boys age 12-13 may train 3-5 days weekly to good advantage.

Should middle-distance runners train one, two, or more times each day?

Mature middle-distance runners no longer question whether they should use one or two workouts daily. If time and circumstances permit, a high percentage train twice daily. Two workouts daily for the mature runner are highly recommended, providing time and individual environmental circumstances are favorable. The morning (or first) training session should be lighter than the evening (or second) workout each day. Recovery must be relatively complete between workouts to avoid chronic fatigue. One workout daily for the high school athlete is usually recommended, although many dedicated high school runners train twice daily. There has been no evidence indicating three or more workouts daily will produce better results than one or two. Some middle-distance runners whose circumstances permit but one workout daily often produce better results than those who train more frequently, although other factors undoubtedly are to be considered in explaining this. The runner who can manage but one workout daily should not develop an inferior attitude for this reason, as it is the quality of training which is important, rather than the quantity.

How many minutes or hours should be spent on each workout?

An athlete training twice daily should make the morning (first) workout lighter than the afternoon (second) session. Morning training may occupy 15 minutes to a full hour, while the evening workout may occupy from 1 to 2 hours or more. International-class athletes frequently spend a total of three hours daily in actual training, one each morning and two hours each evening. A mature athlete who trains but once daily can hardly do sufficient training within an hour, and it is more likely that his training should occupy 1½-2 hours. High school athletes who train twice daily may spend 15-30 minutes on morning workouts, and 45-90 minutes on evening sessions. The majority of high school athletes training once daily need 60-90 minutes for each workout. The 12-13 year old should be able to train properly on workouts lasting 30 minutes. These are, at best, merely arbitrary figures, and in final analysis must be based upon a variety of factors of which the individual differences of the athletes are the most important. The above workout periods do not, of course, include time spent on changing clothes, showering, etc.

How many days each week should one rest during the training period prior to the start of the racing season?

During training prior to starting the competitive season, many international class athletes do not plan rest days. They train every day possible. Their rest days occur when circumstances beyond their control such as illness, injury, and personal problems prevent workouts. Experience has shown that there are usually a sufficient number of these days to provide adequate rest during this period. In the absence of such enforced rest, one day per week without training should be adequate for international class athletes and other mature runners. High school athletes (age 14-18 years) should rest one or two days weekly during this period. Boys age 12-13 will benefit from receiving 2-4 days rest from formal running training each week.

How many days should one rest prior to competition?

During the early competitive season prior to the attainment of desired physical condition, most runners (from international-class through high school athletes) do not rest prior to racing. Instead, they merely ease the training the day before competition. When the early competitive season has passed and a satisfactory physical condition has been attained, most runners should rest one day prior to racing. During late competitive season, and/or before any major race, two days of rest are recommended. Since 12-13 year old boys train with less intensity than older athletes, they do not need special rest prior to racing.

How many months should one train and rest each year?

Modern training is a continuum involving a graduated increase in intensity over an athletic lifetime. Running training and the competitive racing season should total at least 11 months per year for most mature runners. The international-class athlete may take 2-4 weeks away from formal running training at the conclusion of each racing season, but even then he usually engages in swimming, golf, games, and other recreation which generally tends to preserve his physical condition. Dedicated high school athletes whose track racing seasons end about June 1st may advantageously rest 4-6 weeks in June and July before starting preparation for the forthcoming cross-country season which will start in mid-September. These high school runners may also benefit from 4-5 weeks rest in November-December at the end of the competitive cross-country season, prior to beginning preparation for the forthcoming outdoor track season. If the high school athlete is fortunate enough to have a competitive indoor season, then he can afford no more than 2 weeks rest at the conclusion of the cross-country racing season. Since the high school indoor season may begin in January and end in March with the outdoor track season starting in April; athletes who race both indoors and out usually find there is little if any time to rest between these seasons.

What total volume of running should be included in an interval training workout?

Like most questions on training, this depends upon the individual characteristics of the athlete under consideration. As a general rule, except for international-caliber and longer-distance runners, the total training volume for each workout may be two or three times actual racing distance, exclusive of warmup and recovery or slow running. For example, the half-miler may consider such workouts as 15-25 x 110, 8-12 x 220, 5-8 x 330, 4-6 x 440, 3-4 x 660, and 2-3 x 3/4 mile. The miler may consider workouts of 30-45 x 110, 15-25 x 220, 8-12 x 440, 4-6 x 880, 3-4 x 3/4 mile, and 2-3 x 1 1/4 mile. However, mature runners of international-caliber and those training for long middle-distance and long-distance races recognize no such theoretical training boundaries and frequently put in far more total running volume each workout over a prolonged training period. As an example, some mature European 1500m runners are known to do 10 x (15 x 100m in 13-14 seconds. Jog 100m after each. Walk 100m between sets of 15 x 100m) as the morning workout and follow this with an equally intense workout in the evening. However, regardless of what proportions the total running volume may eventually reach, the youth and novice are advised to error on the side of too little rather than too much running in the beginning and early stages of their running career.

Where should one train?

Fortunately good training can be done almost anywhere. Champions have trained and developed in a variety of climates. Pine-needle carpeted paths in forests, beaches, woods, parks, sawdust paths, playgrounds, streets, roads, sidewalks, snow covered fields, and tracks all provide surfaces where training may be done. Athletes may train on practically any surface available, or wherever preferred if there is a choice. Lack of a heated fieldhouse with banked indoor track is absolutely no excuse for failure to train properly. Running may be done on frozen ground and concrete roads without adverse effect on the legs if shoes are worn with soles made of "foam rubber" or "crepe foam", of which there are many varieties.

Is it possible to train outdoors in cold weather, when the ground is covered with snow?

Yes! In the winter, Norwegians, Finns, Swedes, and Russians run daily through the snow in temperatures as cold as 40 degrees below zero (F) with no ill effects. In very deep snow they merely walk and run at speeds which vary according to the footing. To train in very cold weather, a runner should dress in long underwear, track suit, mittens or gloves, cap covering the ears, scarf around the neck, and appropriate shoes. Then he should go directly into the cold weather and snow. Concrete roads usually present the most even surface on which to train in cold weather. In actual practice, because of heat elimination, running in cold weather is much more comfortable and healthful than running in very hot weather. One can often cover considerably more training mileage on cold days than is possible in hot weather. Cold weather and snow are absolutely no excuse for failure to run daily. One can always train in some manner, regardless of weather. Bad weather is an excellent excuse for failure to train in the case of the unenthusiastic, and those lacking in will-power and determination, but those who are really keen, the champions and potential champions, will never permit a minor issue such as cold weather and snow to prevent daily training. One can never truly appreciate the joy of training until he has experienced the thrill of training in cold weather!

What equipment is necessary for training and racing?

A track suit (sweat suit) which buttons or zips high and snugly around the neck, an athletic supporter (nylon-stretch material will cause less galding), shorts (trunks), shirt, socks, and shoes are the basic necessities. For training in extremely cold weather, the additional clothing needed includes long underwear to be worn beneath the track suit, a scarf for the neck, gloves or mittens, and a hat or cap which can be pulled down over the ears. A "hood" type sweat-shirt is often used in bad weather. The shoes necessary are flat-soled warm-up or training shoes (preferably with "crepe foam" soles), and spiked shoes. The spiked-shoes used in cross-country racing are usually identical with those worn in track races. Care should be taken that the spikes are not too long, as there is seldom justification for using spikes longer than ½ inch. If a cross-country race is run partly over cement pavement and the remainder of the course is grass or another relatively solid surface, then consideration should be given to racing in flat-soled shoes. The purpose of spiked-shoes is to gain extra traction. If sufficient traction is gained and no slippage occurs when racing in flat-soled shoes, then spiked-shoes offer no advantage unless they are appreciably lighter. Often flat-soled shoes are more comfortable, which is an additional reason for racing in flats. However, most of the best cross-country runners race in shoes with short spikes unless the course is over an appreciable distance of cement pavement.

During training in very cold weather, a large plastic-film bag (similar to tose used by dry-cleaners for protective covering over suits and dresses) may be worn beneath the sweat-suit, and small plastic-film bags may be worn over the socks and gloves for additional warmth. A thin strip of cotton may be placed inside the mouth between the lips and front teeth to warm the cold air as it is inhaled. Air-proof nylon garments may be even more desirable than plastic bags in cold weather, although more expensive.

Should one train and race barefooted?

The main objections to running barefooted are freezing weather, slipping and intermittent lack of traction, and running over surfaces which may conceal sharp stones, rusty metal such as nails, broken glass, etc. that may cut or puncture the feet. In the absence of these objectionable features, running barefooted may well be faster than running in shoes. The feet may be toughened for barefooted running, and the best way to do this is by running without shoes a few minutes daily, gradually increasing the distance until the feet can tolerate the entire workout without shoes. A few international-class athletes have raced barefooted, but not exclusively so, since they wear shoes when conditions underfoot are not favorable to barefooted running.

How can interval training be used when the wind is blowing with such force that it is extremely difficult to run a full lap around the track at racing speed?

If the wind is quite strong, train on a road relatively free from traffic. Measure and mark the training distances (110, 220, 330, 440 yds., etc.) accurately with a steel tape along the road in the direction the wind is blowing. Run the fast repetition with the wind at your back over the measured distances, recover by jogging back to the starting point with the wind at your face, and repeat the required number of times. The fast runs may seem unusually fast with the wind blowing from behind. Compensate for this by not removing the track suit. The full racing distance or even double the competitive distance may be run on a road with a strong wind at your back. If training in strong wind must be done on a track, then run the fast repetition with the wind, and the recovery interval against the wind. Usually distances no longer than 220 yards may be run with (in the same direction as) the wind on a track.

Is it possible to carry a stop watch while running and obtain an accurate timing?

Yes, but don't carry the watch in your hand, as the motion of your arm will interfere with the balance wheel and render an accurate timing impossible. Put a shoestring through the handle of the stop watch and suspend it around your neck. Let the watch rest in your athletic supporter or in a small pocket in your clothing at the front of your body somewhere between chest and navel. With the watch held securely against your body in this manner, start it as you cross the starting line and stop it as you finish. When doing interval training, read the watch during recovery jogging between fast repetitions of running.

Should one be timed with a stop watch during training?

Timing during training over any distance should be considered on the basis of individual reaction to it by the athlete. Some athletes thrive on timing, while others do not. The stop-watch is just as important to the runner as scientific apparatus and measuring devices are to the scientist. It can be an inspiring mechanism to serve the athlete by accurate measurement of running in a carefully planned training program designed to produce gradual adaptation of the body to the stress of running. The watch is indispensable in developing a sense of pace judgement. But if it is used primarily to measure maximum efforts in training, then it becomes a slave-driver. Factors of dread, apprehension, anxiety, frustration; feelings of helplessness, revolt, and psychological disturbances are involuntary introduced in the athlete's mind. Then the stop watch no longer serves as an inspiration and aid to the gradual adaptation of the body to the stress of running. What might be a mentally pleasant experience in training may instead be harmful to the athlete's psychological attitude toward running if the watch is permitted to assume the role of the slave-driver. The timing of daily sub-maximal repetitions of 110, 220, 330, 440, 660 yards in the training of a middle-distance runner is to be desired, although it is not always necessary. Timing the longer repetition runs of 880 and 1320 yards, 3/4, 1, and 1-1/4 miles at sub-maximal speed is also recommended, although not always necessary. However, in the case of the middle-distance runner the timing of maximum efforts over any distance, especially longer runs, is a matter for careful consideration, because the athlete's psychological attitude toward racing and training may be in jeopardy.

Should one run time-trials in training?

Most athletes oppose time-trials for psychological reasons. If they run poor time-trials, their confidence suffers. If they run fast time-trials, why leave them on the training track? Many athletes claim they submit to the indignity of time-trials only to bolster the confidence of their coaches who doubt their ability. Inexperienced coaches, especially those who have done no competitive middle-distance racing, are often concerned as to whether an athlete will be able to "go the full racing distance" under competitive conditions. This becomes obvious by running repetitions during training at less than full effort over $\frac{3}{4}$ to $1\frac{1}{4}$ racing distance. This type training may be timed, with little danger of adverse psychological results. If a time-trial must be run, it may be worthy of consideration not to clock it!

Should one have a training schedule (workout program)?

The progress which has been made in training, as reflected in track records today which are faster than could have been imagined 50 years ago, has probably come from clear, logical thinking and carefully planned training than from any "new" discovery. One difference between the human and lower species is the ability to think logically, plan, postulate, theorize, conclude, and learn rapidly from experience. We should, therfore, use this ability in improving training through careful planning. The athlete who wants to succeed should always have training plans. These should include both short-range plans for the more immediate goals, and long-range plans for the attainment of future objectives. The athlete must be prepared to change his immediate, day-to-day training plans for the better on the basis of unexpected and unforseen developments. Nevertheless, he should always have training plans - otherwise his training could degenerate to chaos. Not many years ago a minority opinion from abroad denounced training plans and workout schedules as a certain road to "breakdown", and suggested that running by "instinct was the only path to the oasis of success in the wilderness of training. This, of course, is utter nonsense. By "instinct" one does not run very far or very fast unless forced to do so by danger to life and limb. The planning of training and mapping of tentative workout schedules is not a crime, but a procedure of paramount necessity if one expects to succeed in racing. Training should gradually produce adaptation of the body to the stresses involved in running, and this can hardly be done without carefully planned training, accurately graduated in intensity.

How does one distinguish between psychological and physiological fatigue in the training of runners?

Except for actual laboratory analysis, no one has yet found an answer to this question. It is well known that to feel tired (psychological or subjective fatigue) is not to actually be tired (physiological or objective fatigue). Normal athletes differ widely in their tolerance level of both psychological and physiological fatigue. The psychological tolerance level of fatigue may be a defense mechanism of the body. The training value of exercise carried beyond the psychological level of fatigue tolerance is unknown. Some coaches using a 'hurt-pain-agony' philosophy apparently take the psychological fatigue tolerance level as a criterion for training. Using it as a point of reference, they seek to go beyond the psychological fatigue barrier, continually pushing nearer to the limit where the accumulation of lactic acid in the muscles seriously impedes irritability and contractility, or, in other words, the onset of physiological fatigue.

What is the difference between an elementary as opposed to an advanced knowledge of training?

As stated elsewhere, much of our training knowledge today was known 3,000 years ago to the ancient Greeks. In other words, the ancient Greeks knew a lot about "how" to train. They knew that by performing certain workout routines they could expect better results in competition. There is very little evidence to indicate they knew why their training produced better results. Today, we have some of the answers as to why training produces better results. Thus, an elementary knowledge of training implies "how" to train properly. An advanced knowledge of training implies not only "how" to train properly, but also "why" training is done a specific way, and the reason for the effects of training as it is performed.

What is the best diet for racing and training? Is there any food one can eat which will make him run faster?

There is no special diet to make an athlete run faster. There are no data or theoretical implications to suggest that sprints and middle-distance performances can be modified by nutrition. Sugar feeding during a long and exhausting contest such as the marathon does improve performance. The optimal diet for an athlete is not different in any major respect from that recommended to any normal person, but must adequately fulfill energy requirements corresponding to the athlete's physical activity. Runners should avoid excessive amounts of fat. Evidence has been presented indicating that in sports requiring endurance and prolonged muscular work, performance is better maintained on a high carbohydrate diet than on a high fat diet (referring to the diet consumed for several days prior to competition). In final analysis, a normal "balanced" diet of "three square meals" daily seems best. There is no scientific evidence to support claims of ergogenic effects of dietary supplements such as wheat germ oil, blackstrap molasses, kelp, royal jelly, protein tablets or vitamin concentrates (in the absense of vitamin deficiency).

How much time should elapse between the last meal and training or competition?

Eat the last meal at least two hours prior to the workout. Three to five hours should elapse between the last meal and competition. Drink no liquid two hours prior to competition.

Should athletes drink tea and coffee?

High school athletes ordinarily do not drink tea and coffee. This question usually arises at the college level. In the past, tea has traditionally been a part of the pre-competition meal. The caffeine in tea induces a period of stimulation of the central nervous system which is followed by a period of depression. Since the athlete is usually excited and nervous during the period immediately preceding competition, the addition of caffeine to the last meal may not be advisable and may increase his nervousness. The same caution applies to coffee. Both tea and coffee are diuretics, stimulating the flow of urine. Thus they may cause additional discomfort during the competitive period.

Coffee contains about 1½ grains of caffeine per cup, and stimulates the heart, nerves, and kidneys. Millions of people drink 2 to 6 cups daily without harm. Others avoid it because it keeps them awake at night, makes them jittery, or gives them a headache. Physicians restrict coffee in patients who may be harmed by the nerve stimulation it provides. Cup for cup, coffee and tea contain about the same amount of caffeine. Tea leaves contain about twice as much caffeine (2-4%) as coffee beans (1-2%, but well-brewed coffee is usually made approximately twice as strong as well-steeped tea.

Should athletes use alcohol and tobacco (drink and smoke)?

No. Neither alcohol nor tobacco make a positive contribution to athletic performance. On the contrary, both may have a harmful effect.

In regard to smoking, the walls of the alveoli in the lungs through which must pass the exchange of oxygen and carbon dioxide, are thickened when nicotine is forced through them, thus reducing the efficiency of gaseous exchange. There are other known adverse effects of smoking on athletic performance.

The use of alcohol cannot be justified or recommended. In small quantities (such as found in beer), alcohol affects the finer neuromuscular coordinations. In large quantities it affects gross coordinations to a considerable degree. Alcohol to be tolerated by the human machine requires energy that cannot be divided between muscular effort and the oxidation of alcohol. The liver plays an important role in athletics with regard to the conversion of protein into carbohydrate in the process of gluconeogenesis. Thus liver damage through alcohol is an important issue in athletic performance. During exercise the liver must convert lactic acid back into liver glycogen, which can then be reduced into blood sugar for the immediate use by muscles. This sugar is carried back to the muscles for energy or storage as liver glycogen, in a circuit known as the Cori cycle. Liver tissue forms glycogen from simple sugar, and the liver serves as the store house for glycogen. The brain and heart are the chief users of glycogen. Obviously the well-trained athlete can perform at highest efficiency only if his reserve of sugar is not molested by such irritations as the oxidation of alcohol, which will rob the liver of its elasticity and tone. The liver cannot be expected, over a prolonged period of athletic stress, to render efficient service to both the muscles and alcohol. Mixing athletics and alcohol may be compared to burning the candle at both ends. It is now known that even small amounts of beer will adversely affect the body's heat regulatory mechanism 24-48 hours.

What is the limit in terms of the speed any given distance can be run?

The seeds of their own destruction are inherent within the nature of track and field athletics, since standards continue to rise to such heights that youngsters and newcomers may be discouraged from taking up the sport. Yet, within the framework of meaning of the 'glorious uncertainty of athletics' there is one certainty - marks will continue to improve in all events. Any performance by one human, regardless of how excellent, can be duplicated. Some who duplicate the excellent will exceed it, and so it goes. Perhaps but 10%-20% of the world's white population engage in track and field athletics, while hundreds of millions of the world's colored population ignore the sport. Sports medicine and scientific research will undoubtedly contribute to future improvement. Human evolution may well have an effect. Society in the future will be characterized in part by higher living standards, decreased numbers of daily working hours, and increased spare time for devotion to sports. These factors will no doubt result in vast improvement. In final analysis, however, it seems impossible to predict a reasonable ultimate in human performance, since this is dependent upon human evolution and the nature of social existence in the future.

What is the best training for runners?

Running! This means running, running, and more running. Although basically a simple rule, careful examination reveals this is a complicated formula. Running training implies such issues as speed, distance, frequency, volume, recovery, and a multitude of factors which make training for running an intricate art. Nevertheless, running is the major ingredient in the workout diet of any runner. There is no other form of training that can replace running in the training of runners. However, after the full advantage of daily running has been had, the runner should then benefit from other forms of training such as weight training, circuit training, swimming, etc. if time permits.

Should runners use weight-training?

Yes. People are naturally negative, and mostly for this reason, weight-training has long suffered discrimination with regard to its use by runners. Almost without exception the opponents of weight-training have personally never actually used it, but rather they base their opposition primarily on emotion, i.e. "It's no good, because I don't believe in it."

It is still possible to hear old-fashioned ideas and out-dated fallacies about the so-called harmful effects of weight-training. Among these fallacies are the ideas that weight-training produces a "muscle-bound" condition, makes one slow, causes heart-strain, and develops excessively large muscles. The purpose of weight-training is the acquisition of great muscular strength. Strength is the athlete's capacity to exert muscular force against resistance. With increased strength greater power (rate of work) can be developed. Thus, with all other factors equal, the stronger runner should win. Runners should, therefore, use weight-training. However, weight-training is only an adjunct to running, not a replacement or substitute. Running, running, and more running is now, always has been, and always will be the best training for runners. No runner has been known to develop excessive muscle size or a "muscle-bound" condition; but if such a phenomenon should occur, the remedy is quite simple - merely discontinue weight-training.

Should runners include swimming in their training?

Yes. For no apparent reason, coaches of past generations opposed swimming in the training of runners. However, swimming involves no muscular action antagonistic to the basic movement in running, is an excellent means of circulatory-respiratory development during periods of injury to the legs when running is not possible, is especially refreshing after training in warm weather, and provides a most enjoyable means of "active rest" from running training.

How many weeks or months should runners train before the first race of the season?

In the U.S.A., we have sometimes been suspected of entering the racing season with insufficient preliminary preparation. If training is viewed as a continuum extending throughout an athletic lifetime, this question is not of great concern. The beginner should train at least 3 months and preferably 6 months prior to the first race, although such a preparatory period is seldom the case with younger runners. Experienced high school and collegiate runners whose track season ends in June may rest 4-6 weeks in June and July before starting an 8-10 weeks period of preparation for the cross-country season in November. Those who will compete in the forthcoming indoor track season opening in January can afford no more than 2 weeks rest before embarking on a 6 weeks period of training for the indoor campaign. At the conclusion of the indoor season in March, there is no time for rest from training, and preparation is immediately begun for the outdoor season which opens in April, if not before. Those who do not race indoors may rest 4-5 weeks at the end of cross-country season in November before starting a 3 month training period prior to the beginning of the outdoor track season. These rest periods between competitive seasons are by no means manditory, and indeed many runners recognize no period of rest between seasons of racing. It is also well-known that many high school athletes begin their competitive cross-country and track racing seasons with a month or less of preliminary training. This is a fact, rather than a recommended procedure, and is neither recommended nor condoned.

How often should one race?

High school runners often race twice weekly, but the wisdom of this is questioned if any significant amount of training is to be done. There is usually little choice among members of high school and collegiate teams as to the frequency of competition. One race each week during cross-country and indoor and outdoor track seasons is highly sufficient. Only one race of major importance each month in addition to otherwise weekly competition would be preferable; although district, regional, state, and national championships in rapid succession usually preclude this ideal. International-class runners who are at liberty to choose their races often refrain from weekly competition in favor of more time for intensive preparation. They prefer to confine their competitive efforts to one or two races each month.

Is walking or jogging "better" for recovery action between fast repetitions of running during interval training?

No one knows. One minute of walking usually results in as much or more recovery as two minutes of jogging, on the basis of pulse recovery. In jogging contact is broken with the ground and there is a period of "double float" wherein both feet are off the ground during the course of each step, thus the energy requirement for jogging is higher than for recovery walking. Since jogging requires more energy than walking and is physically more difficult, it is generally assumed that jogging has a more beneficial training effect. It is a well known fact that most runners jog for recovery during interval training. However, the physical motions required in jogging at a speed of 2-3 minutes per 440 yards have little, if any, more relationship to the movements used in running at racing speed than do the movements used in walking. It could, therefore, be argued that a greater number of fast repetitions could be run within a given workout period during the time saved by walking for recovery, thus producing a more beneficial total training effect. No experiementation is known to have been done on this issue, and in the absence of proof to the contrary, jogging is generally recommended as the recovery action in interval training.

Are there any exercises one can use to improve breathing which will also improve one's running speed?

This possibility has been the object of occasional speculation, but in final analysis the best exercise known to improve the respiratory movements required of the runner is sprinting and running faster than anticipated racing pace. One should inhale and exhale primarily through the mouth while running.

Should the runner be concerned with the rhythm of breathing in relation to stride cadence?

There may be a respiratory rhythm in relation to stride cadence, but few if any runners are aware of such a relationship. If such a respiratory cadence rhythm is to develop, it will come about, with no conscious effort on the part of the runner, as a consequence of correct training.

At what distance should one race in relation to his sprint speed?

In track racing the slower your natural (or best) speed over 100, 220, and 440 yards, the longer the racing distance you should select. This is a general rule to be applied in accordance with the individual characteristics and abilities of the athlete in question.

Will good training increase one's basic sprint speed?

Native reaction time cannot be changed by training, but basic sprint speed can be improved somewhat through good training. This improvement will be in terms of greater flexibility, decreased muscular viscosity, and greater mechanical efficiency in running. In middle-distance running the important issue is the fact that, although your speed over very short distances may not improve greatly, good training can enable whatever speed you possess to be sustained over longer and longer distances.

At what speed should one run during interval training?

Repetitions of 110 yards may be run at $1\frac{1}{2}$ to $2\frac{1}{2}$ seconds slower than your best 110 yards mark. Repetitions of 220 yards may be run 3 to 5 seconds slower than your best 220 yards. 440 yards repetitions may be run in 1 to 4 seconds faster than your average racing pace. Thus a 4:00 minute miler would run 440 yards repetitions in 59 to 56 seconds. Longer distances than 440 yards may be run at racing pace, but the distance above 440 yards should not exceed half the total racing distance at this speed. For example, the miler may run 660 and 880 yards at racing pace, and the 3 miler may run $\frac{3}{4}$, 1-1$\frac{1}{4}$, and 1$\frac{1}{2}$ miles at racing pace. Repetitions of distances longer than half the racing distance may be run 3 to 5 seconds slower each 440 yards than racing pace. The athlete must, of course, gradually accustom himself to training at these speeds. For all practical purposes, the 110 and 220 yards runs may remain constant at the above suggested speed, while the other distances will alter in speed as the athlete's physical condition improves and he is able to tolerate a faster and faster pace. The speed of the 440 yards repetitions may increase 1 or 2 seconds each 4 to 6 weeks. This increase in speed may cause the average racing pace and the training speed of the longer runs to vary accordingly. It is emphasized that these suggested training speeds are only general recommendations, and they should be altered according to the individual differences of the athlete in question.

Sprints must always be run at absolute maximum effort. There is no such thing as an "easy sprint."

Should runners train for endurance in fall and winter by running longer, slower distances and for speed in spring and summer by running short, fast runs?

In order to answer this question it is first necessary to understand that speed is a relative term as it relates to training. Speed should be considered in relation to racing pace. Anything faster than racing pace may be considered speed training, and anything appreciably slower than racing pace may be considered slow running. For example, the 4-minute miler, whose average racing pace is 60 seconds each 440 yards, would regard repetitions of 440 yards in 58 seconds as speed training, while 70 seconds would be slow training. For the 30-minute 6-miler (75 seconds per 440 yards average racing pace), 70 seconds per 440 yards would be speed training. Regardless of the speed or distance in running, it is nearly impossible to completely separate the training effects and develop either speed or endurance at the exclusion of the other. Long, slow running tends to increase circulatory-respiratory efficiency, which is an endurance factor. It does not reduce speed, contrary to popular belief, and may even facilitate the development of speed, to some extent, through reduction of internal muscule viscosity and increased muscular efficiency. However, endurance is effective only when considered in relation to the specific racing distance. As an example, the development through slow, long distance running of sufficient endurance to run 20 miles at a speed of 6 minutes per mile (2 hours) provides no guarantee that this endurance will be of any effective benefit in racing at fast mile pace. Training with repeated short, fast runs is an excellent method of developing endurance in addition to producing the ability to tolerate the stress of running at very fast pace over middle-distances. With other factors equal, the runner accustomed to many repetitions of 110 yards (in 14 seconds) and 220 yards (in 28 seconds) undoubtedly would have far more endurance for racing a fast mile than the athlete who gains endurance to run 20 miles in 2 hours through slow, long distance running training. The purpose of training is to enable one to run a given distance in competition as fast as possible. No one ever trains to run slower. It is manifestly absurd to train at a slow speed, and expect to race at a fast speed. If the middle-distance runner must choose between training with either long, slow runs or numerous repetitions of short, fast runs, there is every reason to believe he will achieve better competitive results through the use of fast training. Nevertheless, all speeds and distances must be considered without hesitation in seeking the most effective training. Since the objective of training is to run faster (not slower), the implication is clear that fast running (speed training) must form a major portion of the training program, regarless of the season of the year.

How does the training for cross-country competition differ from training for middle-distance track racing?

It differs very little. In the U.S.A. cross-country races are held over relatively fast surfaces, thus they may be considered "speed races" off the track. This element of speed necessitates an approach to training similar in most respects to training for track racing at middle-distances. Our cross-country training begins after a brief lay-off or rest period from the previous track season. Athletes, therefore, tend to view cross-country training and racing as an extended period of preparation for the indoor and outdoor track seasons which follow. Since cross-country races may be longer than the athlete's track specialty, the distances run in cross-country training may, in some cases, be longer. As the athlete is starting a long period of preparation, his training speeds in general may be slower in the beginning and gradually become faster as his physical condition improves and the track racing season approaches. More of the cross-country training tends to be away from the track. Often more longer, continuous runs are included than would be the case during track season. However, since the purpose of training is to enable the runner to race faster (not slower), the element of speed must occupy a major role in cross-country training. Thus by necessity there should be very little difference between the training for cross-country and middle-distance track racing.

What is the pulse or heart-rate test for recovery?

After severe exercise the heart-rate of most healthy athletes is seldom much faster than 180 beats per minute or 30 beats in 10 seconds. Through empirical (trial and error) study it has been determined that after an interval of fast running the experienced athlete should be permitted to recover until the heart-rate drops to 120 beats per minute, or 2/3 of the 180 maximum. When the heart has recovered to 120 beats per minute (or 20 beats in 10 seconds), the athlete should start his next repetition. If the athlete walks for recovery between repetitions of fast running, his heart-rate should drop within 1½ minutes to 120 per minute. If it takes longer than 1½ minutes during interval training, the run was too fast or too long. Generally speaking, the heart-rate should be near 170 to 180 beats per minute after each repetition of fast running. If it is less, the run may have been too slow. While it is not always practical to test the pulse after each repetition, it can nevertheless be used when in doubt about whether an athlete is sufficiently recovered. Runners should be taught to use this test on themselves, checking their heart-rate after fast repetitions by placing one hand directly over the heart and counting the beat for 10 seconds at 30 second intervals with the aid of a stop watch. When the count drops to 20 beats or less in 10 seconds, recovery may be sufficient to continue. In the training of beginners, there is often (but not always) an initial period of some weeks when the athlete's pulse recovery after exercise will be very slow and unfavorable. There is a second stage of about a year or more when the pulse recovery normally takes a short and regular period of time. After running 440 yard repetitions in 75 seconds each, this second stage almost always shows certain characteristics. The pulse will return from its maximum (about 180 beats per minute) in approximately 2 minutes after each repetition and remain at a plateau of about 120 beats per minute for about 30 minutes before dropping. Repeated 440's in 75 seconds will have no ill-effect on the speed of recovery. The heart-rate will return to 120 beats per minute in 2 minutes after the 15th 440, just as it will after the first. Some runners at the second stage will recover to a plateau of 19 or 21 beats in 10 seconds, but few deviate from the normal 20. These 75 second repetitions of 440 yards may continue so long as the recovery remains normal. When the heart-rate fails to return to the normal 20 beats in 10 seconds within 2 minutes after each repetition, the workout should be terminated. Experienced athletes from time to time use repetition running of sufficient distance and speed and sprint training of sufficient distance to prevent recovery within 1½ minutes to the desired 120 beats per minute. The pulse test may in this case still be utilized by merely waiting until the heart drops to the desired 20 beats in 10 seconds before continuing. It is reiterated that the above figures are suggested in reference to walking during recovery.

What should be the duration of recovery between repetitions of fast running?

To a large extent, this depends upon individual difference; and as the athlete achieves better and better physical condition, he may consider reducing the recovery periods gradually. However, certain general considerations may be utilized until the runner becomes sufficiently experienced to decide this question for himself. Recovery is twice as rapid by walking than by jogging (when judged by heart-rate recovery). In other words, 1 minute of walking results in about the same recovery as 2 minutes of jogging. If the recovery action involves walking, it should continue until the heart-rate decreases to 120 beats per minute or less (20 beats in 10 seconds, or less), regardless of the distance of the fast run. If the recovery action involves continuous jogging, thus rendering it difficult to check the heart-rate, the total duration of the recovery jogging should be 2 to 3 times longer than the duration of the preceding fast run. This generally holds true for longer distances if the pace is not too fast. For example, jog 110 yards in 30-45 seconds after repetitions of 110 yards in 15 seconds, jog 220 yards in 60-90 seconds after repetitions of 220 yards in 30 seconds, and jog 440 yards in 2-3 minutes after repetitions of 440 yards in 60-70 seconds. When running repetitions of 880 yards or longer distances at racing pace, it may be advantageous, especially in the interest of saving time, to walk between and use the heart-rate as a guide to recovery.

Can one run middle and long distance races faster in hot or cold weather?

In the absence of the extreme, an athlete should be able to run a given middle or long distance race faster in cool rather than hot weather, primarily due to more favorable conditions provided by cool weather for the elimination of body heat. Officials should avoid scheduling middle and long distances races in hot weather and bright sunshine in favor of staging them in evening twilight so the advantage of cooler weather and less bright sun may be had. The adverse and debilitating effect of high temperature, humidity, and barometric pressure is seldom considered in scheduling races in the U.S.A. Not only is there less oxygen per breath in excessively warm air, but the elimination of body heat is drastically reduced. High atmospheric humidity decreases evaporation of perspiration, thus also reducing elimination of body heat generated through physical effort. This is the obvious reason for the difficulty experienced in running the longer distances in high temperature and high humidity. Cool, dry air materially aids elimination of body heat through contact with the athlete's skin. This cooling effect decreases with the rise in air temperature and/or humidity. Atmospheric humidity and air temperature must be given close attemtion in planning racing pace and training sessions. The stress, energy requirements, and length of recovery period after effort are all increased harmfully in hot or humid weather, or both. The ratio between the athlete's body surface as compared to body mass has a significant effect on elimination of body heat resulting from running. Running middle and long distance races in hot, humid weather under bright sun can be medically dangerous. Most of the few deaths which have occured in races of these distances may be attributed in part to racing in these atmospheric conditions. Putting it simply, an athlete can run faster and more comfortably on a moderately cool day than in hot weather, other factors being equal.

What are the physiological effects of training?

Although all may not yet be known, some of the physiological effects of training are: (a) slight increase in body weight, (b) increased ability to endure effort before exhaustion, (c) decreased pulmonary ventilation during moderate work, (d) ability to attain a greater minute volume of ventilation during exhausting work, (e) slight decline in the rate and depth of breathing at rest, (f) ability to attain a greater oxygen comsumption during exhausting work, (g) greater utilization of anaerobic energy reserves, (h) increased mechanical efficiency as reflected by a lower oxygen consumption for a given volume of work, (i) increased glycogen and creatine content of the muscles, (j) smaller increase in pulse rate during moderate work, (k) increased stroke volume of the heart, (l) lower resting pulse rate, (m) faster return of heart rate and blood pressure of normal following effort, (n) lower blood lactate concentration for the performance of a given volume of work, (o) ability to tolerate a higher blood lactate concentration before exhaustion occurs, (p) reduction in concentration on the specific task at hand required by the higher centers of the nervous system, (q) better heat dissipation during submaximal exertion, (r) improved vascularization of the skeletal muscles, and (s) increased strength of the muscles and improved neuromuscular coordination.

What information should be recorded in the athlete's daily training diary?

A personal training diary should be accurately maintained as an aid to better training. The items recorded daily may include the day, month, year, day of the week, diet, amount of sleep the previous night, time of day the workout starts and ends, place of training, body weight before and after training, fatigue index, brief description of weather (temperature, humidity, wind velocity and direction), and any unusual events in personal activities such as social life or employment which may adversely affect training, surface condition of the training area, and an accurate description of the actual training done. The actual training should include warmup, warmdown, details of weight training, exact description of fartlek and interval training done, exact or estimated times of runs, exact or estimated recovery intervals, exact description of activity during recovery (walk, jog, etc.), sprint times and mileage (in the case of the marathoner). Results of blood tests, description and duration of injuries, daily basal pulse rate, and race results, may also be included. Possible explanations of performances, conclusions, predictions, and recommendations may be made as a result of information accurately recorded on a daily basis. Other items could be recorded but the minimum should be an accurate description of the actual workouts and races. A better understanding of performances in competitions may result from information recorded in the diary. All factors in the athlete's daily regimen are of training significance, and unless recorded daily, many details may be forgotten in evaluating the athlete's total training program during the course of the never ending search for better performances. The benefits available are well worth the small effort involved in the daily upkeep of a training diary.

What is the "fatigue index"?

The fatigue index is merely a simple, numerical, perhaps vague, and certainly personal method by which an athlete may briefly describe in his training diary how he "feels" each workout. This index is kept for future reference. The fatigue index may range from 1 to 9, with 1 indicating that the athlete feels as good as possible, 5 meaning "average", and 9 referring to extreme fatigue. The numbers between 1, 5, and 9 may serve to more accurately define how the athlete "feels". By recording the fatigue index for immediately prior, mid-workout, and immediately after each workout the personal feelings of the athlete may be more accurately assessed in evaluating the effects of training.

What factors should be considered in determining racing tactics?

The following factors are among those which should be considered: (a) Distance of the race. (b) Condition of the racing surface (level, hilly, fast, slow, wet, slick, dry, heavy, cut-up, muddy, sandy, etc.). (c) Weather (hot, cold, humid, dry, windy, rain, etc.). (d) Ability, strength, and weaknesses of opponents, including ability to lead, follow, and sprint at the finish. (e) Current physical condition and state of training of opponents. (f) Personal ability, strength, and weaknesses, including pace judgement and ability to lead, follow, and sprint at the finish. (g) Personal physical condition and state of training. (h) Minimum speed you can afford to lead. (i) Maximum speed you can afford to lead. (j) Minimum speed you can afford to follow. (k) Maximum speed you can afford to follow the leading runner. (l) Number of competitors in the race.

Under what conditions should a runner take the lead and set the pace in a race?

A runner takes the lead for the purpose of increasing the pace, decreasing the pace, gaining tactical position, and sprinting for the finish The front runner has no intention of setting pace for an opponent. Rather his motive in leading is to put as much distance between himself and the opposition as possible while negotiating the race in the shortest time.

What type of start should be used in cross-country and middle-distance races?

Some half-milers use the normal sprinter's crouch start. Otherwise, for all distances above 880 yards, the standing start is recommended.

What is meant by successful racing? Is the winner the only competitor who can claim success?

Winning is not the only criterion by which to judge success in racing. If a runner were to win in a time much poorer than his potential best, he would probably not regard this a successful performance. Success may be judged on the basis of whether the runner accomplishes his objective. Quite conceivably a runner might have a successful racing career and seldom experience victory. The athlete who races far faster than his apparent capabilities might be regarded as highly successful, even though finishing far behind the winner. It seems that successful racing might logically be judged in terms of how nearly the athlete performs to the maximum of his apparent potential.

Does correct training guarantee racing success?

No. Correct training will not insure racing success, but it does make racing success possible, in accordance with the athlete's potential and individual characteristics. Such mental factors as courage, competitive instinct, will-to-win, subconscious desire for victory, capacity to suffer, ability to ignore pain, perseverence, tenacity, fearless determination, intestinal fortitude, and (in the jargon of the locker room) "guts" must be added to correct training to transform racing potential into reality and give any assurance of success. In addition to correct training, there must be developed within the athlete a callousness to fatigue and pain, or an absolute refusal to succumb to the excruciating agony and pain of fatigue. Often the difference between victory and defeat in middle distance racing is the ability of the winner to ignore the same symptoms of fatigue which have caused others to yield. To feel tired is not to be tired. When one feels tired it does not necessarily mean fatigue has set in to the point necessitating the slowing of the pace or decreasing the effort. Physiological tests have proved, beyond doubt, that the winner is usually the most tired at the finish in middle distance racing, and the last finisher is often the freshest. Though the winner is attacked by the same feelings of distress, doubt, frustration, and fatigue as the loser, he nevertheless fights through the psychological and pain barriers to victory.

What role does motivation and mental determination play in successful racing?

Motivation and determination play a major role in successful racing, although the exact degree cannot be determined. As mentioned elsewhere, correct training makes successful racing possible, but this possibility can be transformed into reality only by adding mental determination. Usually, the motivating factors which produce the mental determination necessary for racing success remain largely unknown. Regardless of the psychological motivation present in most champions, younger athletes should realize that even the greatest runners suffer extreme feelings of anxiety and helplessness prior to racing, and are often obsessed with an almost uncontrollable desire to withdraw from competition. Frequently they subconsciously seek socially acceptable excuses for withdrawing or quitting, even simulating injury or illness. The winner is attacked by such intense emotions as often as the quitter, but he is somehow able to control himself and overcome them. No quick or ready solution can be offered to overcome such feelings. It seems best merely to accept such anxiety as a natural consequence of competition, for which there is no known solution. However, the greater the motivation and determination, the less difficulty the athlete will experience in performing in accordance with his racing potential.

How many athletes be motivated to better performances?

Even though the importance of motivation in athletic performance has long been recognized, this recognition has not gone beyond the talking level. No one has developed any certain means of motivating athletes to higher performances. Some athletes want to excell, although no one seems to know why, and these become the record-breakers in many cases. Most athletes feel the game is still the game, not the end of the world, and consequently they seldom set records.

What should be the runner's mental attitude during competition?

Quitting is performing in any way less than best, as it is not necessary to stop running to have quit. Since cowardice is a constant opponent, and the runner must battle his own weaknesses as well as his opponents, there must be a total refusal to succumb to the temptation to quit. Never dwell upon negative thoughts or permit defeatist thinking. Think, instead, of the over-all positive aspects which are favorable to a good performance. Never think of the consequences of possible defeat, and avoid thinking of the actual finish of the race. Instead, concentrate on the technique and tactics of running one phase of the race at a time in proper sequence, according to plan, and do not worry about the finish until it arrives. As an example, the 6 miler should not think of the 23rd lap at the crack of the starter's gun. This might prove an intolerable thought. Rather, he should think of his time at the end of the first 440 yards. Next he should think of his time and position at the end of 880 yards, and concentrate his attention of his efforts only one lap at a time, as the race develops, until the latter stages. There must be a singularity of purpose in the mind of the runner which blocks out all other thoughts except the immediate task at hand - namely - performing to the absolute maximum of his potential. The runner cannot permit his mind to wander even for an instant to thoughts of family, girl-friend, comforts of leisure, or anything other than the actual one-phase-at-a-time progress of the race itself. A wandering mind would be fatal to the concentration essential in producing a maximum competitive effort. The runner must have absolute resolution to win. If he cannot win he must fight for the highest place he can finish and strive, without reservation, to run better than ever before.

Why do men run?

Men might run short distances slowly and on occasion for fun, but the answer must be sought on a different basis when this question relates to competitive footracing. It is impossible to comprehend or identify all the innumerable cross-currents of social influences, racial traditions, frustrations, beliefs, aggressions, impulses, fears, and insecurities that may motivate men to competitive running. There is seldom a single causal motive that can be isolated as exclusively responsible. Usually the motivating factors responsible for competitive racing are neither identified nor recognized by the athlete himself, but they must be of such intensity as to cause the athlete to feel racing is worth the effort involved. More often than not, racing success if directly related to intensity of motivation.

Why should the athlete follow a program of "gradual adaptation to stress" in his training, rather than running as fast as possible in every training session?

The principle of Progressive Resistance Exercise was known to the Greeks, and the legend of Milo lifting the calf daily from its birth to its death as a means of insuring gradual, progressive resistance, is an example. Words of caution about a gradual increase of intensity in training should not be interpreted as suggesting that intensive training is to be avoided. Training must eventually become quite severe for maximum results. However, a plan of gradual adaptation to the stress of running seems the best means of arriving at a state of physical and mental preparation whereby high quality and quantity training in its most intensive form can be safely and economically performed. The human body has amazing powers of adaptation and overcompensation if given the opportunity to exercise them. Vaccinate a man for smallpox with a small dose of appropriate strength vaccine. The body adapts itself to this small infection and overcompensates by producing antibodies of sufficient quantity to ward off and withstand exposure to the disease at a future date. Break an arm, set it properly, and nature overcompensates by healing the break so thoroughly that it is relatively impossible to break the same spot again. Vaccinate the runner with a small does of running, such as 80 seconds per 440 yards type training; the body adapts to this low grade stress and overcompensates in the resistance it produces to this intensity of training. Then, on the basis of this adaptation and overcompensation, the body can, during the excitement of competition, produce a competitive effort at a much faster pace (perhaps 70 to 75 seconds per 440 yards speed, for example). Vaccinate the runner with very short repetitions of high speed running; the body adapts and overcompensates to the stresses involved, and is thus enabled to race over far greater distances at a relatively high rate of speed, even though by necessity not so fast as the high training speed. After giving the body an opportunity to adapt to the stress of one training speed and overcompensates in producing resistance to that particular stress, move gradually and moderately to a slightly more intense training speed. However, just as too strong smallpox vaccine might result in a severe case of smallpox for the patient, so too intense training in the beginning and failure to gradually increase the intensity might tear down the body's resistance to the stress of running. In that case the body fails to produce any concrete adaptation and overcompensation to running stress for use when put to the acid test of racing. Training should therefore gradually produce adaptation of the body to the stress of running, and this can hardly be done unless training is accurately graduated in intensity.

How does one learn to relax while running?

Relaxation is achieved by gradually losing one's self-awareness, especially of the negative aspects of effort and fatigue. This may happen best and most completely by accepting them for what they are, without doubt or fear. Just as in certain war situations admission of fear is considered an effective way of controlling it, so physical expression of fatigue can help to keep it out of mind. Relaxation in running is related to one's approach to life in general. It develops more from unconscious than conscious learning. Relaxation develops out of experiencing with composure the pain of training and anguish of early defeat. All great runners accept discomfort and disappointment as part of running. Through year-round training under all conditions the champion becomes inured to suffering. Good training hurts, for no matter how tough the runner may seem outwardly, every new level of development or intensity of effort brings its own quality of pain. All runners hate the pain of effort from time to time, but they try to accept it, rather than avoid it. They have experienced pain often in the past and survived. They know they will survive again, no matter how intense the pain. Sometimes they achieve a certain degree of satisfaction from the pain, or the ignoring of pain. They learn through experiencing pain again and again that it is not disasterous, but fear of pain may bring on diseaster. To deliberately choose the difficult path in training tends to produce greater running powers and release certain mental inhibitions.

Should the pre-race warmup be identical with the pre-training warmup?

Yes, by all means, possibly contrary to popular belief. Only by using the same warmup prior to both training and competition can you be certain your warmup is sufficient prior to racing. It simply is not intelligent to use a pre-training warmup time after time and become accustomed to it, and then discard it completely for an unaccustomed warmup prior to racing. There may, however, be one difference. In training, the athlete usually goes directly into the workout following his warmup. Prior to competition, the usual warmup may be followed by 5-10 minutes of complete rest. Normally on the day of the race a runner should take his usual warmup. Then he should go to the dressing room, use the bath-room, change from sweaty warmup clothing to dry racing togs, and lie down for 5-10 minutes of complete rest. He should arise 5-10 minutes prior to his race, use the bath-room a final time, go to the track to change into racing shoes and walk and jog until the race starts.

What type of group atmosphere should a coach seek to promote when working with athletes?

This question involves the dynamics of group action, is not readily answered, and is dependent upon many factors. The main issue is dependent upon the attitude and approach of the coach himself to group situations.

The autocratic type ("I will do the thinking, you do the running, and don't question why.") coach works <u>on</u> the athletes. The autocratic coach determines all policies and details, makes all decisions, gives directions piece-meal, bestows punishment and rewards arbitrarily without reason or explanation, and future plans and activities are seldom made known beforehand. Autocratic coaching is self-centered and perpetuates itself by skillful leadership alone. Athletes are deliberately made emotionally and intellectually dependent upon this type coach. In the autocratic atmosphere, hostility, criticism, tensions, and aggressive behavior run high. Although fraught with regimentation, domination, discipline and coercion, autocracy nevertheless can and has worked successfully in the coaching atmosphere as it has in other areas of human endeavor.

The laissez-faire type ("I don't know much about the sport, care less, and feel it's not important enough to bother learning") coach does not work. He is passive and permissive in his approach to training and competition, and leaves the athletes free to do as they please. Studies have revealed aggressive behavior is high in this atmosphere. Needless to say, the laissez-faire group atmosphere is undesirable, and the laissez-faire type coach is in a position to render great benefit to the sport by an early and complete withdrawal from coaching.

The democratic-type ("Lets all work together with go-go-go in getting the job done in the best way possible.") coach works 'with' the athletes, not over them. Policies and details of training are discussed freely, criticism is welcomed, and athletes are encouraged to think for themselves and participate in planning and decision making. The coach proposes alternative procedures and suggests consequences which may be expected. A feeling of belonging and togetherness is fostered. Rewards are given objectively. New ideas are invited by the coach without fear of losing prestige loss through changing his views. He does not jealously consider himself an authority in all events because of his thorough knowledge in one. He is fair, frank, objective, intellectually honest and holds personal motives and ambitions secondary to the best interests of the sport and his athletes.

This superficial examination of autocratic, laissez-faire, and democratic group atmospheres shows the latter would be infinitely preferable.

What is the effect of sexual intercourse and masturbation upon athletic performance?

This is a delicate question which is usally left unanswered or ignored. The emotional and physical effect of sexual intercourse and/or masturbation should have no more adverse or beneficial effect than any other physical and/or emotional experience. However, society today is wraught with legal, social, religious, and moral laws which prohibit extramarital sex and masturbation. When an athlete does so indulge he may be plagued with subconscious feelings of guilt. Furthermore, the human mind may still harbor the ancient taboo which denounces as evil, "bad," and harmful anything which gives pleasure. It is, therefore, the taboo of pleasure and the mental anguish of guilt which will adversely affect athletic performance, rather than the physical and/or emotional experience involved. Sexual relations by married athletes should have no adverse (or beneficial) effect upon athletic performance. Nocturnal emission of semen (wet dream) is a perfectly normal and harmless event, and no sense of guilt should be attached to it. Since extramarital sexual relations and masturbation probably does violate moral and religious principles of most athletes (not to mention possible violation of laws of the land), it may reasonably be expected to arouse sub-conscious feelings of guilt which will adversely affect athletic performance. Therefore, unmarried athletes are advised not to indulge. However, no such caution is directed to married athletes - so long as they confine their efforts to the nuptial aggreement.

What is the effect of "petting" on athletic performance?

"Petting" usually refers to the process of passionate love-making, often with the ultimate (if not immediate) objective of sexual intercourse. It is frequently accompanied by poor ventilation and late hours necessitating loss of sleep. Emotional tension, frustration, and severe anxiety and/or anticipation go hand in hand with petting. It has no known favorable effect on athletic performance.

How much sleep should a runner get each night?

This must be determined by trial and error on an individual basis but, as a general rule, an athlete should sleep at least 8 hours each night. Most athletes in intensive training, especially those training twice daily, prefer more. A nap of 30 minutes at noon is very beneficial, and 30 minutes of sleep directly after a workout should result in more rapid recovery. In fact, the use of a brief nap immediately following very intense workouts is an aid to recovery which has seldom been exploited in the never ending search for more effective training means.

How do the English equivalents of metric distances compare in terms of time differential?

The difference between 100 yards (91.44m) and 100 meters (109.36 yards) is roughly 9/10 second.

The difference between 220 yards (201.17m) and 200 meters (218.72 yards) is approximately 1/10 second.

The difference between 440 yards (402.34m) and 400 meters (437.44 yards) is about 3/10 second.

The difference between 880 yards (804.67m) and 800m (874.89 yards) is roughly 7/10 second.

The difference between 1 mile (1609.3m) and 1500 meters (1640.4 yards) is roughly 18 seconds at high speed, more for slower times.

The difference between 3 miles (4,828m) and 5000 meters (3 miles, 188.1 yards) is approximately 30 seconds.

The difference between 6 miles (9,656.1m) and 10,000 meters (6 miles, 376.1 yards) is about 60-65 seconds.

20,000 meters = 12 miles, 752.0 yards. (Olympic Walking distance).
42,195 meters = 26 miles

42,195 meters = 26 miles, 385.0 yards. (Full marathon distance).

50,000 meters = 31 miles, 120.0 yards. (Olympic Walking distance).

Does it not represent new and revolutionary departures from the generally accepted methods of training to advocate such features as multiple workouts daily, year round training, and weight training?

These features of training are new only if you were previously unaware of them. Although refinements are being made with the passage of time, there is very little that is new under the sun as actually practiced in the world of training. As long as 3,000 years ago the Greeks who participated in the ancient Olympic Games knew much of what we know about training today. Since the ancient Greeks preferred to attribute everything to the Gods and Demi-Gods, they idolized Hermes as the first trainer and coach. The ancient Greeks used running, walking, jumping, dancing, wrestling, games, and various kinds of exercises for the training of their athletes. In addition to such general or all-round preparation, the athletes trained mainly in the game or event at which they expected to compete. The runners ran at first on sand, because this made running extremely difficult; then later when they ran on solid surfaces they had the impression of flying like birds. Hopping, jogging, and skipping were well known and used widely. They used many forms of apparatus designed to put more stress into their exercises, and are known to have worked with weights. For training their feet, they used exercises of running and jumping. Running exercises were: (1) Anatrochamos, or running backwards, (2) Peritrochasmos, or running in circles. (3) Ekplethrizin, which means running forward and backward over a distance of a few meters, lessening the distance each time. Jumping exercises included various jumps, both with one foot and two feet. They climbed ropes and exercised with medicine balls. They rolled big hoops in front of them when running, the main purpose of these hoops being to warm up the athletes. Often they skipped through these hoops, just as we skip rope today. In order to complete their training, the ancient Greeks did fatigue work: they hacked, ploughed, rowed, mowed, and carried heavy burdens. The art of massage was developed to perfection, and used as a part of the warmup, in addition to being used as an aid to relaxation after training. The trainers prescribed various diets in accordance with the games in which the athletes took part. Their training, formerly called "Kataskevi," lasted almost the entire day. The athletes began training in the morning in the stadium or gymnastic hall, and remained until evening. It is important to note that the ancient Greeks trained many hours each day, following a "Tetras" system, or 4-day training cycle which was never interrupted. According to the Tetras, the first day's training was very easy, the second day was very hard, the third day the athletes relaxed or trained very slightly, and on the fourth day they trained moderately hard. The ancient Greek athletes trained a full ten months prior to the Olympic Games, and were not required to work in order to make a living.

This superficial examination of training among ancient Greeks makes it possible to draw certain parallels with present day training. Today, many athletes can meet with success on an international level only if they train twice daily, that is both morning and evening on a daily basis. The athlete, today, who sets about breaking a world record will have to submit to twice daily training of such intensity that it may well exclude other work such as study and occupational endeavor. This is a statement of fact; it suggests no reference as to whether it is desirable or morally correct.

The above should not be interpreted as suggesting the ultimate has been reached, as it seems training knowledge is still in its infancy. There is every reason to believe that application of results of empirical observation and scientific research will continue to favorably influence the character of training in the future.

What comparisons may be made between steeplechase times and times for similar distances in track racing?

Denis Watts ("The Technique of Steeplechasing," Coaching Newsletter, No. 21, April, 1962, page 2.) offers these useful comparisons:

(1) 2 mile flat time = 3,000 meters steeplechase time.

(2) 3,000 meters flat time plus 35 seconds = 3,000 meters steeplechase time.

(3) 1 mile flat time = 1,500 meters steeplechase time.

(4) 1,500 meters flat time plus 18 seconds = 1,500 meters steeplechase time.

(5) The time for running 440 yards negotiating 5 hurdles enroute approximately equals one steeplechase lap with the water jump when the lap is shortened by 6 to 10 yards via the water jump.

The steeplechase layout, using a 440 yard track with the water-jump just to the inside of one curve, is usually about 434 yards per lap. On such a course, 3,000 meters steeplechase = $7\frac{1}{2}$ laps (28 hurdles and 7 waterjumps). 1,500 meters steeplechase = $3\frac{3}{4}$ laps (12 hurdles and 3 water-jumps).

W. N. Coyne ("Notes on Steeplechasing," Coaching Newsletter, No. 8, July 1958, page 8) suggests these approximate time differential factors:

(1) 2 miles flat to 3,000 meters flat, subtract 40 seconds.

(2) 3,000 meters flat to 3,000 meters steeplechase, add 35 seconds.

(3) 2 miles steeplechase to 3,000 meters steeplechase, subtract 50 seconds.

(4) 2 miles flat to 3,000 meters steeplechase, subtract 5 seconds.

Coyne (above) also produced an interesting construction of time differential which is based upon actual clearance time and fatigue time-lag due to clearance of the obstacles. The fatigue time-lag is due to the effect

of hurdling on the runner, and becomes greater towards the end of the race.
Hurdles............time-lag for each hurdle........... 0.4 second.
Multiplied by number of hurdles in steeplechase race 28
Total time-lag for hurdles.......... 11.2 seconds.
Waterjump.........time-lag for each waterjump......... 1.1 seconds.
Multiplied by number of waterjumps in steeple-
chase race.. 7
Total time-lag for waterjumps........ 7.7 seconds.
Total time-lag caused by hurdles and waterjumps
(11.2 plus 7.7).......................................18.9 seconds.
Average time differential between 3,000 meters flat and
3,000 meters steeplechase...............................35 seconds.
Fatigue time-lag (effect of obstacles in steeplechasing on
flat running ability), 35 minus 18.9....................... 16.1 seconds.

What mathematical calculations may be used to determine optimum racing pace and tactics?

In pure sprint races up to and including 220 yards, tactics play a very insignificant role. The sprinter who can maintain his speed longest and decelerate the least should win. The 100 yards sprinter reaches top speed as quickly as possible, which usually takes about 6 seconds. He then strives to hold maximum speed and decelerate as little as possible. The same applies to the 220 yards sprinter. Novice 220 yards sprinters may divide their race into the acceleration at the start (about 60 yards), the "float" or "coast" (about 100 yards), and the finishing effort (about 60 yards). The "float" implies reduction of tension involving only an imperceptable reduction of speed, no change of form, and retaining speed with the least possible effort. Greater relaxation in the arms, dropping the hands slightly in the backswing, and greater relaxation about the hips thus permitting a greater stretch of the thighs, will all help to maintain speed with minimum effort. However, the day will come when top class sprinters run 220 yards under 20.0 seconds without benefit of a "float". At this speed, the 220 yards will be run as a single unit, sprinting as fast as possible with minimum tension the entire distance, with the least possible deceleration.

With regard to 400 meters (440 yards) and 800 meters (880 yards), Toni Nett of Germany has provided mathematical calculations and nomenclature worthy of consideration in determining optimum racing pace and tactics. This has been reviewed by Geoffrey Dyson in "Coaching Newsletter" (No. 12, November, 1959, pp5-7).

A runner's best 100m time (after age 17-18) indicates his potential racing distance: World class sprinters - 10.0 to 10.5; World class middle distance runners - 10.4 to 11.8; World class long distance runners - 11.7-12.5. However, not all distance runners whose time lies within these limits possess the required endurance.

Races of 300-400 m. are known as "battles for oxygen." Oxygen requirements exceed oxygen intake. The greatest oxygen debt is attained at 200 m, after which the speed of running should be adjusted to suit the distance. Therefore, 300-400 m races are not pure sprints.

100m and 200m speed is an essential prerequisite to expert 400m running. World class 400m runners have speed on a par with pure sprinters. A runner's 100m and 200m times express his speed. If the runners best 200m on a curve is doubled, and the resulting figure is subtracted from his best 400m time, the difference will be a numerical expres-res-sion of his "staying power," Stated differently, "staying power" = 2 times best 200m curve time, minus best 400m time. Straightaway 200m time plus .4 second = 200m curve time. Among champions, "staying power" varies between 3 and 5 seconds.

Examples: (1) World record 200m (straight) 20.0 seconds (Sime). Straightaway 200m (20.0) plus .4 = 20.4 (curve). 400m equivalent is 20.4 x 2 (40.8), plus 3 seconds "staying power" = 43.8 seconds. (2). Calculating from 400m time: Best 400m 49 seconds. Best 400m (49), minus 3 sec. "staying power" is 2x best 200m curve, or 46 seconds. 46 divided by 2 gives best200m curve, or 23 seconds. 23.0 (curve) minus .4 gives straightaway 200m, or 22.6 (3). From (b) deduce the 100m time: 22.6 plus .2 second = 22.8 seconds. 22.8 divided by 2 = 11.4 time for 100m.

It is more accurate to assess essential basic sprinting speed from 400m time than to calculate 400m time from basic sprint speed. Not all 10.6 100m sprinters can run 46.0 for 400m. In planning training for the 400m runner, first compare his speed and staying power figures. Then make good his deficiencies. If stressing endurance, devote one-third of the time to speed training. If stressing speed, devote one-third of the time to endurance work.

Pace judgement is important in 400m running.

Preservation time is a runner's best 200m (curve) subtracted from the fastest time he can run the first 200m in a 400m race.

Time loss is the difference between the first and second 200m in a 400m race.

Stayer type 400m runners (who have less speed and therefore slower times over 100-200m) show the smallest time loss, while the sprinter type 400m runners show the greatest time loss.

Preservation time and time loss are closely related. The greater the preservation time the smaller time loss. The smaller the preservation time the greater the time loss. The first 200m of the 400m race must be run with the shortest possible preservation time. What is idled away in the first 200m cannot be made up in the second half of the 400m race.

Example of a stayer (Rudolf Harbig) type and sprinter (Bill Carr) type in 400m competition.

	Harbig	Carr
Best 200m	21.5	21.0
Best 400m	46.0	46.2
1st 200m	22.0	22.1
2nd 200m	24.0	24.1
Preservation time	0.5	1.1
Time loss 2nd 200m	2.0	2.0
2nd 200m minus best 200m	2.5	3.1
Overall loss	3.0	4.2

By increasing 100m and 200m speed, both the stayer and the sprinter type 400m runners can improve their times over the first 200m, readjusting preservation times to advantage.

Stayer:	Previously:	22.5 plus 0.5 = 23.0	plus 25.0 = 48.0.
	Now:	22.0 plus 0.5 = 22.5	plus 24.5 = 47.0.
Sprinter:	Previously:	22.0 plus 1.0 = 23.0	plus 25.0 = 48.0.
	Now:	21.5 plus 1.0 = 22.5	plus 24.5 = 47.0.

Thus improving basic speed can be advatageous in running both first and last 200m intervals in a 400m race.

Rain, wind, track surface, and other factors can all upset the time of the last 200m in a 400m race. Therefore, only the first 200m pace can be planned in advance. Nevertheless, in good class 400m races, the last 200m is very consistent in time. Regardless of whether a minimum preservation time is used or if the runner "takes good care of himself" with a slower first 200m, the time for the final 200m is usually within a range of 24 to 25 seconds. In general, too short a preservation time is better than too long. Preservation times for novices may double, perhaps beginning with as much as 2 seconds, with a time loss of as much as 4 seconds.

(In view of the above recommended minimum preservation time and the fact that the fastest finisher is he who decelerates the least, it would appear that future improvement in 400m times will result from faster running over the second half of the race, as suggested in "Modern Track and Field" by J. K. Doherty.)

It is not unknown for top class 440 yards sprinters to cover the first 220 yards of their race at a speed of only 0.3 to 0.5 seconds slower than their best competitive 220 yards. This event should be run as an endurance sprint involving maximum acceleration at the start and the continuation of such speed as for as long as possible with minimum deceleration.

800m. A runners probable 800m times can be estimated on the basis of his best 400m. No world class 800m runner with a best 400m of 46-51 seconds has achieved a "time loss" for 800m of less than his best 400m plus 60 to 63 seconds. With slower 400m runners, this numerical ratio deteriorates remarkably.

The difference (time loss) between the first and second 400m in an 800m race is from 2 to 5 seconds. Five seconds is not too much time loss in a very fast 800m race. This time loss depends upon the runner's staying power. Staying power for the 800m runner is two times his best 400m, subtracted from his best 800m time.

Formula for determining top class 800m pace: (a) Best 400m time plus 60 seconds. (b) Divide result in (a) by 2. (c) From the result in (b) subtract 1.5 seconds for the time of the first 400m. (d) From the result in (c) add 3.0 seconds for the second 400m time.

Example: Best 400m (47seconds) plus 60 seconds = 107 seconds. (b) 107 divided by 2 = 53.5 seconds. (c) 53.5 seconds minus 1.5 seconds = 52 seconds (1st lap). (d) 52 seconds plus 3 seconds = 55.0 seconds (2nd lap). (e) Preservation time (52 seconds minus 47 seconds) = 5 seconds.

Note that a slower 400m runner would require a shorter 800m preservation time: (a) Best 400m (51 seconds) plus 60 seconds = 111 seconds. (b) 111 halved = 55.5 seconds. (c) 55.5 seconds minus 1.5 seconds = 54 seconds (1st lap). (d) 54 seconds plus 3 seconds = 57 seconds (2nd lap). (e) Preservation time (54 seconds minus 51 seconds = 3 seconds.

Faster times for the first 400m make for faster 800m times. The sprinter type 800m runner is more likely to be overcome by fatigue and must keep a relatively greater preservation time. Sprinters and stayers must have different preservation times. It is wrong to run the first 400m too fast, but this is better than running the first 400m too slow.

The 800m race can be planned only to the half-way mark. There are too many surprises and unknown factors in the second 400m to plan this half of the race. In training the runner must learn to know the pace desired for the first 400m, for he cannot correct matters at the end of the first lap in competition. What has been wasted in the first 400m by slow pace cannot be retrieved on the final lap.

The middle and long distance runner may rely on lap times called out to him during the race. However, the 400m and 800m runners must acquire an exceptional knowledge of pace. But the calling out of intermediate times in 400m and 800m races does not permit the runners to take advantage of the information. It comes too late to be acted upon.

It is possible to assess the likely second 400m time in the 800m race on the basis of the runner's best 400m mark. Thus:

Best 400m	Second 400m in 800m race.
46-47 seconds.	46-47 plus 8.5-7-5 seconds.
48-49 seconds.	48-49 plus 7.5-7.0 seconds.
50 seconds and upwards.	50 plus 6.5-6.0 seconds.

Given a slow first lap, stayers are more likely to run a relatively fast second 400m than sprinters. With strong opposition, (and thus against relatively good and experienced runners), always run the first 400m in the minimum preservation time. If the first 400m is too fast, a runner still has the chance of running either his best-ever time or a very good one. If it is too slow, neither is possible, An idle first lap costs far more than is often realized.

Calculations for beginners should be based on a 66 second differential, rather than 60 seconds for experienced. Thus: (a) Best 400m (46 seconds) plus 66 seconds = 112 seconds. (b) 112 halved =56 seconds. (c) 56 seconds minus 1.5 seconds = 54.5 seconds (1st lap). (d) 54.5 seconds plus 3 seconds = 57.5 (2nd lap).

This gives a time loss of 3 seconds and an 8.5 seconds difference between the first lap time and the best-ever 400m. It gives an 11.5 seconds difference between the second lap time and the best-ever 400m. If, with an 8.5 seconds preservation time, the time loss between the first and second laps exceeds 5 seconds, the preservation time should not be reduced until the athlete has developed sufficient staying power through training to reduce his time loss. Then the preservation time may gradually be reduced. If, after long and conscientious training, a runner's time loss still exceed 5 seconds, then he is unsuited to the 800m distance. However, to duplicate the preservation times and time losses of experienced runners requires many seasons.

Doherty (Modern Track and Field) has recommended a time loss (difference between the first and second 400's in an 880 yards race) of 4 seconds in a 2:02.0 half-mile, 3 seconds for a 1:54.0 effort, and 2 seconds for a 1:46.2 performance.

In terms of maximum performances from a purely physiological viewpoint, a steady, even pace will produce a faster time for all distances from 220 yards and beyond. The body tires less readily when the effort is evenly distributed over the entire race. Theoretically a burst of speed at any time during a race is wasteful of effort and implies that the fastest steady pace is not being achieved. Ideal even pace would be at the maximum speed the runner could sustain for the entire distance, leaving nothing for a sprint finish.

In view of the physiological steady pace optimum, why do 440 and 880 yards competitors follow what may be described as a "maximum acceleration-minimum deceleration" tactical approach to racing? This may be explained by the fact that the energy cost of running increases as the 3.8 mathematical power of speed. Due to the speed of 440-880 yard races, oxygen debt and fatigue products induce exhaustion rapidly. The runner therefore seeks to cover as much of the race as possible at the greatest speed which will still permit him to finish in a minimum time, before fatigue becomes intolerable.

In 1500-mile races, the first half should be slightly slower than the last half for purposes of physical economy and comfort. However, of the world record miles over the past 75 years, only those of Herb Elliott (58.2; 59.9 (1:57.5); 60.9; 55.5 (1:56.4) = 3:54.5) and Peter Snell (60.5; 59.5 (1:59.5); 58.5; 56.4 (1:54.9) = 3:54.4) were run with the first 880 yards solwer than the final half.

As performances rise, runners who expect to win find thay are less often permitted the luxury of reserving effort for a sprint finish. For this reason, superior 1500m-milers tend to run the first half faster than the last, thus following somewhat the "maximum acceleration-minimum deceleration" tactical approach of the 800m-880 yards competiters. This is even more evident in 1500m than mile racing, indicating runners find anaerobic (without oxygen) running becomes more and more inefficient as the distance becomes longer.

For distances beyond the mile, strict even pace running should be the pace pattern for best performances even though this must be altered from time to time to meet the requirements of factors peculiar to any particular race.

How I Train Sprinters

by Fritz Muhle
(West Germany)

How does one recognize a talented sprinter?

Sprinters don't fall into any hard and fast pattern. This becomes obvious from a consideration of our present top sprinters with respect to weight and height. Since we are not able to recognize a sprinter by his outward appearances, one is justified in asking the question: "How may I recognize a very talented sprinter?" The answer: "Among other things, by the leaps and bounds in the evolution of the development of the sprinter."

Organizing a year's training

The year-around training of a sprinter divides itself, in general, into two large stages of development: Winter training (November through April), and summer training (May through September).

First Stage (November-December)

During these two months, the sprinter's training is geared upon the assumption that he has been allowed a complete rest of from four to six weeks from the enormous demands, both physically and mentally, of the summer's competition. At this time he undergoes general bodily development through conditioning work, using all the equipment in the gymnasium. He achieves a general endurance by resorting to the Swedish or Polish speed play and interval-endurance running. (By participating in the interval type of long-distance running, the oxygen debt is consciously kept down.) The slow running should, in addition, build the coordination of the nerves and muscles. The work on running should take place only in the forest; if such a surface isn't possible, then work out upon the track.

Training method

Forest running (twice weekly). Run from one-half to an hour's time in the manner of the Swedish or Polish speed play.

Track training (one time weekly).

1. Up to 10 practice runs at the 200 meter distance. As the the time of these runs, in November add 13 seconds to the best time one achieved at the distance the previous year. In December, add only 10 seconds to it, plus another 17 seconds for the extra 100 meters. In December, add only 10 seconds. Walk or jog 200 meters between each run.

2. Or, run 8 x 300 meters. In arriving at the time for each run, in November take the best time for 200 meters the previous year, and add 13 seconds to it, plus another 17 seconds for the extra 100 meters. In December, add 8 plus 15 seconds, respectively. Walk or jog 300 meters between each run.

3. Or, do a series of repetitive runs in the following sequence: 200, 300, 400, 300, 200 meters. Do one series at a workout in November and two in December. In November, the time differential between each run should be 17 seconds; in December, 15.0 to 15.5 seconds.

	November	December
200 meters	34 secs.	30 secs.
300 meters	51 secs.	45 secs.
400 meters	68 secs.	62 secs.
300 meters	51 secs.	45 secs.
200 meters	34 secs.	30 secs.

Rest between the runs to the extent that a feeling of "joyousness in running" exists.

4. Or, 10 x 100 meters. In November, the time should be 15 sec-

onds, in December 14. Walk back to the start between each run.

Conditioning work in the gymnasium

1. 10 repetitions of a leg-stretching exercise during which the athlete (a) runs over two or three vaulting horses, (b) jumps over two vaulting horses, (c) and then does the straddle split over another.

2. All sorts of calisthenics.

3. Bouncing (springing) exercises on the mat and over a set of hurdles.

4. Work with the medicine ball.

5. Work with weights for the strengthening of the whole body.

6. Games.

The conditioning work in the gymnasium must be in synchronization with the running work in the forest and upon the track.

Second Period (January-February)

Objective; Accustoming the organism (body) and the mental apparatus to an increased running speed. The capacity to run in a relaxed fashion in spite of the increased tempo without causing an excessive tension in the muscles is of the greatest significance.

Training method

Forest running (twice weekly). (a) Run an hour in the pattern of the Swedish or Polish speed play. (b) Do 10 accelerations (bursts) uphill for 150 meters.

Training on the track (1-2 times weekly)

1. Pace work at 200 meters, with the time in January being 6 seconds over the runner's best for the preceding year. In February the time should be 5 seconds over. Rest by walking or jogging 200 meters between each run.

2. Sprinting for 30 meters at about $\frac{7}{8}$ of optimum speed. The number of runs and speed of each run should be adjusted to the runner's state of training at the time.

3. Pace work at 300 meters, with the time being 6 seconds over the runner's best for the previous year at 200 meters, plus 14 seconds for the extra 100 meters. In February, the time added should be 5 seconds, plus 13.5 seconds. Rest between runs by walking 300 meters.

4. Sprint 30, 40, and 50 meters. After each single run, slowly jog back to the start. After doing the whole series, take a somewhat longer rest. Repeat until weariness sets in.

5. Starts over a distance of 40 meters. In January, do them first at a walking tempo, and then go to a jogging rate of speed. In February, begin starts with a jogging tempo and then switch to standing starts.

An example of a week's sprint training at the January-February Stage

One day of running in the forest from 1 to $1\frac{1}{2}$ hours, using the Swedish speedplay system.

One day of training on the track:

1. Long period of warming up with jogging interspersed with calisthenics.

2. Take 18 starts of 40 meters each in this pattern: 6 starts, beginning with walking; 6 starts, beginning with jogging; and 6 standing starts. Stress a relaxed acceleration in each run.

3. Pace work: 4 x 300 meters. The speed for each should be one's best time at 200 meters in the previous year, plus 20 seconds in January and 18 seconds in February. Walk 300 meters between each run.

4. Do two sets of sprints consisting of 30, 40, and 50 meters at a $\frac{7}{8}$ speed. In spite of this increased tempo, remain relaxed.

5. Warm down.

One day of conditioning work indoors:

1. Practice running on the interval pattern with a lot of bounding interspersed with the running.
2. Do some jumping or bounding over chests or boxes and over a set of hurdles.
3. Have some starting practice in an organized pattern.
4. Weight work - 30 to 40 kilograms.

One day of running in the forest:

1. 15 minutes of warming up in the Swedish speedplay manner.
2. 10 accelerations (bursts) uphill over a distance of 150 meters.
3. 10 minutes of easy warming down.

Conditioning Work in the Gymnasium

1. Easy running on the interval principle, interspersing the running with a lot of bounding.
2. Jumping or springing work on mats and over a set of hurdles.
3. Short jumps onto several boxes and over a set of hurdles. In doing these jumps, go from a full knee bend and then from a half knee bend.
4. Do 10 runs over a set of 4 vaulting horses. Go over two horses with the left leg foremost, and over the next two with the right leg foremost.
5. Practice on the wall bars to strengthen the stomach and back muscles.
6. Weight work with an average of from 30 to 40 kilograms.
7. Calisthenics in sitting and lying positions.
8. Starting practice, following this pattern: (a) Walking start; (b) jogging start; (c) skipping start; (d) hopping start; (e) standing start; (f) crouching start without a command.
9. Calisthenics with a medicine ball.

Third Period (March-April)

Lesson to be learned: A broader improvement of the staying capacity (endurance) in order not only to develop a faster tempo, but also to be able to hold this faster pace over a longer sprint-distance.

Training method

Forest running (one weekly):

1. Run about an hour in the speedplay manner.
2. Run downhill 10 times over a sloped distance of 150 meters.

Track practice (2-3 times weekly).

1. Pace running at 200 meters. As to time, in March take the best 200 meter time of the runner for the previous year and add 4 seconds. In April, add 3 seconds. Between each run, walk or jog 200 meters.
2. Do accelerated runs of 200 meters. Stride 120 meters through the curve, and then go 80 meters at the maximum pace to the finish of the 200 meters. Rest between each run by an easy walk of 200 meters to the starting place.
3. From a flying start, run 120 meters, the time to be according to the state of training at the time.
4. Repetitious runs of a series in the following sequence: 200, 300, 300, 200 meters.

	March (13 sec. tempo per 100 meters)	April (12.5 sec. tempo)
200 meters	26 sec.	25.0 sec.
300 meters	39 sec.	37.5 sec.
300 meters	39 sec.	37.5 sec.
200 meters	26 sec.	25.0 sec.

After each single run, rest from 2 to 3 minutes. Between every two series, rest 15 minutes.

5. Pace running at 300 meters. As for time, take the runner's best

time at 200 meters the previous year and add 4 seconds in March, plus 13 seconds for the additional 100 meters. In April, add 3 and 12.5 seconds, respectively. Relax between runs by walking or jogging 300 meters.

6. Starts over a distance of 40 meters. In March, practice both standing and crouch starts without commands. In April, practice crouch starting with commands.

Condition Training or Work

Maintain the building of strength - do no increase it -, because now the running work is put first.

1. Run over a series of boxes, 5 to a series, 10 times with each round being faster than the preceding one.
2. Work with weights.
3. Do bounding runs over a series of mats. Practice jumping over a series of hurdles, going over with the right and left legs in alternation.
4. Calisthenics, practicing with a partner.
5. Practice crouch starts, without and with commands.

An Example or Picture of a Week's Sprint Training at the March-April Stage

One day of running in the forest for 1 to $1\frac{1}{2}$ hours in the Swedish speedplay manner.

One day of training on the track:

1. 20 minutes of warming up work with jumping interspersed in all variations.
2. Take starting practice according to this pattern: 5 from a standing start; 5 from a crouching start without a command; 5 from a crouch with commands.
3. 6 x 100 meters at $\frac{7}{8}$ speed. Relax by walking 100 meters between each.
4. Easy paced run over 200, 300, 300, 200 meters, the time to be determined according to the stage of training. Rest by walking from time to time the distance run.
5. Warm down.

Second day of training on the track:

1. Long warm up in the Swedish speedplay manner.
2. 4 paced runs over 200 meters. Time: Add 4 seconds to the best 200 meter time of the previous year during March, and 3 seconds during April. Relax by walking 200 meters between runs.
3. Long warming down period.

Third day of practice on the track:

1. Warming up.
2. 15 starts in the following pattern: 5 starts from a stand; 5 crouching starts without a command; 5 crouching starts with a command.
3. 6 x 100 meters. In so doing, run 120 meters through the curve at an accelerated pace, and then go the additional 80 meters at the maximum rate. Rest by walking 200 meters between the runs.
4. With a flying start, run 60, 80, and 120 meters. The time should be in accordance with the stage of training.
5. A 300 meter run at maximum pace.
6. Warming down.

A day of conditioning work indoors: Weight work - starts - jumping (springing) practice - practice on wall bars - specialized calisthenics.

Fourth Stage (May-June)

Period of stage of development when the form is fixed. Running work should be done with (or at) a high and maximum pace. Speed can now become better (faster) only through swift running.

Training method

Forest running: To be done occasionally in order to refuel (refresh) one after heavy competition. The pattern of these workouts should be left to the discretion of the individual.

Practice on track (3-4 times weekly).

1. 15 starts over 40 meters with the athlete continuing to 100 meters at a decelerating pace. Go back at once for the next start. After each series of 5 starts, walk a lap.
2. A paced run over 100 meters with the time being only one second over the best time for the previous year. Rest until recovered.
3. (a) 5 starts over a distance of 30 meters. (b) 3 runs at maximum speed over 70 meters. Considerable rest between each. (c) 5 starts over a distance of 30 meters.
4. 2 paced runs at maximum speed over 300 meters. Rest about a half hour between runs.
5. With a flying start, run 60, 70, and 80 meters at maximum speed. Take a lap of easy walking. Repeat up to three times.
6. Up to 5 paced runs over 150 meters, taking the curve at $\frac{7}{8}$ speed.
7. 3 x 800 meters with three sprints of 30 meters each in each of the three runs.
8. A series of repetition runs at the maximum tempo in the following sequence: 40, 50, 60, 70, 60 meters. Rest 15 minutes between each series.
9. Baton-passing practice.
10. 100 meters with a flying start at maximum speed.

An Example of a Week's Sprint Training in the Development Period of May and June

One day of running in the forest, always according to the amount (load) of competition. Tailor this workout after one's own judgment.

A day of practice on the track:

1. Warming up.
2. 12 starts over a distance of 40 meters, continuing to 100 meters in a eased-up manner. After 6 starts, walk 300 meters to rest.
3. With a flying start for each, run 60, 70, and 80 meters at top speed. Have a long recovery period afterwards.
4. A run of 2 laps (800 meters) with three sprints of 30 meters for each of the 2 laps.
5. 100 meters at $\frac{7}{8}$ speed from a flying start.
6. 2 x 200 meters, the time being one second over the runner's best time for the distance. Long recovery period.
7. Warming down.

Second day of practice on the track:

1. Warming up.
2. 10 starts over a distance of 40 meters.
3. A few relaxed bursts of speed through a curve over a distance of 120 meters.
4. Warming down.

Third day of practice on the track:

1. Warming up work.
2. 10 starts over a distance of 40 meters, continuing to 100 meters at a decelerated pace. After 5 starts, walk 300 meters to rest.
3. Three maximum-speed runs over 50 meters with flying starts.
4. 2 x 75 meters at maximum speed.
5. 2 x 100 meters, using a flying start in each case.
6. 1 x 250 meters at maximum speed.
7. Warming down.

If there is competition at the end of the week, then one day of practice on the track is enough. But, if Sunday is free, then a day of light track practice should be added.

Conditioning (during the warming up work)

1. Light weight work.
2. Bounding practice on the turf-up the steps of the stadium - in the playing-field enclosure.
3. Calisthenics.

Fifth Stage (July-September)

Practice during this period is aimed only at preserving the form or condition of the runner.

Training method

Running in the forest: Now and then to enable the athlete to recover from a period of strenuous competition.

Practice on the track: Because of the increased load of competition, the practice days should be lessened. The times of the training (practice) runs and the length of the runs should remain the same, but the number of the runs should be reduced.

Conditioning work: This should now take place at the same period as the track practice. Or, it may be dispensed with entirely.

Returning to track practice, a 20-minute warming up period should precede every hour of actual practice on the track.

Arrangement for Competition

After several months of zealous practice work, each sprinter arrives (comes) to his first competition in a state of tension. It is not always easy to make a good changeover from practice to competition.

The outcome of the first competition can give the sprinter a greater stimulus. The opposite result is, however, also possible. For that reason, when the opening phase of the campaign permits a choice of distances to be run, guide the runner into special distances, into distances that he wouldn't ordinarily be running in competition.

April

At the end of April, have a test run (practice competition). For the 200 meter runner, let him go 300 meters, and have the 100 meter man do 200 meters.

May

From the beginning until the middle of May, let the 200 meter man continue to run 300 meters in practice competition. Have the 100 meter sprinter run a medley of 60, 70, and 80 meters.

In the second (latter) part of May, for test competition let the 200 meter man run 3 races: 100 meters on the curve, 100 meters on the straight, and 150 meters on a combined curve and straightaway. Let the 100 meter man run three races in test competition, too: 75, 100, and 125 meters.

June

From here on, competition with worthy opponents.

(The above is a synthesis of an article entitled, "Wieich Sprinter trainiere," translated from the No. 18, May 1, 1962 issue of Die Lehre der Leichtathletik, and reprinted by permission of editor Toni Nett.)

Sprint Questions and Answers

(We are indebted to former English Chief National Coach, Geoffrey Dyson, for the AAA Honorary Senior Coaching Award questions for 1960. These questions are answered by Eric Broom, AAA Honorary Senior Coach and a leading English sprint coaching authority. Broom has emphasized that these answers represent his own opinions, and may not necessarily coincide with the view of the English AAA Coaching Committee).

Question 1. What are the principles involved in determining the most effective foot spacing for a sprint start?

Answer: Sprint starting positions may be classified into three basic types; the elongated start where the space between the feet varies from 21" to 26", the bullet or bunch start with a foot spacing of approximately 11" to 12", and the medium start with a stance of 14" to 18".

Each of these positions have been favored at different periods during the last 50 years, but it is only during the last decade that our knowledge has had a sound mechanical basis. During the early part of the century the elongated start was much in vogue, but by the early 1920's the bunch start was gaining prominence. This bullet start was accepted only slowly, because by placing the front foot 17" to 19" behind the line it seemed to put the sprinter at a considerable disadvantage, but its popularity received a terrific impetus when the research studies of Bresnahan and Tuttle proved that it was the fastest of all positions in producing clearance of the starting blocks.

It was not until 1952 that further research by Henry proved how misleading this conclusion had been. While it was perfectly true that a sprinter using a bullet start cleared the blocks quickest, he had actually less velocity. Of the positions tested it was proved that the bullet start was the least efficient for the production of body velocity from the blocks. It was found that the medium start, with the back knee somewhere opposite the front foot, was most effective.

From these studies, and from knowledge gained from our coaching experience, we are able to establish certain principles for foot placement in the sprint start. The overriding principle is that the feet should be placed in a position which enables the sprinter to leave his blocks with the greatest possible velocity, on balance, so that he may move smoothly into the full sprinting action. Only careful timing and observation of 20 yards starts will establish these exact positions.

We know that in a sprint start both legs drive as a reaction to the gun. The nearer the rear foot to the line, the greater the flexion of the rear knee and the more inefficient the angle at which the muscles can work. The primary function of the rear leg is to initiate movement, and we must therefore sacrifice time during which muscular force could be applied. As a guiding principle, the angle formed by the rear leg, when in the set position, should be about 120 degrees. This early body velocity provided by the rear leg drive puts the front leg in better mechanical position to accelerate it through a more prolonged application of force. In the set position the angle formed by the front leg will be approximately 90 degrees, but at the end of the rear leg drive, when it will be working alone, it will be in a sounder mechanical position, and have the advantage of not having to overcome body inertia.

An additional guide to placement of the feet is the height of the hips in the set position. Ideally the back should slope slightly downwards towards the shoulders, so that when the shoulders lift slightly at the gun, the rear leg drive will be in one direct line through the body.

When establishing the position of the feet in relation to the starting line, the method most often used is to place the toes of the front foot slightly more than one foot's length behind the line. This approximate position is then made more exact by putting the sprinter into a set position, and moving his foot slightly until he can take up a properly balanced stance. The position of the rear foot is then determined by placing the rear knee on the ground opposite the center of the front foot.

Exact foot spacing for any individual can, of course, only be established by careful experiment, but the medium start position will be found to be the most efficient for almost every sprinter.

Question 2. Describe the typical pattern of acceleration in a 100 yards sprint and give reasons for it.

Answer: The pattern of acceleration in a 100 yards sprint would consist of four phases:

1) Start to 30 yards, rapid acceleration.

2) 30 yards to 60 yards, very gradual acceleration.

3) 60 yards to 85 yards, constant speed.

1) The first phase is one of great acceleration, the sprinter starting from a motionless position on his marks, and attaining approximately 90% - 95% of his maximum speed by the time he reaches the 30 yards mark. This is because the leg drive is most effective at this stage of a sprint. Also, during the start, and at least the first part of this phase, there is considerable forward body lean, made possible by the great acceleration. This body lean makes possible a leg drive which is more directly towards the finishing line. In its stride cycle the foot contacts the ground, moving backwards, directly under the body. The foot thus thrusts backwards into the track, driving the body forwards. At the start, and in the early stages of a sprint, because of low body momentum, the body moves away from the driving foot relatively slowly, enabling driving power to be applied for a relatively long period of time. The drive is thus very effective, and acceleration is rapid.

2) As body momentum increases, the leg drive becomes less effective because the body is moving away from the foot in contact with the track at a greater rate. As the foot lands, under the body, for its driving phase, the body is moving away from it so rapidly that a relatively small period of time is available for power to be applied, and the drive is thus less effective than in the earlier stages of the sprint. With the decrease in acceleration the forward body lean also decreases, and as a result the leg drive is made at a less efficient angle. Thus, from approximately 30 yards to approximately 60 yards, at which point the sprinter will reach his maximum speed, the rate of acceleration is gradual.

3) During the third phase the aim is to maintain maximum speed, and the length of this phase is mainly dependent on the degree of muscular endurance of the sprinter. High quality drive requires maximal contractions, and a top class sprinter succeeds in holding off local fatigue for approximately 20-25 yards. For athletes of less ability this top speed section of the race covers a much shorter distance.

4) From this point on there is a slight slowing down, and the rate of this deceleration is inversely proportioned to the degree of muscular endurance possessed by the sprinter. Even in a 100 yards race, and more so in the longer sprints, the winner is he who slows down the least, and it is the ability to maintain top speed which distinguishes the top class sprinter.

Question 3. In all running, the arms 'take up' the reactions resulting from the actions of the legs. Explain the mechanical principles involved in this. showing how arm action is modified to suit leg action, and give your views on the best arm action for a sprinter.

Answer: All running is a natural movement, and to be efficient the running action must be balanced, which depends on complete harmony between the movements of the legs and arms. One of the prinIples governing movement is that "for every action there is an equal and opposite reaction"; thus, when the legs and hips twist in a clockwise direction the upper body will twist in the opposite direction, and vice versa. These reactions cannot be denied, and in running, where the athlete's contact with the track is momentary, they must be absorbed by his body.

In a normal running stride, as the thigh reaches forward the corresponding hip is also taken forward, and as a reaction to this the upper body twists in the opposite direction - the opposite shoulder moves backward. Exaggerated trunk twistings are not conducive to efficient running, for they throw the athlete off balance. The reactions set up by the leg movements must therefore be absorbed by the movements of the arms, allowing the trunk to remain relatively still and thus maintain the athlete's balance.

To take up the reactions in the upper body which result from the actions of the legs, the arms are swung backwards and forwards from the shoulders. Thus the movement of one shoulder backwards is counteracted by the corresponding arm moving forwards, and instead of the trunk twisting the reactions of the leg movements are absorbed by the movements of the arms.

In all forms of running the shoulders are influenced mainly by the movements of the upper arm, and its action should be backwards and forwards from the shoulder. In sprinting, where leg speed is a vital necessity, the arms are flexed at approximately a right angle in order to shorten the lever and thus accelerate the action. To counteract the reactions from a powerful leg drive the arm action must be forceful and cover a wide range, so the hands are carried to about shoulder level at the front, and to about hip level at the back. In middle and long distance running, in which the leg drive is less powerful and the rate of striding is slower, a less vigorous arm action is required. The hands may be carried a little lower, and the shoulders and arms allowed to swing and twist en bloc, for at this speed of running there is much more time on each stride for the trunk to swing from side to side.

The best arm action for a sprinter should have the following characteristics:

(a) The movement should be directly backwards and forwards from the shoulders, with the elbows kept close to the side. An action in which the arms travel across the body is ineffective in taking up reactions, and while a slight inward path is permissable I would not advocate it.

(b) The arms should act independently of the shoulders, as though the upper arms were connected by a pin to the shoulder and free to move as on a toy doll. The angle at the elbow should be slightly greater than 90 degrees, so that the hand in the backward movement travels beyond the hip.

(c) The action must match the leg action in force and range of movement. The arms actually lead the legs, and a high quality leg drive is only possible when the arm action is in tune with it.

Question 4. Discuss the relative importance to the sprinter of strength, muscular and general endurance.

Answer: Muscular strength, the capacity to exert muscular force against a resistance, muscular endurance, the capacity for continuous performance of relatively heavy localized work, and general endurance, which shows itself in the ability to perform activity of medium intensity involving the whole body, are some of the components of fitness. An example of the first would be the leg drive against the track in sprinting; the second enables the sprinter to maintain the necessary high quality stride; and the third is what we generally know as circulo-respiratory endurance or stamina, and reveals the efficiency of the heart and lungs. Fitness for a particular activity demands differing degrees of development of these, and other components.

Sprinting is a relatively simple event, and is basically dependent on two factors; the number of strides that can be taken in any one second, and the length of each stride. Stride speed, or cadence, is a natural quality of sprinters, which can be little influenced by training. Stride length, however, if we ignore length of limb, is dependent on mobility in the hip joint, in a forwards/backwards phase, and on leg strength. The more powerful the leg drive, the greater the stride length. Sprinting (races up to and including 440 yards) demands a high degree of muscular strength in the form of power. Power is force x velocity, or in other words, strength applied at great speed, and is attained when a sprinter's naturally speedy muscular contractions are combined with great muscular strength. This powerful leg drive must be balanced by the arm action, and thus it can be seen that development of a high degree of all round strength and power, particularly in the legs and upper body, is of vital importance to all sprinters.

A 100 yards sprint can therefore be described as a series of maximal muscular contractions produced as rapidly as possible. We know, however, from tests made with grip dynamometers that when maximal contractions are made rapidly one after another, local fatigue soon sets in and the sprinter is faced with the same situation. Even in a 100 yards race there is a slowing down over the last 20 yards or so, due to the onset of local muscular fatigue, and it is over this past part of the race that a sprinter who has a high degree of muscular endurance will slow down the least. Because of his ability to fight off the effects of local fatigue he will be able to maintain a high quality drive. In the longer sprint races, 220 and 440 yards, muscular endurance becomes even more important, for while the rate of drive in the longer race decreases, the duration of the race increases.

In top class sprinting, therefore, muscular power is of prime importance, and muscular endurance, which depends to a large extent on muscular strength, is vital to enable this power to be applied over the maximum distance.

General endurance, which is a measure of the efficiency of the circulo-respiratory system to supply oxygen and glycogen to the working muscles, and to remove carbon dioxide and other waste products, is of relatively little importance in the short sprint. During this phase of highly concentrated muscular activity the working muscles demand more oxygen than the lungs can immediately supply, and an oxygen debt is incurred which can be repaid after the race.

In the longer sprints however, the general endurance factor becomes increasingly important. The capacity of the oxygen debt is limited, and because of the increased duration of the effort, much of the oxygen required must be supplied during the race. The degree of general endurance must therefore increase as the sprinting distance increases.

It is clear then that muscular strength, and muscular endurance, which are closely associated, are vital to sprinters of all distances, and that general endurance is not required in the short sprint, but becomes increasingly necessary in the longer races.

Question 5. "Progressive resistance exercise" is a term widely used in the coaching of Athletics. Define its meaning, describe the physiological changes it can bring about, and explain how it can be applied in training for these events.

Answer: Progressive resistance exercise is that which imposes steadily increasing loads on the athlete with the object of improving basic fitness. This type of exercise, which usually takes the form of weight training or circuit training, is based on the "principle of progressive loading". The load or resistance against which the athlete works in weight training is progressively increased, in its simplest form, by adding weight to the bar, or increasing the repetitions; and in circuit training, by increasing the repetitions or by raising the rate of work by reducing the total time.

Through intelligent application of the principle of progressive loading the 'hard core of fitness' may be improved. The components of this core are the basic physical qualities: muscular strength, muscular endurance, power and circulo-respiratory endurance, each of which is required, in differing degrees, in sprinting. All of these qualities may be developed through sprinting itself, and for some of them I would advocate this, but in the main they are more rapidly developed, and to a higher level, by means of progressive resistance exercise.

Sprinting is a 'power' event, and as such demands a high degree of muscular strength, which is best developed through weight training. When training for strength the guiding principle is to use near maximum poundages and low repetitions. With resistance of this nature the movements will of necessity be performed slowly, and some coaches fear that this will lead to 'slow muscles'. This, of course, is not so because the 'muscular intention' is for a fast movement, and the muscles do in fact drive at maximum speed, but because of the great resistance the action is slowed. It is only when this 'drive' is employed that near maximum resistance can be used.

For strength training Isometric Contraction possesses all the essentials. The resistance is immovable, and is therefore in excess of a weight an athlete could move, and the one six-second contraction required is the ultimate in low repetitions. It must be remembered however, that this form of training affects only the strength factor; endurance, either local or general is not improved.

Weight training, when light poundages and high repetitions are used, can be used to develop muscular endurance, which is closely related to strength, but for this quality I prefer to use circuit training during the winter months when little outdoor work can be done, and a great deal of high quality repetition sprints when it is possible to train outdoors. These sprint repetitions would take the form of maximum speed 80s, 110s, 150s for the short sprint specialist, and longer distances for the 220 and 440 men. This type of training is in itself a form of progressive resistance exercise, and a build up would take place as fitness improved.

In a similar way circuit training may be used to raise the level of general endurance, but this quality is best developed by repetition running.

Question 6. "What has been idled away in the first 200 meters cannot be made up in the second half of the race". Discuss this statement concerning the 400 meters and outline its implications with regard to speed-distribution.

Answer: One of the most important factors in one lap running is speed distribution, and ideas of how the race should be run have changed without attitude towards the event. When 400m was considered to be a middle distance run the method adopted was similar to that used for 800m, basically even pace running, and the race was broken into three parts; sprint, coast, sprint. If, for instance, the athlete's target time was 52 seconds, he would run the first 200m between $1\frac{1}{2}$ and 2 seconds faster than the second, i.e. 25 to 27 seconds. This method is generally known as the British method.

The event is now regarded as an endurance sprint, and what has become known as the American method, where the first 200m is run exceptionally fast and where there is a difference of as much as four seconds between the first and second half of the race, is now favored. This method does not think of the race as having three parts, but rather a single unit where the athlete runs as smoothly and as fast as possible all the way. We know that a sprinter cannot hold his top speed for long, and that deceleration will set in during the second half of the race, but this deceleration should be gradual and smooth - like clockwork running down. In a correctly run 400m the strong finisher is the sprinter who slows down the least, and if a runner is able to increase his pace at the end of a 400m race he has distributed his effort badly, and, in consequence, not returned his best time. The theory behind the American method is "maximum speed, minimum deceleration".

Today, nearly all races are run in lanes, and the key to success is the ability to distribute effort throughout the race. The important thing is that the athlete should return the best possible time of which he is capable, and with staggered starts which may mean he may see little or nothing of his opponents, this is dependent on pace judgment.

When deciding the pace at which the race is to be run,the most important single factor is the sprinter's best performance over 200m. In good class races the time taken to run the full 400m is determined very largely by the time taken over the first half of the race. Within limits the time taken for the second 200 meters will be constant. If the athlete runs a relatively slow first 200m, with the idea of saving effort for a fast finish, his over-all time will invariably be slower. The race must be regarded as a sprint and the pure speed of the runner must be used to its best advantage. This means running the first half of the race only a fraction of a second slower than the best time for that distance. In the case of a mature top class sprinter this would be as close as 0.5 seconds to his best time, and for a runner of less ability about 1.0 seconds would be added. A breakdown of top class performances over the last few years has established that best times are returned only when the time for the first 200m is within 0.5 seconds of the sprinter's best time for that distance.

Question 7. Write short notes, giving your opinions on (a) Coasting, (b) Turn running, (c) The value of artificial aids in training for speed (e.g. down-hill running), (d) The advisability of increasing stride length.

Answer: (a) Coasting. We know that it takes a sprinter running flat out about six seconds to reach his maximum speed, and that he can hold the top speed for a further 15 yards or so. After that deceleration sets in, and to minimize the loss of speed the sprinter coasts or floats. This most difficult part of the race is of vital importance to the 220 yards and 440 yards man, and only experience will give him the feel of the coast, and determine the distance of it in relation to his capabilities.

The sprinter should not think of this phase as a reduction in speed, but rather a reduction in tension. His thoughts should be on maintaining his speed without fighting for it. Most coaches feel that a slight loss of speed is inevitable, but this may not occur immediately, particularly if the sprinter has been trying too hard. In fact, this lessening of tension will facilitate the holding of top speed.

In my view very slight modifications to the normal sprint action may occur, but these are rarely conscious to the sprinter. His hands may drop a little, and there may be slightly more hip swing, but these are results of more relaxation of the muscles directly unrelated to the sprinting action. With experience the sprinter will feel this release of tension and use it to maintain full speed with the least possible effort.

(b). Turn running. Good turn running is mainly a matter of good balance and a great deal of practice, and furlong and quarter sprinters should not neglect this aspect of their training. The natural tendency for the runner to be pulled outwards has to be overcome, and because of this it is impossible to sprint as fast on a turn as on a straight. In fact, the generally accepted differential between a straight 220 yards and a full curve race is 0.4 seconds.

A first principle of turn running is to keep well to the inside of the lane, and to facilitate this a slight inward lean is required. The amount of lean demanded by different curves will be found by practice. No real adjustment to the normal sprinting action should be made, except perhaps to lower the inside arm slightly on sharp bends, and with practice the sprinter will learn to negotiate the turn with a minimum of interference to his action. Training should include plenty of full speed bend running, with particular emphasis on keeping a smooth path on the inside of the lane, and keeping this path as he comes out of the curve and into the straight. When starting on a turn the starting blocks should be placed on the outside of the lane in order to allow the initial driving strides to be in a straight line across the corner. In addition to this, relay starts on a bend should be practiced from both a standing and crouch start, so that the sprinter becomes skilled at accelerating into a curve. The skill of turn running, once acquired, will pay great dividends, and practice of it will form an interesting aspect of a sprinter's training.

(c) The value of artificial aids in training for speed (e.g. downhill running). In a normal sprinting stride the supporting foot contacts the ground directly beneath the body, and the driving or propulsive phase takes place behind the body. In other words, sprinting is a pushing event.

We know that in sprinting it is possible to achieve a near maximum stride frequency of about 4½ strides per second, and the object of downhill running is to raise this level, and thus bring about an increase in performance. Although downhill running gives the impression that the legs attain a speedier movement, this is not so. Because of the greater body lean encouraged by gravity the driving foot contacts the ground further under the body than it would normally do, thus reducing the length of stride, and also reducing the time in which the foot can apply force against the track. Thus, although the feet contact the track more frequently the duration and efficiency of their drive is reduced, because of the enforced 'pattering' brought about by downhill running. It is clear therefore that attempts to increase leg speed by such means will not be effective.

(d) The advisability of increasing stride length. Sprinting, if we refer to first principles, consists of two basic factors: stride length and rate of striding or cadence. We know that training has little or no effect on the latter; the speed of muscular contractions being a natural quality, this fact giving a basis of truth to the saying that "a sprinter is born and not made". It is obvious therefore that if a sprinter is to increase his speed he must work on the other factor - stride length. If a sprinter can increase the length of each stride, while maintaining the same cadence, he will cover the ground at a greater rate.

Lengthening the stride by pushing the leading foot out in front as it contacts the ground, or by excessive bounding, will simply lead to a lower rate of striding, and a consequent loss of speed. Instead the stride must be lengthened by increasing the power of the leg drive. To be effective this increase of power in the drive must be coupled with the same rate of striding; to improve stride length at the expense of stride speed would be useless. This increase of power is achieved by developing a higher degree of muscular strength, not only in the legs, but also in the upper body. Coupled with this must be increased mobility in the hip joint - more "split" between the legs - so that the power may be used over a greater range in order to produce a longer stride.

General Warmup Exercise Program

by Gustaf Laurel
(National Coach of Sweden)

1. Trot relaxed on the entire foot about 1 mile in 6-10 minutes.

2. Walk with an easy stretch of the hips. Push forcefully on hips with hands placed behind hips for ½ minute.

3. Hip walk or competition walk. Marked hip work and good push with foot. Increase speed until fast walk speed, increase to a jog and light running in half speed for about 175-200 yards-repeat.

4. Stretching of lower leg muscles and heel tendons 15-20 times each leg.

5. Heel-toe walk. Roll-up on the complete foot, stretch knee and ankle with force and increase speed to walk with double bounce on each step as in skipping.

6. Double bounce walk or skip. Diagonal arm movements with loose shoulders as in running, thereafter with forceful arm swing forward-backwardward and high knee lift. Trunk upright. About 100 yards.

7. Fast trot with short steps, loose hanging shoulders and arms. 15-20 seconds.

8. Jog with heel kick against seat or buttocks, lifting the thigh back and up. Fast tempo 2-3 series of 20-30 yds. using skip steps. Trot between series.

9. Stretching of the posterior thighs. Stand with feet not far apart, bend trunk forward, move left hand to right foot, right arm back and up. Stretch right knee during exercise, bend left knee as body weight goes to left side. Change over to opposite side 10-12 times. Shake loosely and relax your shoulders and legs.

10. Mark time with light trot (or move slowly)with high knee lift. Start in a slow tempo with good rhythm and fully complete movements. Increase tempo when rhythm and knee lift and under control. Knee should be lifted 90 degrees against body, which should be upright. Keep lower leg relaxed. 2-3 series of 15-25 double steps.

11. Stretching of hips and front of thighs. Walk with long steps and knee-falls. Turn body with heavy arm swing to same side. Do 2-3 stretchings on each step. 10-12 times altogether.

12. Fast Starts. Start from light trot, changing tempo each 3-4 steps. Begin with hips low and well forward. Step off with force and long drive, marked arm movements. See that the trot is done completely relaxed, go over to "float" and slowly decrease speed. About 5-6 trot in between.

13. Jump with both feet close together with twist of hips alternating left and right. Turn shoulders to opposite side 10-12 times.

14. Skip Run. Going from light jog to skipping, as in paragraph 6. Arm movement parallel forwarded upward-backward. Repeat in opposite direction. Loose shoulders. About 100 yards.

15. Running sideways. Every other step goes behind the other. Marked turn of shoulders and hips to opposite sides. Good running rhythm with evenly measured steps behind as well as in front of leg. About 50 yards with each side in running direction.

16. Stretching of breast musculature. During walk, pull and stretch arms forward and backward with a walk rhythm. 1-21314 10 times.

17. Jump in series. Hop forward with full stretching of body. Series of 8-10 hops. Increase number of hops successively. Light trot between series.

18. Bend sideways during walk with arm pull and after stretching, all with the walk rhythm. Right 1-2, left 3-4, 10 times to each side.

19. Swing legs out and forward, making time with small hops. 10 times each leg.

20. Knee lifts and forward swinging motion of lower leg, like a hurdler, single or double arm movements meet the floor, 10 times each leg. The exercise takes place during light jog.

21. Swing legs forward, backward, while steadying yourself at each. Swing each leg with full relaxation in hip and knee joints. Main purpose are high swings backwards, keep body upright. 10 times with each leg.

22. Swing leg sideways, in-out. The exercise performs similar to exercise 21, but with straight knees. 10 times in each direction with both legs. Chosen for individual needs. Some strength exercise should be included in the warmup before the exercise training. For arm and shoulders, (1) Push-ups (2) Chip-ups. For stomach and trunk muscles, (1) Sit-ups, (2) leg raise from sitting position, (3) on the floor on your back with legs together and moving them from side to side, (4) while sitting on the floor, hands to toes like closing a pocket knife.

The warm-up concludes with increased speed in running or other forms of hard breathing exercise, according to special training programs.

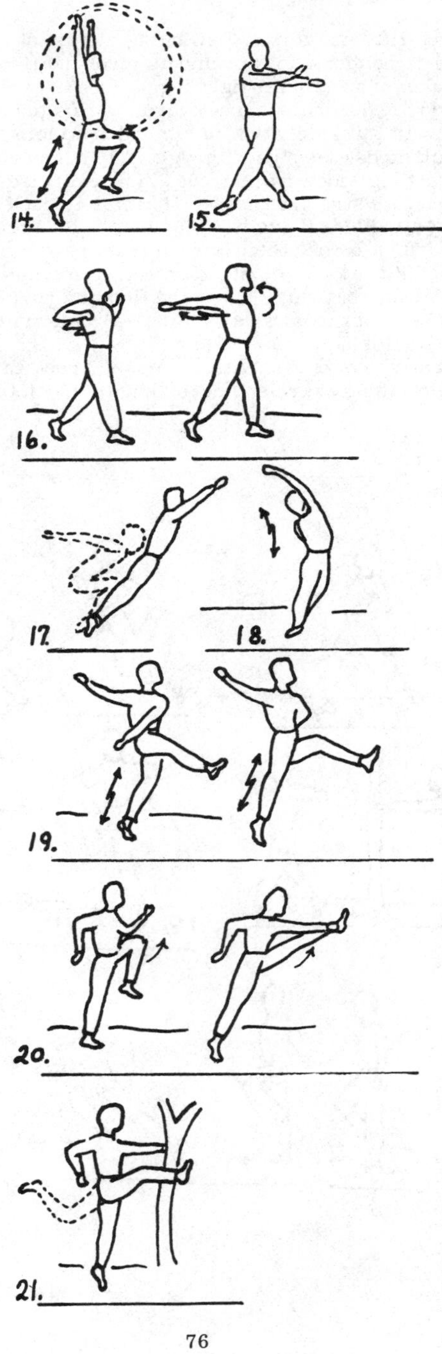
14.
15.
16.
17.
18.
19.
20.
21.

Lydiard Method of Training Runners

by Arthur Lydiard (New Zealand)

(The following article was translated and synthesized by Charles Sullivan, Track Coach, Pioneer High School, San Jose, California, from the No.4, January 23, 1962 and No.5, January 30, 1962 issues of Die Lehre der Leichtathletik, published in Berlin, Germany, and is reprinted by permission of Editor Toni Nett of Stuttgart, Germany.)

The recent successes of Peter Snell make it well worth the while of any coaches of the middle and long distances to consider the training methods employed to develop him and his countryman, Murray Halberg. Their coach, Arthur Lydiard, gives a detailed and thoughtful presentation of his training methods and the principals on which they are founded.

The basis of Lydiard's success seems to be the development of a carefully wrought training program, detailed in every respect, whose goal is to bring along the runner in such a way as to have him on a given day, well planned in advance, ready to put forth his top performance. This training plan is predicated on the idea that the runner is to train the year round. Starting soon after the end of the previous season, he begins a program of marathon training which lasts approximately four months. From here the runner enters a one-month transitional training period, followed by a three months specialized schedule which leads the runner, as Lydiard puts it, to the "run of the year."

Lydiard argues from the outset that most good middle distance runners are capable of negotiating 440 yards in 50-52 seconds. Since to run 880 yards in 1:50 requires simply to run the equivalent of two 55 second 440's, it would seem to follow that the main problem is not one of speed but of staying capacity. For this reason, although certainly not neglecting speed work for the half-miler, he stresses the development of endurance.

During the first training period Lydiard tests his athletes' increasing capacity by careful checks of the declining pulse rate. This, he says, "is a confirmation by the organism that the heart has become larger and stronger." Runners who have never run cross-country are initiated with 30 minute runs which are increased until they are capable of handling the "marathon schedule."

The following plan calls for no less than one hundred miles per week during the initial four-month training period. Fractions following distances in the schedules indicate degree or intensity of effort, which are explained at the end of this article.

Marathon training (four months, for both middle and long distance runners). Monday; 10 miles over hills and along roads or cross-country at $\frac{1}{2}$ effort. Tuesday: 15 miles at $\frac{1}{4}$ effort effort over hills and roads. Wednesday: 12 miles fartlek (speed-play). Thursday: 18 miles, $\frac{1}{4}$ effort.. Friday: 10 miles, $\frac{3}{4}$ effort on road. Saturday: 20 miles, $\frac{1}{4}$ effort. Sunday: 15 miles, $\frac{1}{4}$ effort.

It will be noted that the above schedule, and those which follow, calls for a seven-day training regimen each week. Lydiard indicates that this marathon program is the basis for his success and that future preparation would be meaningless without this background. He also suggests that during these early months the runner may employ gymnastic exercises for the loosening and stretching of muscles over the entire body. He rejects outright, however, the use of weights. He stresses this position metaphorically by arguing that his runners "need the muscles of a stag, not a lion." Halberg has never lifted weights.

A period of transitional training now follows for one month. At this time the runner continues a fairly intensive type of cross-country training, as well as running on the track for additional preparation. Off the track the runner is required to negotiate a one mile hill course, of which one-half mile is gradual incline. At the base of the hill and at the top there is a 440 yards even stretch. The athlete covers the course four times per day. The level portions are run at an easy jog. The hill itself is run at a much livlier speed. Running on the incline should be done with a springy stride, which will tend to strengthen the legs and also stress good knee action. Lydiard recommends short sprints enroute during the longer runs. Track running is begun according to the following schedule. The following distances are in yards and miles. The training on Sundays is always "long distance jogging."

Transitional training (one month, for both middle and long distance runners). First week. Monday: 440, $\frac{1}{4}$; 700 with 30 sprint on command; 440, $\frac{1}{4}$, Tuesday: 3 x 220, $\frac{1}{2}$; 4 x 50, $\frac{1}{2}$; 440, $\frac{1}{4}$. Wednesday: 2 x 220, $\frac{1}{2}$; 2 x 100, $\frac{1}{2}$; 1 x 100, $\frac{3}{4}$; 2 x 50, $\frac{1}{2}$. Thursday: mile with 50 sprint every 220. Friday: rest. Saturday: 4 x 220, $\frac{1}{2}$; 1 x 100, $\frac{3}{4}$. Second Week. Monday: 440, $\frac{1}{4}$; 700 with 30 sprint; 440, $\frac{1}{4}$. Tuesday: 440, $\frac{1}{4}$; 2 x 220, $\frac{1}{2}$; 440, $\frac{1}{4}$. Wednesday: 2 x 100, $\frac{1}{2}$; 700 with 30 sprint; 220, $\frac{1}{4}$. Thursday: 2 x 220, $\frac{1}{4}$; 3 x 100, $\frac{1}{2}$. Friday: rest. Saturday: 3 x 100, $\frac{1}{2}$; 700 with 30 sprint; 220 $\frac{3}{4}$. Third Week. Monday: 2 x 220, $\frac{1}{2}$; 3 x 100, $\frac{3}{4}$. Tuesday: 3 x 220, $\frac{1}{2}$; 3 x 100, $\frac{3}{4}$. Wednesday: 2 x 440, $\frac{1}{2}$; 100 all out. Thursday: 6 x 220. Friday: rest. Saturday: 440, $\frac{1}{4}$; 10 x 100, $\frac{1}{2}$ Fourth Week. Monday: 3 x 220; 100, $\frac{3}{4}$. Tuesday: 2 x 700, $\frac{1}{4}$. Wednesday: 2 x 440, $\frac{1}{4}$; 700 with 30 sprint. Thursday: 2 x 700, $\frac{1}{4}$. Friday: rest. Saturday: 10 x 50, $\frac{1}{2}$; 2 x 700, $\frac{1}{4}$.

The next three months are devoted to the careful preparation of the athlete for his "run of the year." Individual differences are special problems which require the coach to tailor the plan to his runner's needs. But there must be a plan to begin with. During the last six weeks the coach must work closely with his runner and alter or augment the plan wherever it is deemed necessary.

Training for 880 yards (800m) runners (three months).

First Month. First week. Monday: Mile $\frac{3}{4}$; 6 x 30 yard starts. Tuesday: 6 x 880, $\frac{1}{4}$; 2 x 100, $\frac{3}{4}$. Wednesday: Starts with sprinters; a few 300's stressing pace. Thursday: 880 with 8 x 50 sprints enroute; 6 x 300; 1 x 300, $\frac{7}{8}$. Friday: 2 miles, $\frac{1}{2}$ (even pace). Saturday: 6 x 50 yard starts; 6 x 300; 1 x 300 all out.

Second Week. Monday: 1320, $\frac{1}{2}$; 6 x 30 yard starts. Tuesday: 3 miles (running at alternate speeds, 100 fast in each 440, then remainder at medium speed). Wednesday: starts with sprinters; a few 300's for pace. Thursday: 20 x 300, medium pace. Friday: 3 miles, $\frac{1}{2}$ (even pace). Saturday: 12 x 100, $\frac{3}{4}$, 4 x 50 yard starts; 1 x 220 all out.

Third Week. Monday: 1 x mile, $\frac{1}{2}$; 6 x 30 yard starts. Tuesday: 6 x 50 yard starts. 2 x 100, $\frac{3}{4}$; 1 x 300, $\frac{7}{8}$, Wednesday: starts with sprinters. A few 300's for pace. Thursday: 880 with 8 x 50 yards sprints enroute; 6 x 330; 1 x 220, $\frac{7}{8}$. Friday: 2 miles, $\frac{3}{4}$ (even pace). Saturday. 880, $\frac{1}{4}$ until last 300 - then $\frac{3}{4}$; repeat until 10 x 880 completed in this fashion.

Fourth Week. Monday: 1320, $\frac{3}{4}$; 6 x 30 yard starts. Tuesday: 3 miles (same as in 2nd week). Wednesday: starts with sprinters; several 300's for pace. Thursday: 20 x 300. Friday: 3 miles even pace. Saturday: 10 x 880, $\frac{1}{4}$ (same as third week).

Second Month. First week. Monday: 2 miles, $\frac{3}{4}$. Tuesday: 10 x 440, $\frac{1}{4}$. Wednesday: starts with sprinters; several 300's for pace. Thursday: 3 miles, $\frac{3}{4}$; 3 x 50 yard starts. Friday: 6 x 220, $\frac{1}{2}$. Saturday: 6 x 880 (first 580, $\frac{1}{4}$ & last 300, $\frac{3}{4}$); 2 x 880 (first 580, $\frac{1}{2}$ & last 300, $\frac{7}{8}$).

Second Week. Monday: 2 miles, $\frac{3}{4}$. Tuesday: 10 x 440, $\frac{1}{2}$. Wednesday: starts with sprinters; several 300's for pace. Thursday: 3 miles, $\frac{3}{4}$; 3 x 50 yard starts. Friday: 6 x 220, $\frac{1}{2}$. Saturday: 8 x 880 (same as first week).

Third Week. Monday: 2 x mile, $\frac{1}{2}$. Tuesday: 1320 time trial. 6 x 50 yards starts. Wednesday: 6 x 440 at 880 pace. Thursday: 2 miles (with 32 fast bursts enroute, or one each 110); 3 x 50 yard starts. Friday: 6 x 220, $\frac{1}{2}$. Saturday: One mile run.

Fourth Week. Monday: 2 x mile, $\frac{1}{2}$. Tuesday: 1320 time trial. 6 x 50 yard starts. Wednesday: 6 x 440 at 880 pace. Thursday: 2 miles (same as third week). Friday: 6 x 220, $\frac{1}{2}$. Saturday: 440 yard run.

Third Month. First Week. Monday: mile, $\frac{3}{4}$. Tuesday: 880 time trial; 4 x 50 yard starts. Wednesday: 4 x 440 at 880 pace; 2 x 440 all out. Thursday: 2 miles as last week. Friday: 6 x 220, $\frac{1}{2}$. Saturday: one mile run.

Second Week. Monday: 1 x 660, $\frac{3}{4}$. Tuesday: 880 time trial; 4 x 50 yard starts. Wednesday: 4 x 440 at 880 pace; 2 x 440 all out. Thursday: one mile with 16 fast striding bursts enroute; 6 x 50 yard starts. Friday: 6 x 220, $\frac{1}{2}$. Saturday: 880 yard run.

Third week. Monday: 12 x 220, $\frac{1}{2}$. Tuesday: 1 x 660, $\frac{3}{4}$; 4 x ; 50 yard starts. Wednesday: 1 x 440 at 880 pace; 1 x 440 all out. Thursday: one mile (same as last week); 6 x 50 yard starts. Friday: 3 x 220, all out. Saturday: 440 yard run.

Fourth Week. Monday: 6 miles jogging. Tuesday: 3 x 220, $\frac{7}{8}$. Wednesday: 1 x 440, $\frac{7}{8}$. Thursday: 3 miles jogging. Friday: rest or very light jogging. Saturday: "The run of the year."

Training for mile (1500m) runners (three months).

First Month. First Week. Monday: 2 miles, $\frac{1}{4}$. Tuesday: 4 x 880, $\frac{1}{4}$. Wednesday: 12 x 300; 1 x 880, $\frac{1}{2}$. Thursday: 6 miles, $\frac{1}{4}$. Friday: 6 x 220, $\frac{1}{4}$. Saturday: 1 mile, $\frac{1}{4}$; 1 mile, $\frac{1}{2}$.

Second Week. Monday: 1 x $1\frac{1}{2}$ miles, $\frac{1}{4}$. Tuesday: 1320, $\frac{1}{4}$. 2 x 100, $\frac{3}{4}$. Wednesday: 1 x 440, $\frac{3}{4}$; 6 x 220, $\frac{3}{4}$; 1 x 440, $\frac{7}{8}$. Thursday: 6 miles, $\frac{1}{4}$. Friday: 6 x 220, $\frac{1}{4}$. Saturday: 20 x 440, $\frac{1}{4}$.

Third Week. Monday: 2 miles, $\frac{1}{2}$. Tuesday: 6 x 880, $\frac{1}{4}$. Wednesday: 1 x 880, $\frac{1}{4}$; 1 miles, $\frac{1}{2}$; 440 all out. Thursday: 6 miles, $\frac{1}{2}$. Friday: 6 x 220, $\frac{1}{4}$. Saturday: 1 x 1 mile, $\frac{1}{4}$; 1 x 1 mile, $\frac{1}{2}$.

Fourth Week. Monday: 1 x $1\frac{1}{2}$ miles, $\frac{1}{2}$. Tuesday: 1 x 880, $\frac{1}{4}$; 1 x 880, $\frac{1}{2}$: 1 x 880, $\frac{3}{4}$. Wednesday: 4 x 440, $\frac{1}{4}$; 4 x 220, $\frac{1}{2}$; 1 x 440, $\frac{7}{8}$. Thursday: 6 miles, $\frac{1}{2}$. Friday: 6 x 220, $\frac{1}{4}$. Saturday: 20 x 440, $\frac{1}{2}$.

Second Month. First Week. Monday: 1320, $\frac{1}{2}$; 880, $\frac{3}{4}$; 440 all out. Tuesday: 4 x 440, $\frac{1}{2}$; Wednesday: 6 x 880, $\frac{1}{2}$. Thursday: 6 miles, $\frac{3}{4}$. Friday: 6 x 220, $\frac{1}{2}$. Saturday: 20 x 220, $\frac{1}{2}$.

Third Week. Monday: 2 miles with 32 x 50 yard sprints enroute. Tuesday: 3 miles time trial. Wednesday: 1 x 880, $\frac{3}{4}$; 8 x 100, $\frac{3}{4}$. Thursday: 1 x 11 mile, $\frac{3}{4}$. Friday: 6 x 440, $\frac{3}{4}$. Saturday: 880 yard run.

Fourth Week. Monday: 2 miles with 32 x 50 yard sprints enroute. Tuesday: 1 mile time trial. Wednesday: 2 x 880, $\frac{1}{2}$; 1 mile, $\frac{3}{4}$. Thursday: 6 x 440, $\frac{3}{4}$. Friday: 3 x 220, $\frac{3}{4}$. Saturday: 1 mile run.

Third Month. First Week. Monday: 3 miles with 48 x 50 yard sprints enroute. Tuesday: 1320 time trial. Wednesday: 6 x 440, $\frac{3}{4}$. Thursday: 3 miles, $\frac{3}{4}$. Friday: 3 x 220 all out. Saturday: 880 yards run.

Second Week. Monday: 1 x 1 mile with 16 x 50 yard sprints enroute; 3 x 100 all out. Tuesday: 1 mile time trial. Wednesday: 6 miles, sprinting 50 yards each 440 throughout; 3 x 100 all out. Thursday: 1 mile time trial. Friday: 3 x 220 all out. Saturday: 1 mile run.

Third Week. Monday: 1 mile time trial. Tuesday. 2 miles with 32 x 50 yard sprints enroute. Wednesday: 880 yard run. Thursday: 3 miles, $\frac{1}{2}$. Friday: 3 x 220, all out. Saturday: 880 yard run.

Fourth Week. Monday: 6 miles jog. Tuesday: 3 x 220 all out. Wednesday: 1 x 440, $\frac{7}{8}$. Thursday: 3 mile jog. Friday: 3 mile jog. Saturday: "The Run of the Year."

Training for three mile (5,000m) runners (three months).

The first seven (7) weeks of this three months period is identical to that described above in the training of the mile runner.

Second Month. Eighth Week. Monday: 3 miles with 48 x 50 yards sprints enroute. Tuesday: 3 mile time trial. Wednesday: 2 x 880, $\frac{1}{2}$. Thursday: 6 x 440, $\frac{1}{4}$. Friday: 6 x 220, $\frac{1}{2}$. Saturday: 1 mile run.

Third Month. First Week. Monday: 3 miles with 48 x 50 yard sprints enroute. Tuesday: 3 mile time trial. Wednesday: 6 miles with 24 x 50 yard sprints enroute (one sprint each 440). Thursday: 6 x 440, $\frac{3}{4}$. Friday: 6 x 220, $\frac{3}{4}$. Saturday: 880 yard run.

Second Week. Monday: 1 mile with 16 x 50 yard sprints enroute. 3 x 100 all out. Tuesday: 3 miles time trial. Wednesday: 6 miles with 48 x 50 yard sprints enroute as on previous Wednesday. Thursday: 2 miles, first mile $\frac{1}{2}$ effort and second mile $\frac{7}{8}$ effort. Friday: 6 x 220, $\frac{3}{4}$. Saturday: 3 mile run.

Third Week. Monday: 3 mile time trial. Tuesday: 2 miles with 32 x 50 yard sprints enroute. Wednesday: 880 yard run. Thursday: 6 miles, $\frac{1}{2}$. Friday: 6 x 220, $\frac{1}{2}$. Saturday: 1 mile run.

Fourth Week. Monday: 6 miles jog. Tuesday: 3 x 220 all out. Wednesday: 1 x 440, $\frac{7}{8}$. Thursday: 3 miles jog. Friday: 3 miles jog. Saturday: "The Run of the Year."

Training for six mile (10,000m) runners (three months).

The first six (6) weeks of this three months period is identical to that described above for the mile runner.

Second Monday. Sixth Week. Monday: 2 miles with 32 x 50 yard sprints enroute, or one sprint each 110 yards. Tuesday: 3 mile time trial. Wednesday: 1 x 880, $\frac{3}{4}$; 8 x 100, $\frac{3}{4}$. Thursday: 1 mile, $\frac{3}{4}$. Friday: 6 x 440, $\frac{3}{4}$. Saturday: 1 mile run.

Eighth Week. Monday: 3 miles with 48 x 50 yard sprints enroute, or one sprint each 100 m. Tuesday: 3 mile time trial. Wednesday: 2 x 880, $\frac{1}{2}$; 1 x 1 mile $\frac{3}{4}$. Thursday: 6 x 440, $\frac{3}{4}$. Friday: 6x 220, $\frac{1}{2}$. Saturday: 6 mile run.

Third Month. First week. Monday: 3 miles with 48 x 50 yard sprints enroute as on previous Monday. Tuesday: 3 mile time trial. Wednesday: 6 miles with one 50 yard fast burst of speed each 440. Thursday: 6 miles time trial. Friday: 6 x 220, $\frac{3}{4}$. Saturday: 3 mile run.

Second Week. Monday: 1 mile with 16 fast bursts of speed enroute; 3 x 100 all out. Tuesday: 3 miles time trial. Wednesday: 6 miles with one 50 yard sprint each 440. Thursday: 6 mile time trial. Friday: 6 x 220, $\frac{3}{4}$. Saturday: 6 mile run.

Third Week. Monday: 10 x 220, $\frac{1}{2}$. Tuesday: 6 mile time trial. Wednesday: 880 yard run. Thursday: 2 miles with 32 x 50 yard fast bursts enroute. Friday: 6 x 200, $\frac{1}{2}$. Saturday: 1 mile run.

Fourth Week. Monday: 6 mile jog. Tuesday: 3 x 220 all out. Wednesday: 1 x 400, $\frac{7}{8}$. Thursday: 3 mile jog. Friday: 3 mile jog. Saturday: "The Run of the Year."

Training for the marathon runner (three months).

First Month. First Week. Monday: 20 x 220, $\frac{1}{4}$. Tuesday: 15 miles, $\frac{1}{4}$. Wednesday: 2 miles with 32 x 50 yard fast bursts enroute. Thursday: 18 miles, $\frac{1}{4}$. Friday: 1 mile, $\frac{1}{2}$. Saturday: 22-28 miles. Sunday: 15 miles jog.

Second Week. Monday: 20 x 440, $\frac{1}{4}$. Tuesday: 15 miles, $\frac{1}{4}$. Wednesday: 2 miles, with 32 x 50 yard fast bursts enroute. Thursday: 18 miles, $\frac{1}{4}$. Friday: 1 mile, $\frac{3}{4}$. Saturday: 22-28 miles. Sunday: 15 miles jog.

Third Week. Monday: 15 x 220, $\frac{1}{2}$. Tuesday: 15 miles, $\frac{1}{2}$. Wednesday: 3 miles with 48 x 50 yard fast bursts enroute. Thursday: 18 miles, $\frac{1}{4}$. Friday: 3 x 880, $\frac{1}{2}$. Saturday: 22-28 miles. Sunday: 15 miles jog.

Fourth Week. Monday: 15 x 440, $\frac{1}{2}$. Tuesday: 15 miles, $\frac{1}{4}$. Wednesday: 3 miles with 48 x 50 yard bursts enroute. Thursday: 18 miles, $\frac{1}{4}$. Friday: 2 x 880, $\frac{3}{4}$. Saturday: 22-28 miles.

Second Month. First Week. Monday: 3 miles time trial. Tuesday: 15 miles, $\frac{1}{4}$. Wednesday: 6 miles time trial. Thursday: 18 miles, $\frac{1}{4}$. Friday: 6 x 220, $\frac{1}{2}$. Saturday: 22-28 miles. Sunday: 15 miles jog.

Third Week. Monday: 3 mile time trial. Tuesday: 15 miles, $\frac{3}{4}$. Wednesday: 6 miles time trial. Thursday: 18 miles, $\frac{1}{2}$. Friday: 3 x 220, all out. Saturday: 22-28 miles, $\frac{1}{4}$. Sunday: 15 miles.

Fourth Week. Monday: 3 miles time trial. Tuesday: 15 miles, $\frac{1}{2}$. Wednesday: 6 miles time trial. Thursday: 18 miles, $\frac{1}{4}$. Friday: 3 x 220 all out. Saturday: 22-28 miles, $\frac{1}{4}$. Sunday: 15 miles.

Third Month. First Week. Monday: 10 miles, $\frac{1}{2}$. Tuesday: 3 miles, $\frac{1}{2}$. Wednesday: 15 miles, $\frac{1}{2}$. Thursday: 6 miles jog. Friday: 3 miles jog. Saturday: Run 26 miles. Sunday: 1 hour jog.

Second Week. Monday: 6 miles jog. Tuesday: 6 miles jog. Wednesday: 15 miles, $\frac{1}{4}$. Thursday: 15 x 300 yards. Friday: 6 x 220, $\frac{1}{2}$. Saturday: 1 hour running, $\frac{1}{2}$. Sunday: 15 miles jog.

Third Week. Monday: 2 miles with 32 x 50 yard fast bursts enroute. Tuesday: jog 12 miles. Wednesday: 6 miles, $\frac{1}{2}$. Thursday: 15 miles jog. Friday: 3 x 220, $\frac{3}{4}$. Saturday: 3 miles run. Sunday: Jog 1 hour.

Fourth Week. Monday: 3 x 220, $\frac{3}{4}$. Tuesday: 1 mile, $\frac{3}{4}$. Wednesday: Jog 6 miles. Thursday: Jog 3 miles. Friday: Jog 3 miles. Saturday: "The run of the year."

Speed Tables:

Best 220	$\frac{3}{4}$ speed	$\frac{1}{2}$ speed	$\frac{1}{4}$ speed
22	24	27	31
23	25	28	32
24	26	29	33
25	27	30	34
26	28	31	35
28	30	33	37
30	32	35	39
32	34	37	41

Best 440	$\frac{3}{4}$ speed	$\frac{1}{2}$ speed	$\frac{1}{4}$ speed
52	55	58	61
54	57	60	63
56	59	62	65
58	61	64	67
60	63	66	69
62	66	69	72
64	69	72	75
66	71	74	77

Best 880	$\frac{3}{4}$ speed	$\frac{1}{2}$ speed	$\frac{1}{4}$ speed
1:46	1:52	1:57	2:02
1:49	1:55	2:00	2:05
1:52	1:58	2:03	2:08
1:55	2:01	2:06	2:11
1:58	2:04	2:09	2:14
2:01	2:07	2:12	2:17
2:10	2:16	2:24	2:29

Best mile	$\frac{3}{4}$ speed	$\frac{1}{2}$ speed	$\frac{1}{4}$ speed
4:00	4:06	4:13	4:20
4:10	4:16	4:23	4:32
4:20	4:26	4:33	4:44
4:30	4:36	4:43	4:56
4:45	4:51	4:58	5:14
5:00	5:06	5:16	5:32

Best 2-miles	$\frac{3}{4}$ speed	$\frac{1}{2}$ speed	$\frac{1}{4}$ speed
8:30	8:50	9:10	9:30
8:40	9:00	9:20	9:40
8:50	9:10	9:30	9:50
9:00	9:20	9:40	10:00
9:20	9:40	10:00	10:20
9:40	10:00	10:20	10:40
10:00	10:20	10:40	11:00
10:30	10:50	11:10	11:30
11:00	11:20	11:40	12:00

Best 3-miles	$\frac{3}{4}$ speed	$\frac{1}{2}$ speed	$\frac{1}{4}$ speed
13:00	13:30	14:00	14:30
13:20	13:50	14:20	14:50
13:40	14:10	14:40	15:10
14:00	14:30	15:00	15:30
14:20	14:50	15:20	15:50
14:40	15:10	15:40	16:10
15:00	15:30	16:00	16:30
15:30	16:00	16:30	17:00
16:00	16:30	17:00	17:30

Best 6-miles	$\frac{3}{4}$ speed	$\frac{1}{2}$ speed	$\frac{1}{4}$ speed
27:30	28:10	28:50	29:30
28:00	28:40	29:20	30:00
28:30	29:10	29:50	30:30
29:00	29:40	30:20	31:00
29:30	30:10	30:50	31:30
30:00	30:40	31:20	32:00
30:30	31:10	30:50	32:30
31:00	31:40	32:20	33:00
32:00	32:40	33:20	34:00
33:00	33:40	34:20	35:00

Mihaly Igloi's Training Method

by Jan Mulak

(This article originally appeared in the April, 1962 issue of "Lekka Atletyka", published in Warsaw, Poland. The attention of the reader is invited to the possibility that the training methods described herein may not necessarily be identical in every respect to those employed by Igloi today. Robert Z. Opiola, translator of this article, has indicated the possibility that precision in meaning between the original article and this translation may vary to some small degree. It is believed that this is the first article ever appearing in English specifically describing the methods of this world-famous Hungarian molder of champions.)

The training used by Mihaly Igloi (Hungarian coach residing in the USA, formerly with the Santa Clara Valley Youth Village, and now associated with the Los Angeles Track Club) is not an ordinary combination of up to date training knowledge. Like the majority of originators of methods for training runners, Igloi formerly ran with his athletes. As a result, he not only understands training, but has also experienced it. His original contribution to training methods was the introduction of repeated series of short, fast repetitions of running.

Although Igloi was formulating and crystallizing his system during the time Emil Zatopek was enjoying his greatest victories, Igloi was not influenced by the authority of Zatopek's success. Igloi enriched his workouts with a wide variety of distances of running repetitions which gives the impression of almost baroque exaggeration.

Igloi's methods are in direct contrast with the simplicity of Zatopek's training. The training of the fabulous Czech can be expressed in a short, simple formula: 5-10 x 200m, plus 20-40 x 400m, plus 5-10 x 200m. Zatopek's interval training was divided into three series (200, 400, 200m), with a relatively long (200m) jog for recovery following each repetition of running. This training developed the capacity for oxygen consumption necessary in long distance running.

Igloi introduced sets or series of short, intense repetition of running, which produced a high oxygen debt. This oxygen debt was repaid during the recovery periods between sets of fast, short repetitions. Thus the athletes using this method developed the ability or capacity to tolerate greater oxygen debt. The running of sets of repeitions over short distances at high speeds enabled Igloi's athletes to achieve excellent competitive results over a wide variety of distances - as was the case with Paavo Nurmi, but on a higher plane...to an extent that would have been impossible with old-fashioned training methods. The Hungarian system enjoyed the advantage of variety over the monotonous training of Zatopek. Furthermore, Zatopek's training had limitations with regard to the development of speed.

Under this system, Igloi divides the year's training into three general periods, and plans along this general outline:

PERIOD	TRAINING SPEED	DISTANCE OF REPETITIONS	NUMBER OF REPETITIONS	SERIES OR SETS OF REPETITIONS
I. Main period.	Racing speed plus relative speed of the athlete.	100-400	10-20	2-3

II. Training for competitive condition.	Relative speed of the athlete plus light speed.	50-100	5-10	5-6
III. Racing period.	Racing speed plus relative speed of the athlete.	50-200	3-6	3-4

From the above table it is obvious that the training during periods I and III is the same, except that in III the repetitions are shorter, run at a faster speed, and interspersed with competition.

The repetitions of running are as short as possible, especially in the spring. The speed is so important, according to Igloi's pupil Gyula Antal, that any kind of endurance training which might lower the athlete's speed is not permissible. Accent in this training is on "light speed" run at a fast pace, but with only relatively small oxygen debt being accumulated, and on rhythm. In other words, the repetitions are run faster than medium speed for a given distance, but with a definite accent on fast pace rhythm. Training at a fast pace rhythm over many short repetitions makes it easier to run at a slower pace over longer distances. Competitor and friend of Igloi, Andras Csaplar (who coached the tiny Josef Kovacs by using the methods of Germany's famous coach, Woldmer Gerschler, progressing from longer to shorter and faster repetitions), wrote that Igloi employs mostly 100, 150, 200, 300, and 400 meter repetitions...seldom using 1200 and 1800 meter repetitions, as these are used only occasionally to verify racing fitness prior to competition.

If the athlete lacks endurance, Igloi improves this by gradually lengthening the distance of the repetitions run at racing speed. For example, 2 x 200m at racing speed might be gradually lengthened to 15 x 300m, up to a maximum of 2 x 1200m.

Basing himself on general principles, Igloi has improvised, to a certain degree, individual units of training by varying the speed of individual repetitions in order to provide great diversity of running stimuli and thereby cause the body to react as nearly as possible to the stress requirements experienced by the athlete in actual competitive racing.

Igloi himself writes, "I do not train my pupils according to a workout pattern made long in advance. As a rule, I plan the training from day to day, depending upon how the athlete feels, environmental conditions, the training objective, etc."

With such a system, it was impossible to plan in advance the times of the repetitions quoted below in the training of Istvan Roszavolgyi, since they are a report of the training which he actually accomplished, and are not the copy of a training schedule planned in advance. Because of this, the stop-watch is seldom used by Igloi, except to occasionally verify the speed of the various repetitions. As a result, this training is largly based upon the confidence of the athletes in Igloi, and their obedience to him. The athlete is frequently surprised with the variation and variety in his training assignments. He does not have to think about his workout program, and he loses no sleep over training schedules. Thus the training is psychologically easy on the athlete. After workouts, the next most important issue is rest, with sleep put ahead of food. Undoubtedly this removes pressure from the athlete, but it does not develop within the athlete a knowledge of training. This is why the Hungarian athletes often failed when Igloi was not present to direct their every move.

Whole Year's Training

Starting November 1st, the intensity of the new yearly cycle was increased rapidly until December, decreased from December until January, and gradually increased until April. The general intensity decreased during racing season. The first two training periods (periods I and II, above) give the foundation for the results during racing season. Racing preparation is completed by short, fast training "punches" (sprints) during a three-week period of intensified training prior to an important meet. A runner with an endurance background may limit himself to one week's special preparation before racing.

Professor F. Rossner, builder of Austrain power in Alpine skiing, considers this system justified only under conditions of the long European competitive season, during which time it is so difficult to sustain high form over such a prolonged period.

In preparing runners for record-breaking results using this system, one should strive to obtain maximum results in a relatively short period, using maximum economy of the athlete's physical resources. "Unnecessary work and all superfluous efforts have to be eliminated from the training of a runner", maintains Igloi. This principle, observed to the point of almost exaggeration, led to almost complete elimination of general bodily development in the training of Hungarian runners, causing in the foremost representative of the Hungarian school of training an almost emaciated physical appearance.

This training is not without its negative side. Igloi's athletes set most of their world records in Budapest, the scene of their training camps. They failed entirely in the European Championships at Berne, and the Olympic Games at Melbourne. It is interesting to note that other Hungarian athletes (Lajos Szentgali and Josef Kovacs, for example) who were trained according to other methods did achieve success on these occasions.

The preparation of the athlete for best results on a specific date required complete rest and peace of mind, such as Igloi secured for his athletes prior to competition in the Honved Club of Budapest. Great nervous tension of the type experienced prior to competition in the European Championships and Olympic Games, plus changed training and resting conditions were sufficient to upset and "unregulate" the ideal competitive environment Igloi was able to create in Budapest. Too often it ended in failure.

The Hungarian system gave consideration to how the athlete feels in planning the training. The Swedish "fartlek" system also gave much consideration to the feeling of the athlete. However, in the fartlek system the athlete himself was the judge of his feelings, whereas in the Hungarian system Igloi decided how the athlete felt. This did not give the well-grounded foundation in the Hungarian runners on which to base harder pace training.

An important problem which absorbed the attention of the famous Hungarian coach was how to get the human organism accustomed to a great amount of work so that more running could be done during one day. In search of a solution, Igloi did not hesitate to break the normal routine of the day. One daily workout leaves too much time between training sessions. Moreover, in the case of training applied exclusively in the afternoon, such training is limited by the given amount of effort for each athlete which should not be exceeded. Dividing the training into two parts makes the body's work easier and creates a condition whereby the training can be made much more intense.

Igloi has found that the most effective way to train is twice daily (two workouts each day). There were experiments with three and even four workouts daily, but Igloi returned to twice daily training. Morning, directly after the night's sleep, is the best time for the training in preparation for the basic afternoon session. The athlete can adapt himself to the new routine of morning training, just as the early morning worker becomes accustomed and adjusted to starting work at dawn, especially if he starts the new routine of morning training early in life.

The diversion of daily training into two workouts resulted in a tendency to increase the volume of the morning session. The afternoon workout consisted of from two-thirds to three-fifths of the total daily training. Thus the morning workout did not in the least have the character of a mere warm-up, although it gradually prepared the body for the greater effort later in the day. The nature of the morning workout is determined entirely be the athlete's "feelings" and lasts about one hour. It is based on the principle of interval training, involving short repetitions of light running, e.g., 2x100m plus 2x200m plus 2x300m plus 2x100m plus 2x60m. The first 100m repetitions are run at a speed not faster than 20 seconds. The speed of these repetitions increase as the athlete becomes "warmer".

The recovery after each repetition of running is taken by jogging half the distance of the previous run, e.g., jog 50m after each fast 100m; jog 100m after each fast 200m; etc.

Let us now examine the way the above described principles were put into effect. The examples of Igloi's training methods were published by F. Rossner on the basis of a report of the training of ex-world record holder at the 3000 meter steeplechase, Sandor Rozsnyoi, the yearly training of Istvan Rozsavolgyi, and the training of Sandor Iharos just before he set a new world record at 5000m (13:40.6) in Budapest on October 23, 1955.

The Training of Sandor Rozsnyoi

(as told by Sandor Rozsnyoi) This is a schedule of the training assignments given by Igloi. The speed of these repititions of running is described in percentages relative to the maximum possible speed by Rozsnyoi for the specific distance is question at the particular stage of his overall training.

January: Day 1. 16x100m. 5km at steady speed. 150m run, 150m jog. Day 2. Exercises indoors. Day 3. 16x100m. 400m 60%. 300m 70%. 200m 80%. 100m 90%. Day 4. Rest and Finnish sauna bath. Day. 5. 16x 100m. 6-7 km run, accelerating gradually from 20% to 60%. 1km with 5-6 x60m sprints enroute. Day 6. Exercises indoors. Day 7. Rest and sauna bath.

February: Day 1. 10x100m. 6km at steady speed. 100m 60-80%, jog 100m. Day 2. 16x100m. 2x(5x300m 60-70%. Jog 100m between). Walk 400m between sets. Day 3. Exercises indoors. Day 4. 10x100m. 8x (200m 60%. 100m 80% of racing speed. 100m 80%. Jog 100m after each). Day 5. 10x100m. 800m 50-60%. Walk 300m. 8x100m 50%. Jog 50m between. 800m 50-60%. Walk 500m. 6x100m 70-80%. Walk 5m after each. Day 6. Exercises indoors. Day 7. Rest and sauna bath.

March: Day 1. 16x100m. 2x(10x150m, jog 100m between). Day 2. 10x100m. 4x(400m 60% jog 400m. 100m 40%, jog 50m. 100m 40%, jog 50m). Day 3. 16x100m. 5x(200m 70%, jog 100m. 100m 60%, jog 100m. 100m 60%, jog 100m. 100m 60%, jog 100m). Day 4. 10x100m. 6-7 km, accelerating gradually from 20% to 70%. 10x100m 50% every second repetition, and 90-100% on alternate repetitions. Jog 100m between. Day 5. 10x100m. 2000m 50-60%, or 2x1000m 60%. Day 6. Exercises indoors and sauna bath. Day 7. Rest.

April: Day 1. 10x100m. 8x150m, 50m jog plus 200m walk after each. 6x100m, jog 50m between. Day 2. 10x100m. 2x(4x300m in 49-50 seconds. Jog 100m between. 6x100m, jog 50m between). Day 3. One hour run in woods, part of which is run at racing speed. 5x200m in 33-34. 6x100m lightly. Day 4. 10x100m. 2x(5x200m in 34-35 seconds, jog 100m between. 6x100m lightly, jog 50m between). Day 5. 10x100m. 2x(10x120m 80%, jog 80m between. 6x100m lightly). Day 6. one hour light run in woods or rest. Day 7. 1000m in 2:45-2:50, or cross country race.

May: Day 1. 16x100m 8x(200m 70%, jog 100m. 100m 70%, jog 100m. 100m 70%, jog 100m). 6x100m 100%, jog 100m after each. Day 2. 16x100m. 4x400m in 64. Jog 200m between. 5x100m 50%, jog 50m between. 6 x100m 100%, jog 100m between, or 2x800m in 2:08. 5x100m 50%. 6x100 m 100%. Day 3. One hour run in woods at changing speeds. 16x100m, running 100% effort every second repetition. Day 4. 16x100m. 10x200m in 32-33 seconds, jog 200m between. 6-8x100m 100%, or 2x(4x300m in 48). Day 5. 16x100m. 2x(10x120m, jog 80m between). Day 6. One hour run in woods. 20x100m 50-60%. Jog 50m between. Day 7. 1200m in 3:14-3:15. 800m in 2:07. 400m in 65.

June: Day 1. 10x100m. 2x(8x150m 70%, jog 50m between). Day 2. 20x100m. 2x800m in 2:06-2:07, or 2x400m in 62-63, jog 100m between. 10 x100m 80%. Day 3. 6km in the woods at changing speeds. 200m fast and 200m slow. 12x100m 80-90%, jog 50m between. Day 4. Paced 1200m in 3:10-3:12. 200m 60%, 200m jog. 4x100m 80%, jog 100m between. 100m 80%, jog 100m. Day 5. 16x100m. 10x120m 80-90%, jog 80m between. 6-8 x60m 100%. Day 6. 5-6 km rhythm running. 1-2 400m in 62, rest 3-4 minutes between. Day 7. Race.

The Training of Istvan Rozsavolgyi

(as told by Gyula Antal) This is a record of the training actually performed by Rozsavolgyi, and not a schedule of training assignments prepared in advance. The times quoted for the individual repititions of running were those achieved, and not necessarily those at which the athlete was aiming.

December: Day 1. 10x200m in 30. 400m light running between. 5x300m in 45-48, 100m light running between. 5x600m, 800m lightly between. 20x100m, 50m lightly between. Day 2. 20x100m. 4x800m. 20x100m. 20x100m. 4x800m. 10x100m in 14. Day 3. 10-15km fartlek. Day 4. 10x100m in 20., jog 50m between. 10x300m in 45-48, jog 100m between . 5x600m in 1:40, jog 200m between. 10x100m, jog 50m between. 10x300m, jog 100m between. 10x100m in 13-14. Jog 100m between. Day 5. 10x200m in 32, jog 100m. 10x100m in 15, jog 50m. 10x300 in 45-48, jog 100m. 20x100m in 15, jog 50m. 10x200m, jog 100m. 10x100m, jog 50m. 10x300m, jog 100. 10x100m in 13-14, jog 50m. Day 6. 10x100m in 13. 5x300m in 40-41, jog 100m. 10x100m. Day 7. Rest.

April: Day 1. 2x(4x300m in 45, jog 100m. 10x100m in 15-18, jog 50m. 6x300m in 45, jog 100m. 10x100m, alternately in 16-18 and 14-15, jog 50m). Day 2. 5x(5x200m in 27-28, jog 100m. 6x100m in 15, jog 50m). Day 3. 10km fartlek. 15x100m, jog 50m after each. Day 4. 5x300m lightly. 5x300m fast. 5x300m very fast, 5x300m lightly. 10x100m in 16. 6x300m in 80%. 10x100m fast. 10x100m lightly. Day 5. 10x(10x100m. One series of 10 fast and next lively rhythm, alternately. Walk 400m between series). Day 6. 10x150m moderate speed. 2x(3x400m in 55-56, jog 300m between. Walk 400m between sets). 10x100m lightly, jog 50m. 10x100m fast, jog 50m. 10x100m lightly, jog 50m. Jog 400m between each set of 10x100m. Day 7. Light cross-country run.

June: Day 1. 3x(4x150m in 20, jog 50m. 6x100m in 15. jog 50m. 6x150m in 20, jog 100m. 4x100m lightly, jog 50m.) Day 2. 10x100m in 15, jog 50m. 3x400m in 52-55, jog 100m. 3x200m, accelerating entire distance. 6x100m in 15. 2x400m in 52. 10x100m acceleration sprints. Day 3. 6km cross-country. 100, 200, 1000 and 3x100m. Day 4. 3x(6x 200m in 26, jog 50m. 4x100m in 15, jog 50m. 300m acceleration sprint. 6 minutes easy running between sets). Day 5. Rest, or in case of a race on Day 7, repeat the training on Day 1. Day 6. 3x(6x100m, jog 100-150m. 200m maximum). Day 7. Morning warmup or rest.

The Training of Sandor Iharos

(as told by Andras Csaplar) This brief example of Iharos' workouts does not by any means tell the entire story of his training. It contains only the most essential elements.

Tuesday: 5x400m in 56.8; 56.8, 57.6; 57.6.

Wednesday: 25x100m

Thursday: 15x100m. 10x300m in 45. 6x600m in 1:37.

Friday: 40x100m.

Saturday: 14x100m. 6x1500m 5x100m.

Sunday morning: 12x100m. 6x100m, finishing fast at the end of each.

Sunday afternoon: 5000m race.

Deeply contemplated and rich in diversification and variety, Igloi's methods have been authenticated by the excellent results of the great Hungarian trio, Sandor Iharos, Istvan Rozsavolgyi and Laszlo Tabori. Igloi's system of training is based to a large extent upon his personal intuition and ability to sense and interpret the reaction of his athletes to the various workouts. The success of the methods employed by Igloi has therefore been the achievement of the individual. Igloi's secret is an uncanny ability to sense and detect the "feeling" or reactions of his athletes to training and adjust their workouts according to individual differences--an ability not transferrable to others. This is why those who tried to copy his methods in Hungary after Igloi's departure did not achieve results, generally speaking, worthy of mention. Now, with the retirement of Rozsavolgyi and the fading of Iharos, the might of the Hungarian runners is past history.

When Igloi left Hungary for the USA, he took his "secrets" with him. After two years of struggle on the margin of American track and field athletics, the talented Jim Beatty has come under the direction of the Hungarian master. Beatty, thanks to the training and guidance of Igloi, has advanced rapidly to the elite of the world's runners.

C.C. Training for Sprinters and Others

by A. P. (Tony) Ward,

(British AAA Honorary Senior Coach)

In Britain, the middle-and long-distance runner has three main factors to consider when dealing with his training program: (1) cross-country racing (2) climatic conditions (3) length of and prospects for the track season. As these vary from district to district and even from athlete to athlete, it is extremely unwise for coaches and athletes to set down any rigid system of training for all to follow. I believe that the decline in British running standards between 1958 and 1962 can be traced, in part, to this factor.

If standards in middle- and long-distance running have declined somewhat during this period, British sprint standards have improved and we can point to a number of world-class dash-men who have emerged - Peter Radford, David Jones etc. This has come about because there has been a realization that sprinters in this country must train on much tougher lines than their counterparts in America, where climatic conditions are more favorable and moreover, where all-the-year-round competition, outdoor and indoor, is more prevalent.

Sprinters

In dealing, first of all, with a sprinter's winter training program, I do not recommend cross-country racing for sprinters during the winter, despite the obvious attraction of almost weekly racing and its consequent motivation. Racing of this sort is bound to nullify the sprinter's speed and there are other ways that he can obtain his stamina - in other words his stamina must be of a functional type and obtained by a lot of continuous sprinting. I believe that a sprinter must aim at increasing his power during the winter, and so at least two of his sessions per week will be devoted to weight training. Poundages etc. must be worked out by the individual coaches and athletes but a general recommendation of a weight training program in this period is:

Power Cleans	-	Repetitions to Maximum
Bench Press	-	Repetitions to Maximum
Abdonimal Curl	-	3 x 10 repetitions, progression by increasing the poundage
High Step-Ups	-	3 x 10 repetitions, progression by increasing the poundage
Alternative exercises:		
Military Press	-	Repetitions to Maximum
Straddle Life	-	3 x 10, as above
Two Hands Snatch	-	Repetitions to Maximum

Once a month the sprinter should attempt the three Olympic Lifts for motivation.

On the track a great deal of work will be done in the October - December period, when the weather is fairly mild but often wet. After January, for about four or five weeks, work out of doors can be limited owing to snow and ice.

Interval running over 150, 300 and 440 yards should be done during this period with the athlete progressing by adding to the number of repetitions attempted and by reducing the interval jog in between. Thus:

October	December
8 x 150 with 3 mins. in between	15 x 150 with $1\frac{1}{2}$ mins. in between
6 x 300 with 5 mins. in between	9 x 300 with 3 mins in between
4 x 440 with 6 mins. in between	6 x 440 with 4 mins in between

Again, the above are only a general guide and will depend on the sprinter's fitness-state when the training begins.

Technique practices

In addition to interval-running, the sprinter should work on technique practices at various times during his program, though I believe that the technique practices and conditioning work must be kept separate. Some technique practices are:

(a) Start practice - generally speaking sprinters spend far too much time on this aspect of their race and become fabulous over the first 25 yards only. A minimum of 65 yards should be run: 40 yards acceleration and 25 yards decelerating. Each start-practice should be positive - working on a particular point that the coach has mentioned.

(b) Improving stride length through 'line-running' i.e. find out sprinter's normal stride length and then set out a series of lines about six inches further apart. Let the sprinter take a fast run at the first line and then attempt to hit each line by driving harder, by raising the knee and thigh and trying to keep cadence and normal sprinting action. At first all semblance of normal action is lost but constant practice, during this period, brings the desired result, with no loss of leg-speed.

(c) Bend running. Timed runs around the bend and on the straight for comparison, then practicing at 'relaxed running' around the bend, aiming at the same times.

(d) Sprinting, concentrating on a wider range of movement of the arms.

(e) 'Pattering'.

Continuous relays, parlaufs and some easy Fartlek should be introduced into the program, to avoid monotony.

After December/January, the above program should be continued as far as possible by the sprinter who has no indoor competition. Obvious adjustments will have to be made by the athlete who has a fairly busy indoor program. The switch to faster work and toning-up for the track season will obviously depend on many factors - dates of important races etc. - and must be left to the discretion of athlete and coach.

Middle-distance runner

In considering his winter-training the top-class middle-distance runner must first of all decide the place of cross-country in his career. If he believes that cross-country racing is an ancillary to his track racing, then he will train accordingly; but, if he considers cross-country equally or more important then his training will be different again.

I believe that too much cross-country racing - such as we have in Britain - ending as it does with the big, long races in March, can do much tearing down of the training an athlete has put in and that, in addition, the athlete, always with his eye on next week's race, will not undergo a progressive winter training program. Thus, I believe that a top class middle-distance runner must use cross-country racing judiciously, constantly bearing in mind the state of his training at a particular time and the affect of racing on his program.

Between September and December the distance runner should aim at a high mileage, which should be accomplished at a reasonable rate - never developing into a steady plod. While not agreeing with Lydiard that every middle-distance runner should aim at achieving 100 miles a week, certainly every top class 5000 meters runner and above should eventually aim at this total, achieved by 1½ hours quality work per day. During this period he should keep away from the monotony of track training by planning his training to take in mainly Fartlek, road running and cross-country running during a 7-day period. He should aim to get as much variety in his training routine as possible - often travelling to entirely new areas for a training session: regular distance-running training camps at week-ends are excellent for this purpose. Thus a typical week's work during this period would be: Sunday: 20 mile run. Try to include as much variety of terrain and surface as possible in such a run.

Monday: $1\frac{1}{2}$ hours Fartlek - aiming at 10 miles. This must be a 'fast and slow' session with variety in terrain and distances covered.

Tuesday: 5 to 10 miles fast run on road, followed by $\frac{1}{2}$ hour weight training session, i.e. two exercises - power clean, bench press.

Wednesday: Track session: 440, 880, $\frac{3}{4}$ mile interval running or parlauf.

Thursday: 1 hour Fartlek. Followed by $\frac{1}{2}$ hour weight training session, i.e. abdominal curl, snatch, furls.

Friday: 3 to 5 mile run or 1 hours Fartlek.

Saturday: Cross-country race or parlauf or rest.

It will be noted that weight training is included. I believe that this will be a most important facet of training for the middle-distance runner of the future - that the 13-minute three-miler will have to possess a high weight strength ratio, as well as endurance. If the middle-distance runner cannot, for some reason or other, fit in a weight-training session, then he should certainly plan a program of isometric exercises which he can carry out any time during the day.

Quality running

Obviously by December the runner will be doing his best performances over cross-country. During the New Year, however, he will be thinking more in terms of quality running, gradually speeding up as the track season approaches, with more emphasis on track work and interval training. His weight training program will continue. Thus, a typical week's work mid-way during this period would be:

Sunday: 20 mile run.

Monday: Track: 440 yards interval running. Progression by increasing the number of repetitions and decreasing the interval jog.

Tuesday: 1 hours Fartlek. Increase the speed of fast running and lengthen the jogging, followed by $\frac{1}{2}$ hour W.T. session.

Wednesday: Track: 880 or $\frac{3}{4}$ mile interval running session. Progression as above.

Thursday: 5 mile fast run, followed by $\frac{1}{2}$ hour W.T. session.

Friday: Track: 220 or 330 yards interval running. Progression as above.

Saturday: Cross-country race or parlauf or rest.

Typical tract progression for 14 minute 5000 meters runner.

January

10 x 440 in 70.0 with 3 min. in between

5 x 880 in 2:25 with 5 min. in between
3 x $\frac{3}{4}$M. in 3:40 with 8 min. in between
20 x 220 in 35.0 with 2 min. in between

March

20 x 440 in 70.0/69.0 with 2 min. in between
8 x 880 in 2:20 with 4 min. in between
6 x $\frac{3}{4}$M. in 3:35 with 6 min. in between
40 x 220 in 34.0 with 1 min. in between

Once a fortnight the athlete could include a multiple training session, e.g.:

4 x 880 with 4 min. in between
6 x 440 with 2 min. in between
10 x 220 with 1 min. in between
15 x 110 with $\frac{1}{2}$ min. in between

The aim being in this session to run each distance at a faster pace than the previous i.e. 2:20; 68; 33; 15.0.

The time for increasing the speed of the fast runs and of making other necessary adjustments will again depend on many factors - dates of major races etc.

From the above it can be seen that three factors are considered of importance - that increase in power is of importance for top-class middle-distance runners; that variety is necessary in any training program; that progression is important from week to week. Such progress can be vital in the coach's motivation of his charges and a training diary should be kept, plotting not only week by week progress but season by season.

Cross-country season

In Britain, to may devotees of distance-running, the cross-country season is the highlight of the year's athletics, with the track season secondary in importance. Many coaches believe that the British cross-country season, spreading as it does from October to a grand climax in March, with a mammoth National Championships and a self-styled International Championship, is too long and enduring, aims at quantity rather than quality and detracts from track performances. Equally many top-class athletes and coaches disagree. Briefly, the cross-country season begins with inter-club and League races over 5 miles between October and December, when the country championships - usually over 7 miles - take place. These are followed early in the New Year by the Inter-Country Championship and the Area Championships. Then follows the National Championships over 9 miles and finally the International Championship. Courses in Britain are, in the main, tougher than those on the continent of Europe, which are flatter and faster.

The road racing season usually covers the same period of time but is concentrated in September and early October and again in April, between the cross-country and track season. Road relays are popular at this time and the main road relay between the leading clubs is the popular London to Brighton. Road races vary between 5 and 20 miles in length.

The track season in Britain covers a period between the end of April and the end of September. County championships occur at the end of May or the beginning of June and are followed by the Area Championships and the AAA National Championships. The main international fixtures usually come in August and September.

Marathon racing, in the main, covers the same period of time as the track season. Though the AAA Championship usually comes in August, the Windsor to Chiswick Marathon - the Polytechnic - is considered of equal importance by many and is staged in June. There are no county or Area marathon championships. Sometimes the longer races are staged - the London to Brighton run is an annual event and the Road Runners Club stage a 100 mile Bath to London run.

All in all then, distance-running and cross-country running plays an important and integral part of the track and field scene in Britain. The clubs - which form the backbone of the sport in the country - are often mainly of the harrier type, with the cross-country section the main part.

British tradition

It is this tradition which has, in the past, given Britain such great strength in depth in most distance-running events and from which the Albert Hills, Sydney Woodersons and more recently the Tullohs, Hymans, Ibbotsons and Piries have emerged. All had a great amount of distance and cross-country running in their formative years of running. Taking the majority of top-class British runners into account there certainly seems massive evidence to back the Russian-Estonian coach, O. Karikosk's, contention that specialized training for distances at school (13 to 17 years) can have an adverse affect on young athletes, for, only a fractional percentage of the English schoolboy half-mile and mile champions become top-class senior athletes.

Progress in training in the future will undoubtedly follow the pattern of past years and doubtless national temperament will play a big part in determining the systems which will be followed. In pronouncing sanddune training for all, the effervescent Percy Cerutty failed to note that the Finns (using snow) and the English (using mud) had trained over similar terrain for resistance and that the open-air life of Portsea was particularly suited to the Australian temperament. The methodical Germans, ever-eager for methods which would bring them international success, obviously found that interval-training suited their teutonic approach to sport, much as the Swedes had developed Fartlek as a method which suited them. The English runners - the majority of whom feign coaches - tend to employ rather hit-and-miss methods of training, to follow popular vogues of training and to keep in mind their beloved cross-country where the underdog has a chance to shine. Thus the British have great strength in depth in the 5000 meters and 10000 meters events but only a few runners at the pinnacle of world-class performances. The New Zealanders, so similar in temperament and outlook to the English, have followed fairly similar methods - Lydiard in his initial learning of the art of coaching read F.A. Webster, who followed the works of Arthur Newton as his gospel in distance running. So, most methods can still be traced back to the single factor that distance-runners must do a lot of running to succeed.

I believe also that weight training and other forms of progressive exercise will play an ever-increasing part in the preparation of world-class performances and the - 13 minute, 5000 meter runner and the 27:30, 10,000 meter runner of the future, together with the 2-hour marathon runner, will be more mesamorphic than ectomorphic in body-build and be capable of power-running in the region of 3:58 for the mile. The basic training method for the next decade or so, will undoubtedly still be interval-running and athletes will chose from other methods of conditioning those which suit them best. Coaches and athletes must, surely, come to realize, that the recent great dogmatists of training offer more in terms of motivation to their athletes than any significant trend in training or special knowledge. More and more the importance of psychology in track will come to be realized and the knowledge of sports medicine will be put to use, with coach and physiologist and physician working together towards deeds that we today deem impossible.

Training of Runners in Poland

by Tadeusz Kepka,
(National Coach of Middle-distance runners in Poland).

Present results obtained by Polish runners are the result of several years of hard work started as far back as 1952 when the specialization of coaches was introduced. Prior to 1952, runners of Poland did not produce noteworthy results according to international athletic standards, and several errors were observed in their training methods.

Foreign methods (sometimes not entirely correct) were often literally copied, even though they represented only narrow sections of certain training periods. Furthermore they were by no means suitable for Polish boys and girls, owing to the entirely different climatic conditions as well as to the different types of physical build of competitors which are seen in this country.

We had to adapt to our environment and to the physical characteristics of our athletes such types of training which could give us the required positive effects. Our method of training today is known as "Polish running-play." Here are the most important items in our training plans.

Division of the year in correlation to the calendar of competitive events

The yearly training in this country is divided into four periods, since we have only one (outdoor) competitive season. We have no indoor season whatsoever, nor any cross-country season.

1. **Intermediate period, between Oct. 15, and Nov. 15.** In this period, competitors slow down their training, applying in principle easy running workouts, without strict forms of endurance and speed work. This period is also used for treatment of any possible injuries with mud and saline baths, etc.

11. **Preparatory period, between Nov. 15, and March 31.** This period is designed for the endurance work-outs and building up stamina by cross-country running (mostly in woods).

111. **Pre-competition period, between April 1, and May 15.** In this period, attention is primarily given to the endurance and speed work. Competitions at other than racing distances are run during this period. These serve as an analysis of the training performed so far. Thus middle-distance runners specializing in 800m take part successively in the races of 1,000m, 500m, and 400m. The "metric mile" (1500m) specialists run 2000m, 1000m, and 800m. The distance runners participate successively in 2000m, 1500m, and 3000m races.

1V. **Competitive period between May 15 and October 15.** This is a long period of competition during which athletes participate in races of their specialty. Each weekend they run typical distances such as:

Half milers......... 400m, 800m, and 1000m.
Milers .... 400m, 800m, 1000m, 1500m, 1 mile, 2000m.
Distance runners....800m, 1000m, 1500m, 3000m, 5000m, 10,000m and 3000m Steeplechase.

Interval training

Polish runners, having at their disposal very favorable cross-country conditions (many woods with soft, springy grass and moss paths), give up entirely their training at the stadiums and on the track.

The cross-country training is based on several forms of play and games which are not strictly and accurately planned because often they are determined by the shape and condition of the ground and cannot be planned in advance.

Transferring the training into the woods was also determined by the objectives to be accomplished. They were somewhat too extensive to be attained at the stadium. The daily work out of a runner in this country lasts about 2 hours, during which he sometimes runs as much as 20 km, ($12\frac{1}{2}$ miles). It would be difficult to train on the track in unfavorable city conditions (industrial and motor car fumes in the air, monotony of circling the track, etc.). By running in the woods, on the other hand, an athlete feels much better physically. The green color of nature delays his mental fatigue. Running past trees and shrubs gives an impression of much greater speed. A runner feels better, gains confidence, and is satisfied with his running. Furthermore, he avoids the monotony of training, because many surprises await him on his way. Sometimes while running longer endurance-building distances he must jump over ditches, fallen trees, and bushes. At times, he is compelled to sprint up a steep slope, or (as it happens during the winter) run in knee-deep snow which requires much more of his attention and effort. He seldom knows what will be the next obstacle for him to negotiate.

During the winter period, our athletes cross-country training takes place sometimes in very low temperatures or in very strong winds.

In summer no amount of heat or rain can prevent our runners from their work-outs. Training under such difficult climatic condition gives the athlete strength and a high degree of stamina. Some of our training is done in the mountains during winter for two reasons.

1. **Physiological:** The entire physiological system of a runner operates under an entirely different condition of oxygen supply. This includes a) Living at the height of about 900m above sea level. This is higher than in the normal environment of the majority of athletes who live at the average altitued of 500m above sea level. b) Pure mountain air. c) The choice of alternating the content of the air during one training session with altitude above sea level changing between 900m to 2000m. These workouts sometimes take place at low temperatures in strong wind, and in deep snow.

2. **Development of Strength:** All kinds of running up steep slopes in deep snow, as well as long distance mountain hikes (up to 30 km, or 18 $\frac{3}{4}$ miles in 4 hours of non-stop marching) gives the runner something indispensable in terms of strength in his legs and hips. This cannot be obtained by indoor calisthenics.

There are three types of running in interval training:

a) Jogging - a fundamental, easy means of work in building endurance, applied as 60% of the total training. In jogging the strides are about 1.20m long, upper part of the body loose and relaxed, and the heel moves low above the ground and passes forward as quickly as possible. The speed of jogging is about 4-5 min. per 1 km, or $1\frac{1}{2}$-2 min. per 400m.

b) Easy striding - a more intensive means of training than jogging, less often used and applied only in the form of short distances during the warm-up or at the end of a training session. Easy striding consumes about 10% of the total training time. In easy striding the upper body remains upright as in jogging, and can be inclined slightly forward, the step is a bit longer (reaching up 4'11"-1.50m) the heel moves higher above the ground than in jogging and moves forward as fast as possible, with the speed increasing to $3\frac{1}{2}$ to 4 min. per 1 km., or 85-96 seconds per 400m.

c) Running for endurance or pace running as it is called in this country is the third most intensive, and important part of the training of our runners.

Pace running is divided into the following distances, the lengths of which are correlated to the specialty of the runner:

Half-milers run long distance of 1200, 1000, 800; Middle-distances of 300, 200m.

Milers run long distances of 1600, 1000m; middle distances of 800, 600m; and short distances of 400, 300m.

Long middle-distance runners negotiate long distances of 3000m, 1500m; middle distances of 1000, 600m; and short distances of 500, 400m.

The speed at which the individual distances are run depend on the training period and on the runner's state of physical condition.

One point worth of particular attention when speaking of pace running is that this type of training is also done over cross-country areas mostly in the woods, with the athletes wearing field or basketball shoes or running barefooted. The pace running distances are not marked, and the athletes approximate the distances of their pace running repetitions. They recover between repetitions of pace running distances by jogging or easy striding. The duration of recovery between pace repetitions is very short and the athlete begins the next repetition while still breathing deeply. However, this duration of recovery between pace repetitions is not planned in advance, and actually the length of recovery is left to the judgement and preference of the individual athlete.

d) Speed - The last means of building endurance. Sprint work is used in the training of Polish athletes at every workout. Beginning in the late winter or early spring, one day of training in each week is devoted exclusively to speed training.

When an athlete trains and covers quite long distances in the woods, he often encounters fallen trees, bushes, ditches, streams, fences, and other obstacles which he must clear, thus changing the rhythm of his running. In running pace repetitions he must often change the rhythm of running 2-3 times following the obstacles encountered.

We have introduced a special "hurdle training" into cross-country or woods work-outs of our runners. It consists of hurdling with good technique over bushes, shrubs, fallen trees, fences, and temporary hurdles made of dry boughs and twigs collected in the woods.

This facilitates an early mastery of hurdle technique and aids subsequent participation in 3000m steeplechase races. Furthermore, such training increases the range and flexibility of hip joing movement. This has a great and positive influence on relaxation, ease of stride, and the efficiency of running technique.

Middle Distance Training in Borneo

by Anthony M. Traill
Shell Oil Company coach of Borneo and former National coach of Pakistan

Requirements

A consideration of the great middle and long distance runners of recent times shows that they do not display such similar physical characteristics as one might expect. None appears to possess all the gifts which would suit him to these events, and some are even at a disadvantage from one point of view or another, such as length of limb, symmetry of structure, or lightness of body. Again their training is far from identical and differs widely in certain respects.

This suggests that there is still a long way to go before the ideal combination of the perfect type, and the most effective method of training, is achieved in each distance event. This is undoubtably true, hence the present world's distance running records, magnificent though they may be, are in fact still far from the limits of human capability. Thus these events present a fine challenge and wonderful possibilities for those athletes with natural gifts and real greatness in them.

Since, however, the achievements realized by distance runners are similar, they must also resemble each other in many important features of both their make-up and their methods. It is these resemblances which are of particular importance to the ambitious athlete, as they will tell him clearly what are the most essential ingredients of success. The athlete needs to consider first the physical and mental characteristics commonly found in these runners in order to assure himself, before undertaking serious training, that he is cut out for these events, and to decide which particular one should suit him best.

Physical Characteristics

Broadly speaking distance runners are light of build and of average height, or a little above it, with long and slender limbs. World record holder for the mile Herb Elliot, (3:54.5) and ex-world record holder John Landy have approximately identical height and weight figures of 5' 10½" and 146 lbs.: these may be regarded as typical and roughly ideal for their specialist event.

The physical qualities which are primarily responsible for giving the runner greater staying power or stamina are: (1) A light body. (2) A large powerful heart, (large stroke volume). (3) Rich blood, (high hemoglobin content and high red corpuscle count). (4) A good blood supply to the working muscles, (high capillarization of muscle). (5) Strength and quality of the essential muscles.

Other factors which play a part are flexibility of the joints, and ease of movement arising from rhythm, skill, and co-ordination.

Body weight is largely a question of inheritance, but in some cases may be effectively reduced. All the other qualities which are essential to endurance may be steadily developed or improved by regular and suitable training, which for maximum results must be maintained for several years and combined with a first class diet, adequate rest, and sound health habits.

Unlike skeletal muscle, heart size is not related to body weight, thus a lightly built man may possess a comparatively large heart. The greater the distance to be run, the more important the factor of pure endurance becomes, therefore the lightest athletes with the best developed hearts may excel in the longest events, namely the 10,000 meters and marathon. Popov, the Russian marathon champion, has a body weight of only 120 lbs. with an exceptional heart volume of 1200 c.c. This last value may be compared with that of the average sprinter, jumper, or thrower of only about 600 c.c. Bikila Abebe, the marathon victor at the Rome Olympics, scaled only 140 lbs. although 5' 9" tall.

The examination of numerous middle distance specialists has disclosed heart values ranging from about 750 to 900c.c. with proportionately low body weights. Paul Schmidt, the German 800 meters champion, has the favorable figures of 873 c.c. heart volume, and 132 lbs. weight. It is important to note that the large, strong heart of the distance runner is more the product of training than inheritance, and that such an efficient organ is healthy and more conducive to long life than a smaller, weaker one.

The superiority of the heart as a pumping organ, of the highly trained athlete over that of the untrained, is made clear by the following comparative figures. The volume of blood pumped through the untrained heart may rise from 4 liters per minute to 20, but that of the trained heart may increase to 40 or more.

Stamina and endurance are chiefly limited by the amount of volume of oxygen, which can be supplied to the working muscles in a given time. This depends chiefly upon factors (2), (3), and (4) listed above. Thus besides the power of the heart to pump blood to the muscles, also of vital importance is the capacity of the blood to carry oxygen. This is largely decided by the hemoglobin content of the red corpuscles and the concentration of these in the blood (surface area).

Blood that contains 14.5 gms. of hemoglobin per 100 c.c.s is said to be 100%, while 5,000,000 red corpuscles per cu. m.m. is also standard. By regular and sound training coupled with a first class diet the athlete may raise his blood values far above these figures. Some of the distance runners given blood tests at the 1960 Olympic Games recorded 18 grms. hemoglobin per 100 c.c., or about 120%, and a 6,500,000 blood count.

Athletes in endurance events aiming for top class results should expect a blood test to give them over 105% hemoglobin and a $5\frac{1}{2}$ to 6 million count(erythrocyte or red cell). Such tests should be obtained regularly - about once a month - from a local medical center, as one indication of the athlete's degree of fitness and health

The remaining principal factor which decides the oxygen supply to the muscles is the number of blood vessels supplying them, (capillaries). Prolonged training brings into use resting or dormant ones, and results in the growth of others. Some experiments have shown the increase in capillaries due to training to be as much as 45%.

Pulse rate checks (heart beats per minute) are also useful in indicating the degree of fitness and the suitability of training exercises. Highly trained distance runners generally have a pulse much slower than average owing to the greater pumping power of their hearts, and the superior quality of their blood. A normal resting pulse is about 72 per minute. Some athletes, such as Emil Zatopek, have shown a basal pulse rate of below 50, and many, like Gordon Pirie, below 60. The basal pulse should be taken lying down, and before rising in the morning. During the day, while resting in a sitting position, it will be about 10 beats faster.

Training, such as prolonged daily runs of several miles, produces a gradual fall in the resting pulse rate, and thus demonstrates its benefits. During strenuous exercise the pulse will rise to $2\frac{1}{2}$ to 3 times its resting value (appros. 180), but tends to be less in the fitter athletes. A method of testing by taking pulse counts, whether a training exercise was too light or too severe will be described under training methods.

As the competitive distances become less, pure speed must become relatively more important, and also therefore, the physical qualities largely responsible for producing it. These are: (1) Muscular strength and power. (2) Flexibility and length of limbs. (3) Skill and correct technique in running movements.

From (1) and (2) it may be seen that those who excel at the shorter distance events will tend to be taller and heavier. The outstanding example in this respect is Tom Courtney, the 800 meters champion of the 1956 Olympics, who scaled 183 lbs. and stood 6' 2". He possessed exceptional basic speed having been credited with a 9.7 100 yards and also a 21.0 220 yards. This was his greatest asset as with such size he must have had less staying power than some of his smaller rivals, but was running relatively further below his peak speed. Generally speaking the large, heavily built athletes are only able to succeed at the events requiring explosive power; namely the sprints, throws, and jumps.

The qualities of strength, suppleness, and skill or technique which are so important to speed, can be continually developed by any determined athlete regardless of his natural gifts.

Mental Characteristics

Without the requisite strength and attitude of mind, the physical characteristics, however outstanding, will never become fully expressed in athletic performance.

Certain mental qualities are common to all great distance runners of the past and present, and these may be regarded as more responsible for their success than anything else.

Without exception, distance running champions possess: (1) Desire: to succeed - to excel - to prove themselves to themselves, - and to others. (2) Determination and Courage: to triumph over all handicaps, obstacles, and difficulties. (3) Industriousness: a willingness to work, and a capacity to derive great satisfaction from physical effort and achievement. (4) A Love of Running: as a form of movement and exercise, - as a sport.

Basic Training for the Middle Distances

After considering and assessing the physical and mental requirements of the distance runner, the next step is to produce a basic training plan for developing them, as required by the individual concerned.

The general scheme which follows is designed only for the middle distances, i.e. ½ to 3 miles, as it is considered unwise to attempt the longer races early in ones career, and before some success at the shorter ones has been achieved.

The 440, 220, and 110 yards times suggested under Interval Running, are merely suitable examples, and should be modified by the athlete and/or coach to suit the individual. The complete plan is intended mainly to act as a framework on which the athlete may build his schedules.

In the early stages, as may be seen, the training is similar for all the middle distance events. A little more emphasis on speed for the 800 meters/880 yards and on the distance covered in training for the 5,000 meters/3 miles is all that need be born in mind. If so little variation between training for say the 800 meters and 5,000 meters is wondered at, then it must be pointed out that the qualities to be developed are basically the same. Those that tend to differentiate the 800 meter man from the 5,000, are largely the inherent ones of natural physique and speed, and mental attitude. Other differences will depend on the actual individual, rather than his event, and each man's training in its details must consider these.

The middle distance events are: 800 meters; 1500 meters; 3000 meters steeplechase; 5000 meters. Or 800 yards; 1 mile and 3 miles.

General Plan

The formula which spells success in all track events is:
Stamina plus Strength plus Suppleness plus Skill = Speed in performance
(Endurance) (Power) (Flexibility) (Technique)

Basic training must apply the simple but effective principle that great stamina, endurance, and running strength may be gradually developed through sheer running mileage in training of the right type.

By employing the various forms of running training described below, the greatest effect is achieved and basic speed and technique improved at the same time.

A program of special exercises may provide a most effective means of directly developing strength and power, and suppleness and flexibility.

Specific technique work for mastering the correct crossing of the barriers and the water jump for the steeplechasers, is the only other type of training required.

The Mileage Targets

These are the key to success by ensuring that the athlete runs far enough in training.

The average athlete who aims at reaching championship class must set a total mileage target in training of at least 1500 miles of running in the 1st year of serious competition. About 1200 miles of these should be completed before the major competitions of that year.

An annual mileage of 1500 or 1200 in 9 months breaks down to an average of 30 miles per week. The number of training sessions per week should be not less than 6 to 8 (maximum 12). These may be either (a) long or (b) short: (a) long - 1 hr. average duration - one per day. (b) short - 35 minutes average duration - two per day. One in early morning, one in afternoon. The average mileage for a long session: 6-8 miles. The average mileage for a short session 3 - 4 miles. Target no. 1 is a mileage of 350 - 400 miles in the 1st 3 months of training.

All the most successful middle distance runners of recent times, such as Halberg, Snell, Elliot, Bolotnikov, Kuts, and Zatopek, have run over 3,000 miles in training annually. This may appear a tremendous amount of work, but in fact it isn't. It requires an average of only 9 miles per day, and this takes a trained athlete less than 1 hour of actual running.

To those to whom running is a pleasure and a natural exercise, and who also achieve world acclaim for their performances on the track, this is not a hardship but a task to be welcomed and enjoyed.

A target, therefore, of 1,500 miles per annum is easily within the capabilities of any young, enthusiastic, and healthy athlete, requiring an average of only 30 minutes of actual running per day.

Remember, to be a runner, you must run, and run, yet run within yourself, and run to enjoy it!

The Types of Running Employed

(1) Fartlek, (2) Cross Country, (3) Interval Running and Pace Judgement work. (4) Time Trails and pure Speed Work.

(1) Fartlek. This is "speed play" or playing at running. Its keynote is enjoyment. The athlete runs at a variety of speeds as the mood takes him. He must also choose the terrain; grass, road, path, beach, forest, so as to provide as pleasant a variety and scene as possible.

Uphill and downhill as well as level surfaces must be included. Steep uphill work is a particularly important part of training. The strain is never great in Fartlek, since the emphasis is on pure joy in running, nevertheless sufficient mileage must be covered in each session - not less than 3 and an average of 6.

Once a week or month a "Big Run" should be held, and the distances completed in them progressively increased as follows: Big Run, 1st month, 12 miles - time 1½ hrs., Big Run, 2nd month - 14 miles - time 1 3/4 hrs., Big Run, 3rd month - 16 miles - time 2 hrs.

Target no. 2 is a 20 mile run on the Fartlek principle, completed in 2½ hours to 3 hours in the 3rd or 4th month of training. It will require courage and determination, but represents a great triumph. "Big Runs" are also to be performed in subsequent months. They should be over the same course of 20 miles, but with the time taken for each reduced according to the ability to do so.

Stretches of walking during Fartlek training may be counted as mileage provided that: (a) It is brisk and springy, with the athlete deliberately rising up and down on his toes. (b) The walking spells are only for 2 or 3 minutes at a time, and never longer than 5 minutes. An important principle to observe is that of keeping on the move all the time, however slowly. The end of the run should be in the form of limbering down.

(2) Cross-Country. This differs from Fartlek as follows:

(a) Performed at a steady pace throughout: variations of speed occur only where the surface compels it.

(b) No walking. The emphasis is on more and more relaxation and better rhythm of movement. During all running activity the athlete must think about imporving his technique or skill in running, looser forward swing of the lower leg in recovery; short, natural, free stride; very loose back and shoulders. N.B. Relaxation is a 'letting go' of muscles during activity which must be continually practised and improved.

(c) The distances run do not increase - the minimum 3 and the maximum 6-8 miles - but the times taken must be progressively reduced.

Start with the speed of 6½ to 7 minutes per mile for the 6 mile course, i.e. 40 to 45 minutes total time, and 6 minutes per mile for the 3 mile course, ie. 18 minutes total time.

Target no. 3 is to reduce the 6 miles to under 36 minutes (6 minutes per mile) during the first 2 months and 3 miles to 16 minutes 30 seconds or less. In a few months it should be possible to cover 6 miles in less than 32 minutes, and 3 miles in under 15 minutes 30 seconds.

Targets 1, 2, and 3 are not really difficult to achieve; they require chiefly faith, patience, will power, and running as a daily habit and way of life. Yet they are so important that reaching these goals alone means that the athlete is already in a position to surpass all his previous performances on the track by a striking margin.

Commence with 3 Cross Country and 3 Fartlek runs per week of 3 miles each.

(3) Interval Running and Pace Judgement Work. This is a form of training which aims directly at developing stamina, strength, skill, and speed for a chosen event or events; in this case the 800 meters, 1500 meters, 3,000 meters steeplechase, or 5,000 meters, which ever is the athlete's chosen event or events.

The total distance covered in a training session of this type is generally less than in Fartlek or Cross Country, but the intensity of effort reached at the climax of the work is greater, and this is the vital part of it.

The factors involved are the distance run (D); the Interval of rest between each run (I); the number of repetitions (R); and the time of each run (T). Remember the word - D I R T !

The distances to be employed are principally: (i) 440 yards. (ii) 220 yards. (iii) 110 yards.

The recovery intervals are fixed at 2 minutes approximately: - (never more than 3 minutes). The repetitions: - for 440, minimum 4, maximum 10; for 220, minimum 6, maximum 16; for 110, minimum 10, maximum 30. Times taken: - commencing at 68-70 seconds for the 440. 32 - 34 secs. for the 220. 14-15 sec. for the 110 according to ability.

Thus the first interval running sessions may be as follows:

D I R T = (a) 440 x 4 in 68 secs. with 2 mins. rests. (b) 220 x 6 in 32 secs. with 2 mins. rests. (c) 110 x 10 in 14 secs. with 2 mins. rests.

The repetitions (R) are gradually increased as improving condition permits until the sessions become: (a) 440 x 10 in 68 secs. condition permits, (b) 220 x 16 in 32 secs. condition permits, (c) 110 x 30 in 14 secs. condition permits. When this stage is reached the times (T) are reduced and the procedure repeated for example: - (a) 440 x 4 in 64 secs. Procedure repeated, (b) 220 x 6 in 30 secs. procedure repeated, (c) 110 x 10 in 13 secs. procedure repeated.

Note that (a), (b) and (c) are separate sessions for different days. It is suggested that they are done in this order.

A guide that the repetitions are not too many, or the time too fast, for the stage of fitness reached may be obtained by a pulse rate check. Exactly 2 minutes after completing the last run the pulse rate should have fallen to about 20 per 10 seconds.

Use a whistle and stop watch as required to assist in setting the correct pace. A coach or fellow athlete must assist here.

Pace judgement laps at speeds at which it is estimated an actual race could be run must be prescribed for practice later, as demanded by time trials and competitions.

(4) Time Trials. These sessions are always short from the point of view of distance, never totalling more than the minimum 3 miles per work out. The intensity of effort however, invariably reaches the highest peak, since the athlete is running flat out in an endeavor to beat his previous best time over a specified distance.

He should approach these attempts with exactly the same attitude of mind as actual competition: with the same determination, the same controlled nervous tension, the same courage. He should endeavor to visualize the great crowd watching in anticipation, and imagine that his rivals are running with him; for to succeed now is to succeed 'then'.

Like interval running and pace judgement work, time trials always take place on the track.

The distances over which trails are to be held are as follows: - 60; 100; 220; 440; 880 yds; 1 mile; 2 miles.

There would be one time trial session per week, with the above distances tackled in rotation in the following order: -1st week -60 and 220 yds. (same day), 2nd week - 100 and 440 yds. (same day), 3rd week - 880 yds., 4th week - 1 mile., 5th week - 2 miles., 6th week - Repeat.

The important distances of 3 miles and 6 miles will be taken care of the cross country sessions for the time being. Time trials in these, however, may occasionally be run on the track instead of over the country, if desired. 330's and 660's will be added later when the emphasis switches from endurance to 'speed' training.

A performance graph of the results obtained should be drawn and kept up to date by the athlete or coach to show potentiality and strong and weak points. This is useful and encouraging, and it makes it possible to predict what the athlete may expect to achieve next season in actual competition.

Two time trials per day will be held at a later stage to develop the ability to withstand tough heats in competition, and to tackle more than one event.

Specimen Training Sessions

Week One

Mon. a.m. - 3 miles Fartlek., p.m. - Interval Running: (i) One mile warm up run - slightly increase the pace of each succeeding lap (440's) e.g. lst. 95 secs.; 2nd 90 secs.; 3rd 85 secs.; 4th 80 secs.; Total time approx. 5 min. 50 secs. (ii) 5 to 10 mins. stretching and limbering exercises. (iii) 4-440's in 68 secs., each with 2 mins. rest in between. (iv) Check pulse recovery rate. (v) One mile limber down. Decrease the speed of each lap. e.g. 80 - 85 - 90 - 95 or 75 - 80 - 85 - 95. Total mileage for the day. 6.

N.B. At the end of the last run the pulse rate should be about 180 per minute, unless the work is too east. The important check to take, however, is the one after 2 minutes rest. This should show that the pulse beat has fallen to 120 per minute; that is from 30 per 10 seconds to 20 per 10 seconds approx. If it has not, then the work is too severe or the athlete is not well.

If the pulse recovery is satisfactory and every lap has been completed comfortably in 66 secs., then one more lap must be added in the same session next time. Attempt to complete this extra lap in 66 secs also, and do not add on another one until this can be done without strain as indicated by the pulse test.

Tues. a.m. - 3 miles Fartlek (varied work in about 20 mins.) p.m. 3 miles Cross Country (time 17 mins. 30 secs. to 18 mins. at even pace). Total mileage - 6.

Wed. a.m. 3 miles Fartlek. p.m. - Interval Running. (i) 1 mile warmup jog. (ii) 10 mins. exercising (in the shade). (iii) 220 x 6 in 32 secs. (iv) Check pulse rate. (v) 5 laps (440) limber down - 75 - 80 - 85 -90 walk the last lap rising from the heel right up onto the toes in each forward stride. (Spring heel walking). Total mileage - 6.

Thurs. a.m. - 6 miles cross country (in approx. 40 mins.) p.m. Rest Mileage for the day - 6.

Fri. a.m. - 3 miles Fartlek. p.m. - Interval Running (i) 5 laps ($1\frac{1}{4}$ miles) warm up 95 - 90- 85- 80 - 75. (ii) 10 mins. exercising. (iii) 110 x 10 in 14 secs. (full 2 mins. inter val between each with very slow jog back to start.) (iv) check pulse rate. (v) 1 mile even pace in 5 mins. 40 secs. (85 per lap). (vi) Spring heel walk - 2 laps.. Total mileage - 6.

Sat. - Rest.

Sun. a.m. - Time Trials: or p.m. (i) $1\frac{1}{4}$ mile warm up as above. (ii) 10 mins. exercising. (iii) 60 yds. x 2, full speed, time taken. Ease down on crossing finish of each, and run on relaxed to complete 110 yds. 220 x 1 full speed. Ease down and jog 440 yds. (iv) $1\frac{1}{4}$ mile limber down. Total mileage - 3.

N.B. Time keeper and starter are required for the time trials.

During interval running jog very slowly to start in the 2 mins. recovery period. Shake arms and legs loose for relaxation.

Total mileage for week: - 33.

Week Two

Mon. a.m. - $3\frac{1}{2}$ miles Fartlek (20 minutes) p.m. - 3 miles Cross Country (17 mins. 30 secs. pace) Mileage for day - $6\frac{1}{2}$.

Tues. a.m. - $3\frac{1}{2}$ miles Fartlek. p.m. - Interval Running. (i) $1\frac{1}{4}$ miles warm up. (ii) 10 mins. exercising. (iii) 440 x 5 in 68 seconds. (iv) Check pulse recovery. (v) 1 mile limber down. Spring heel walk. Total mileage - 7.

Wed. a.m. - 6 miles cross country (38 to 40 minutes even pace). p.m. - Rest. Total mileage - 6.

Thurs. a.m. - $3\frac{1}{2}$ miles Fartlek. p.m. - Interval Running. (i) $1\frac{1}{4}$ miles warm up. (ii) 10 mins. exercising (iii) 110 x 12 in 14 sec. (iv) Check pulse recovery. (v) 1 mile even pace - 85 seconds laps. (vi) Limber down jog and spring heel walk 660 yds. Total mileage - 7.

Fri. a.m. - $3\frac{1}{2}$ miles Fartlek. p.m. - $3\frac{1}{2}$ Fartlek, or Cross Country. Total mileage - 7.

Sat. a.m. - Rest. p.m. - Rest.

Sun. a.m. - or p.m. - Time Trials: (i) $1\frac{1}{4}$ miles warm up. (ii) 10 mins. exercising. (iii) 100 yds. at full speed - timed. (iv) 440 yds full speed. (v) $1\frac{1}{2}$ miles steady run and limber down. Total mileage - 3

Total mileage for week - $36\frac{1}{2}$.

Week Three and Four

Schedules for these will follow the same pattern as the above. Two interval running sessions per week should be sufficient at present. In the third week substitute 220 distance for 110, i.e. 220 x 6 in 30 seconds. For the fourth week return to 440's.

A training program should always be regarded as being flexible so that it may be adjusted to suit the actual requirements of the moment, such as the time and facilities available and condition of the athlete.

It is in order to interchange the time trials and rest day or any other sessions.

In weeks three and four the Fartlek distances may be slightly increased as the need is felt. At all costs the previous level of mileage must be maintained, and actual running speeds reduced in order to do so if necessary.

The Fartlek, the cross country, and the easy runs in training may be regarded as quantity work, the interval running and time trials as quality work. At present the emphasis must be on quantity rather than quality.

Middle Distance Training in Yugoslavia

by Leo Lang
(National Coach for middle and long-distance runners in Yugoslavia.)

Training of youth

I am of the opinion that we start coaching youth for long-distance running a little too late. Here science still owes us an exact answer as to the time of safe beginning. But we also know from experience that it takes at least five years to reach class results in long-distance running.

In my opinion we should gradually start with long-distance running at 12 years of age, and indeed with a more playful workout. Perhaps we should start with twice a week in the first year. By this I do not mean training as individuals, but rather running with a juvenile group. This gives greater pleasure and strengthens the desire for gradually more intensive running. I always put a somewhat older boy in such a group. One, who has already mastered the method, and who understands the mentality of youths.

Here is an example of training for youths in long-distance running. For the last three years I have experimented with a group of boys. They started at 12 years of age. In 1958 the average age was 15. The lads practiced twice a week in the first year, two to three times in the second, and three times in the third, but only rarely four times a week. It was a gradually increased light interval training.

The best in the group, just 15 years old, made the following results in the outdoor season of 1958: 100m, 11.9; 400m, 52.1; 800m, 1:58; 1000m, 2:36; 1500m, 4:12; 2000m, 5:56. This youngster, for example in December 1958 trained one afternoon (temp.46° F) as follows: 8 x 200m, in 32 secs with two to three minute jog intervals. He had 130-150 heat-beats after running and 110-100 before the beginning of the next repetition. The workout was under control of a physician. I am of the opinion that by gradually increasing this sort of training with youth from the 12th to the 20th year of age, 90% of the later personal best results can be reached.

Training methods for adults.

For all that we know today about running, we must first thank great runners like Nurmi, Haegg, Harbig, Zatopek, Bannister, the Hungarians (under Igloi), Kuts, the Cerutty school, and today's Polish school. I have not been able to mention everybody important because of lack of space.

All in all, practice has worked out the basic principle of training: By repeating shorter runs than the event, and running in the same or faster tempo than racing speed. This basic principle differs from earlier methods which were based on longer runs than the competitive event, but slower than racing speed. This new conception has evolved in the last 20 years. Based on the experience and findings of the above mentioned pioneers of new methods, and my own experience from working with the Yugoslav middle and long-distance runners I would like to describe my methods with the following main elements.

1. Repetitions of short runs with short jog intervals.

About this I will, as the best, give an example from my practice. An evening of training with one of my athletes, who has seven years of training behind him, who is now 26 years old, ran in December 1958 as follows:

6 x 100m, in 16-17 secs.with 20 sec.jog intervals, with a 2 minutes rest at the end, followed by -

5 x 200m, in 32-33 secs. with 40 sec. jog intervals, then 3 minutes rest.

10 x 100 m, in 16 secs. with 20 sec. jog intervals, then 2 minute rest.

10 x 400m, in 66-67 secs. with 60-70 sec. jog intervals, then 3 minutes rest.

5 x 200m, in 33-34 secs. with 40 sec. jog intervals, then 2-3 minutes rest.

6 x 100 m, in 17-18 secs. with 20 sec. jog interval.

The weather conditions were: 46° F without wind. The athlete ran in a sweat-suit, with rubber soled shoes at 5 p.m. - four hours after his midday meal. It was an athlete who trains every day. Breathing difficulties occurred occasionally, but quickly disappeared. It was an anaerobic workout (without oxygen) of medium intensity. The use of strength was maximum 70%.

Kutz used jog - intervals between his 400m runs of only 30 secs. under the same circumstances, but in winter he too, on an average used 70 secs. jog-intervals. He made these short intervals purposely to avoid complete recovery. This could be expressed best by the number of pulse beats: After the run it was up to 170 beats per minute and before the beginning of the next run it was 130. According to the old theories the recovery should be greater, and one should have waited till 90 heart beats a minute. Today we do not think this purposeful.

2. Longer repeated runs with longer jog - intervals.

The distance of the training runs here is from one to two -thirds of the distance of the athlete's competitive event. The speed is significantly greater than in a race. These runs are repeated only two or three times. Here is one example: Twice 1000m, in 2:37,8 (for my athletes) a jog-interval of 10 minutes and 1000m, in 2:38. The pressure on the respiratory system is greater than during the above mentioned interval work. It is an anaerobic workout of a much greater intensity. The use of strength here is 90%.

These repeated runs are made all the year through, in winter as in summer. In winter the purpose is learning to endure a fast tempo for a longer time, and so bring the athlete to a condition similar to that in a race; to adapt him for the event and its specific conditions. In summer they serve as a base for specific racing adaptation (physiological purpose) and also for the purpose of giving the runner the opportunity of testing his built-up racing ability. These runs also feed his self-confidence a short time before competition (psychological base).

3. Slow runs without repetition.

The distance of these runs is one-half to one-third longer than the competitive event. Tempo: half speed. Here there is no pressure on the respiratory system so it is an almost aerobic workout (running with a balance between the used and the receipt of oxygen - steady state). The purpose here is to adapt the organism to run in balance for a longer time, and the aquisition of general mental and bodily perseverence (general endurance).

Period	Training Speed	Distance of Repetitions	Number of Repetitions	Series or Sets of Repetitions
I. Main period	Racing speed plus relative speed of the athlete.	100-400	10-20	2-3

II. Training for competitive condition.	Relative speed of the athlete plus light speed	50-100	5-10	5-6
III. Racing period.	Racing speed plus relative speed of the athlete.	50-200	3-6	3-4

From the above table it is obvious that the training during periods I and III is the same, except that in III the repetitions are shorter, run at a faster speed, and interspersed with competition.

The repetitions of running are as short as possible, especially in the spring. The speed is so important, according to Igloi's pupil Gyula Antal, that any kind of endurance training which might lower the athlete's speed is not permissible. Accent in this training is on "light speed" run at fast pace, but with only relatively small oxygen debt being accumulated, and on rhythm. In other words, the repetitions are run faster than medium speed for a given distance, but with a definite accent on fast pace rhythm. Training at a fast pace rhythm over many short repetitions makes it easier to run at a slower pace over longer distances. Competitor and friend of Igloi, Andras Csaplar (who coached the tiny Josef Kovacs by using the methods of Germany's famous coach, Woldmer Gerschler, progressing from longer to shorter and faster repetitions), wrote that Igloi employs

Additional longer training for runners over 500m and up.

a/ Repeated runs over a course of 1000m to 5000m

b/ Endurance runs over a course of 8000m to 18000m

Additional training for marathon runners.

a/ Repeated runs over distances from 3000 to 15000m.

b/ Endurance runs over distances of 20, 30, 40, 45 km. of this the main training is 75% on a grass surface, and 25% on a marathon course. Of these 25% should be run on roads. This distribution will spare the legs, which are here especially heavily taxed.

Various training interpretations.

We have tried various kinds. Here I would like to mention two variations on three matters, with which, in spite of contradictions, good results are obtainable.

1. The training workout. On the one hand: (1) Training with interval and repetition running at the same speed or faster than the speed of the event. On the other: (2) Training with interval and repetition running slower than the speed of the event.

11. The trainings plan and the use of the stop-watch. On the one hand: (1) A fixed plan for a long time in advance. Here one mostly uses the stop-watch and runs on the track. On the other: (2) A firm plan is made up for a week ahead at the most, but even on the day of the workout one must adapt to momentary state of health and disposition of the runner. Here one will run less on a course and use the stop-watch sparingly.

111. Training adapted to the type of runner. The types being: (1) A runner with greater basic speed. (2) A runner with greater natural endurance. Here are two opinions of international experts: the first wish to stress the training on the existing natural strong points, and endeavor to develop these still more. The others prefer to improve the natural weaknesses of the runners.

Seasons.

These days long distance running takes up a lot of time. One must train every day, and for 4 months of the year it is best to train twice daily. In this way one can generally attain up to the average of 15 to 20 km a day. We employ a cycle of 7 days, and after that we repeat again from the beginning. Our seasons of the year are as follows:

I. Period: 15 November - 31 January (the first preparatory step).
II. Period: 1 February - 31 May (the second preparatory step).
III. Period: 1 June - 15 October (competitive training).
IV. Period: 16 October - 14 November (active recovery).

The coach during the jog-interval.

From experience I have learned that during the recovery jogging intervals it is well to leave the runner alone. Every remark made by the coach is an extra stress. The athlete is preparing himself, and because of this one should not disturb him. At that time I am always a certain distance away from the athlete and speak to him only if he wishes to ask me something. I constantly observe him carefully and take the pulse beat only from time to time. The remainder of our conversation takes place after the workout. The coach must keep especially inquisitive spectators far from the athlete, because they distract him.

Other things to think about in long-distance running.

The warmup. After the warmup it is customary to take a 20 minute rest. I think this, especially before a race, is too long. Before the race we put in a lively last five minutes. I believe that we are going the wrong way. We must experiment with the duration of the warmup and the length of the rest before the race. This best done before unimportant races.

Learning the sprint finish (kick). It seems that to a certain extent speed is an inborn factor, and yet by training it is possible to improve the ability to sprint. The kick is not so dependent on the basic speed of the runner as it is on his ability to accelerate at the end of the race. Professional literature says that in the sprint finish these muscle fibers must be used, which for the greatest part of the race for economical reasons, were not in use. To learn the sprint finish we use a tested method, e.g. 3 to 5 times 300m with 3 x 30m wind sprints (spurts) thrown into each run.

Warming-down (cooling off). Cooling off after the training or race takes about ten minutes of running and walking. I believe that we have avoided many muscle injuries with this cooling off.

Running technique. I am of the opinion that the shorter lively rhythm is better, that it consumes less energy, and that it is more easy to "turn on" acceleration. Nevertheless, one must find the best rhythm for each individual runner. Zatepek, for instance, in a 5000m race had a stride of 5'11" (1.80m). Popov in the marathon (he is 5' 3½" - 1.61m tall) had a stride of 5' 3" (1.60m).

Breathing. All my runners use the "two rhythm" e.g. they take in their breath in two strides, and let it out in the next two.

Weight training. Yugoslav long-distance runners have also begun with weight training, but have only three years of experience with it. We think, however, that it has not been bad. We believe in the correctness of this work, and even this belief is psychologically important. We make use of the weights beside the usual body building exercises. We started with 55 lbs. (25 kg) and have repeated 4 - 5 various exercises, until we repeated them 10 times, one after another. We repeat this three to four times in one evening. We have used this method nearly 200 workouts. After 10 repetitions we give ourselves 1 - 2 minutes to recover. Later after 3 months we increased the weight to 66 and 88 lbs (30 and 40 kg.) Today this is the main weight with which we practice. Only rarely with some exercises do we use 132 lbs (60 kg.). Except for the competitive season, we have been using weight-training all the year round, and only from time to time in the competitive season. The youths practiced with weights from 36 to 44 lbs (15 - 20 kg.).

In Yugoslavia working hours are mostly from 6:00a.m. to 2:00 p.m. or 7:00 a.m. to 3:00 p.m. Only the merchants have their work hours cut in two, from 8:00 a.m. to noon and again from 4:00 to 7:00 p.m. in the evening. 90% of the athletes work in the various professions. Because of these favorable working hours the Yugoslav long-distance runners have their day set out favorably for training as they always have the afternoon free. This is especially important in winter because of early sunset. In Yugoslavia in winter it is dark at 5:00 p.m.

The Track and Field clubs are scattered all over the country. The altitude of the various regions is on an average between 10 and 400m above sea-level. During the holidays in summer or winter one can train in the mountains in the northwest of the country. Here the height is 1000m above sea-level. The temperature on the Adriatic Coast in the winter is from 0-12° C and in the other parts it fluctuates from 18° to 32° F. In summer we have from 77° to 104° F in the shade on the coast and from 68° to 95° F inland.

Our grass is inferior to the English or Scandinavian grass because of our heat and dry climate. Therefore our long-distance runners have to look for better grass terrains in the city suburbs, and sometimes rather far away. In my home town, Zagreb, good grass is 6000m away from the dressing room, but it is worth while getting there. The marathon runners use the grass strips bordering the highways. Most of the training is done in linen (cloth) shoes with somewhat thick rubber soles.

To end, here are our records: 5000m, 13:58.8 Mugosa, Belgrade, 1956. 10,000m, 29:07.6, Cervan, Belgrade, 1962. Marathon, 2:20:26. Skrinjar, Tunis, 1960.

(The above article originally appeared in the No. 22 issue of "Die Lebre-der Leichtatletik" dated June 2, 1959. It was translated and systhensized by Mr. Lang and Mr. Rajko Miler, National Coach of long and triple jumpers in Yugoslavia.).

Cross Country in India

by K.O. Bosen
(Chief Athletics Coach, Indian Railways Sports Association, Madras, India).

The term cross-country running positively bears the trade mark of the British regime in India. This branch of athletic competition means different things in various part of the world. In many countries, cross-country running is primarily road racing. Certain parts of Europe indulge in racing through deep woods and hilly practice which is widely used for training. The original cross-country races were the hare and hound races introduced in the English public schools, which really were cross-country obstacle races over the toughest terrain possible.

In the early days, cross-country competitions in India were strictly organized races over measured obstical courses. These races formed a part of the physical training programs set up for the Armed forces of the country - Army, Police, Fire Service etc. - The English medium high schools all over the country enforced cross-country competitions which were actually road races that ranged from $1\frac{1}{2}$ to 4 or 5 miles on a country road within the vicinity of the school. Each school had its own distance and course and the competition formed part of the schools athletic program for the year. There was no organized training for the race as such. It was all taken in ones "stride" so to say. These races were run once a year at an appointed time during the track season, then entirely forgotton for the rest of the season.

Off season program

To-day, the emphasis in training, the world over, has brought home to our athletes the importance of training off the track. Our athletes use cross-country running as an off season conditioning program. They use a variety of courses that all come under the same heading - cross-country - but follow quite another trend - Fartlek. Training is done along the sea shore, up hill or a steep bridge, on the road, on the lawns of a park or golf links, but all follow the Fartlek pattern very closely.

Most of the top coaches in the country have made trips abroad with teams and have had the opportunity to discuss and study the training methods of foreign athletes and coaches. Many Indian athletes have been abroad and have returned home with a great desire to supplement their training with cross-country work during the morning session while the evening session is confined to track training. This type of "twice-a -day" training it appears has come to stay of late. Not so long ago athletes and coaches shrugged the idea away for fear of staleness.

Our athletes have learned to enjoy this morning cross-country-cum-calesthnic program. From the dash men down to the marathon runners, jumpers and throwers, each one has his daily dose. The degree of intensity and bulk of work put into this session varies with the event and the individual. None of these athletes train to become cross-country runners but the carry over value is good for general endurance of all events on the athletic program. Actually, cross-country running is indispensable to the development of middle and long distance runners throughout the world. Here in India the coaches make no effort to push the boys to work hard at it. The athletes have just taken to it quite naturally, and from practical experience they have found it a necessary part of their training to help to condition them both physically and mentally for the long track season ahead. In order to stay on top in their specific track events it has become evident there is no possible substitute for running - you just got to run and keep running those miles away.

For Sprinters?

Quite a few coaches and athletes insist that cross-country running is detrimental to sprinters in particular. They believe it takes too much out of them to be beneficial to the development of speed. While training to be a cross-country specialist and enter for regular competitions is one thing, the use of such training by sprinters I believe is a typical developer during the conditioning period and early season. Cross-country running spread over with calesthenic exercises, depending upon the individuals ability and condition, should form a must with every sprinters schedule. Naturally the sprinter will cover less training miles than a middle or long-distance runner. Besides, the intensity of training will also be different for the sprinter.

Milkha Singh, Makhan Singh, Silveira and Ferrao are but a few of our leading sprinters who apply this type of cross country training as part of their schedule. Milkha Singh is reported to have out run some of our top middle and long-distance men over a six mile cross-country run last season. His speed is still with him (1963) in spite of what the critics say. Only two weeks ago he produced a 21.5 200 meters around a bend and a 46.3 400 meters while he literally flew home with the baton in an easy 10.5 in the 4 x 100 meters relay. The use of mild cross-country training has positively helped Nicky Ferrao, our 100 meters representative for the Asian games at Jakarta. His previous best sprint was a mediocre 10.8 for the 100 meters. This season he has brought home a convincing 10.6 and followed it up with 10.7 against a head wind within four days of the first run. I have no doubt whatever about the value of cross-country training for a sprinter, leave alone the middle or long-distance runners.

Since we in India are not sold on the idea of cross-country competitions and have no particular season as such, the recommendations pointed out for distance runners are entirely based on personal views. As mentioned earlier, I am one who considers the use of cross-country as indispensable to the development of middle and distance runners throughout the world. The schedule outlined is during middle season for a 14 minute class 5000 - 10,000 meters runner.

Two sessions

Training is split into two sessions. The morning period consisting of cross-country training and calesthenics, and the evening hours alloted to repetition work on the track. This training plan is predicated on the idea that the athlete is one who trains the year round. Starting after the previous season ends, he begins a program based on the marathon runners long build up period. During this part of the year evening work is only light Fartlek and calesthenics. We call it the early season, a conditioning period lasting about five months. We have practically no competitions whatever during this period. Up North is the long dry summer and down South the humid monsoon climate. From about August through to the middle of November is a gradual transition period called the middle season. Competitions are few and on state level. Regular interval training on the track is done 5 days a week during the evening session with cross country training in the morning. Then follows the long competitive season from December through to February. The morning sessions are confined to light restful Fartlek and calesthenics while the evenings are spent on short but brisk work-outs interspread with trials and long easy work.

Middle season training - (one week) 5,000-10,000 meters

	Morning	Evening
1st day:-	6 to 8 miles over hills, road or across country at ½ effort - calesthenics 15-20 min.	1. 15-20 x 200m in 28-30sec. each. Jog 1½ -2 min. after each.

2nd day:-	50 to 60 minutes on the beach, over sand hills and on the shore at a steady pace - calesthenics 15-20 min.	2.	5-6 x 600m in 1:35 -1:37. Jog 200m after each, plus 3-4 x 1200 m in 3:15-3:20 each. Walk 5 min. after each.
3rd day:-	40 to 50 minutes cross country on grass lawns in park, Fartlek type. 15-20 min. calesthenics	3.	15-20 x 400m in 64-66 each. Jog 2-3 min. after each.
4th day:-	One hour jog across fields and grounds 15-20 min. calesthenics	4.	Accelerations. 8-10 x 100m. 4-5x200m. Walk and jog 200-300m after each.
5th day:-	6 to 8 miles over hills, road or across country at ½ effort - 15 - 20 min. calesthenics.	5.	Alternate 800 and 2000 m repetitions. 4-5x800m in 2:06-08. Jog 400m after each. 2-3 x 2000m in 5:30 - 34. Walk 5 min. after each 2000m.
6th day:-	50 to 60 min. on the beach over sand hills and on the shore at even pace - 15 - 20 min. calesthenics.	6.	Light work - Train as you feel.
7th day:-	Rest.	7.	Rest or time trial.

The performance of track and field the world over has indicated a great percentage of improvement in middle and distance events than ever before. Records keep tumbling with every meet. It would almost appear that we have only made a beginning; yet, I am quite aware of how far we are from achieving our real potential in this sphere of athletics called running. New training methods or new emphasis on certain details of training in running do occur from time to time and yet I feel such new methods as we have seen often have not kept pace with performance. I support the argument that this world wide improvement in performance of track, especially in middle and long-distance races, has resulted much more through greater intensity of work over more months of the year, and through more years of active interest at all age levels, rather than as a result of improved techniques and their efficient learning.

We have a tendency of assuming that as professional specialits in athletics we know a great deal about our sport and how best it is coached and developed. Yet a survey of compiled questionnaires along this line has always brought no satisfactory or factual answer. There is always little agreement among coaches, not merely in details but in basic ideas. The wide range of methods adopted by coaches the world over is very marked and changable. The true explanation of development for the future could lie in the adoption of even harder work methods over more training hours and an indifference towards ultimates in achievement of records. We need greater co-operation from the sports minded scientists, coaches and athletes, much more exactly and precisely than is now possible.

Trifles make perfection, and perfection is no trifle -'Michelangelo.'

Cross Country Running in Australia

by Al Lawrence

When speaking of cross-country running to an Australian, there is a very strong possibility that what the questioner means, if he is a foreigner, and what the Australian thinks he means, may be two different matters. To clarify this statement, let me say that to an Australian, the cross-country season is a time of the year when there is athletic competition separate and distinct from track running. During this period the athlete may, and usually does, run in road races, occasional track races before an international football game, and true cross-country running. The time of year when this program takes place is from the beginning of May (autumn in the Southern Hemisphere), and the season closes early September (spring in the Southern Hemisphere).

There is tremendous emphasis placed on cross-country running in Australian athletic circles. To a middle-distance and long-distance runner, the season is considered absolutely essential, and over the past five years cross-country running has gained wide acceptance as an off-season necessity for all track athletes. Even the majority of Australian women athletes undertake a rigorous winter training program of cross-country running.

The organization of the cross-country season in Australia is left primarily to each state. The competitive program carried out by the state of New South Wales is indicative of the Australian cross-country season in general. In early May the clubs (the backbone of Australian track) begin their harrier season. The races will vary from 2 miles to 4 miles and may be run on road or cross-country courses, depending on the location of the club. A series of interclub races will be initiated in late May, and in mid-June a New South Wales relay championship will be held. This race, a 4 x 5 mile road race, is open to every athletic club in the state and a club may enter as many teams as it desires. The New South Wales cross-country championship follows in mid-July. This race is over 10,000 meters with a teams race held in conjunction. A junior 5,000 meters championship (under 19 years) is held on the same day, with an under age 17 1-mile championship for sub-juniors. The cross-country championships are keenly contested and big fields enter all races. Normally about 150 starters contest the race.

Two weeks after the cross-country championship a 10 miles track championship is run. This race also has a teams race in conjunction with the individual title and is held on one of the horse race courses in Sydney. From the first two state championships a team of six is chosen to represent the state in the Australian cross-country championship over 10,000 meters in early August. The Australian championship is held in the capital city of each state by turn. After the Australian title the true road racing season begins. The middle of August sees the first state road running title conducted - a modified marathon of 15 miles with a teams race included. In early September or late August the final race of the year takes place. This is the state marathon championship and teams title. Every second year an Australian marathon championship is held with four runners from each state contesting the title. In some circumstances individuals from each state may be allowed to start in one of the Australian championships.

It can be seen, therefore, that the Australian cross-country season caters for every class and type of athlete. The champions have the state and Australian championships to aim for; the strong club runners have the teams races to aim for that are held in conjunction with the various championships; and the moderate runners can secure competition through the various club events. For track runners and shorter distance men who do not desire the competitive cross-country season, there are occasional appearances if desired in special events at international football games.

Training for cross-country should not be thought of as being too far removed from ordinary middle-distance training. There are, however, minor variations of this type of training. Australians in general work two or three days each week on the track during the cross-country season. This theory applies in reverse during the track season when most long distance and middle distance runners train two or three days each week on the cross-country.

I believe that there are three main aspects to be considered by any athlete when training for cross-country running:

A. The psychological approach that is used while preparing for the cross-country season.

B. The various changes of technique for different terrain.

C. Normal conditioning and training.

Without any of the three a runner will never realize his potential competitively during the season. A certain psychological approach is needed for cross-country running, and a certain attitude of mind is required. This attitude is difficult to define. Perhaps the best way to explain this is to simply say that unless a runner approaches the cross-country season with the thought in mind that he intends to concentrate solely on this season with the exclusion of all other considerations, he will surely fail to produce anything like his true potential. Cross-country running is definitely not a sport for half-desire athletes. The individual must go into the season and blot out any thought of the track season following. The theory that I put forward is that the runner must enter the season wanting to do well and not be concerned with what will occur several months hence. I have personally found, and most of the great distance runners that I have come in contact with during the past few years support me, that when I enter the cross-country season with the main objective a buildup for the coming track season, I invariably have my worst season. This does not mean that the buildup for the track season is not a very valid consideration. The buildup will naturally occur, however the thought of it should be thrust to the back of the mind while the job on hand is fully concentrated on.

Attitude. An athlete who enters the cross-country season with the thought of the approaching track season clouding his consciousness will not produce his best efforts. The great cross-country champions that I have associated with all agree that they pull down a type of curtain over their minds when they enter this season. Although one must always plan ahead, and this includes the season following - the essential thing in sport is "now." Sometimes by looking too far ahead, we miss fields to conquer that are right at our feet.

I have never known a great cross-country runner that was not a great track runner, but I have encountered many great track runners who could not make the grade when it came to cross-country running. Although these runners may rationalize as to the reason for their failure, in most cases it was simply a question of not applying themselves completely to the job on hand. These athletes candidly state that they hope and expect to run well in the cross-country, but their main consideration is to prepare themselves for the approaching track season. It appears logical to me that with this built-in "mental block" before they begin the cross-country season that it is no surprise that they fail to produce the results they desire.

One of the acquired skills of cross-country running is the ability to adapt a technique suitable to running over the various terrain that is encounted during a race. My former Australian coach emphasized the importance of following certain rules while running cross-country:

A. Never overstride in the early stages of a race.

B. Balance at all times is a most important consideration and must be consciously worked for.

C. Knowing the technique for running up and down hills was essential, however, once learned there was no need to work hard continually over hills.

D. What you do to your opponents before you arrive at a hill is vital strategy.

E. Training for cross-country does not vary much from the training of a 10,000 meter track runner except for small refinements.

The danger of overstriding is particularly prevalent among beginning cross-country runners, although many experienced runners are likely to make the same fatal mistake. The real difficulty appears to be in the fact that without specified measurements every 440 or 220 yards such as in track running, the inexperienced runner tends to run too fast in the early stages of a race. The fast pace generally results in the runner overstriding. Once committed to an overstride, what occurs when the runner is forced to cut his speed? His stride shortens, his rhythm is impaired, and his whole sense of balance is literally ruined. When this happens the runner cannot even rely on his knowledge of technique to save him. He becomes a "plodder." It then becomes sadly evident to the runner concerned that he must make drastic concessions to his whole running action - the inevitable result is that the runner cannot make the necessary adjustments, and he is defeated. There are many great champions of track who have failed to make it in cross-country because of this fault. I always make a point of concentrating on an understride during the first 300 years of any cross-country race, until I work into my normal racing rhythm. Once this rhythm is attained, correct balance naturally follows.

Balance is another essential requirement for the cross-country runner. The nature of the terrain in this sport demands an action that is quick to recover after any disturbance in the rhythm of a runner. Once again this demands, as well as technique adjustments, an attitude of mind. The problem of encountering a rugged part of a course, having to check stride slightly, change running technique, and recover back to normal racing stride tends to bother many runners. The short stride is a benefit here, also, for it is not so difficult to recover balance from this action. Take the case of the long-strider. He moves over the track and flat ground beautifully, but his long-flowing stride keeps him in the air much longer than the shorter, economical one. The long-strider hits a patch of muddy ground for example, he becomes unbalanced, and his rhythm is lost - usually with disastrous consequences. One can readily see that a sense of balance and the ability to quickly recover from breaks in rhythm are essentials in cross-country running. This will be acquired by conserving stride length and concentrating on balance during a race. A sense of balance comes through rhythm, and rhythm comes from running slowly at long distances and from much track running at medium pace. In other words it must be worked at on terrain and at a pace where it can be consciously worked on.

Learn the technique of running the hills and practice often and diligently. Once learned, however, do not overdo hill running. I have found through personal experience that consistent hill running in training through the competitive season tended to "flatten" me. Once the technique is learned for running the hills, there is no extra benefit (except for the change in terrain occasionally) to be derived from training consistently on hills. In fact there are indications - without too much documentation I must confess - that there is a certain saturation point in hill training, after which the runner begins to weaken.

Running down the hill is often a sadly neglected area of the overall technique, yet here many races are lost, and even experienced runners come to grief. The main danger is to lose control and come off the bottom of the hill too fast. The position is somewhat similiar to a car coming down a steep hill out of gear. Then, once again, we meet our old friend "overstriding." At this stage of the race it is absolutely essential to hold one's self together at all costs. The runner should develop an action whereby he can use his body as a brake to check his forward momentun if needed. By landing heel first on steep hills the athlete has a natural brake. If the runner needs to increase his speed going down hills of a slighter gradient he can do this quite easily by dropping his arms slightly and leaning forward. The weight of his own body will assist him then. At no other stage of a race, however, should the athlete be more aware of the necessity of holding himself together.

Sometimes lost in the desire to learn all there is about running the hills, both up and down, is one essential fact: much depends on how a runner arrives at a hill as to how successfully he will negotiate it. Therefore it is absolutely essential that a runner be well versed in all phases of cross-country running. This certainly does not mean that one area should be concentrated on at the neglect of others. Cross-country running entails everything from the start of the race to the finish, and no part should be minimized. The runner should always be fully aware that being proficient in one area of this many-phased sport - is not good enough to get the job done.

To my way of thinking there is not a great deal of difference in the training for cross-country and that of training for 10,000 meters on the track. However, cross-country running offers more of a challenge to the athlete. It may appear paradoxical, but even though an athlete should thrust the thought of the coming track season to the back of his mind during the cross-country season, he must never lose sight of the fact that this is the time to undergo a tremendous pre-season buildup - both physically and psychologically. A runner who knows he can finish a 15 mile training run (or further) will have no qualms thinking about a track race of up to 10,000 meters. This trend of thinking is exemplified by such athletes as Peter Snell (NZ) who ran a competitive marathon less than two months before he set the current world records for 800 meters, 880 yards, and 1 mile. Snell is also New Zealand cross-country champion.

Training for a sprinter during the cross-country season

This season is a valuable time for the sprinter to work on many aspects of his technique when there is very little pressure on him. Training during this season, at the same time, will give him many advantages over his sedentary opponent who sits out the winter months and talks of what he intends to do in the spring. The great advantages of cross-country running and training for the sprinter are: it puts running into the legs, it keeps a sprinter's legs loose and supple, it develops the heart and lungs, and it prevents fat - the enemy of every athlete - from accumulating around muscle.

At a recent lecture I heard Abilene Christian coach Oliver Jackson say that a sprinter who could not run a reasonable 440 in competition was a disgrace to track. I will project Coach Jackson's theory a little further and say that the sprinter who cannot build himself up to run a easy 5 miles in training during the cross-country season ought to take up another sport. In Australia we have many women who can easily run 8 or 10 miles; any male runner who cannot at least duplicate this feat should hang his head in shame.

A possible schedule for a sprinter who is not going to race during the cross-country season, but who wishes to pursue a full and vigorous program of training might undertake the following:

Monday: Weight-training - the program would depend on the particular characteristics (physical) of the individual concerned.

Tuesday: 12 x 220 at 30 secs. choose own recovery - may be alternated with 8 x 330 at 45 secs., or 8 x 440 at 62.5.

Wednesday: 10 x 110 at 13 secs. - 6 to 10 starts in full track suit.

Thursday: Weight-training.

Friday: 3 x 1 mile at 5.16 to 6 mins. - choose own recovery.

Saturday: rest.

Sunday: 5 to 10 miles very easy running on cross-country - the distance should be gradually built up.

All running should be done in flat soled shoes, and if possible on a grass track or measured length of parkland. The sprinter will find that a program such as the one outlined above will build in tremendous strength, yet at the same time, allow him to eliminate style faults while he trains. The sprinter of today is a more complete athlete than his contemporary of several years ago, and having natural speed is not the only requirement for championship running. He must work to develop all his talents if he wishes to be in the vanguard of competition, in these days of superlative performance in high-powered track.

Training for cross-country racing.

I have already stated that I believe that there is very little difference in the type of training needed for the track distance runner and the cross-country runner. The main difference, to my way of thinking, is the attitude of mind. One technical aspect works for the cross-country runner much more than his track brother, however. The cooler weather during the fall and winter allows him to log a bigger volume (mileage) of training. This is a good time to get running into the legs and build up for the coming track season. Once more it must be emphasized through that once a runner has committed himself to a cross-country season - he should obliterate all thoughts of other running, except the season on hand.

For the actual preparation I advocate ten days training and one day rest. Two days each week should be set aside to train on varied terrain at a speed where the runner can concentrate on cross-country technique. The other days should be devoted to normal middle-distance training except for one day which is set aside for the runner to strive for long distance. A typical 10 day program might be as follows:

1st day: 10-12 x 800 at 2.20-2.30 -440-880 recovery

2nd day: 20x 300 at 41-43 secs - 220-440 recovery

3rd day: 10-12 miles run - concentrate on form and technique on hills.

4th day: 2-30 x 440 at 75-80. 110-220 recovery jog.

5th day: 6-10 x 1 mile at 4.50-5.20. 440-880 recovery jog.

6th day: 10 miles easy running over cross-country.

7th day: 15 x 220 at 30-32 secs. - 440 recovery jog.

8th day: 15-20 miles easy running.

9th day: 440 -880 - 1320 - 1 mile - 1 mile - 1320, - 880-440 (all at 75 sec. per. 440 - all with 440 recovery jog.).

10th day: 6 x 880 at 2-5 to 2-12. - 880 recovery jog.

11th day: rest.

The above represents a generalized training schedule for a top-class runner at 10,000 meters cross-country.

To my way of thinking, there will be no revolutionary training trends in cross-country or running in general for the next few years. If one traces the developments of distance training through the past 50 years, he will notice that except for one big step forward, as far as training methods go, there have only been a series of refinements of existing methods. The big "breakthrough" came with the advent of the zatopek theory of distance running training. Here, for the first time, definately proven principles known to scientists were applied to physical aspects of training.

Zatopek. Once sport physiologists had established that the heart - the driving force in distance running -could be actually trained and developed when it was worked, allowed to recover slightly, and then worked again, the way was open for a pioneer like zatopek to evolve a new concept of distance training. Zatopek reasoned that by running a fast 440 followed by a slow 220, training could be developed to work in harmony with scientific knowledge. Zatopek made a tremendous impact on the distance running scene and had a good lead on the rest of the world for five years. Will anybody ever forget his three gold medals - 5000 meters, 10,000 meters, and marathon - in the Helsinki Olympics? Yet, like many great discoveries, Zatopek's theory abounds with simplicity. A fast 440 (the heart is worked), a jogging 220 (the heart recovers), then the cycle is repeated. Could anything be more simple?

If one takes careful note of all the great training methods since that time they will notice that this is the underlying theory throughout. Other athletes, of course, have improved on Zatopek's training ideas with subtle variations of the work-recover-work theory. Even the training done by the fabulous New Zealanders is saturated with Zatopek's ideas. In the case of the New Zealanders, however, an added refinement is the introduction of marathon training with their fast and slow running. It is this long running plus the fast and slow running that gives this small nation the edge on the rest of the world in this area of track.

In conclusion I would say that there will be no major drop in world distance times in the next five years, although I would qualify this statement by saying that times will be reduced. It would appear that a new breed of athlete is beginning to make his presence felt in distance running today. This is the young "super-athlete" who is physically much superior to his athletic contemporary of 10 years ago. It is to these runners that I look to for new records. At this time it is hard to imagine another scientific "breakthrough" as revolutionary as Zatopek's for several years. I am convinced, however, that the champions of tomorrow must work hand-in-hand with scientific knowledge, and the record-breakers will be developed through the medium of sport's laboratories.

(Al Lawrence placed third in the 1956 Olympic 10,000 meters and enjoyed a successful four years at the University of Houston).

How I Train Middle Distance Runners

by Bertl Sumser (West Germany)

I should like at the very beginning to emphasize that all my comments, all my statements concerning training days, times, and recovery rests, above all each sort of training load, refer to runner of the top class who already have behind them several years of training (5 to 6 to 7 years) and who have, or are aiming at this year, 800 meter times less than 1:50.0 and 1500 meter times less than 3:45. The training loads of the younger, developing runners are, to be sure, the same in methods of training, but differ in time, in the number of runs and the arrangement of the recoveries and must, in particular, make allowance for the individual peculiarity and the stage of development. Just as in the development of young runners, patience is everything! Unfortunately, however, the ambition of the trainer is frequently greater than that of his protégé!

At the start of my comments I should like to stress an essential point: "The form and the kind of training shape the organ, the muscular system - the whole organism!"

This physiological knowledge is and must be the guide and we can't help but consider first of all the physiological processes which take place during a run. In this connection I shall point out very shortly only the most salient features.

On the whole there are two points of view to which it refers: 1. How great is the capacity to take in oxygen? 2. How high is the oxygen debt which the runner is able to incur?

Both of these factors, oxygen intake capacity and oxygen debt are the chief criteria, the most far reaching, which determine and also limit the load.

Tests have yielded the following results: For a race in about 1:50 an 800 meter runner requires about 27 liters of oxygen. During the run he himself can take in, however, only 9 to 10 liters. Therefore, he runs his race with an oxygen debt of 18 liters, i.e. 1/3 oxygen intake in contrast to 2/3 oxygen debt.

For his run in about 3:45 to 3:43 the 1500 meter runner requires about 40 liters of oxygen. However, his intake capacity is only about 18 liters. In take and need almost balance. However, the debt still predominates and becomes even more of a factor with faster times.

We now know that the heart and circulation are responsible for the ability to take in oxygen; the very complicated chemical reactions in the muscle are most largely responsible for the oxygen debt. The special reaction, which enters into the working muscle, is the occurrence of acids, especially of lactic acid. This increase of lactic acid is all the stronger the lesser the oxygen that is available. Therefore, through proper training methods we must strive to supply more oxygen to the working muscle and, in addition, to diminish the effectiveness of the lactic acid. The former is a "transportation problem" (heart/circulation training); the latter an increase of the so-called alkali reserve to neutralize the acid or an accustoming of the system to the high oxygen debt. From this, therefore, we see how one factor overlaps another, how achievement is rendered by the system as a whole.

That goes to show us that the training of middle distance men must be organized versatily in order to do justice to all physiological requirements and in order to attain an optimum adaptation of heart and circulation and overall muscular structure.

Now let us turn to those methods of training which are available to us:

1. Endurance Running

Under this we understnad a rhythmic easy run in the forest, over a cross-country course, uphill and downhill, over long distances of an hour or more duration. During the months from November to March this easy long endurance running is a wonderful and restful means of training which unfortunately is used by us all too infrequently during this time of year. (Perhaps because it is too simple?) Our top level courses for middle distance runners have begun for years now on Friday afternoon with such a run for $1\frac{1}{2}$ hours in the forest and open country.

2. "Speed Play" (Fartlek)

Under this we understand a continuous running and jogging over varying distances in varying time, the nature adapted to the cross-country course. At first the distances are long, the time easy. From November to the end of December: 2000-3000-3000-2000 meters with recovery jogs, time for 1000 meters about 4 minutes. From January to March the distances become shorter, the speed increases; 1000-1600-2000-1600-1200-1000 meters, likewise with recovery jogs, speed for 1000 meters gradually reaching 3 minutes.

With time and with good surface conditions even light sprints can be inserted repeatedly (longer recoveries necessary). The inventiveness of the runner (with regard to the particular cross-country course) and the knowledge of the results which he wants to attain are, in the final analysis, for the determined personal organization of the speed play! It should never, however, result in an exhausting run. Good health and pleasure must be realized from such a run.

The modus operandi of both: adaptation of heart and circulation, regulation of the breathing process, improvement of the capillary transfer process.

3. Interval Endurance Run

Under this we understand a frequent repetition of distances (in my opinion not to exceed 300 meters) at the same relatively slow speed and same recovery (rewarding recoveries!). The intensity of the stimulation is not very high. However, through frequent repetition, and with it we come to the modus operandi, we attain an optimum adaptation of heart and circulation with time.

Examples: November and December: 25 to 30 x 100 meters, time 17.5 to 16.0, recovery jog: 50 to 60 seconds; or: 20 to 25 x 200 meters, time 36.0 to 34.0, recovery: 50 to 60 seconds. The times gradually decrease and can reach 15.0 to 14.5 on the 100 meter basis, 32.0 to 30.0 on the 200 meter basis. In the final analysis the pulse rate is the deciding factor. For almost all of our runners it varies between 180 and 120.

4. Repetition Runs (Speed Runs)

Here we distinguish between two forms of speed runs:

a) A Frequent repetition of high intensity stimulation with recoveries which take into account the preceding stimulation, but do not represent a complete recovery (interval speed runs).

Examples: 8 x 200 meters, time 27.0, with 2 minute recovery jog, gradually attaining: 8 x 200 meters, time 26.0, with 2 minute recovery jog, continuing with: 8 x 200 meters, time 26.0, with 90 to 60 second recovery jog, in order to have as the final goal: 6 x 200 meters, time 26.0 to 24.5, with 60 second recovery jog. The goal must be: during the course of time to spawn ever shorter recoveries for given high loads.

In order to reach this goal we begin January/February on the 400, 500, and 600 meter basis (see table) and change as of March to the 300,

200, and 100 meter basis, thus from slower to faster times although, of course, the 400 and 500 meter distances are interspersed during the succeeding months (fewer runs, but increased speed).

b) Runs of greater, yes at times greatest, intensity and long recoveries up to almost complete recovery:

For example, for the 800 meter runner on a training day in June: 300 meters in 34.5 to 35.0, with 6 to 8 minute recovery; 500 meters in 64.5 to 65.0, with 10 to 12 minute recovery; 600 meters in 81.0 to 83.0; or a 1200 meter run in 3:00 to 2:58. For the 1500 meter runner on a training day in June: 500 meters in 68.0 to 69.0, with a recovery of 6 to 8 minutes; 600 meters in 84.0 to 85.0, with a recovery of 10 to 12 minutes; 800 meters in 1:55 to 1:56; or a 2000 meter run in 5:30 to 5:35.

The modus operandi: adaptation of muscle metabolism, entrance of a high oxygen debt, increase of the alkali reserve and of energy, adaptation to the products of a high hyperacidity.

5. Sprint Runs

At this point we must touch upon the distinction between sprint runs, which serve the advancement of pure speed (high stimulation, fast speed, long recovery periods) and sprint runs which contribute to the capacity to maintain speed over a distance (speed endurance), therefore the occurrence of muscle metabolism and thereby actually falling within the scope of speed training (high stimulation, fast speed, short recoveries). Not only the one, but also the other must be.

Examples (assumed for the month of June): a) 10 x 100 meters (flying start) in 11.0 to 10.8 with a recovery of a 3 to 4 minute walk (pure speed training); b) 10 x 50 meters at 7/8 speed with 50 to 60 meter recovery jogs (muscle metabolism work) - increase of the alkali reserve, appearance of a high oxygen debt).

The latter is probably the optimum form of speed training. I have observed Halberg and Snell in this form of training during their stay in Leverkusen. They ran 15 x 40 meter dashes with 60 meter recovery jogs (therefore over a total distance of 1200 meters), and in regard to their effort one can recognize the high efficiency which this training has. Incidentally, I noticed that Halberg and also the marathon runner occasionally carried out this training over 3 miles (50 yard dashes - 60 yard jogs)!

6. Special Conditioning

It is imperative during the winter months and has as its goal: training of the entire muscular system for indefatigability through small and gradually medium loads over long durations (frequently repeated!). This training must be intensively organized, and must be real training! By all means it is good policy to pursue this conditioning training once a week during the summer months, in easy form of course.

In conclusion of the above, the athlete must know the special modus operandi of the method of training; he must know why today he carries out this, tomorrow that, program in order that he can economically and even more independently organize his training.

The Use of the Training Method During the Course of the Year and its Difficult Points.

In general it can be said that the training road leads over endurance runs, speed play, interval endurance runs and the special conditioning training to speed runs! From quantity to quality! One aspect must be thoroughly understood: as the interval endurance run and endurance run are the optimum forms of the adaptation of heart and circulation for the long distance runner, so the speed run is the most efficient and most condition producing means of training for the middle distance runner, here in particular for the 800 meter runner. That in no way excludes the interval endurance run as an essential means of training during the competitive season. Indeed, it is especially indispensable for the 1500 meter runner. However, here the speed run also gives condition.

Now before I give a general view of training during the special periods of the year, I should like to clarify the goals, especially in regard to the importance of speed training.

Proof of Achievement.

An 800 meter runner, who wishes to run under 1:50, must be able to execute the following training on a day (end of June to the beginning of July; a long warmup of 30 minutes at the start and a long jogging, decelerating while jogging, of 20 minutes at the end are assumed in each case):
6 x 200 meters in 25 to 24 seconds with 60 to 90 second recovery jog; or:
5 x 300 meters in 37 to 38 seconds with 90 to 120 second recovery jog: or:
200m in 25 with 200m recovery; 300m in 38 with 300m recovery; 400m in 54 with 400m recovery; 300m in 38 with 200m recovery; and 200m in 24.
or: 1200 meters in or better than 3:00.

A 1500 meter runner who wishes to run under 3:45 must be capable of running (end of June to the beginning of July): 10 x 300 meters in 40 seconds with a 60 second recovery jog; or: 300m in 43 with 200m recovery; 400m in 58 with 300m recovery; 500m in 73 with 400m recovery; 600m in 90 with 400m recovery; 300m in 43 with 200m recovery; and 200m in 25.
or: 4 x 800 meters in 2:00 with 400 meter recovery jog; or : 2000 meters in 5:30 or better.

Training of the 800 Meter Runner.

Now, however, we shall examine the development of the training and the use of the training method during the course of the year. First for the 800 meter runner, whereby we take 1:50 as a basis.

November, 4 days of training per week

1 day: 12 to 15 kilometer endurance run;

1 day: ½ interval endurance run plus ½ conditioning work;

1 day: ½ endurance run of 6 to 8 kilometers, plus ½ conditioning work;

1 day: interval endurance run. (Interval endurance run alternated with the 100- and 200- meter distances; therefore: 20 x 100 meters, time in 17.0 seconds, recovery jog of 50 seconds; or: 15 x 200 meters, time in 36.0 seconds, recovery jog of 60 seconds)

December, 5 days of training per week

1 day: speed play over 12 to 15 kilometers;

1 day: ½ interval endurance run, 20 x 100 meters in 17.0 seconds, plus ½ conditioning work;

1 day: 10 to 12 kilometer endurance run;

1 day: ½ interval endurance run, 15 x 200 meters in 36.0 seconds, plus ½ conditioning work;

1 day: 10 to 12 kilometer endurance work. (In speed play distances of 2000, 3000, 3000, 2000 meters, which are run in about 7:30, 11:00, 11:00, and once again 7:30, are inserted.)

The months of November and December therefore serve as the foundation. They provide the basis of the easy, long training and the interval endurance run. The conditioning work in these two months is characterized by: versatility, ease, form of play and consists of: gymnastics, partner exercizes, medicine ball, wall bars, spring work, light weights (20-25 kilograms), games.

January and February, 5 days of training per week

1 day: 10 to 12 kilometers of speed play (1000, 15000, 2000, 1000 meters);

1 day: ½ interval endurance run, 20 x 100 meters in 16.0 seconds, plus ½ conditioning work;

1 day: speed runs on 400-, 500-, or 600 meter basis;

1 day: ½ interval endurance work, 15 x 200 meters in 34.0 seconds, plus ½ conditioning work;

1 day: speed runs (mixed distances, i.e. 200, 300, 400, 500, 300, 200 meters).

To be observed: with speed play the distances are shortened, the speed raised a bit (1000 meters, 3:10 to 3:20; 2000 meters, 6:40). The time for the interval endurance run is likewise lowered a little, with the recoveries remaining the same.

Speed training is taken up though only at the distances of 400, 500 and 600 meters (see especially Table 1).

The conditioning work is to be carried out with the aim of continually developing the entire muscular system.

March, 6 training days per week

1 day: 8 to 10 kilometer endurance run to recovery;

1 day: ½ dashes, 10 x 60 meters, plus ½ conditioning work;

1 day: speed runs on a 500 or 600 meter basis;

1 day: ½ interval endurance run, 15 x 200 meters in 33.0 seconds, plus ½ conditioning work;

1 day: speed runs on a 200 or 300 meter basis;

1 day: speed runs, mixed distances.

To be observed: of the six days of training three serve as speed training, whereby on one day the 500 or 600 meter basis is selected, on another day the 200 or 300 meter basis has the priority, and on the third day the mixed distances are in effect as, for example, 200, 300, 400, 300, 300, 200 meters (the time is taken from Table 1), or: 3 x 1000 meters in 2:50, 2:40, 2:50 with 600 meter recovery jog or 2 x 1200 meters in 3:15 to 3:10 with 800 meter recovery jog.

The sprint work is resumed. It serves to promote speed, requiring therefore greater recovery periods. It begins on the 60 meter basis and gradually switches over to 70 to 80 meters.

April, 6 training days per week

1 day: 6 to 8 kilometer endurance run as a restful run;

1 day: speed runs: sprints over 10 to 12 x 40 to 50 meters, 3/4 speed with 50 meter recovery jogs;

1 day: speed runs on a 300 or 400 meter basis;

1 day: interval endurance run, 15 x 200 meters, time: 32.0 seconds, recovery 60 seconds;

1 day: speed runs on a 100, 200 or 300 meter basis;

1 day: speed runs: either mixed distances, or 2 x 1000 meters in 2:35, or 3 x 800 meters in 2:05 to 2:02, or 1 x 1200 meters in 3:05 to 3:10.

Before I now carry the training schedule a step further, as well as one can in general, I must emphasize the following:

1. A training schedule or a training plan is better than nothing at all.

2. Such a plan should never, however, to considered as a mandate! It should only indicate the general direction!

3. All statements about times, recoveries, number of runs are likewise only guides! The load and dosage have to be arranged entirely according to the condition of the runner, his training state, weather, and track condition. The load is never allowed to go so far that the well-being of the runner is strongly disturbed! The load on the next training day must be arranged largely in accordance with the state of recovery following the

effort of the preceeding day!

4. If complete recovery and training enthusiasm has still not occurred, so it becomes only jogging or complete rest.

5. In each case the training program is established with the athlete before each training, whereby the trainer has to take into consideration all factors. The extent of the training determines itself however!

May The first races begin. They show the trainer and athlete how far the achievement level has progressed, where it is still lacking, and toward what direction the training must be geared. However, it is preferable to allow the runner to run the distances "all out" in training at the end of April and the beginning of May (time 1:53, 1:54 with 400 meter intermediate time, 56.0; 500 meters, 70.0 to 71.0; 600 meters, 84.0 to 85.0) and not wait for the first race. Here he runs unencumbered and can construct for himself an exact picture of reactions during and following the race which yields the most essential indices for the designing of further training.

You see therefore that it is very difficult now to form a schedule. if I nevertheless do, I realize that it is incomplete. It can only be general instruction.

May, 5 training days per week

1 day: sprints: 10-12 x 100 meters with running start as speed training;

1 day: speed runs on a 200 meter basis:

1 day: interval endurance runs 10 x 200 meters, time 32.0 seconds, recovery: 60 seconds;

1 day: speed runs on a 300 meter basis or 10 to 12 x 50 meters, 7/8 speed, with 60 meter recovery jogs;

1 day; restful long endurance run as a recovery run.

Speed, speed endurance, and speed consistency are in the foreground. Days with easy, long, and restful endurance training are inserted. This same training is also continued during the months of June and July.

Especially during these months it depends upon the knowledge and the instinct of the trainer to sense the correct dosage in the load; however, unfortunately here one can begin to notice a basic error. From November on the athlete has devoted himself to a systematic and methodical training cycle, the goal constantly before his eyes of bringing the greatest achievement, of being able to bring about the desired success. Yet scarcely has the first race occurred than he is thinking only of the next race, is training for it, or is even taking it easy in training in order then to be in the race, and already his thoughts are again passing on to the next race. The exhausting trips come up, the training cycle is interrupted! The goal must be here: the emphasis is on the fashioning of top performers through their participation in competitive running and on the adjustment of the training cycle with this in mind. In exchange for few races, however, run good races! Only in this manner can he achieve the desired success, which in turn justifies the preceding heavy training program.

During the main months, end of June, July, and August, the proper scheduling of training and starts is of paramount importance.

Only the intelligent athlete, who can impose limitations upon himself, will have the best results!

Now we shall turn to the long middle distance, the 1500 meters.

Training of the 1500 Meter Runner

If we were to examine the achievements of the great middle distance runners we would find out that a very good 1500 meter man achieves an equivalent good performance over 800 meters sooner than vice versa. Naturally there are exceptions: Paul Schmidt could run 3:42.5, Roger Moens ran the mile under 4 minutes and Stephan Lewandowski ran 3:41.1 and 1:46.5.

When we look into the training of the "long" middle distance runner, the word "long" is self-explanatory.

At the outset I emphasized that oxygen debt and oxygen intake are almost balanced for the long middle distance runner and this is the essential point which is to be taken into account in the method of training.

Wherein now lie the real differences and features?

1. The proper endurance run is carried out over longer duration: up to 1½ hours.

2. It is exactly the same with speed play. It can go up to 1½ hours, although at the beginning of the training period longer distances are repeatedly inserted. As the distance is shortened, the pace is increased and there are more frequent repetitions.

3. The interval endurance run appears increasingly in the program. The ratio to the speed running is 1:1 during the months January through April i.e. two days interval endurance running and two days speed running. In the interval endurance run the number of repetitions is increased. (30 x 100, 25 x 200, 20 x 300)

4. Regarding speed running I am of the opinion that, in the last analysis, only the speed running training gives condition, is also advantageous to you, and should be given preference from the beginning of May.

We shall now stick to speed running. While the stimulations are higher and more intensive for the 800 meter run, they are not as high as for the 1500 meter run. However, they do extend over a longer duration. In any case, I have had the best experiences with runs over 600 meters, 800 meters, 1000 meters several times and the mixed distances of 300, 400, 500, 600, 300, 300, 200 meters, gradually reaching racing time. In my opinion it is here that the best adaptation of the entire organism is executed; however, here the great and intensive stimulation must come unconditionally, occasionally over 15 to 20 x 50 meters at 7/8 speed with quite short recovery jogs. Therefore, high stimulation over a short time, short recovery jogs and frequent repetition! Of course that hurts and requires a great strain and self-conquest; however, it must be! Such a strenuous day is followed by a calm, restful, restrained one. Out of this combination must now be found the correct dosage.

We want runners with fighting spirit! These are the runners who succeed in mobilizing their last strength in the final race! Fighting spirit springs out of the training spirit! And we want trainers who do not allow the training load to be forced down the throat of the athlete, who do not succumb to every fad which is enjoying great popularity, and who wish to strive for good will. The knowledge of the thing is a prerequisite. The development during the formative years must take place with patience, foresight, and care; however, during the final phases of the development of the runner large loads must occasionally be inserted. We can achieve more than we think and believe!

In as much as the development over the entire year bears such a marked resemblance to that of the 800 meter runner, I will not repeat it, but only present a 14 day program (preparation for the German Championships):

July 14-15. Regional championships, heats and finals at 1500 meters, possibly even 3 x 1000 meter heats and finals.

Monday, July 16, 1 hour easy running and, in addition, 2 x 2000 meters in the slow speed of about 6:00;

Tuesday, July 17, interval endurance run, 20 x 200 meters, time in 32 seconds, recovery 60 seconds;

Wednesday, July 18, 30 minutes of jogging (accelerating while jogging), 12 to 15 x 60 meters, 7/8 speed, with 60 meter recovery jog (about 20 seconds), 20 minutes of jogging (decelerating while jogging) - relax!!!

Thursday, July 19, 5 x 600 meters, time 86 to 87 seconds with 400 meter recovery jog (about 4 minutes);

Friday, July 20, one hour of easy running;

Saturday, July 21, 4 x 800 meters, 2:00 to 2:02 with 5 to 6 minute recovery jog;

Sunday, July 22, forest: one hour of restful easy running;

Monday, July 23, 10 x 300 meters, time 40 seconds, recovery 60 seconds;

Tuesday, July 24, 1200 meters, time 3:00 to 2:58;

Wednesday, July 25, interval endurance run, 15 x 200 meters, time 33.0 to 34.0, recovery 60 seconds;

Thursday, July 26, 1/2 hour of easy jogging;

Friday, July 27, travel time and 1/2 hour of jogging in the evening;

Saturday, July 28, morning: 1/2 hour of jogging, afternoon: 1500 meter heat;

Sunday, July 29, final.

No races occur during the interim. The trials serve entirely as the preparation and in dosage and load conform completely to the condition and well-being of the individuals. Here, however, a certain rhythm must be found in the load in order that the athlete "run with desire" in the heats!

As far as was possible in the limited time that was my conception of the training of the middle distance runner. Immense still is the number of influences which are not exclusively of an organic, bodily nature and yet, in the final analysis, contribute to great performances.

"Subjective emotional results as frames of mind of enjoyment or non enjoyment, determination and inner drive, self-conquest, inertia, temperament are several of the fundamental factors. The will-power to achieve determines how far the organ power can be driven." (Thörner)

Without this will to achieve there is no achievement!

(The above is a synthesis of an article entitled, "Wie ich Mittelstreckler trainiere," by Bertl Sumser, which was orginally published in the No. 8 issue of Die Lehre der Leichtathletik dated February 20, 1962. It was translated from German by Glenn B. Hoidale, and is reprinted by permission of editor Toni Nett.)

Table 1 Speed Work for the 800 meter Runner (Achievement; 1:50.0)

	January	February	March	April	May	June	July
50/60m			8-10 x 50;$\frac{3}{4}$S	8-10 x 60; $\frac{3}{4}$S	8-10 x 50;$\frac{7}{8}$S	12-15 x 50;$\frac{7}{8}$S	12-15 x 60;$\frac{7}{8}$S
100m			10-12 x 13.0	10-12 x 12.5	10-12 x 12.0	10-12 x 11.5	10 x 11.0
200m		10 x 27.0	10 x 26.5	8 x 26.0	8 x 25.5	6 x 25.0	6 x 24.5-24.0
300m		10 x 42.0	10 x 41.0	8 x 40.0	8 x 39.0	6 x 38.0	5 x 37.0
400m	8 x 66.0	8 x 64.0	8 x 62.0	6 x 60.0	5 x 59.0	4 x 57.0-58.0	4 x 56.0-55.0
500m	6 x 80.0	6 x 77.0	5 x 74.0	5 x 73.0-72.0	4 x 70.0	3-4 x 69.0	3 x 68.0
600m	5 x 100.0	5 x 96.0-94.0	5 x 90.0	4 x 88.0	4 x 86.0	3 x 85.0	2 x 83.0
1200m			3:12-3:10	3:08	3:04	3:00	2:58

In addition mixed distances: 200-300-400-300-200 or: 300-400-500. $\frac{3}{4}$S and $\frac{7}{8}$S = $\frac{3}{4}$ and $\frac{7}{8}$ speed.

Table 2 Speed Work for the 1500 meter Runner (Achievement; 3:45.0)

	January	February	March	April	May	June	July
50/60m			10-15 x 50;$\frac{3}{4}$S	10-15 x 60;$\frac{3}{4}$S	10-15 x 50;$\frac{7}{8}$S	10-15 x 60;$\frac{7}{8}$S	10-15 x 60;$\frac{7}{8}$S
200m			15 x 28.0	15 x 27.5	12 x 27.0	12 x 26.5	
300m	12-15 x 47.0	12-15 x 45.0	12 x 43.0	12 x 42.0	10 x 41.0	10 x 40.0	10 x 40.0
400m	10 x 66.0	10 x 64.0	10 x 62.0	8-10 x 60.0	6 x 58.0	6 x 57.0	5 x 56.0
500m	8 x 82.0	8 x 80.0	6-8 x 78.0	6 x 75.0	6 x 73.0	6 x 70.0	
600m	6-8 x 100.0	6-8 x 96.0	6 x 93.0	6 x 90.0	5 x 88.0	5 x 87.0-86.0	8 x 86.0
800m	5-6-8 x 2:25	5 x 2:20	5 x 2:15	5 x 2:10	4 x 2:05	4 x 2:02	4 x 2:00
1000m	5-8 x 3:05-3:10	4 x 2:50	3-4 x 2:45	3 x 2:40	3 x 2:35	3 x 2:32	3 x 2:30
2000m		5:50	5:45	5:40	5:35	5:30	5:30

In addition mixed distances: 300-400-600-400-300-200-100 or: 300-600-600-600-300-200-100. $\frac{3}{4}$S and $\frac{7}{8}$S = $\frac{3}{4}$ and $\frac{7}{8}$ speed.

C.C. Training for Middle Distance Runners

by Chicks Hensley
President, New South Wales Coaches Association,
Matraville, Australia

For an athlete to be successful in any section of track and field athletics he must have both speed and strength.

In my opinion cross-country training is of great assistance in the development of the strength that is required to help an athlete maintain a high rate of his speed for any event.

Training for a considerable period over hilly courses helps to develop the muscles, heart, lungs, in fact every part of the body including the mental approach to an event, because running over steep grades requires a considerable amount of determination.

In recent years men like John Landy, Herb Elliott and Peter Snell have shown what can be done by athletes who are prepared to cover long distances over hilly courses.

The strength that they have shown in their races has been outstanding. To be a world champion today an athlete must have a considerable amount of natural speed as well as strength. Let us take Peter Snell as an example. Peter is reported to run the 220 yards in 22 seconds and in the 880 yards, runs at an average of approximately 26.25 seconds for each of his 220 yards. This is almost 84% of his top 220 yards speed. In the mile he averages approximately 29.25 seconds for each of his 220 yards or about 75% of his top speed. While Landy and Elliott both had at least as much developed strength as Snell they were not as fast over the sprint course. An athlete who had much more speed than these three great athletes was Tom Courtney, former world 880 yards record holder. Tom Courtney with a 21 seconds 220 yards to his credit could only maintain about 79% of that speed for the 880 yards and in running the mile in 4:07 he was only able to maintain about 68% of his top speed.

So in the future an athlete with the speed of Courtney and the developed strength of Snell could run 1 min. 40 secs. for the 880 yards and 3 mins. 44 secs. for the mile. This example is typical of what will be needed by the world champion of the future, in all track and field events.

During the track and field season there is very little time to develop this strength and so the usual practice is for the athlete to use the winter season for this purpose. It should be done gradually and over a period of years, starting from early age. Some of our 15 year old boys in Australia regularly run distances of up to 15 miles as part of their middle distance training.

For the sprinter and the very young middle distance athlete who has done very little cross-country training, I suggest that he commence with slow daily runs over easy C.C. courses of about three miles and increase the distance and the toughness of the course as they become used to this type of winter training. The distance could be increased by up to one mile per day per month, but this will vary with the individual and it is for his coach to decide as to how much he can do. A common mistake is to try and increase the distance too quickly or at too fast a pace.

The 5,000 meters and 10,000 meters athletes should train up to 10 miles a day with one long run per week of about 20 miles. As they will be racing on occasions during the winter they will have to ease this training down a few days before the race.

There are three variations in C.C. training that I advise. (1) Running very fast uphill and easing on the down hill and flat sections. (2) Continuous running at even pace both up and down hill. (3) Running downhill very fast and easing on the uphill and flat sections. This helps to develop the muscles in a different way each day and allows them plenty of time for recovery.

Use No. 1 method Monday and Thursday. No. 2 method Tuesday and Friday. No. 3 method Wednesday and Saturday. Long easy run on Sunday.

This method of training helps an athlete develop his hill running technique which is so important in the saving of energy and is usually the deciding factor in the result of a cross country race.

For running up steep grades an athlete should shorten his stride and lift his knees higher than usual, similar to running up stairs. To do this it is necessary to use the sprinters arm action as an aid to the higher knee lift.

Down hill running requires no knee lift as it is necessary to keep as close to the ground as possible to avoid the jolting that occurs when a normal stride is used. This is similar to running down stairs, the main action is from the knees down with very little arm action. Thus up hill running uses and develops the arms and thigh muscles, while in down hill running these are rested to some extent and the work is done by the lower part of the leg that has not been used to its fullest capacity on the up hill run.

There are two places where a normal strider feels the strain of hill running and where he is always inclined to ease the pace. They are on the top of the grade and on the completion of the down hill run. These are the places where the athlete who has developed his hill running technique should apply the pressure. This technique is varied according to the grade of the hill, the steeper the grade, the shorter the stride and the higher the knee lift.

At the present time Dave Power of Australia is typical of the world-class distance athletes. He has a speed of 23 seconds for the 220 yards and maintains approximately 68% of his speed to run 13 minutes 30 seconds for the 3 miles. He covers the six miles at 64% of his top speed to record 28 minutes. In the future when athletes with a speed of 22 seconds for the 220 yards develop their strength as he has done, then they will record 12 minutes 57 seconds for the three miles and 27 minutes 10 seconds for the six miles.

So the trend of the future will be more speed and more strength.

Harrier Running in New Zealand

by Jim Bellwood
Editor of the New Zealand Amateur Athletic Coaches' Association Monthly Bulletin, and Honorary Advisor to the N.Z.A.A. Coaches' Association.

Nature has blessed New Zealand with a temperate climate, an undulating mountainous terrain, and a lush green carpet of pasture, and bush which is liberally bounded by rivers, streams, lakes and sea shore. These natural assets are significant. They provide the variety and beauty which makes running pleasant, plus the type of natural obstacles which help to develop great strength and stamina. Moreover, because winters are mild and the heat of summer is tempered by cool sea breezes, running out-of-doors without undue discomfort is possible all the year round.

As a result, competitive running of some sort goes on constantly. Track starts in October and continues until April, harrier running starts in April and continues through to August, and the road racing season holds sway for the remainder of the year.

All this activity is administered by the New Zealand Amateur Athletic Association through nine district bodies or "Centers" and the clubs and schools. In many instances each type of running is handled by a separate sub-committee, and, in some cases, by separate clubs.

The early season harrier runs are mostly of an easy social type. In fact, the social side of harriers is much more pronounced than in track. Club runs usually start and finish at the home of a club-member or a club-room, where showers and refreshments can be provided to punctuate proceedings. It pays to finsih with the leaders or it may mean cold showers, cold drinks and empty plates!

Possibly for this reason, runners are divided into "fast", "medium" and "slow" "packs" and starting times are adjusted so that there will not be too great a gap at the finish. Each "pack" has a leader or captain who keeps the runners together, dictates the pace, and demonstrates how to tackle obstacles and various types of terrain.

For some runners, these "social runs" remain the main attraction throughout the season, but for those keen on racing, the major activities comprise "open runs". These are races sponsored by individual clubs and open to harriers from any part of the country or even overseas. By making an application to their "centers", clubs are granted a specific date for their "open" runs. The bulk of these races are handicap, but some are "massed start" with sealed handicaps unknown to the individual runner until he finishes. As a rule, both individual and team winners are sought, plus individual and team fastest times. Some harrier races, like the 68 mile Wellington to Masterton run over a range of mountains, are relays.

Many of these runs have become traditionally famous. This fame often stems not so much from the race itself but from the hospitality of the hosts. As I said earlier, the social side of harriers is very strong, and the dinners and celebrations which wind-up proceedings are usually something to remember. Moreover, visitors usually live for a day or so in the homes of members of the host club and this practice founds some splendid life-long friendships.

All high schools run their own annual cross-country in which participation is virtually compulsory, plus an occasional dual team fixture and an annual six-man team fixture of two grades between all schools in a district. The schools' own run isusually in three age grades (under $14\frac{1}{2}$, under 16 and under 19 on Oct. 1) and the inter-school fixtures are in two age-grades (under 16 and under 19 on Oct.1).

District or center and national races come at the end of the season. Some centers run a ten-man team event and then, on a later date, a six man team and individual event. On the basis of performances in these events, centers then pick six men to contest the national race. In these six-man races the first four count for the team title. Center championship races are provided for "colts" (boys under 16 years), "juniors" (boys under 19 years), seniors and women. The national races are for "juniors" and "men". Cross country for women is flourishing in some centers and is particularly strong in Auckland and Canterbury who stage an annual home and away fixture. A national race for women seems imminent.

Because of it's team basis and attractive social side, harrier running is more popular with the average performer than track. In Auckland alone, with a population of about 500,000, there are no less than 1,200 registered harriers. This figure takes no account of schoolboys and various clubs of middle-aged sedentary workers who run purely for fun and as a means of keeping fit.

A great many harriers treat the track season light-heartedly or participate in some other summer sport. Some run only for the social enjoyment and as a build-up for track, and some seem to thrive on all-the-year-round racing on track, country and road. This year, for instance, after particularly heavy track season, both Snell and Halberg carried on with serious cross country racing. Snell won the Auckland center and national harrier titles, but Halberg skipped the big races although he has several previous national cross country titles to his credit.

All our top track runners participate in harriers to a greater or lesser degree. Usually they vary this degree from year to year according to how they feel physically and psychologically. Consequently, although one of our top track runners often carries off the big harrier titles, the cross country specialist, who is usually just below the top rung on the track, and who usually races lightly in the summer, also has a very fair measure of success. His greater skill at clearing fences and negotiating rough ground, sometimes proves too much for better runners.

As seems to be the case elsewhere, training methods in New Zealand vary. Most of us have inherited some of the independent pioneering spirit of our grandfathers, so there is plenty of diversity in ideas. There are those who think it does not matter what you do so long as you do more of it than anyone else and there are those who seek the short-cuts through quality rather than quantity. To confuse the issue, successes are achieved by both groups of extremists, but the most consistent results seem to come from somewhere between. It is certainly clear that no worthwhile results can be accomplished without a great deal of hard work, but for the sake of those who run for fun and as a means of recreation, I personally hope that some of the quantity can be profitably replaced by quality.

Fortunately, the tremendous fund of accumulated knowledge on the working mechanism of the human body is now adequate and clear enough to point the way. How to interpret and apply this knowledge simply and effectively is another problem. Here again the spirit of independance enters, so that interpretations vary widely.

From my point of view, one needs a solid base from which to plan. To achieve this only two basic principles need to be kept in mind. Firstly, never lose sight of the fact that the human body will do really well only what it is regularly accustomed to doing. Secondly, it is necessary to be ever conscious of the fact that the development of latent talent in the individual depends on the harmonious cultivation of strength, speed, stamina, style, suppleness and relaxation. These various physical qualities are the links in the chain between effort and output. As their proportional significance varies from individual to individual and from event to event, it is the individual and the event that must be studied and analyzed.

With these two principles ever in mind, the training of the cross country runner is straightforward. In the first instance it is necessary to make sure that he gets plenty of running at racing speed over the identical type of country he will encounter in his important races - i.e. the same sort of hills, the same sort of terrain and the same sort of obstacles generally. All this work to be of the interval-training type.

Secondly, we must analyze the individual to find his weaknesses and then plan his training with a bias towards those activities which will "strengthen the weak links". Then we give him up-hill running, swampy ground running and sand-hill work for strength; short-interval work for speed; long-interval, "fartlek" or long-steady-pace running for stamina; fast, downhill overstriding or high-knee-up-hill for suppleness; personal coaching for style; and conscious training for relaxation. I know, of course, that qualities like relaxation can be cultivated automatically by running in a state of partial fatigue regularly; that style can be influenced by driving, springy up-hill running, by carrying weights etc.; and that other physical qualities essential to the complete harrier can be cultivated almost automatically through various types of running. All I really want to stress here is that the important thing is to make sure that no link in the chain is overlooked and that training schedules are balanced for the individual with the object of developing each latent faculty fully. Our harriers must also spend time and effort learning to clear, fences, gates, creeks and mud patches economically.

Don't run away with the idea that all New Zealand runners train to a scientifically based system. Many train without a system at all and still reap a measure of success. Almost in the same category are those who adopt the training schedule of the champion, and those coaches who have a hard and fast schedule for all, regardless of individual differences. There is a tendency to forget that no two individuals are alike and "one man's meat can be anothers poison". Some athletes are doing huge amounts of every type of training hoping that they will work in the right amount of the right sort successfully. Some of them get good results, but I think they would do better by selecting the type of work they most need and going for quality. These athletes are like the sufferer of a specific vitamin deficiency who takes regular doses of every known vitamin to remedy the position. The result is effective, but expensive.

No summary of cross country training in this country would be complete without reference to the system used by Arthur Lydiard in developing such runners as Snell, Halberg and Magee. The unique aspect of Lydiard's system is that of change in emphasis. First comes the marathon training phase. Then, this is dropped and followed by a mixture of long and short interval work on a very tough hill circuit. Finally comes another complete change to mostly very short interval work interspersed with very easy long runs and racing. Arthur Lydiard himself believes that the significant aspect of his training is the long, marathon runs. This was also a feature of Cerutty's system, but I still don't think it is the complete answer. I know a great number of runners who have adopted such work without success. To me, the attractive features of Lydiard's work are the hard, hill-circuit workouts, which are particularly suited to the development of strength; the changes in venue, which give a new psychological stimulus to the athlete; and the long easy runs which intersperse the very short interval training to once again shift the emphasis and provide mental and physical relaxation.

Judged on a population basis, New Zealand seems to have the greatest cross country runners in the world. How this comes about can only be conjectured, but as I said at the outset, climate and environment certainly play a significant role. Gosta Holmer, Chief Swedish Coach, believed that the key to his system of "fartlek" training lay in the psychological stimulus of a pleasant, changing environment. New Zealand has as much or more to offer in this respect plus climatic conditions which enable out-of-door training to go on constantly. General organization of the sport engenders a pleasant friendly spirit and comparatively large numbers of participants and this in turn produces a solid top. The right sort of leadership and inspiration from officials and coaches has also had its impact, but this is also true in other countries and I want to confine myself mostly to factors which are peculiar to New Zealand.

Herbert Schade's Training Methods

by Herbert Schade

(This is a synthesis of an excerpt from the German Track and Field Union school at Nainz, Germany from January 5 to 7, 1962, which was presented as an introduction to a general discussion of middle-distance running by the former German 5,000-10,000 meters champion, Herbert Schade, who placed 3rd in the 5,000 meters at the 1952 Olympic Games in Helsinki.)

It would be foolish, unwise and presumptuous for a trainer or a coach to believe that his training method alone promises "open sesame".

Examination and comparison of the various training methods of the Russians, of the Poles under Jan Mulak, of the Hungarians under Mihaly Igloi, of the Czechs under Emil Zatopek, of the New Zealanders under Arthur Lydiard, and finally the Australians under Percy Cerutty shows us quite clearly just how varied the methods are. And yet they have all led to world records.

The training of Emil Zatopek is the most familiar to us. After World War II his method set training for running on a basis which, though familiar to us today, was quite new at the time.

Pure interval training over distances of 200 and 400 meters almost always run exclusively according to feeling. It happened that in Zatopek's case the difference between load and interval was barely discernable.

Emil Zatopek's method was very simple and uncomplicated. His main forte, however, was his tremendous will-power.

The Poles, among them especially Jan Mulak, were the first who recognized that Zatopek's method had, to be sure, launched the performance rocket, but that it was far from the final solution.

My Greatest Mistake

I am firmly conviced that the greatest mistake of my own career was too much fast interval-training. In my preparation for the Olympic Games of 1956, I trained only at distances of 200, 300, 400 and 600 meters and regularly had a daily load of 25-30 x 200 meters in 27/28 seconds separated by jogs of 200 meters, or 30 x 400 meters in 61/62 seconds with each fifth leg in 58/59 seconds, separated by jogs of 200 meters, or 20 x 600 meters in 95/96 seconds separated by jogs of 300 meters, or even a twice daily training whereby I executed 20 x 300 meters in the morning and 25 x 400 meters in the evening in the aforementioned times.

As I reflect on this daily load I ask myself just where an increase in efficiency would have been possible at the time. Such a load would certainly not be expected today of our best distance runner - Horst Flosbach.

Perhaps the sole advantage of my drilled method of training was that it made me enormously hard and allowed my performance during the racing season to remain nearly constant from beginning to end. However, the prime result, a run under 14:00.0, was denied to me.

Not Only Short Interval Runs

Jan Mulak, whose training is known to us under the expression "Polish running game", incorporated even longer distances into his training program. The training of the Hungarians was likewise elastic. Along with the short distances there also timed runs, frequently over 800 meters, which went at a very fast pace of course.

Both countries, Poland as well as Hungary, were successful with their methods, back of which government support and control played an important role and was, indeed, the main-spring. It may, however, lead us to believe that both countries produced great world class runners on the basis of a successful approach to their theory of training as demonstrated by such runners as the Poles Chromik, Krzyszkowiak, Ozog and Zimny and by the Hungarians Iharos, Rozsavolgyi and Tabori, whereas even now a certain stagnation is already appearing on the horizon.

All of the aforementioned Polish and Hungarian runners were and are, in part, currently still of world class. But what stands behind these so-called "first élite"?

On the basis of what is known to us of the Iron Curtain countries it seems that they failed to bridge the gap to their own current class athletes in spite of the systematic care with which they conducted the recruiting and selection of the athletes. Behind their own world class athletes is a void which is not to be overlooked. Yet doubtless new names have to emerge in Poland and Hungary. Of course one has to allow for the fact that once again during the past season in Hungary two new runners became known for the first time.

No Training Pattern

The real reason that the countries referred to have failed up to now to maintain a consistent supply to their achievement peak is, as I see it, that their method is unconditional and is used also by the junior without restriction and distinction.

In my opinion it is in the following that the essentials of our training work lie:

It would be wrong to believe that the same training method can be used by several runners without change or variation. A training program can, of course, be established on purely scientific foundations, knowledge and calculations, but in practice the person himself stands at the focus, the individual with all his strengths and weaknesses.

If a training program is to be used successfully by an athlete, then first of all I have to study this runner in detail. Apart from his current performance curve, body condition (poorly developed or muscularly well developed) plays a decisive role. These factors are absolutely crucial in determining the degree of load which I can demand of the athlete.

Training Only After a Hard Day of Work For Us

It is no secret that in many countries the sport receives extensive assistance from the government. Athletes in these countries can carry out their training according to the wishes of trainer and coach without cares and wants and develop unhindered at any time of day. In our case, however, all are employed or are in college. They all must put in their hours of work. This, therefore, requires that the training load always be in the evening hours, i.e. after a hard day's work. These facts, with which we have to live, no doubt force us to look for and proceed along the proper course.

Above all in the main training period, November to March, we have, except on weekend, only the cinder track or at best park paths at our disposal for our training. How delighted I would be to transfer the whole training work exclusively to the forest!

Many Roads to Performance

My current opinion of training is the result of numerous conversations with well-known foreign athletes and trainers. All of these conversations and discussions confirmed for me very quickly the fact that many roads lead to success or cause failure.

In problems of training which are not clear cut or which are basically different my decision is, today, based exclusively on my own training experiences and the knowledge gained from them.

The training program is, no doubt, decisively influenced only by the performance readiness of the individual athletes. However, experience does not yield performance readiness without the proper mood, no proper mood without pep, no pep without recreation. A good trainer or coach must, I dare say, be able to recognize during the warm-up just which loads he can subject his protégé to on this day.

No Twice Daily Training For Us

At this point I should like to say that this has been viewed with disfavor on the basis of our financial status and our basic requirements.

With some reservation I should like to stress, however, that a light workout in the morning hours, i.e. before the start of the day's work, is not of value to a well conditioned athlete as a training workout but, on the contrary, as a light activity, as a scarcely noticeable stress, which the organs almost demand.

The Warm-Up

Yet we can state that many athletes execute a warm-up which is too humdrum. The dull monotony of a jog has never yet contributed anything. By its very nature limbering-up must be relaxed, quick and loose. Slow start, fast run with variations of skipping, fast tripping, vigorous knee lifts, limbering-up exercises. The warm-up should not be intensified near the end before the real training (possibly, however, before competition, since in competition one has to warm up more rapidly; therefore, intensification is inserted here).

The Prime Time For Preparation: November to March

Our most important training period lies in the interval from November to March. It is during these months that the foundation for a further organic development must be established with the aim of carrying out the complete proposed training plan from January.

Daily training is fundamental. Yet no rule is without exception. Occasionally individual days of rest can and should be inserted.

How Do I Stand On Weight Training?

It is obvious that at this stage of the training we cannot dispense with it. A weekly indoor work-out of $1\frac{1}{2}$ to 2 hours is imperative during the main training period. In that connection we prefer to work with light weights, instruction in take-off power, work on wall bars, leather box, leather bench, a lot of motion in hopping and squatting, work with the medicine ball and partner exercises. Only care is to be taken that all starts of motion are light and loose (without cramps). All muscle bundles from the tip of the hair to the sole of the foot must be actuated indoors by thorough work. Even during the season a weight workout should not be omitted completely. It would suffice to bring a $7\frac{1}{2}$ kilogram (16 pound) shot vertically to arm's reach alternately with the right and left arm following each training session.

Run Training From November to March

Do not copy the following instructions on training methods during the main training period, but regard them solely as a guide:

Basically the length of the training distances plays no crucial role in training. The difference lies primarily in the number of runs, the time, and the rest.

During the aforementioned months (November to March) I train most expediently at the following distances: Short; 100, 200 meters; Middle; 1000, 1200, 2000 meters; Long; All work upwards of 2000 meters.

It may be shown medically that interval work at 100 and 200 meter distances is most profitable. For adjustment and preparation in the scheduled training plan I say yes to these short distances. However, from my own experiences I object emphatically to training exclusively and uncompromisingly only at these short distances.

Training Plan, November to March

1st day: indoor workout of $1\frac{1}{2}$-2 hours.

2nd day: middle distance (track): 10-12 x 1000 meters in 3:10.0 to 3:12.0 or 1200 in 3:45.0 to 3:47.0, with recovery jogs of 400 meters in 3:00.0 to 3:10.0 in each case.

3rd day: long distance (street, park): easy run up to 25 kilometers.

4th day: middle distance (track): easy 6-7 x 2000 meters.

5th day: short distance (track): 50-60 x 100 meters in 17-18 seconds, separated by 50 meter recovery jogs in 25-27 seconds, or 30-40 x 200 meters in 35-37 seconds, separated by 100 meter recovery jogs in 50-54 seconds.

6th day: long distance (forest): 3 kilometers, 6 kilometers, 3 kilometers; concluding with 10 easy 100 meters.

7th day: long distance (forest): 1-2 hours of speed play (walking-skipping).

In regard to the detailed training days 6 and 7, I maintain that they were a determining factor for Horst Flosbach during the main preparation time of the preceding season.

"Speed play", which was first carried out by the Swedes under Gösta Holmer, comprises a great many things of course and very few are clearly defined. Profitably it is only be correct dosage: a long run with repeated changing of loads and relaxations over shorter and longer distances; diversified through interspersing of stressed skipping up to 15 minutes, likewise stressing of fast walks with intensive, rhythmic arm motion (as already has been practised by the Finns under Arne Valste for 20 years).

Let us not forget that Percy Wells Cerutty with his self-willed training method, particularly in his training quarters at Portsea, also favors an analogous training, partly over sand trails, hills and mountains.

Transition Training, April to May

I consider the months April to May as a time of transition at the beginning of which most of the German cross country championships are already over. Thus the cross country athlete has carried out his training preparatory to the track season and does not require special preparation.

Yet time and again we observe that in this event there are specialists who hardly play an appreciable roll during the peak season.

The cross country championships are followed by a short period of rest of about 2 weeks during which the training is carried out with diminished load. Obviously it would be wrong to interject a complete period of rest.

Performance Training From June

In the section on performance training which now follows, the point is to prepare the athletes slowly for their main task. In contrast to the training work during the main preparation period (November to March) we are now in favor of more short distances. However, here it seems advisable to change over slowly since many runners judge this transition to be difficult.

Just as during the training for maintenance of condition, speed play is also retained in this training method. Only now it may not be worked with the same intensity. Skipping and walking are now omitted. Speed play is limited to one hour.

The following training distances are scheduled: Short, 100, 200, 300, 400 meters; Middle, 600, 1000, or 1200 meters; Long, only forest training 1500-3000 meters.

Notes On The Training Days

1st day: 25 x 200 meters in 30-31 seconds, recovery jog of 100 meters between each in 50-54 seconds.

2nd day: 10 x 300 meters in 43-44 seconds or 20 x 300 meters in 46-47 seconds, recovery jog of 200 meters between each in 1:40.0

3rd day: 20 x 400 meters in 65-67 seconds, recovery jog of 200 meters between each in 69-70 seconds, recovery jog of 100 meters.

4th day: 10 x 600 meters in 1:35.0-1:38.0, recovery jog of 300 meters between each in 2:30.0.

5th day: 5 x 1200 meters in 3:18-3:20.0, recovery jog of 400 meters between each in 3:00.0-3:10.0.

6th day: forest: 1.5 kilometers, 3 kilometers, 1.5 kilometers, 3 kilometers in a free and easy style.

7th day: one hour of speed play.

8th day: 1. 5 x 100 meters in 15-16 seconds, recovery jog of 100 meters between each (400 meter jog); 2. 5 x 200 meters in 30-32 seconds, recovery jog of 100 meters between each (400 meter jog); 3. 5 x 300 meters in 45-48 seconds, recovery jog of 200 meters between each (400 meter jog); 4. 5 x 400 meters in 67-68 seconds, recovery jog of 200 meters between each (400 meter jog); 5. 5 x 300 meters (as in 3); 6. 5 x 200 meters (as in 2); 7. 5 x 100 meters (as in 1).

Now it is mandatory to be adroit in the application of fixed training methods.

In no case are those of 1-8 to be utilized in the numberical order given. On the contrary, they must be mixed in training; after a hard day of load a lighter training must be prepared for the following day.

The training program under the 8th day has proved to be a very tough load. Consequently, this form should be used only once every eight days.

Maintenance of Condition Following the Championships

An athlete who has carried out all of the aforementioned training steps must and can retain his condition for quite a long time. Following the high point of the season, the German Championships, he will try to race many times and who can blame him.

At this stage the training must conform completely to the competitions. Yet to insist now on a daily high load in training would be wrong; it must, on the contrary, be so selected that the training of the athletes occurs almost like a game. The same training conditions can nevertheless be employed with slight load. Also I see again in this phase a great advantage in shifting many of the training days to the forest.

On "Crash Training"

In my opinion crash training is nothing more than an aid, a stopgap so to speak, and even then it is only to be used by athletes who have years of track training behind them.

Before one decides on crash training it is an unconditional prerequisite that the athlete has completed a normal training several months previously. If his training must be interrupted, on whatever basis or by whatever circumstances (illness, job, etc.), better results are likely to be achieved through pure interval work over 100-, 200-, 400 meter distances. The condition thus achieved will not, however, last very long.

In 1958 illness forced me to interrupt my training. Three weeks prior to the German Championships in Hannover I was still determined to get into gear by 14 days of crash training. For all that I was still fourth in the 10,000 meters with a time of 30:18.4. Subsequently I continued with my usual training and regained my normal form just before the end of the season.

Change Training Distances Occasionally

If one had trained an athlete for 2 or 3 years according to a certain training method, it would seem advisable to give him new stimuli, therefore a stimuli change, by means of new distances and loads.

A well-known long distances runner of past years, whose training program consisted almost exclusively of middle or longer distances, managed to attain an increase in performance with 20 x 400 meters in 69-70 seconds which absolutely could not have been predicted.

No Spikes in Training!

In order to guard against the risk of injury it is advisable to conduct the entire training only in running shoes - those without spikes.

Competition Planning is Necessary!

However, training and readiness for achievement are not alone sufficient for an athlete to realize great achievements but, because of the record performances which are demanded these days, a well thought out set of season long instructions is imperative. In this connection I am, today, firmly convinced that Horst Flosbach is solely indebted to a well thought out competition planning for his performance increase in 1960 and for his participation in the 1960 Olympic Games. In order to reach a lofty goal one must, once in a while, to able to forego a start and, what is more, forego an ever so tempting trip abroad. Also not to be overlooked by us is the large number of races which, unfortunately, must be curtailed or else we shall trod the same course as did Sweden and Finland before us.

Even at the start of the season the trainer or coach should draw up, at least in rough outline, a firm plan of competition with his protégé and undertake with that also the task of continually protecting his athlete, coordinating the invitations, and effecting the cancellations.

I know that this will never be possible without difficulties and vexations, since the "reason" on many promotors often follows quite strange paths. If one cannot proceed without vexations at this time, then one should at least spare the athletes from them.

Competitive Development (Performance Development)

As far as possible during the first month of the season no special distances should be run. Here invitations to competition over 1500 meters, 2000 meters and 3000 meters offer a sufficient choice to us. It is also to be recommended that the first competitions not be carried out right away against basically stronger opponents.

Steeplechase

In the running phase, training for the 3000 meter steeplechase is no different from long distance training.

After a complete training program from the primary training period to (and) inclusive of the training for competition a runner has so much energy and endurance that he can conditionally last out the steeplechase distance without hesitation.

Quite crucial for the steeplechaser, however, is a natural take-off power. If a runner is not naturally endowed with this pre-requisite, it will not be possible to reach international performance standards.

In addition to the "running training" the hurdles technique and the water jump technique are now added. The barriers should be run over.

In this connection, however, it is to be noted that the barriers, as opposed to the hurdles of the 400 meter hurdles, are rigid. Therefore hitting the barrier conceals a very great injury hazard for the steeplechaser. This is true all during the last third of a 3000 meter steeplechase, where the take-off power, nimbleness and agility fade away naturally.

For the mastery of the barrier technique we avail ourselves of the same preparation used in the training of a 400 meter hurdles runner.

It is best to learn to train for the water jump technique at a jumping or pole vault area. Place a barrier in front of the pit. In doing so care is to be taken that the run-up remains on the grass. Consequently, conforming to the conditions of competitive steeplechase, the barrier can be jumped from a slow start up to a race speed run-up. It is important in negotiating the barrier that the spikes of the runner's shoes reach over the bar and the upper part of the body be bent slightly forward. The number of jumps which can be required of an athlete on the training day depends purely and simply on his bodily structure. Here it is obvious, as with many details in training, that subtle intuition is necessary.

During the period of competitive training practice interval runs over barriers. Bring the runner to the point that he can jump with either foot.

I consider it wrong to lay out markers at the barriers, i.e. at the water jump, before a run. For when can these even be adherred to? The battle against the competition and the exhaustion leaves no time for the competitor to concentrate on prepared markers. For it is only with courage and determination that one can take a water jump.

Final Considerations

Viewed in the long run, achievement and success come only to those who train daily. In long distance running achievement can only be reached by hard work, spartan ways of life, doing without the allurements and charms of everyday life.

It is absolutely possible to set world records at the age of 22 or 23 and, sportwise, to be an old man at 27 or 28. The relatively few years, in which the athlete stands at the zenith of his ability, must be utilized correctly. However, after the athlete's competitive career he still has enough time left to recover "lost ground and so-called pleasure". On the cinder track it is not the years of life or how old a competitor is classified, but it is the years of competition which are of value.

In addition to our own training methods and views we must be tolerant and recognize the opinions of others! By a closer examination we shall discover that the "common guideline" which passes through training is the same in many cases. The one leans toward the left, the other toward the right. Therefore let us try to find the "common guideline".

A proverb says: "Many roads lead to Rome!" This proved to be true at the last Olympic Games in the truest sense of the word, theoretically in many special talks and discussions at the edge of the competition and through the evidence of the great running on the track.

Paavo Nurmi once said: Any trainer can train mediocre men: an ace, however, only through special unremitting work." We should continually keep in mind these words of the great reticent one.

(The above article was translated by Glenn B.Hoidale from the No. 9, February 27, 1962 and No. 10, March 6, 1962 issues of "Die Lehre der Leichtathletik," and is reprinted by permission of Editor Toni Nett.)

Developing Stamina in Athletes

by N.G. Ozolin, Moscow, USSR

The important quality of endurance is a vital one for all athletes, especially those specializing in forms of sport that require prolonged movements. From a physiological point of view endurance is characterized by the ability to carry out extended work loads and to combat fatigue. This ability is governed by the activity of the cortex, which determines and regulates the work capacity of all bodily organs and systems. It further depends on the preparation of the muscular, cardiovascular, and breathing systems and on other systems and organs.

A deterioration in the efficiency of the central nerve apparatus is the main element in a chain of processes which characterize the development of fatigue. The fight against the organism's fatigue is above all else a fight of the higher nerve centers for the preservation of their working capacity.

The athlete's stamina also depends on the perfection of technique, the ability to carry out movements freely and economically.

Finally, it depends to a considerable extent on his will, on his psychological condition, and this again testifies to the predominant significance of the central nervous system.

Thus endurance is determined by many functions of the organism and does not depend only on the working capacity of the heart, lungs and muscles, as has still recently been maintained. Stamina in sport is attained by instruction in technique and tactics, by increasing the functional capabilities of the organism, and by training the will power. Many methods are used to achieve this end. They are applied as part of a year-round training system extending over many years.

Endurance can be divided into two types: "general" and "special."

General and special endurance.

General physical preparation of the athlete includes many-sided development of his organs and systems, a high level of their working capacity, and the art of coordinating various movements. In particular, and important aspect of general physical preparation is the ability to carry out prolonged work involving the action of many muscle groups and placing great demands on the cardiovascular and breathing systems. This ability is called general endurance. It is indeed general, in that it enables each well-prepared athlete (in any form of sport) to cope with extended work of large or moderate intensity, in comparison to the person not participating in athletics.

But a runner specializing in short distances will not show much stamina in a marathon; a pole vaulter, competing over several hours, cannot maintain a good pace for 1500 meters; etc. Thus there exists a special (specific) endurance, peculiar to a certain aspect of sport. This endurance results only from repetitions of the actions involved in this form of sport.

The main road to developing special endurance.

As a result of Elfimov's (ref.1) laboratory experiments plus observations in practice, it can be stated that for the development of special endurance in middle-, long-, and ultralong distance runners the pace in training should be slightly faster than race pace. In the laboratory, we measured the amount of endurance developed in three groups of middle distance runners after the first group had run in place at an average pace

(230 steps per min.), another group had run at an increased pace (260 steps per min.), and a third group at maximum effort (300 steps per min.). Their pulse and breathing rates were measured before and after the training. The average results of the experiments are given in table 1:

Table 1:

test group	training pace (steps/min.)	Duration of run "to the limit" at a pace of 230 steps/min. prior to training	after the training pd.	Increase in working capacity (%)	Duration of run "to the limit" at pace of 260 steps/min. after the training period
1	230	52.3 sec.	72.3 sec.	38.3	35-40 sec.
2	300	52.0 sec.	98.6 sec.	89.6	44-52 sec.
3	260	54.3 sec.	106.3 sec.	95.8	59.65 sec.

("To the limit" means to the point where fatigue interferes with normal movements.). Thus the greatest increase in working capacity was attained by the group which trained at faster than race pace but not at maximum effort.

Methods for developing endurance. (The various methods are listed in table 2.)

General endurance can be acquired by doing a wide variety of calisthenics throughout the year, as well as by more frequent training sessions and games of all sorts. But the most important method, at least for runners, is thru continuous running at slow paces. (For several reasons, walking may not be a good method for runners to use.)

The more steady the pace in a race, the easier it is to turn in one's best time, because changing the tempo interferes with the coordinating functions of the organs and systems. An even pace promotes an economical use of available energy, a better operation of the biochemical processes, and most important of all it creates a more favorable situation for the central nervous system.

The pace of the long, steady practice runs, designed to build up general stamina, must be relatively slow so that there will not be a heavy load placed on the cardiovascular and breathing systems. A stable condition is maintained between the oxygen debt and the actual consumption of oxygen. The pace for beginners should be around 2:20 to 2:50 per 440, lasting for only 5-8 min. at first; for girls, about 2:50 - 3:20 per 440. For more experienced athletes the pace can be faster, e.g. 2 min. per 440 for sprinters, 1:50 per 440 for middle and long distance runners.

Table 2. Methods of developing general and special endurance in athletes.

Main purpose	**Name of method**	**Contents of method**	**Main application**
Devel. of general endurance	Steady pace	Negotiating a distance at an even pace, gradually increasing the distance	For all athletes
Devel. of general endurance; active rest	Cross-country	Running, or walking on skis, at medium or easy efforts over rugged terrain	For all athletes

Devel. of general and special endurance	Gradual drawing-up	Negotiating a distance and gradually increasing it each workout while keeping the pace constant; then gradually decreasing the distance while increasing the distance while increasing the pace	For novice distance & middle distance runners
Devel. of special endurance	Standard	Covering the distance at which the athlete will be competing	For all athletes
Devel. of special endurance	Repetition	Repetitions at maximum effort with average rest intervals	For sprinters, throwers, jumpers, etc.
Devel. of special endurance	Repetition	Repetitions at faster than race pace with long rest intervals	For middle - & long distance runners
Devel. of special endurance	Repetition	Short repetitions, following more prolonged training, at race pace or slightly faster, with very short rest intervals	For developing finishing ability
Devel. of special endurance	Increasing - decreasing	Repetitions at maximum effort, first gradually increasing & then gradually decreasing the duration of the training session	For sprinters
Devel. of special endurance	Increasing	Repetitions at maximum of effort gradually increasing the duration of the workout	For sprinters
Devel. of special endurance	Decreasing	Same, but gradually decreasing duration of workout	For sprinters
Devel. of special endurance	Interval	Covering at race pace short distances which add up to the full racing distance, gradually decreasing (to zero) the rest intervals between each stretch	For middle distance men and sprinters

Devel. of general endurance	Mixed	Alternating slow runs with easy walking	For novices
Devel. of special endurance	Sprinter's variable	Alternating short accelerations at medium and maximum effort with short decelerations	For sprinters
Devel. of special and general endurance	Distance man's variable	Continuous alternation of efforts faster than race pace & active rest in the form of very moderate work	For middle distance & especially for long distance men
Devel. of general endurance, and active rest	Variable restoration	Continuous alternation of moderate efforts with active rest in the form of very easy work	For all athletes
Devel. of general endurance	Fartlek	Continuous alternation of various efforts, in the country; running at varying paces plus walking	For all athletes

Main purpose	**Name of method**	**Contents of method**	**Main application**
Devel. of special endurance	With accelerations	Running while increasing the pace from slow to maximum, done repeatedly	For sprinters & middle distance men
Devel. of special endurance and sense of pace	Pace	Runs at a set pace at distances less than, equal to, and greater than the racing distance	For middle- & long distance runners
Devel. of special endurance	To the limit	Running without stopping to the point where fatigue prevents the correct fulfillment of the exercise	For all athletes
Devel. of special endurance and check of training	Control	Covering 3/4 - 4/5 of the basic racing distance at race pace or slightly faster	For middle & long distance men

Devel. of special endurance	Tactical	Covering racing distance at slightly slower than race pace, but altering the pace according to a curve, as in actual competition	For middle
Devel. of special endurance	Competition	Covering the basic distance in the best time possible	For all athletes

In taking these runs the athlete should not tire quickly. Only towards the end of the workout should he experience some muscle fatigue and difficulty in breathing, but even here he should feel capable of continuing on for some time. If fatigue sets in rather early and the workout seems difficult, the pace should be reduced.

For more experienced athletes the variable pace method can be used to develop general endurance. This is done in parts, in the country, etc., running first one min. at average speed, then 1-2 min. slow, again faster, etc., for a relatively long period of time (1-2 hours). The intensity of the workout is increased by making the workout longer in duration, but doing more faster stretches, and by cutting down on the number of slow stretches.

During the preparatory period of the yearly training cycle two workouts a week should be devoted to developing general endurance. Adding a 10-12 min. warmdown onto normal workouts does a great deal in developing general endurance. An extended warmup can also be used. During the racing season less (but still some) attention should be given to general endurance.

Special endurance for distance runners is acquired thru three main methods: varying pace, repetition, and pace methods.

The varying pace method (interval training) consists of a continuous alternation of stretches at faster than race pace with stretches of active rest in the form of slower movements (e.g. 80 x 150m fast with 50m jogging after each 150). In this type of workout an oxygen debt is repeatedly built up and the organism becomes capable of maintaining a stable condition or of having a lower oxygen debt during even-paced running at the racing distance. The rest intervals should be short, not more than 1-2 min. The sum of the fast stretches should not be more than 1.5-2 times as much as the athlete's racing distance. As the latter decreases, the number of repetitions (as well as the distance and speed of each fast stretch) becomes less (e.g. 80 x 400m for a marathoner, 20 x 200m for a 3,000m man).

The repetition method is utilized to a much lesser extent among distance runners. It consists of taking a distance less than (about 1/5-1/8 of) racing distance and repeating this distance several times at faster than race pace. The stretch is repeated until the time becomes slower. Rest periods should be long enough to allow the runner to cover the distance is the desired time, but should not exceed 20-25 min.

The pace method, less popular still, involves a steady covering of the racing distance at slightly slower than race pace.

For middle distance runners, methods of developing special endurance vary considerably according to the racing distance (i.e. according to the length of time of the racing effort). In general, all those who race for 3-5 min. fall into one group, and those who race for a lesser period fall into a second group. For the former group the methods utilized are much the same as those for distance runners, with the repetition method playing an increasingly important role as the racing distance shortens.

Many unsuccessful attempts have been made to apply the varying pace method to 800m runners. As one example, S. Arkharov in 1951 tried workouts of 20 x 200m in :28.3-:28.5 sec., jogging 200m between each. But he was only able to repeat his previous year's best of 1:52.2; however, he did run what for him was an excellent 1500m (3:56). Thus the varying pace method is important for the 1500 but not for the 800m.

For those whose racing time extends from 30 seconds to 2:00 min. the repetition method is very important for developing special endurance. However, the speed of these repetitions should not be "all-out." Experiments by A.A. Pugachevski with 800m runners showed that they failed to improve by doing workouts such as 15-20 x 100m at nearly maximum effort. This is understandable since short all-out efforts accustom the organism to working on very little oxygen intake, such as is the case with sprinters. Generally speaking, one should take half the racing distance and do 2-4 repetitions, or until the times begin slowing down significantly. Care should be taken to get enough rest between repetitions, in workouts of this type. Laboratory and track experiments with 800m runners were conducted by Elfimov and Ozolin (refs. 1 and 2). When the test runners were doing 400m repetitions, it was noted that the second rep. was usually slower than the first. They found that in order to run identical times for the first two reps., 15-20 minutes rest (not more, not less) was necessary. (With 3 min. rest the second 400m run was about 7 secs. slower than the first. This gap decreased to about 0 secs. for 15-20 min. rest, but taking more than 20 min. also produced a slower and slower second 400m.) Additional tests by Elfimov with two groups of 800m runners, each of which did 20 training sessions of repetition 400m running, showed that the group taking 20 min. rest between reps. improved their 800m time by 4.2-5.1 secs., whereas a second group taking 7 min. rest improved by only 2.1-2.5 secs.

The repetition method should, however, be supplemented with the standard, pace, and interval methods for runners in this area. (See table 2.)

Developing qualities of will power.

The training of mental qualities is one of the most important aspects of improving an athlete's stamina. Unfortunately, the majority of coaches fail to devote enough attention to this.

The development of stamina is closely connected with the development of persistence and tenacity, industriousness, willingness to bear difficulties, confidence in one's powers, ability to muster maximum strength, and the will to win.

To develop persistence and tenacity it is necessary not only to be striving towards a goal but to believe in its attainability. An easy goal is reached more quickly. The real fruits of actual training strengthen one's self confidence and one's ability to attain higher goals. It helps if the coach cites examples of cases where complete novices have become famous athletes largely thru tenacity, persistence and the will to succeed.

The best method for inoculating athletes (especially those unaccustomed to real work) with industriousness is by having them fulfill definite assignments in training: complete one more exercise today than yesterday; cover a distance in a selected time; cover a given amount of mileage in a workout; etc. Doing these things of course strengthens one's self confidence, while not doing them can have the opposite effect.

Training sessions for those lacking tenacity and persistence should often be group sessions. When everyone is doing the same thing it is "uncomfortable" for anyone to stop before the task is finished. Competitions should often be used, e.g. seeing who can do the most number of exercises, who sticks up with the leader the longest, whose team does best in cross-country relays, etc.

One of the greatest difficulties in running, walking, etc. is that of carrying out prolonged work when fatigue is really setting in and is encouraging the athlete to give up the inner battle within himself. One cannot develop stamina without having fought against fatigue and overcome inclinations dictated by the mind. In training for endurance the athlete must first of all get used to long, continuous work, exceeding that of his racing event. For example, a marathoner can do workouts of 3 hours of continuous running, thus getting among other advantages the psychological boost that he has spent more time on his training run than he will in the race. Another method is that of Zatopek: forcing oneself to increase the pace when fatigue begins to set in.

Confidence in one's abilities and a willingness to fight against tough odds are very important qualities in athletes. The athlete's thoughts prior to training and competition are of prime importance for his success. He should think of covering the distance faster, hanging with the record holder all the way, etc. If he thinks of the difficulty or impossibility, he has already lost. Lack of self confidence and doubt in one's ability to perform the task lower the tone of the nervous system, interfere with the stimulation and inhibit relationships in the cortex, distort the dynamic stereotype, and lead to the rise of other directions of thinking and to uncoordination.

A coach can help the athlete overcome such vital negative influences as indicision and fear of competition and of a sporting battle. He can speak of the athlete's great potential and compare his height, weight, speed, etc. to that of the top runners, showing him that many record holders have the same general physical data as other people and that they achieved success only thru persistent and tenacious work.

From physiology it is known that everyone possesses a tremendous potential physical energy. This energy, however, does not appear in ordinary circumstances. A simple desire is not enough to bring it out. Rather, a powerful emotional jolt is needed. In life many cases are known of this phenomenon. Its nearly instantaneous implementation is related mainly to the central nervous system. And as we know from physiology, the action of this system can be improved and strengthened thru training. Such training should involve first of all daring - the daring to attack not only personal records but world records as well, and the setting of high goals in general. Additional important training aids are handicaps, where one is placed at a relative disadvantage.

Actual competition has great significance in teaching the athlete to evoke large physical efforts as well as in developing all the desirable mental qualities mentioned above. The coach should first of all encourage those who did not do well and should explain to each individual that defeat in sport is the road to victory. Furthermore, it is necessary to be willing to train and compete under unfavorable circumstances, such as soft and slippery tracks or roads, rain, headwinds, etc. Under conditions such as these one best receives the mental preparation needed for success in similar circumstances in important competition.

Methods of developing endurance and the resulting condition of the athlete.

Which methods of developing endurance help produce the best time over the basic racing distance? To study this problem in relation to the 800m run, experiments were conducted with 16 groups of girls (285 people), all of whom were in good physical condition but were not specially trained for running. The methods compared were the gradual drawing up, repetition, and standard methods (see table 2). Prior to the start of the experiment everyone was given a time trial over 100m and over 800m. In testing all 3 methods the training sessions were held twice a week, after a general warmup taken by everyone.

in the case of the gradual drawing up method 5 groups (87 girls in all) participated. The first general stage consisted of 8 workouts, each one involving the running of a gradually lengthened distance (600m, 800m, 1000m, 1200m, 1400m, 1600m, 1800, 2000m) at the same slow pace (70 sec. per 200m). The second general stage consisted of 6 workouts wherein they ran a shorter and shorter distance each workout (1800, 1600, 1400, 1200, 1000, 800m) while gradually increasing the pace. After these 14 workouts, extending over 7 weeks, the overall average 800m time improved from 3:22 to 3:02 (table 3).

Another 5 groups (71 girls) were used to test the repetition method. The workout consisted of 4 x 200m with 5 min. rest between each run. Pace of the 200m runs was always quite a bit faster than race pace. The workout in general was difficult and they often dropped out on the last 200m. Twelve training sessions were held over a 6 week period. The average 800m time improved from 3:20.4 to 3:09 (table 3).

The standard method consisted of putting everyone thru an 800m run every workout, striving for best time. Six groups (127 girls) were used. After only 3-4 workouts they began to complain about not wanting to do the run. Monotony in the training lowered the working capacity. The interest diminished practically in proportion to the number of training sessions, and this undoubtedly affected the times. After 12 workouts, over a 6 week period, the average 800m time did not improve, and in fact became worse (table 3). Such lack of success calls for a closer look at this phase of the experiment. Out of the original 127 girls, 57 were excluded, having completely lost interest in the run and hence not trying to train in the workouts. Of the remaining 70, the average 800m time progressed as follows: before the experiment - 3:11.9; after 6 workouts - 2:58.6; after 12 workouts - 3:20. This indicates that for purposes of accelerated training this method may be useful.

Table 3. Averaged experimental results on effectiveness of training methods.

Name of training method	Group no	No. of subjects	100m run (average time) before the expert.	100m run (average time) after the expert.	800m run (average time) the expert.	800m run (average time) the expert.
Gradual drawing up	1	13	17.2	16.5	3:20	3:01
	2	18	17.8	15.8	3:23	3:10
	3	19	17.0	16.1	3:21	3:00
	4	19	17.3	16.0	3:21	3:00
	5	20	17.3	16.4	3:25	3:01
Repetition	6	13	17.0	16.4	3:10	3:07
	7	17	17.5	15.8	3:24	3:03
	8	17	16.7	15.6	3:18	3:18
	9	20	17.6	16.2	3:24	3:07
	10	14	18.3	16.9	3:26	3:10
Standard	11	24	16.9	15.8	3:03	3:07
	12	21	17.1	15.9	3:06	3:28
	13	21	17.0	16.0	3:17	3:13
	14	23	16.0	16.8	3:02	3:14
	15	20	17.6	16.7	3:04	3:17
	16	18	18.5	16.4	3:33	3:13

A comparison of the three methods examined is given in the following tabulation:

Training method	no. of subjects	100m run (average improvement, in secs.)	800m run (average improvements, in secs.)	remarks
Gradual drawing-up	87	1.16	19.9	
Reptition	71	1.84	11.4	
Standard	127	0.90	Deterioration of 4.5	Had improved by 13.3 sec. halfway thru the experiment

Thus for novices not trained for running, the gradual drawing-up method turned out to be the best.

Planning the Training and Developing Endurance.

The development of stamina should be done on a year-round basis. But at different times of the year each should receive different emphasis. As a guide for the work distribution, data of G.I. Nikiforoff concerning national caliber athletes is given in the following table.

Type of workout (see table 2)	Total mileage during preparatory period (December - April)	Total mileage during racing season (May - October)
For 5000m and 10,000m runners		
Steady pace	170	238
Variable pace	125	212
Cross-country	138	244
Repetition	36	52
With accelerations	15	23
For marathoners		
Steady pace	320	419
Variable pace	484	688
Repetition	135	127
With accelerations	21	-
Slow run with high knee lift and long strides	16	42
For walkers		
Steady pace	188	188
Variable pace	130	134
Repetition	15	-
Cross-country	212	212
Walking	313	513

Although much hard work is necessary to get to the top, one should always remember that the main thing is not the quantity of the training, but the quality.

References

1. Elfimov, I.T., 1954, The Effectiveness of Various Running Tempos and Rest Intervals in Repetition Training for a Middle Distance Runner; Dissertation, State Inst. of Physical Culture, Moscow. (In Russian.)

2. ________________, and Ozolin, N.G., 1955, Effectiveness of various rest intervals during repetition training; Theory and Practice of Phys, Culture., No. 9. (In Russian.)

(The above was translated and synthesized by Gar Williams from the book entitled "Developing Stamina in Athletes," by N. G. Ozolin, published in Moscow in 1959.)

Visit With Dr. Woldemar Gerschler

by P. Sprecher,
(Professor of Physical Education, International d'Athletisme)
(translated by Brother G. Luke, F.S.C.)

On a trip to Germany I was able to stop for a few days at Frieburg, Germany where one of my friends lives - a professor of Physical Education at Turenne College.

For a long time I hoped to be able some day to hear Dr. Woldemar Gerschler and learn from his own mouth the fundamental principles of what is generally called "interval training".

When in 1952, Josey Barthel became Olympic Champion at 1500 meters, the name of Gerschler, forgotten for thirteen years, returned to everyone's lips; he recalled the memory of both Rudolph Harbig and the surprising victory of J. Barthel.

Interval training, explained and commented on in the press, became popular then, overshadowing the Swedish method (Fartlek). The great majority of runners adopted the interval method entirely or in part. Numerous performances have proved its effectiveness, and the names of Zatopek, Kuts, Pirie, Jungwirth, among others, are there as confirmation. However, it is necessary to state that this method has been diversely employed. It is also necessary to state that a good number of coaches, in interpretation and application, have had a tendency to make the workout too easy, notably in regard to proposing times for given distances, that are too slow.

I was then able to speak with Dr. Gerschler, who had just returned from a trip to Spain and Portugal. He went there to give some recent findings concerning cardiac research and their significance. He was able to give me one hour and fifteen minutes of his valuable time, and without hesitation he began the conversation himself. It was a veritable course in cardiac physiology, remarkable in every respect. He expressed himself in practically faultless French. He is, incidentally, equally fluent in English.

Basic Principles. 1. Physical exercise, everybody knows, increases the heart beat, Rest slows it down. 2. Repeated physical exercise-such as is found in training, diminishes, eventually, the number of beats for the same volume of blood for a given time. 3. The volume of blood in the body is constant for a given individual. Then, if the heart beats diminish for the same volume of blood, the quantity of blood pumped at each beat is increased in volume.

Certainly this has been known for a long time, but it remains to be found what the optimum amount of physical exercise is in order to arrive at systematic improvement. After long and patient work with the celebrated German cardiologist, Dr. Herbert Reindel, Dr. Gerschler is not in a measure able to establish a physiological law. Three thousand cases, that is to say 3000 persons without special characteristics, have been examined and it can be said that they represent the average person.

The Gerschler-Reindel Law

After these 3000 experiments had been carried out for 21 days, it appeared that the heart did not at any time surpass 180 beats per minute in the course of physical exercise - 180 beats represents a limit.

From this point (180 beats), the heart is permitted 1 minute, 30 seconds to return to 120 or 125 beats per minute; if it takes longer, it is because the effort demanded is (1) either too violent, or (2) too long.

In the second case, the distance to be run should be shortened. One minute, 30 seconds also represents a limit. When the pulse has returned to 120-125 beats per minute, the runner is able to - and ought to - begin running again, even if the heart took less than 1 minute, 30 seconds to recover.

In resume, what is most important is:

1. Bring the heart to 120 beats per minute by a preliminary warmup - not only by running on the track but also by exercise of all kinds - in order to begin the workout effectively.
2. From this point, the runner does a given distance - 100, 150, or 200 meters in a given time which will bring the heart up to about 170-180 beats per minute.
3. Soon afterward, the heart ought to take a maximum of 1 minute, 30 seconds to return to about 120 beats per minute. This time could be shortened however, but what is important is the return of the heart to 120 -125 beats per minute. When this occurs, the runner should being running again.

Before doing this article, I experimented with all this on myself. (I am now 38 years old). I was satisfied with 15 times 100 meters in 15 seconds each. After each effort my pulse was 165; I recovered by walking, and after 1 minute and 30 seconds I had a pulse of 122.

Dr. Gerschler insists very much upon the following theory. It is the recovery effort which strengthens the heart; that is, while the pulse if returning from 180 to 120 a minute. This recovery effort can be walking at the beginning and later on become a slow jog. After such a workout for 21 days the heart volume can be increased by one-fifth. It is evident that there also exists a limit fixed by the hereditary characteristics of the individual. Dr. Gerschler cited to me the case of a young 18 year old girl who came to visit him after having undergone an open heart operation. He was fully successful at the end of 21 days of very delicate work.

What gives all the value to this law - and by the same token, these workouts - is its application to anyone for any kind of predetermined exercise, of course, in proper proportion.

I was very much interested in asking Dr. Gerschler, who is director of the Institute of Physical Education of Freiburg University, a few questions. Two of these seemed of special interest.

"Do you think that a runner can gradually change over to a racing distance longer than that which can generally be considered his specialty?" His response came immediately in a precise and clear fashion:

"The change to a longer racing distance does not have to be gradual. One can advise it when he is sure that the subject is capable of it through his heredity and his physical make-up. A very careful examination is necessary. However, it is not absolutely proved that the longer racing distance will be satisfactory on first trial."

Dr. Gerschler then cited to me the case of Herbert Schade, who certainly reached his peak in the 5000 meters, according to his physique and natural qualities. That is, Schade, no matter what type of training he did, would not have done any better. It is necessary then to discover the best event according to the ability of a given individual in order that he attain the best performance without injuring his health.

To my second question: "What do you think of the Swedish Method (Fartlek)?" He answered me, "It is not exact."

And this is true for the most part because there is no check upon the accuracy and effort of the runner who uses it. Never have I heard it stated that it (Swedish Method) was supported by precisely exact statistics such as the measurements of heart beats at various moments. However, we must not see in this thought of Dr. Gerschler a condemnation.

Marcel Hansenne, in the October issue of "Sport and Life" mentions two names together; Gerschler and Gosta Olander of Sweden, illustrating for all those who are interested in running two concepts generally considered as opposed. According to my humble opinion there is no conflict, and here is why.

The Swedish concept, according to what has been written for us, does not depend so much on physiology as a science. It is admitted at Volodaen in Sweden that whoever presents himself at the Chalet of Olander is physically in condition. The training by its nature does not require, it seems, any physiological tests be passed, and the fact of feeling able to run again after a given effort is sufficient.

This is undoubtedly true - based on the psychological plan, but that does not completely satisfy Dr. Gerschler, who, as a perfect scientist, likes to have every guarantee. And he is right because the runner is thus constantly checked, thus avoiding possible errors in training (which are always possible) because of excessive enthusiasm or an understandable euphoria, if one is too much taken up with the method.

That this Swedish Method is more pleasant is indubitably true. To practice on the shore of a lake, as can be the case in Sweden or Finland, is completely different from the "routine menu" - 50 x 100 meters - that Dr. Gerschler proposes for certain runners. However, this is not "psychological torture" as Marcel Hansenne pretends, but a scientific manner of proceeding. There is no doubt that if Dr. Gerschler could use the Nordic countryside, his method based on timing would have an undeniably supplementary attraction (romanticism and science thus being a service to each other) but in any case a lake and a mass of dunes are not sufficient in themselves to uncover certain physiological factors indispensable to our knowledge referring directly to the cardiac mechanism. It is not two men with their respective opposing concepts that should be proposed - at least not to the mind of those who read such an interview as this - but rather two systems to be joined. The following must be the logical synthesis without which exact and superior results (as concerns yet unsuspected human possibilities) cannot come to light or even be imagined:

One, to utilize first the method of Dr. Gerschler in order to determine scientifically what the subject is capable of.

Two, to undertake physical conditioning according to an agreeable natural method.

The Swedish concept cannot in any case constitute of itself alone a point of departure. Not being scientific, it cannot be compared, and by the same token, counseled or even preferred as a means of research for better performance. It is far from being infallible.

With cardiac observation on the one hand and natural qualities on the other, the German method is not only incontestable but even indispensable.

And then to return to more verifiable matters - if we consider the physical workout alone, the methods matter little from the moment that the running recommences when the heart has returned to 120 beats a minute - without ever having surpassed 180 after a recovery interval of 1 minute, 30 seconds at the most.

Finally, whether we use a stop-watch in order to follow and verify the heart-beat or whether we use personal judgment in order to decide when to resume running - it makes no difference, so long as there be rigorous agreement with a physiological plan. But the latter method assumes that the average person can arrive at that degree of development of judgment. I would like to think this possible, but I am personally inclined to doubt it.

In any case, this should not in any way stir up sterile polemics because, despite its laudable romantic character, the delightful Scandinavian summer of itself alone is insufficient to produce a sound theory for method of physical training.

Marathon Running

by Leonard G. "Buddy" Edelen
(Holder of the world's fastest time over the full marathon distance).

Training for the marathon can be both interesting and exciting. The athlete need not necessarily possess a lot of natural speed. Endurance is the important issue, and unlike shorter track races, one need not depend on great natural speed. It is important to utilize what natural speed one has and even more important, to develop the endurance which is so necessary in marathon running. The marathon is exciting because merely to finish a marathon, a distance of 26 miles 385 yards, is a wonderful achievement which one can reflect upon for the rest of his life.

It is not necessary to be able to run a fast mile to run a fast marathon, although the current trend seems to be that the faster one can run the mile the faster one can expect to run the marathon, providing he possesses the mental tenacity to develop the necessary endurance. It never ceases to amaze me how an athlete can run close to his maximum speed for a specific distance, yet carry on and run twice as far at approximately the same speed. For example, my best 3 miles is only 13:51, yet I have run under 14:00 minutes for 3 miles enroute to a 28:00 minute six mile. If the athlete can only negotiate a mile in 4:45, I am convinced it is possible for him to average 5:10 - 5:20 for the full marathon distance ... a speed which would assure him of a world class marathon time.

Natural Speed Not Necessary

My best 880 is 1:57 but only during two seasons of my 10 year career have I achieved a sub 2:00 min. 880. In 1963, for example, I ran 13:51 for 3 miles, 28:00 min. for six miles, 48:28 min. for 10 miles and 2 hrs. 14 min. 28 sec. for the marathon, yet my best 880 was only 2:02. My best 440 is only 55 seconds and yet I have run 58 seconds at the end of a 3 mile. Again, natural speed is not the most important issue in marathon running, but merely the ability to sustain what speed one has.

It is also interesting to note that man seems to gain endurance with age ... not only in running, but as regards laboring generally. It is reasonable to assume that an athlete can maintain roughly the same volume and intensity of training from year to year, yet improve simply due to the fact that he is gaining endurance through maturing physiologically. Also, the physiological maturity enables him to tolerate a heavier training load which should result in an improvement in his racing speed.

Another reason why I find the marathon an exciting event is that one has such a great distance to run in attempting to improve his time. Pity the poor sprinter. How much improvement can he hope to make when he has only 100 yards to run? His improvements can usually be measured only in terms of tenths of a second. Also, he cannot console himself with the fact that when he is 28-30 years of age he will necessarily be running much faster.

I feel it is best that the athlete who wishes to become a marathon runner first attempt races at a shorter distance. For example, he should run a few races on the road over 6 miles and 10 miles. Then attempt a few at 15 or 20 miles. After this, he will be ready to tackle his first marathon. No matter how much training he has done, he will usually find the first marathon far more difficult than he envisioned. The last 6 miles can seem an eternity ... the last 3 miles can seem longer than the first 23 miles. Races over the shorter distance will make the last few miles easier, although there is no such thing as "an easy marathon". Anyone who describes a marathon race as easy is only speaking in relative terms.

I think it is highly important for the athlete not only to run shorter road races before attempting his first marathon, but also to be prepared for this grueling event by making sure he has put in the necessary quantity and quality of training. I personally feel this consists of one long run each week of 20-23 miles at a steady pace, a mid-week run of 12-15 miles, a faster pace than the longer run, a high volume workout of repetitions of 440's or 880's at a medium pace with relatively short recovery, and a small amount of repetition sprint work. Many athletes and coaches will undoubtedly disagree with me on the latter, but I have found that the repetition sprints have contributed immensely in improving my marathon time. I also feel that twice a day training is essential. The faster repetitions enable the athlete to run well over the shorter distances while preparing him to run a fast marathon. Also, it affords tremendous variety to one's training and decreases the possible boredom of the training from day to day.

Typical Winter Training

A typical training week for me in winter is as follows, subject of course to slight alterations from time to time depending on how I feel, the weather conditions and important races. Sunday morning, I run continuously for 22-23 miles. I always start slowly and gradually increase to a steady pace. I usually run the last 10 miles quite hard. Sunday evening I go out for a 5-6 mile run usually at a slower pace, but I do about 10 x 110 yd. fast strides enroute. If I am tired from the Sunday morning run, however, I sometimes forego the evening run. Monday morning I usually carry my clothes to the school where I teach some 4½ miles from my home. Therefore my Monday training merely consists of 4½ miles home in the evening at a fast pace. However, on occasions I take my clothes to school on Sunday, thereby enabling me to run to school Monday morning. It might be best to merely do the 4½ miles home or rest on Monday, since I am often tired from the 30 miles from the day before. Also by running just once or resting I am sufficiently recovered to complete a good double session the next day. Tuesday, I run 4½ miles to school at a steady pace in the morning and in the evening I usually run 4½ miles home at a steady pace, then jog a mile to the sea front. There, on the road, I try to run between 20 and 25 x 440 in 68-70 seconds with 60 seconds jog after each. I jog a mile back home for a taper-off. At times however, I run 4½ miles home at a faster pace and then run fewer 440's with the usual 60 second jog. If the wind is particularly strong I sometimes choose to do faster 440's with the wind in 66 seconds with a full 440 recovery jog against the wind. Wednesday I run 4½ miles steady to school. Then, in the evening, I run approximately 15 miles at a faster pace than my Sunday run, but well within myself. I usually run the last 5 miles quite hard. Thursday, I run 4½ miles to school, then either at noon, or after school I run 2-3 x (10-15x110) yd. sprints. I try to run these at 14-15 seconds with 110 jog between, and a 3-5 minute jog between the sets. I end this session by running 4½ miles home as I feel. Sometimes it is quite fast. Other times it is a little more than a jog. Friday, I run 4½ miles to school, and often in the evening I do a 5 mile run at a steady pace. If I am tired, or if the race on Saturday is relatively important I do not run Friday evening. Saturday, I usually race for my club. In England one races almost every week. I usually treat most of these races as part of my training, often doing a 5 mile run in the morning before the race in the afternoon. If the race on Saturday is very important with International competition, I prefer two days of complete rest. Obviously, the above schedule results in a great volume of running each week, but it also includes tremendous variety. It enables me to race reasonably well over any distance.

In marathon running there is certainly no substitute for experience. I know this is true with other track events as well, but I think it is especially true of the marathon. One simply must run a number of marathons to gain this experience. I suspect most experienced marathoners view their first marathon as the worst. That was my experience, and I am sure this is the case with many. This is because the athlete really has no idea of the distance he must run. Presuming that he has done the necessary mileage including the weekly run of 22-23 miles, he still cannot possibly imagine how difficult those last few miles can be until he has run them. I have seen great runners over the shorter distances full of confidence, and running extremely well at 17 miles, yet at 20 miles they are almost jogging. This brings me to pace. If one must err in pace judgement, far better he run the first half of his race too slow than too fast. If is difficult to know just what pace one can tolerate when running the marathon. Attempting a pace which is too ambitious usually results in disaster the last few miles!

Marathon Pacing

The fastest times in the marathon have invariably been achieved by athletes covering the latter part of the race at a faster pace than the first part. Ideally, of course, one should run at an even pace for the full 26 miles, 385 yds. Since this is most difficult it is therefore best to run a bit slower for the first half or three quarters of the race, and then be full of run in the later stages. One must be well trained and experienced to attempt tactical fast bursts of speed during a marathon since the bursts tend to disrupt the rhythm of the run and can waste valuable energy. These fast bursts or rushes afford the advantage of disheartening one's opponent as he has no idea how long the burst will be or how frequently they will occur. The opposition will invariably assume that you must be in a superb state of fitness to even attempt these tactics during such a long grueling race. However, such a tactic should be used with considerable discretion.

There appears to be a difference of opinion as to whether or not it is necessary, or advisable to take liquid refreshment during the marathon. It can be argued that the body loses much liquid during the race, and this should be replaced during the race or dehydration will set in, putting an added strain on the heart and the circulatory system. However, I have personally found that taking liquids often serves to upset the stomach, causing in some instances diaarhea. The higher the temperature, of course, the greater the need to drink liquids during the marathon. It might be advisable to experiment with drinking liquid refreshment during long training runs. Thus the body can become accustomed to this and later it will not be such a shock to the system during the race.

Finally, to become a good marathoner, one of the most valuable prerequisites is tremendous determination. One cannot attach too much importance to the mental tenacity required in marathon running, not only in racing but also in training. To sustain a tenacity of purpose is most difficult, particularly during the marathon race. The miler knows that in just over 4 minutes the pain of severe effort will subside. The three miler realizes that it only lasts for about 15 minutes. The six miler must suffer some 27-33 minutes. But the marathoner must be able to tolerate pain and fatigue for over two hours. Admittedly, the pain is not so intense during the entire stages, but it is gradual and cumulative for more than 26 miles!

An athlete may never become a world class marathon runner, but I can assure you the satisfaction and wonderful feeling of achievement to be derived from completing this 26 mile 385 yard grind makes the effort more than worthwhile. After all, if you can run 26 miles 385 yards without stopping, you can at least console yourself with the fact that there cannot be too much wrong with you ... physiologically anyway!

Tactics in Long Distance Running

by Vladimir Kuts (USSR)

It is said that there is no accounting for taste in regard to tactics of running. Ostensibly each tactic is fine only if it results in victory. As everyone knows, one doesn't sit in judgement of victories.

Is this really the case? Is any tactic perfect? The running tactic is the plan of action of the runner in competition both before the start and during the run. The plan of action can be quite different depending on the goal which the athlete wants to reach, be it to set a record, to attain a predetermined time, or to win.

Before proceeding I wish to point out that there are many possibilities for tactical action. However, I intend to examine only two of them which were frequently used by the strongest long distance runners during recent years at internationally stacked competitions. The one plan of action I shall designate as the "record tactic", the second as the "competitive tactic".

1. The most Progressive Tactic

Many times it is said of a runner that he has run foolishly because he began his finish drive much too soon and therefore could never become a good athlete by this means; he simply doesn't understand how to distribute his energies. Such "sins" are generally committed by beginners. One can easily hoodwink a young, relatively inexperienced, although well trained, runner by bringing him out of his pace and taking victory, which he seemingly already has in his pocket, away from him.

I remember my sad experience in Budapest in 1953. At the time I was the only participant who had the task of running the 5000 meters in under 14 minutes. Up to that time only the Swede Gunder Hagg and our own Anufrieyv had succeeded in this. I was not badly prepared, having previously won the silver medal at the 4th World Youth Festival in Bucharest, beaten only by Emil Zatopek.

The start came. I had no plan for the individual laps and plunged head over heels in the race at almost a sprint speed. The time at 4000 meters was about 7 seconds faster than at the same point in Hagg's world record run. My next pursuer, the Hungarian Jozsef Kovacs, was more than 100 meters back. At that point, however, my superiority came to an end. My indiscretion caught up with me after exactly 10 laps. My "tactic" punished me cruelly in the fifth kilometer. My speed slackened inexorably and no effort of the will was capable of withstanding the fatigue of the body. My entire lead was very quickly lost in the last two laps. In the home stretch Kovacs overtook me. I dragged myself laboriously behind him at the finish. Thus ended my first attack on the world record.

When I later analyzed my failture, I came to the conclusion that the reason for the failure had been my inadequate tactic. During the run I was only concerned with myself. I did not pay attention to the positions of my opponents, did not take into account their ability and, most important, I rushed off from the start without estimating and budgeting my own energy properly.

Requirement for Fast Time

I have not mentioned this example to bring discredit upon the record tactic. On the contrary, I advocate it fully and look upon it as the most progressive, most daring, but, at the same time, the most difficult. It results in victory and consequently a new best performance only if all of the following conditions are observed:

1. Good training condition, which is developed from good all-around physical preparation;

2. Ideal pace judgment;

3. Knowledge of one's own strengths and a previously conceived plan of running which is adhered to for the entire distance as well as the individual laps;

4. Knowledge of the special features of the run and the potential of each of the opponents.

Only when a runner has learned to adhere to all of these prerequisites can he afford to bolt off to a sizeable lead, especially during the first part of the race.

In this connection it must, however, be understood that one retains the lead for the entire distance.

During the winter of 1953/54 I prepared myself for the European Championships which were to be held the following August in Bern, the capital of Switzerland.

Along with my training in the forest and on the track my preparation contained a detailed study of all my expected opponents, their running styles, their racing tactics, and their training methods. I ran imaginary laps with Zatopek in the Olympic Stadium in Helsinki, accepted battle with the wily and devoted Englishman Chataway, and repeated my Budapest run with Kovacs. I endeavored to defeat them. In my imaginary race one half year before Bern I failed to defeat any of them even once. However, I had the desire to outdo them all in order to give my country the first world record in long distance running on the track.

I knew that none of my dangerous opponents took me, a little known long distance runner, seriously as candidate for the title of European Champion. That just suited me. Thus no matter which tactic I would use it would come as a surprise for the runners with whom I would start in Bern. In the cross-country run for the prize of the newspaper "L'Humanite" I observed my future opponents (I placed third at the time) and realized that the tactic chosen by me for the European Championships promised victory for me.

In Bern the previously determined tactic came into use. I opened up on my opponents right from the start and, according to the precisely adhered to prearranged time schedule, widened the gap to them lap by lap. The first 1000 meters was covered in 2:44.0, 1500 meters in 4:10.7, 2000 meters in 5:36.7, 3000 meters in 8:23.9, and finally 5000 meters in 13:56.6. Differences from the time schedule of 1 to 2 seconds were allowed for. From the newspapers I later learned the opinion of Emil Zatopek, whose world record I had lowered at the time: "I am glad that Kuts won, that he carried out his battle for the championship without all sorts of maneovering and ruses, that he did not conceal himself behind the backs of the other runners, and that he did storm forward gamely, resolutely and courageously."

During the race I adhered to my tactical schedule of a uniform pace as, by the way, did my opponents. It showed that my tactic of long distance running was the best'. This new grain which I had fortunately found had to be secured. Therefore I subsequently continually endeavored to hold a uniform pace at the highest possible speed for the entire distance. With this tactic I have twice set world records in the 5000 meter run: in Belgrad in the fall of 1955 and in Rome in the fall of 1957. It may be observed from the table how I followed the race plan.

Cumulative Lap Times

Belgrad

Lap	1	2	3	4	5	6
Planned	1:03.0	2:09.0	3:15.0	4:22.0	5:29.0	6:36.0
Executed	1:04.0	2:10.0	3:17.0	4:23.0	5:29.0	6:35.0
Lap	7	8	9	10	11	12½
Planned	7:43.0	8:51.0	9:59.0	11:05.0	12:11.0	13:46.0
Executed	7:43.0	8:49.0	9:57.0	11:05.0	12:12.0	13:46.6

Rome

Lap	1	2	3	4	5	6
Planned	1:01.0	2:05.0	3:12.0	4:18.0	5:24.0	6:29.0
Executed	1:00.5	2:06.4	3:10.8	4:18.4	5:24.8	6:30.8
Lap	7	8	9	10	11	12½
Planned	7:35.0	8:41.0	9:47.0	10:53.0	11:58.0	13:34.0
Executed	7:36.8	8:41.6	9:46.8	10:53.0	11:59.1	13:35.0

2. Variations of the "Record Tactic"

Today no long distance runner any longer doubts that a prearranged tactic is necessary for success in racing. Above all it has to be very elastic. At the start one is sometimes not able to foresee the overall behavior of his opponents during the race. Results in long and middle distance running come not only from adherence to a prepared race schedule but also depend on the ability to switch tactics during the course of the run. Here one cannot be oblivious to the opinion of Franz Stampfl, the track and field expert, who wrote: "Fame, reputation and standing of the runner can markedly influence his choice of tactic. For a known runner the choice of tactic is difficult, because all of his tactical habits are known and it is only seldom that a tactic can be employed which can deceive the opponents. He is observed much too keenly by them."

Prior to the XVI Olympic Games in 1956 I found myself in such a difficult situation. With my tactic of breaking away quickly from my opponents and then running a steady speed, I was able to get the jump in 1954 in Bern. Two years later the factor of surprise was no longer present. I knew that the English runners would follow hot on my heels provided that I did not alter tactics and would be in position to pull out the win shortly before the finish by utilizing their greater speed. Before the Games my training condition and my endurance were about the same as those of my most important opponents. I resolved to outmaneuver them tactically and for this purpose I prepared a new variation of the "record tactic". I intended to take the lead at the start and then unexpectedly change the pace sharply by switching from a steady pace to running with intermediate spurts and by this means break down the strengths of my opponents. According to my calculations even well trained and strong willed runners could not stay with the telling intermediate spurts without special training.

I practiced my contemplated tactical variation for four long months prior to the trip to Melbourne and then used it in the 10,000 meter run. I varied the pace so often and so unexpectedly by increasing and decreasing the pace that there were times when my prime opponent, Gordon Pirie, who was following at my heels, almost ran over me. The intermediate spurts had so weakened Pirie that in the 20th lap he gave up the chase and finished the race in 8th place although he had the opportunity to place 2nd or even to become an Olympic winner in the event that I had remained with my old tactic.

After my victory in the 10,000 meter run, I could no longer use the tactic of breaking down the resistance of my opponents with distance to surprise those with whom I still had to battle at the 5000 meter distance. Several other runners could have stuck out the intermediate spurts, which were too much even for Pirie. If they were to succeed in bringing me out of my pace, then surely a runner could be found who had reserved his strengths and who could overtake me in the home stretch.

The 5000 meter run began. Tabori took over the lead in the second lap, went to the inner edge of the track and slowed the pace. Lightninglike I made up my mind to break away from the main field and to lead the run in the fastest possible steady racing speed which I could hold to the end. That is just what I did. I overtook Tabori and the lead. Of course I had to be constantly on the alert, at each moment prepared to tactically face my opponents whom I could not see behind my back. At each moment I expected Pirie or Chataway would close ranks to me with an intermediate spurt. At the same time I also knew that with this speed each intermediate spurt of my opponents would signify an error. After each intermediate spurt a speed decrease always follows to wit and here I ran a steady fast speed so that an opponent had to drop back again after he had caught up with me. Thus it happened to Chataway who tried to take over the lead in the eighth lap with a strong intermediate spurt. This intermediate spurt proved fatal for the Englishman. At the finish he wound up in eleventh place, although he did not participate in the 10,000 meters and could, without doubt, have taken a medal in the 5000 meters.

The tactic I chose proved to be correct. Thanks to my maximum, steady race pace I was able to pull away from my pursuers by 40 to 50 meters in the ninth lap and from this moment on I was racing solely against the clock and set my second Olympic record in this race.

Four years later at the 1960 Olympic Games in Rome the New Zealander Murray Halberg sensibly used this tactic to break away from his opponents. During the first three kilometers of the Olympic 5000 meter final he was striving solely to maintain contact with the main field. Up to the seventh lap the Pole Kazimierz Zimny, the Australian Albert Thomas, and the German Hans Grodotski alternately led. Yet they all steadfastly refused to break away from their opponents although such runners as Friedrich Janke, Kazimierz Zimny, and Hans Grodotski were definitely strong enough to lead from start to finish. They all adhered to the waiting tactic and no one took the initiative of setting a fast pace. Only in this way can it be explained why the strongest long distance runners in the world covered the first 3000 meters in a modest 8:19.3.

The tactical error of his opponents resulted in an advantageous position for Halberg. He ran behind the leaders, observed them keenly and, diagnosing the situation correctly, took over the lead at the end of the eighth lap and thereupon put on a determined intermediate spurt. Halberg's opponents didn't grasp the situation in time. When Grodotski woke up and took up the battle with the New Zealander, Halberg had already pulled away to a lead of 30 to 40 meters. It was practically impossible to make up such an advantage. The speed of Halberg and Grodotski was almost the same. Halberg was the Olympic winner with a personal best time of 13:43.4. Grodotski finished 7 to 8 meters behind him.

A Steady Fast Pace is the Best

Now, in conclusion in regard to the record tactic, I repeat that I look upon it as the most progressive:

1. Thanks to this tactic my performances improved from run to run, from year to year. In my first 5000 meter run I had a time of 17:34.9. Five years later, the "record tactic" mastered by this time, I established my last world record with 13:35.0. Altogether I managed to set 5 world records and 10 Russian records.

2. This tactic brought me great moral satisfaction. Even when

I had to swallow defeat twice at the hands of English long distance runners (1954 in London and 1956 in Bergen) I ran personal best times. If I run faster today than yesterday then this tactic helps me to run faster tomorrow than today.

In using the "record tactic" the runner has the opportunity to achieve a best performance since by running away from the opponents from the start and then holding a steady fast pace for the remainder of the distance the leader can expend his energies fully and effectively. A vivid example of this is Pyotr Bolotnikov's excellent run in the 1960 Russian Championships in Kiev. Using the "record tactic" he attained the sparkling time of 28:18.8 in the 10,000 meter run and thus improved my world record by more than 11 seconds.

3. The Competitive Tactic

The "competitive tactic" is diametrically opposed to the "record tactic". Here the runner tries to win irrespective of the resultant time. As a rule, the long distance runner does not give an outstanding performance or set a record with this tactic, but gains a string of victories instead. A long distance runner of international class has to start a dozen times a year, yet his goal is not always to set a record or national team to place first and bring in the most points. Such a situation arises if the results of team meets are valued according to place rather than according to actual achievement.

In applying the competitive tactic the runner allows his opponent to lead, follows closely behind him, observed all his actions keenly (in order to surprise the leader at the opportune moment), overtakes and wins. The art of this tactic is based on staying within the pace (within reason) set by the opponents, having the ability to sensibly judge energy fluctuations with distance and using all unanticipated intentions of the opponents to one's own advantage, in other words understanding how to react correctly to attain the established goal during the course of the battle. As a rule the "competitive tactic" of such runners results in a fast and efficient victory with all energies concentrated on the last spurt. The longer the spurt, the greater the chance for success.

In the 1960 Olympic Games in Rome Pyotr Bolotnikov was very successful in the application of the "competitive tactic". Of the 33 runners who started in the 10,000 meter run in Rome easily half were in a reasonably strong position to place among the first six. As far as I was concerned, Bolotnikov had the best chance for the gold medal. However, we did not have the right to overlook his strongest opponents, the German Grodotski, the Pole Krzyszkowiak and Halberg, the Olympic winner from New Zealand.

At first Yevgeniy Zhukov led the field. When Bolotnikov took over the lead in the second lap and tried to pull away after the first kilometer, it was felt that he had selected the "record tactic" (detachment from the opponents). However, it seemed so only at first. The Soviet long distance runner was experienced enough to know after about seven laps that it is dangerous to play hare for such strong and fast finishing opponents. As soon as the group of his strongest opponents had cut the gap to him, Bolotnikov sensibly ceded the lead. In the fourth kilometer Sandor Iharos took the lead and Bolotnikov, conserving his strength, ran in third position. The pace set down by the future winner was, however, too fast for Iharos and the others who were now quickly peeling off one after another from the lead. Their pace slackened inexorably. From the 9th to the 14th lap the lap times were between 70 and 72 seconds. The Soviet runner now knew that although his opponents had decided to take the lead they feared the fast pace like fire.

In the 15th lap Bolotnikov's plan of battle was made evident to his opponents. He resolutely took the lead and intensified the pace. He ran the next three laps in 67 to 69 seconds per lap. At the proper time Aleksey Desyatchikov supported Bolotnikov in his goal of increasing the pace and thereby running away from his opponents by closing ranks to Bolotnikov and following closely at his heels. This intermediate spurt by Bolotnikov seemed to be the first attack on my Olympic record and was a shock for his opponents. The German Grodotski and the Australian Power, obviously seeing through the purpose of the Soviet runner, gave chase and picked up the pace of the runaway. Furthermore, Power took over the lead with an intermediate spurt, led the field in the 19th and 20th laps and still had enough strength to hold the fast pace started by Bolotnikov. Bolotnikov now appraised the situation sensibly: twice he had set down a fast pace, twice he had tried to free himself from his opponents and twice his opponents cut the gap to him, holding his race pace as long as they could. With such strong opponents it was risky for Bolotnikov to attempt the same tactical maneuver a third time. Therefore he moved up to remain closely on the heels of the leader up to the last lap.

From personal experience I knew only too well how intensely Bolotnikov could concentrate all his energies on a long haul final spurt. When my German neighbors in the stadium grandstand saw Grodotski in the lead in the last lap they shouted: "Hans - Win!" I could not resist and called: "Pyotr - Go!" At this point the runners still had 300 meters to run. Bolotnikov shot past Grodotski and finished the race in a glittering 28:32.2. In the last 300 meters he made up a whole five seconds on the German, almost unheard of in the annals of long distance running! The faculty of being able to sensibly vary the tactic with distance brought the Olympic victory to Bolotnikov.

4. Which Tactic is the Better?

Now, of course, the question arises as to which tactic is really the better.

I take the view that beginners in long distance running should hold to the "record tactic", according to which the battle is geared to the best possible time and thereby serves to expose the real potential of the runner. With the "competitive tactic" a young runner can win a few races all right, but without willingness to set the pace, without spending himself complet ly, he will scarcely realize good performances.

I carried out my military service in the Baltic Fleet together with the well-known long distance runner Sergei Protonin. When I reached performance class III (5000 meters in at least 17:00) Protonin was already in performance class I (5000 meters in at least 14:50) and was, furthermore, champion of the Navy and Estonia. The years passed and Protonin could not meet the champion standard (14:05) although he won race after race. Once we went to the starting line together. I exerted myself to the limit of my energy because, with such a strong opponent, I believed that I had to run at the fastest possible speed. How great was my astonishment however when Protonin ran quietly behind me, did not attempt to take the lead or to bring me out of my pace. In the last lap he tried to overtake me to be sure, but it was already too late! As a result of this run I rose to performance class I. This was my personal best time.

Protonin, on the other hand, had a time which he had attained many times previously and which he also repeated later.

Now when I think back to this time I am firmly convinced of the fact that the failure of this doubtlessly endowed runner to develop further was due to his one track tactic. He used the competitive tactic in all his races, and didn't try to battle for the entire distance in order to attain a best performance.

Scientific Researches

Only when a long distance runner used the "record tactic" can he fully determine his potential. An interesting research in this direction has been carried out by the Soviet physiology professor W. S. Farfel together with the speed skating trainer M. P. Sokolov. They analyzes four variations of energy distribution as a function of race distance: 1. steady pace throughout the entire distance; 2. a relatively slow start with gradual increase of speed; 3. fast start with gradual decrease of speed; 4. very fast start with a subsequent decrease of speed and a renewed speed increase up to the planned speed.

Their research showed that the most favorable energy distribution is given by the fourth variation. This distribution of energy with distance is typical of the runner who used the "record tactic". I have experienced the advantages and on the basis of my experience I can say that runners who want to run a good time must first learn the "record tactic" and only then the " competitive tactic".

(The above article originally appeared in the No. 4 issue of Legkaya Athletika, 1961, published in Moscow, Russia. A translation of the article has beenpublished in the No. 39, issue of Die Lehre der Leichtathletik, dated October 3, 1961. It has been translated and synthesized by Glenn B. Hoidale.)

Running on Snow

by P. Bolotnikov and Y. Travin
Honored Masters of Sport, USSR

The idea of year-round training for athletes participating in all types of running, jumping, and throwing in warm, dry weather has proved effective. It is of equal importance to run in snow as part of the winter preparation during the conditioning period so as to strengthen and develop the organism and improve form. Besides, training in snow affords great pleasure and tends to remove the boredom of intensive physical activity when done indoors. It is therefore not without purpose that leading athletes in Russia have included walking and running in snow in their training programs.

Snow running may be used in training for many different purposes improving one's general physical condition, developing stamina, strength, speed, and even learning and mastering certain skills. The experienced runner utilizes every little change in weather to make his training more effective. If the weather proves more unfavorable than usual (frost and freezing wind) it automatically intensifies the training load, while a dry crust of frozen snow provides yet another variation in training.

Outdoor training may occupy up to 70% of the total time in training during the winter months. For a five day a week winter program, three workouts may be done entirely on the snow. It is not absolutely necessary to always have a well prepared surface of snow for training. The type of snow surface, depth, gradient up or down, temperature, and other weather conditions, however, need to be very carefully considered in choosing and arranging the schedule. Most often the best suited snow covered courses are in the parks, forests, and along fenced country roads. Here there is less interference of traffic, and the surroundings provide shelter from the icy wind. It is of great importance to be well clad and comfortably dressed so as to keep warm yet retain freedom of movement. Below a lightweight but roughish-weave outer training suit it is necessary to wear woolen sweater, woolen undergarment next to the skin, and ski-tights or skating breeches.

It is particularly desirable to conduct training in rugged terrain where it is necessary to run up slopes of different steepness, or run obliquely across the slope when tired, and run at faster pace down hill for variety and speed. Running on a well-packed snow and specially leveled snow tracks or nicely rolled ski-tracks is used for improving speed and mastering skills. But running in deep, loose snow is usually for the purpose of developing stamina and to a certain extent strength.

A snowy surface is hence definitely not an obstacle to training, but rather an aid and a challenge to the aspiring champion. Any type of snowy surface (soft, fluffy, damp or sodden, sticky, or frozen hard) has its own beneficial effects, while providing a pleasant change of training venue. However, one important point which must not be neglected when running in snow is footwear. Running on even and leveled snow tracks can be done in ordinary training shoes or spiked shoes stitched with a felt sole. On deep snow and brittle frozen snowcrust it is better to use either ski or skating shoes (with the soles fitted with spikes or covered with felt). In damp sodden snow it is advisable to wear rubber or waterproof shoes or leather sports shoes which are greased in order to protect the feet from moisture. The shoe should be one size larger than normal so that a pair of extra inner soles may be put into them, and so that an extra pair of woolen socks may be worn.

If snow training is started for example in December, one must increase the quantity of the training very gradually up 'till February, and then increase only the intensity of training thereafter while maintaining the same quantity as before. Thus, for a middle distance runner it is sufficient to train for a distance of 5 to 10 Km. and for longer distance runners 15 to 25 Km. during the preliminary winter work while maintaining a uniform speed in running over slightly rugged terrain. During the latter part of the winter season training it is necessary to increase the intensity gradually. This is possible by increasing the speed and by running in deeper snow and on sloping surfaces in 100-300 meter repetitions, and on flat surfaces of 300-500 meter repetitions.

Such outdoor winter training should not be over-strenuous and exhaustive. Running on snow should be easy, natural, and relaxed. It is very useful to perform different jumping exercises, especially triple jump exercises, and easy "pop-up" jumps with four steps on snow. The resistance offered by the soft surface as well as the effort put into up-hill running, forces a high knee action which is particularly effective in intensifying the work load.

Each outdoor workout should finish with slow running and walking, followed by very light gymnastic exercises (calisthenics). The use of walking twice a week up to 3-5 hours is particularly good for developing one's physical condition and stamina. To increase the intensity of work one may adopt fast race walking, alternated with short bursts of fast running and longer stretches of easy running for recovery, while the training area itself may become gradually a more rugged terrain.

The duration of such training sessions on snow will depend largely on the weather, temperature, humidity, wind velocity, and the condition of the snow itself. The usual duration of one training session may extend over 90-120 minutes. If there is wind stronger than three feet per second (two miles per hour) and the temperature is quite low, it is advisable to shorten the workout time to 40-60 minutes, and conduct the training in the forest or other naturally protected area where the wind can not do great damage to the athlete's organism.

To avoid the effects of cold and frost bite during outdoor winter training the athlete must be cautioned not to stand still for any considerable length of time, but rather to keep moving constantly, particularly after intense running. Observing the basic rules of hygiene, one can train outdoors effectively in cold and snow throughout the entire winter.

(The above article was reprinted from the December, 1962 issue of "Legkaya Atletika" magazine, published in Moscow, Russia. Pyotr Grigorievich Bolotnikov is world-record holder and 1960 Olympic Champion in the 10,000 meter run.

Weight Training of Russian Runners

by Edgars Laipenieks
(Track Coach, University of Denver).

I observed the Russian distance runners for one full week before the USA vs USSR dual meet in Stanford, California during July, 1962. They went out each morning and afternoon for training. In the morning they started at 6:45 a.m. away from the stadium, running on a golf course and dirt roads. This morning workout lasted from $1\frac{1}{2}$ to 2 hours. It varied every morning, and the schedule was never identical. It was characterized by first a long easy warmup lasting 30 minutes, followed by 15 to 30 minutes of continuous real running at $\frac{3}{4}$ full speed. The 1500 meter and 800 meter groups, after warmup, ran together in one group, for their remaining running was faster and did not last as long. All runners used flat soled shoes and warmup suits. After the running they did free exercises, body building stretching, jumps, etc. Then they changed into spikeshoes, and did some speed work, in repetitions of 100 to 300 meters, varying each day, lasting 15 to 20 minutes. After each repetition the rest period was progressively shorter. For the longer distance runners the morning speed workout distances were 300 to 600 meters, also with progressively shorter rest periods after each repetition. None of the runners were timed with stop watch during this morning workout. Only the total running time was controlled and apparently determined beforehand.

Weight training. Immediately after the speed work all runners were driven back to the Stanford University weight-room. Weight-training was performed each and every morning, but varied in length of total time. The weight workout consisted of three characteristic types: (1) general body building, (2) stretching exercises, and (3) leg development exercises to improve and strengthen the amplitude of leg extension.

In general each type of exercise consisted of a number of repetitions and sets.

The weight depended on the size and physique of the athlete, and each athlete was apparently free to choose his own starting weight. After 3 or 4 sets of the same weight, the weight was increased 10 - 20 lbs. Also, the rest time between sets became progressively shorter.

Now, for details of each type of exercises:

(1) The general body building exercises. The starting weight was 60 to 70 lbs. The starting position was with the barbell on the floor, the man standing behind it with legs slightly bent, hands with palms down grasping the barbell, feet parallel, a few inches apart. The man then jerked the weight in one motion over his head, throwing one leg forward and one back. The legs were very slightly bent, the front foot resting flat on the floor, the rear foot resting on the ball of the foot. Then, without pause, the athlete brought the weight to the floor, bringing the feet together as it was lowered. Then again, without a pause, the exercise was repeated. This exercise was continuous and rythmical, without any pause whatsoever. The forward leg was alternated with each repetition. In each set the repetition number was not definite, perhaps 7 to 10, varying with each man so as not to produce any strain. The number of repetitions was increased with each set, and the rest time was shortened. After each set the athlete walked and jogged, waiting until the breathing and pulse returned close to normal (1 to 2 minutes at the beginning)before performing another set. The number of sets again varied with the individual, but the minimum was 5 to 6 sets.

(2) Stretching exercises. These are the usual ones performed by all runners, and also serve as a recovery period before the final weight train-

ing (below). The athlete's breathing and pulse return to normal before he starts the final weight-training period.

(3) Leg development exercises. The weight is increased about 50%, so as to put some strain on the legs and ankles. The barbell is placed behind the head, permitting it to rest entirely on the shoulders and back, using the arms only to help balance the weight. The athlete then jogs about slowly. During the jogging he keeps the toe of the foot generally in contact with the floor, lowering and raising the heel, thus exercising the leg extensors. The time and number of repetitions and sets again varied with the individual. The average total time was about 6 minutes each, while the long distance runners exercised continuously 5 to 6 minutes without resting.

As most of us know, the strength and amplitude of leg extension is very important in running. The difference can be seen in competition with those who do not pay sufficient attention to this development.

This particular weight training sequence is used only during the competitive season. During the off-season the weight training is more intensive. Besides the ones I have described, they perform other heavier weight exercises.

The weight-training is discontinued two days before competition, and the morning workout is limited to only warmup and some speed work. After the weight training the men jog or walk in a relaxed manner to the shower and massage. All this is done before breakfast. Before this morning workout they drink something hot, like tea with sugar and lemon or milk

There is nothing "mysterious" about the 32 year old Russian who this year (1962) established a new Russian record in 1500m at 3:41. This was the result of weight training, which he started intensively during the past year. This shows how an athlete's speed can be maintained and can progress in this class even at an "old" age, thanks to weight training.

Middle Distance Running

(We are indebted to former English Chief National Coach, Geoffrey Dyson, for the AAA Honorary Senior Coaching Award questions for 1960. These are answered by Ronald A. Jewkes, AAA Honorary Senior Coach, and a leading English middle distance running authority. Jewkes has emphasized that these answers represent his own opinions, and may not in some instances represent the view of the English AAA Coaching Committee.)

Question 1. A gradual diminishing of speed is indicative of well apportioned effort. Discuss this statement with particular reference of the half mile event.

Answer: At distances of one mile and over, experience shows that the fastest times are achieved where the pace is almost even throughout. Tactical considerations may inevitably cause slight variations of this, possibly at the expense of a fast time.

In the half mile event, however, the speed factor is equal in importance to stamina and there is an increasing tendency nowadays to regard the race more in the nature of a sprint. Meredith set the pattern for modern half mile running in this manner and thereafter the object became to get to the 440 yard mark at the greatest speed which would still allow the runner to complete the whole distance in his minimum time. Thus if he reached the finish without running himself right out, he had not exerted the maximum effort.

In the sprint - stamina events such as the 440 and 880 yards exhaustion builds up comparatively quickly as the oxygen debt develops together with the concentration of lactic acid in the system, but this process nevertheless takes an appreciable time and it is advisable to cover the greatest possible portion of the race before the burden becomes intolerable. This factor also tends to make the first part of the race faster. In any case it is almost impossible to accelerate over the last portion and any calculated attempt to do so usually results in tieing up. The winner of a close race is likely to be the man who decelerates least rather than the one who accelerates most. Conversely if an athlete is able to approach anything like a sprint at the finish he clearly has not run fast enough earlier on.

The pattern of the race should therefore be somewhat as follows: At the gun the athlete should accelerate as fast as possible so as to reach his optimum speed at the earliest possible moment and to gain his best tactical position. This requires considerable effort for a matter of only a few seconds. He should then settle down to maintain the same style and speed throughout the bulk of the body of the race. If his style and relaxation are satisfactory this requires very little additional effort. At around the 660 yard mark, however, some deceleration is inevitable with the onset of fatigue. An increased effort will be required to offset this and as the race approaches its termination the effort has to be steadily increased as the muscles of the shoulder and upper body which have been resting hitherto are brought into full play. Care must, of course, be exercised that the arm action is not over emphasized or the trunk will be forced upright and the tendency to tie up will be increased. It may be added that psychologically if the first half of the race is covered in less than half the probably over all time the athlete gains confidence from his belief that he has some seconds in hand for the second half.

When therefore the coach detects a very small diminution of speed throughout the race and the athlete finishes in good style, but without the ability to run much farther, he can assume that the effort has been well apportioned. Confirmation of this belief is to be found in the very fine coaching manual written by Ken Doherty who analysed the 220 yard sectors of 33 races run in under 1 min. 52 secs. He found that in 29 of these first 440 yards was run faster than the second 440 and that the pattern for the best time of 1 min. 50 secs. was with sectors 26.5, 27.0, 27.8, and 28.7. Experience in fast run races performed since the book was written amply confirm his findings.

Question 2. Some maintain that a distance runner should "build up from below" - by running races well below his distance - especially in the early part of a season before progressing to longer distances. Do you agree? Give reasons for your answer.

Answer: In distance running the main requirement is stamina but all too few distance runners give adequate consideration to the development of speed without a modicum of which all the stamina in the world is useless in competition. Stamina and speed can be developed simultaneously to a certain extent by the judicious planning of interval running. But mere interval running together with competition at the one particular distance of the athletes' choice is hardly adequate to produce the adaptibility required for the big time competition.

Broadly speaking, bearing in mind the probable weather conditions, the bulk of the stamina is acquired in the winter while the maximum speed is further exploited in the spring and early summer. In England most of the distance runners compete at cross country in the winter and by March many one milers and most of the three milers will have worked up to distances of 9 miles - usually in heavy mud and deplorable weather. Few tracks are floodlit and the evening training is nearly all on roads. During this period any track work (seldom more than twice a week) takes the form of repetition or interval 440's, 660's, or 880's and usually on a heavy soggy track. The athlete will thus have become accustomed to a steady heavy grind and will require to be shaken out of it. The coming of the better weather, lighter evenings and more frequent track competition gives the opportunity to remedy this by placing the accent on speed. For three to four weeks (longer for a half miler) the fast intervals are reduced, shortened and speeded up and thereafter the athlete seeks competition at a shorter distance. Thus in the early season the half miler competes at 440's the miler runs halves and the three miler runs miles. After about a month of this together with the training applicable to his own speciality the athlete then moves to his own track event quite fresh and ready for the long track season which stretches from at least May until October.

Thus while winter training builds from above, summer competition in the early part of the season builds from below.

Towards the end of the season, after the international meetings, the athlete is well advised to have a few easy competitions at the distance greater than his own. This provides a welcome mental change and also helps him to move easily into the stamina work planned for the following winter. This will first take the form of a great deal of slow running at a comfortable pace and interval running with many longer and comparatively slow intervals. The seasons should thus dove-tail into one another in a continuous (and almost unbroken) sequence to build the next season on the foundation of the last.

It may be added that a progression in competition distance also should occur throughout a distance runner's career.

Question 3. In the past 12 years, fairly definite ideas have been formulated on how runners should use interval running at different stages of training. Give your views on, and examples of, the principals which govern the building-up and use of this form of training.

Answer. The object of interval running is to build both speed and stamina simultaneously. The coach prepares the program by selecting a portion of the racing distance which the athlete then runs at around racing speed. This is repeated many times with a calculated "rest" jog between these fast intervals so that a considerable amount of continuous running is performed. The total distance covered in the fast intervals might be twice or three times that of the racing event so that the athlete gets used not only to traveling fast but also to doing so when he is feeling fatigued. It will be seen therefore that the coach's problem is to solve simultaneously the several variables such as the number, distance and speed of the fast intervals together with the distance jogged and time taken over each of the "rest" or recovery intervals.

The subject is therefore both vast and controversial with several schools of thought. For instance, one believes that the best results accrue from a great number of comparatively slow intervals. Another prefers a smaller number of intervals performed at a speed very much faster than racing pace. Another thinks that the jog between should be so fast that the athlete reaches the point for the performance of the next fast interval in a condition in which he is just able to do so. Yet another believes that since the main object is to accustom the athlete to tolerate fatigue it is best to make him tired with a fairly hard run or fast warm up before putting him onto a reduced interval session.

One system is not necessarily correct nor another completely wrong. The coach must attempt to find out what suits a particular individual and then the secret of success would appear to lie in not being too rigid but rather to start in the autumn with a large number of comparatively easy fast intervals. When the athlete has got used to the volume of work the number of fast intervals should be gradually reduced while the speed is increased. The process should be continued over a period of at least six months until a smaller number of intervals is being performed very much faster than racing pace.

Thus a four minute miler in October would commence to do 10 x 440 (70), 440 or 330 jog. Or 6 x 660 (1:50), 440 to 660 jog. Having got thoroughly used to this type of work (plus cross country, weights and circuits) for a couple of months he would reduce the rest intervals and perhaps the repetitions to something like 8 x 440 (70), 220-330 jog; or, 5 x 660 (1:45 - 1:50), 440 jog. In about February he might speed up to 8 x 440 (65), 220-330 jog; or, 5 x 660 (1:40) 440 jog and alter a few of the sessions to 3 x 660 (1:40), followed by 4 x 220 (30). In March he should work towards reducing first to 8 x 440 (62), 220 - 330 jog and then to 8 x 440 (60), 440 jog while most of the 660's should be replaced by 8 x 330 or 10 x 220 at faster than mile racing pace. There should also be some top speed three-quarter miles.

Thus the emphasis on stamina which occurred in the autumn and early winter is very gradually changed until in March and April it turns to speed. During the season, interval running should be reduced to the point where it maintains speed, stamina and fitness without producing frequent exhaustion. The emphasis will naturally remain on speed.

Question 4. In all running the arms are used for balance; they "take up" the reactions resulting from the movement of the legs. Outline the mechanical principles involved in this, showing how leg and arm actions are modified in the middle distances, and in distance running.

Answer: Newton's Third Law states that to every action force there is an equal and opposite reaction force.

When a man stamps on the ground a resistance force is exerted by the earth against his foot exactly equal to the force which his foot exerts on the ground. Force is imparted to the earth.

A man running however, has his foot in contact with the ground for too short a time for the drive to be absorbed by the earth and in consequence the reaction force is imparted elsewhere. In fact it is indicated by a lateral turning motion of the upper body and particularly of the shoulders. This effect can be observed more closely if the athlete is asked to run with his arms held firmly down his sides. At each drive of the right leg his right shoulder is thrust forward while the left moves back. Thus the reaction to the drive causes a shoulder roll in opposition to the hip turn and this is accentuated by the thrust of the recovery leg coming up.

This shoulder roll has to be absorbed by the action of the arms and is achieved by thrusting the bent right arm forward and slightly across the body during the period when the right leg is driving. Thus the faulty tendency is partially neutralized and the coach must gradually adjust the force and range of the action to produce a harmonious and relaxed movement.

It may be added that as the leg drive is absorbed in the end by the arm action it follows that any arm drive is best absorbed by the leg action. Thus a powerful back and forward upper arm drive encourages a more powerful leg thrust.

In sprinting a very powerful leg drive is required as speed is of paramount importance and no consideration is given to conservation of energy or economy of effort. This drive is not achieved by stamping on the ground but rather by accentuating the high knee lift of the opposite leg. And thus, again, we have made use of the reaction force.

In middle distance running however, conservation of energy is important and thus a more relaxed style is desirable. The stride is shorter, the knees are not lifted so high and the arm movement is a little lower and less vigorous. It must be adjusted and blended harmoniously into the whole flowing movement so that the shoulders are kept to the front. If a sprint arm action were maintained when running a middle distance race a turning of the shoulders is apt to occur in opposition to that of the hips.

Likewise an even more relaxed arm movement will be required in distance running. The arms will be carried straighter and lower and barely across the body at all and the swing will be only just adequate to offset the slight turning of the hips produced by the action of the stride.

Question 5. Write short notes on: (a) Front running, as opposed to "running from behind." (b) The value of Fartlek training. (c) Weight and circuit training for the track athlete.

Answer. (a) Front running as opposed to running from behind. Front running in middle distance racing implies taking the lead at an early stage and endeavoring to stay there until the tape is reached. Running from behind signifies the playing of the waiting game by running behind the leader (s) and then accelerating past at the appropriate moment of the athlete's choice.

Front running has the advantage that the athlete gets a clear run against the inside of the track and without obstruction so that he runs the shortest possible distance. He is able to settle quickly into his own cadence and rhythm and he avoids the present day deplorable tendancy to buffeting and being boxed in. He needs superb pace judgment and complete confidence in his own ability however and is not likely to be successful very often unless he is easily the best performer in the field.

The great disadvantage is that the whole of the field benefit from his pace setting, they all have him constantly under observation and he has the worry of not knowing what is going on behind him. At any moment of their own choosing one of the rear runners can "jump" him without warning and can take over the lead before he can recover from the surprise.

Observations over hundreds of middle distance races run in England indicate that the front runner hardly ever wins unless he is vastly superior to the whole of the other competitors. The winner is almost invariably the "brainy" man who runs in second or third spot and then "kicks" at the psychological moment.

(b) The value of Fartlek training. The word is Swedish and means "speed-play", implying running for pure enjoyment. Yet if you mention it to the Swedish athletes you will find that most of them have never heard of it and few ever perform it.

The idea is to run continuously on soft paths at varying speeds and distances without any set plan as and when the mood takes you. This is of course a very natural activity, for what can be simpler than to run fast when you feel good and the going is pleasant and to take it easy when you are tired? This naturally develops a feeling of self dependance and encourages you to try different distances. It needs no track and can be fitted into any time of the day to suit the requirements of work or meal times. It is also a psychological change from the routine of track training and the tendancy to run longer distances contributes to the athlete's indifference to fatigue and to the development of a relaxed carriage and stride. The soft going builds up soft muscle and from this point of view is a splendid recuperative agent.

The main disadvantages of too great a proportion of the training sessions being spent on this type of work are that it does little to develop the pace judgement so necessary to a track runner, it brings the athlete to his optimum fitness rather more slowly than is the case with other systems and it does not develop the absolute maximum speed required for 880 and mile. It is very individualistic and in any case can be performed only in the few cases where there is suitable country readily accessible.

On the whole, fartlek is probably most useful as a psychological change from the grind of endless track training and is helpful if performed say once or twice per week.

(c) 1. Weight training for the track athlete. This is invaluable in correcting any weakness and then producing the sheer animal strength which in a modern civilization is becoming all too rare. The tendancy these days is for the athlete to be educated, filled with statistics, technique and training schedules but to be just not strong enough to run. In middle distances particularly, the arms and upper body are often neglected and become mere passengers. Weight training is probably the speediest remedy for this by making them able to do useful work.

The idea of some ten years ago to do several sets of many repetitions using light weights and a whole series of exercises is now being supplanted by a system whereby about five of the most appropriate exercises are selected and then only three of four repetitions of each are performed using the heaviest weights. There is an enormous variety of these exercises and this is not the place to go into them in detail.

It may be added that quick results must not be expected. It seems to take about three years of perseverance before the full benefits are apparent in the track runner.

2. Circuit training for the track athlete. Circuit training is a system of repeatedly performing several severe exercises at maximum effort and speed regardless of fatigue. It thus acts quickly on the cardio-vascular system so that in a short time the athlete is brought to breaking point and still worked at his maximum capacity for a period longer than he would normally be running in competition. Circuits usually take about 15 to 20 minutes.

Examples of the exercises are:- heaving to the chin on the beam, dipping on parallel bars, high step ups, jumps reaching high with the hands, rope climb, lifting a log, press up, trunk curls and 6 x 50 yards sprint. Experience indicates that circuit training is more effective if weight training exercises are included such as squats, press above the head, jumping on and off the bench with a dumbbell in each hand, curls, swings and abdominals.

Circuit training can be done either in the gym or in a small area outdoors, by a large number of athletes doing the exercises in rotation, and in a very short time. It is exceedingly valuable for the middle distance man in the winter, especially in bad weather. It should, however, be used only as a training aid and not as a main source of running fitness. It should therefore take up only one session per week or alternatively be performed in a reduced form twice a week after a lighter running session.

Conclusion: The best training for running is running. Weight training, circuit training and tests and measurements are only either aids or barometers. The coach already has many problems to decide with track, country or road, fartlek, interval, overdistance or under distance and should resolve each case individually, being always mindful of the fact that his job is to help the athlete to achieve his maximum potential at the earliest possible moment.

Question 6. "Insofar as physiological limit is involved in setting records, a steady pace will result in a faster time in distance running. And yet, in competition, the physiological requirements for the fastest time must often be modified to suit the psychological means of winning the race." Discuss this statement in relation to the running of the mile and 3 miles.

Answer: The mile and three miles are primarly stamina events and therefore call for the greatest possible conservation of energy. The distances are too long to admit of an early development of a large oxygen debt or a concentration of lactic acid in the bloodstream without necessating a considerable reduction in the pace. It is therefore desirable for the athlete to run to a pre-arranged schedule of equally timed laps calculated to take him to the tape at as near as possible to the point of his personal complete exhaustion. Only thus can he achieve his fastest time.

There has been a number of classic record races which lend weight to this opinion. A typical example was Bannister's first four minute mile where he was assisted to run even laps by the unofficial pacing of his friends Brasher and Chataway. A similar sequence occurred when Ibbotson set a new world record in 1957 when he was guided through about equal laps by Blagrove. It is perhaps significant that the authorities evidently became so disturbed at deliberate attempts on records in this manner that it was decided not to ratify any more where it was suspected that assistance had been thus afforded by "hares" or "pacers". As regards the three miles in the world records variously set by Pirie, Green and Chataway the laps were equal within a small tolerance which would have been humanly difficult to eliminate. It may be added that records at these distances have seldom been set "accidentally" in a normal thrilling contest where the first consideration was to win the race and the setting of the record purely incidental.

In track athletics however the main object is to win races and with this in view the experienced performer will adopt a plan designed to get himself to the tape first, irrespective of whether he is currently the fastest runner. For this reason Zatopek developed a system of varying his pace so as to break up the rhythm and upset the schedule of any rival attempting to stay with him. Kuts then perfected this system and was able to run almost an interval-training type of race, so great was the differential between his fast and his slow laps. It is true that these tactics failed when he ran against Chataway and both broke the world record. Chataway beating Kuts on the run-in. But it must be remembered that in different races soon afterwards, both broke that record by a substantial margin indicating that an even paced clash would have resulted in a faster time. Kuts was more successful in the Melbourne 10,000 meters when Pirie tried to hang onto him and run his race but was killed off. The winning time was well below Pirie's fastest and had Pirie been able to run an even paced race there is no knowing what the result would have been. At some points he would have been well ahead, but at other times over 50 yards behind and it is terribly difficult to ignore a reputable opponent who is deliberately trying to break up the pace in this manner. As it was, however, Kuts' frequent and unexpected bursts of 220, 330, and even 440 so demoralized the opposition that one after the other they largely abandoned hope.

To turn again to the mile it is interesting to note that although Elliott is a superb performer and could probably win anyway, it is usually in the third lap (which is normally the slowest in most miles) that he puts in the effort which breaks the opposition. He did this in 1958 when he set a British record after trailing the field for over two laps.

There is a wealth of talent in British middle distance running at the moment with so many of approximately equal talent that all races are tactical. The first three quarters of the race or thereabouts, is usually slow and most competitors rely on the "kick" to win on the run-in. The front runner seldom wins so nobody wishes to sacrifice his chances by being the "hare".

Question 7. "Given a slow first lap in an 880 yards race 'stayers' are more likely to run a faster second lap than "sprinters". Give your views on this.

Answer: 880 runners may broadly be separated into two classes which for convenience are called "sprinters" and "stayers". The "sprinter" is the man who can run 440 or 880 and who generally finds the longer distance is the absolute maximum he can manage. The "stayer" is the one who can run 880 or mile and who generally finds the 880 a trifle short for him and who consequently is inclined to finish fresher.

The 880 has now become such that the bulk of successful competitors are sprinters who concentrate largely on the theory of maximum speed at the start and minimum deceleration which is not quite so applicable to the stayers. In consequence, not only is the first lap generally the faster but in fact the four 220 sectors are run at a steadily reducing speed so that the first is the fastest and the last the slowest. The stayer tends to be run off his feet initially but begins to pick up fast towards the end when the sprinter is tiring rapidly. Thus the stayer wants to slow the pace initially but accelerate at about the bell. Another point is that the sprinter is usually running at the extreme of his capacity in both time and distance and if the pace is slow he finds it unduly irksome and then as he tires he finds that he is incapable of changing the cadence to enable him to burst into his sprint pace. In this case the stayer has usually succeeded in taking the sting out of the sprinter's finishing kick.

Continuous Running Training

by Toni Nett

Training for General Endurance

Whether we investigate the total training of the short distance, the middle distance or the long distance runner in all its details, we will always discover continuous running to be an indispensable element of that training. This will take the form of long warm-ups and perhaps some kind of running cross-country or in the woods. Endurance training is running without interruption at a relatively slow pace over a relatively long period of time. The pace can be even or perhaps preferably, with moderate variations, faster and slower.

Interval Training is Monotonous

The weakness of interval training on the cinder track is its great monotony. Indeed, one does have to possess a high degree of tenacity (doggedness) for this and it is not to everyone's taste to knock off 30 or more repeats - depending on the length of the run and the disposition of the athlete - on an artificially designed track in constantly monotonous, often depressing, surroundings. For this reason alone one finds practically all the best distance-runners doing supplemental work in the fields, meadows or woods over a relatively long distance at a slow pace. Most distance-runners do not feel right if they are not able at least once a week to do 10, 20, or even 30 kilometers (6, 12, or even 18 miles) out where they are relieved of the monotony of interval training on the track with its tediously unchanging background. Out in the open they feel released, exalted, and are only half aware of their exertions. We must not overlook the fact that the spiritual element is often as essential in preparation for good performance as the physiological and often the two work hand in hand. There must be variety.

Good Training for the Circulation

But it cannot be said that the effect of continuous running is limited to the psychological. It also has an effect on the training of the circulatory system even though this is obviously not as strong as that of interval training. We must keep in mind, however, that distance training used to be thought of as the only known method of achieving a "large heart" (athletic heart). In all the older sports-medicine textbooks and treatises the effect of continuous running training on the expansion or enlargement of the heart was pointed out again and again. Now this cannot have changed all of a sudden. Interval training only surpasses distance training in effectiveness but this is to be understood only as a difference in degree, not a basic difference in kind. A favorable "beat-volume" (stroke-volume) will also be present in continuous running if - as we know today - the "beat-volume" is the real stimulus for the enlargement of the heart cavities (Reindell). The most favorable "beat-volume" occurs when the heart beat count is approximately 130 to 150 per minute (Reindell). Certainly continuous running might also be included here for presumably the heart beat count lies between these limits since the tempo is faster than the jogging in the recovery intervals of interval training. Thus continuous run training also enlarges the heart and is therefore a good supplementary method of mild circulatory training especially if the runner alternates slightly faster and then slightly slower speeds to vary the slow pace. It is a kind of "disguised interval work".

Prof. Nocker said it thus on one occasion: "The practice in the training camps in East Germany (for longer middle-distance and long-distance runners) goes like this: after getting up in the morning, a run of perhaps 10 kilometers (6 -miles) in a relatively easy tempo, sometimes faster, sometimes slower, that is, a 'disguised interval-work'. In my opinion this is likewise a direct training of the circulatory system." (To this they add interval training in the forenoon and sharp speed work in the afternoon.)

The circulatory system also comprises the blood vessels, including the very minute ramifications which we call capillaries. These tiny blood vessels which serve in transporting oxygen and carrying away metabolic waste products, undergo effective training (as in interval training, which is basically also continuous running although at a different speed). This means their number is increased and they are enabled to open more quickly and more completely. Thus, they are able to deliver more oxygen and carry off more waste matter.

Significance of Capillarization

Although Dr. Reindell now considers the importance of capillarization of the musculature to be far less significant to endurance performance than heart enlargement, other physiologists have been and are convinced of its equally great importance. Prof. Nöcker emphasizes this especially: "For endurance performance, -- resistance to fatigue is the decisive factor. The capacity for taking in oxygen, therefore, plays a leading part. The ability to take in oxygen, on the other hand, is closely coupled with the superficial blood-vessel system, particularly the capillaries. Thus it is to be understood that the first reaction of a muscle trained for endurance is an increase in the capacity for complete blood suffusion (supplying blood to muscles) through an increase in capillaries. Investigations of rabbit muscles have shown that not only are more capillaries formed, but that cross-connections between the capillaries have also increased. A substantially improved oxygen exchange is thereby made possible. If one were to try to grasp the change quantitively, one would find that there is a doubling of capillaries per muscle fiber and that the connections between the capillaries increase as much as 3½ fold. Thus every muscle fiber is surrounded by a thicker network of capillaries. Along with the intensified capillarization there is also an increase in the total diameter which results in a slower blood flow. This prolongs the contact between the blood and the tissue so that oxygen is delivered in larger quantities. It is in this fact that one of the causes of the increased arterio-venous difference in oxygen content in the blood of the trained athlete can be found.

How does Capillarization Come About?

The capillarization of the musculature seems to be subject to the same laws of stimulus and adaptation as we have described in the adaptation of the heart. There we found that a most favorable beat-volume occurs only at medium speed. The sports-medicine people say the same thing about capillarization:

> "The stimulus for new formation of the capillaries appears to be the lack of oxygen or the acidification of the tissue such as occurs at the beginning of a physical exertion. In analogy to other observations in muscle physiology and in the clinic, the fact seems to obtain here also that mode-rate stimuli produce stimuli of optimal (most favorable) influence on capillarization while too mild or too strong stimuli may actually have a deleterious effect--" (Dr. Hollmann).

According to this, slow walking or strenuous sprinting would not bring about increased capillarization.

But obviously, not only the tempo but also the amount of blood suffusion plays a great part in capillarization. "The importance of capillarization of a muscle was demonstrated by Maison and Broeker. For several months they had some people training the extensor musculature of the fingers with a special ergograph. The fingers of both hands were trained but with the difference that the blood-flow--to and away--in the right arm was interfered with by a tourniquet (blood-pressure sleeve). The endurance of the finger musculature of the left hand, with the unhindered blood-supply, increased substantially while the increase in the right hand was negligible. This experiment proves that an adequate blood-supply is necessary if the endurance of a muscle is to increase in the course of training." (Dr. Hollman)

The extent of the blood suffusion of the muscle is also quite great during endurance training for continuous running goes on at a slow or medium tempo and above all, for a considerable period of time (sometimes for hours). Dr. Von Aaken has for years persistently pointed out the favorable conditions brought about by continuous running training for endurance and capillarization of the musculature (by running while the oxygen supply replenishes itself, not under oxygen debt).

There can be no doubt that this is true.

What is General Endurance?

The concept of "general endurance" is usually very sketchily explained in the literature and requires somewhat more precise definition in reference to running training as compared with specific endurance or "special endurance."

We know that special endurance is related to and limited by the length of the distance of the run. A given distance is to be covered in the shortest possible time, that is, as fast as it can be done. The task here is that of "given distance in given time." Every run for time of distances up to 10 kilometers ($6\frac{1}{4}$-miles) brings about a more or less extensive oxygen debt since here a real "steady state" (equilibrium between expenditure and intake of oxygen) is not yet possible. The extent of the oxygen debt will, of course, vary with the length of the run. Running under oxygen debt, however, is always the most uneconomical kind of running, even though it may be unavoidable. Yet this uneconomical form of exertion of the organism is only a second step, the second stage in the adaptation of the organism. The first step should be the more economical kind, where sufficient oxygen can be taken on while running, that is to say, while running at a slow pace. The first step is the necessary preparation of the organism which should take place at the stage of general endurance training through continuous running. This encompasses the entire, the total organism and adapts it in the direction of endurance. It is a general exercise of the organism in the economy of metabolism, of the work capacity of the circulatory system and the coordination of the totality of inner organic activities thus leading to a general capacity for withstanding fatigue. It is not tailored to or limited by any specific distance but is rather the basis for "special endurance" which is more efficiently attainable through sprint training, tempo-run (speed run) training and interval training.

Prof. Nöcker and his colleagues put it this way: "A real dose of general endurance work, necessitating great patience on the part of both athlete and coach, is a decisive factor in further building up special endurance. The more thoroughly and carefully the foundation of general endurance. The more thoroughly and carefully the foundation of general endurance is constructed, the higher the structure of special endurance which can be erected upon it."

The bio-chemist Prof. Jakowiew of the USSR bases his continuous running training on the metabolism as follows: "It is an exercise to enable the organism to run in a 'steady state' as long as possible. Hence for a distance runner, running with interruptions and repeats will not suffice. For the attainment of general endurance, continuous running is indispensable in order to give the organ practice in economical metabolism.

Therefore it is essential for the distance-runner to establish, through supplemental continuous running, a conditioned (by training) reflex focus on economical exertion and to spread out the functional capacity of the organism over a considerable period of time. All this can not be accomplished merely be repeated runs over sections of the total distance, even if the number of repetitions is large. It can only be accomplished by running a distance which is longer than the race distance. Even from the standpoint of the metabolism (total metabolism, increase in the supply of glycogen) it is advisable for the distance runner to supplement his training with occasional continuous running (over-distance) and not to depend on interval training alone."

General endurance is also important for the speedster, though in another sense. Here it is a part of the preliminary preparation to enable him to carry speed work and sprint training over a long enough period of time. Here it is more of a "warm-up" of the total organism, a readying of the organism for fast and all-out muscle and nerve exertion.

Continuous training can perhaps be compared, in running at any and all distances, with the part played by a slow warm-up before the workout or competition. Nowadays no one believes in the absurd idea that any great performance can be demanded of the organism without a sufficiently long warm-up. It should be just as self-evident that general endurance must first (or concommitally) be developed before one can proceed to concentrate on building up special endurance.

Moderation in Continuous Running Training

Just as excess can change any blessing into a curse, so it is with continuous running. As Prof. Jakowiew emphasizes, too much running at "economical speed" ("steady state") also has disadvantages. It does not make enough demands on the muscles and therefore does not contribute to accustoming the organism to operating under anaerobic conditions (running under oxygen shortage). When practiced to excess, such (economical) exertions do not favor improvement of potentialities of anaerobic reactions and with too frequent use actually lead to a reduction in these potentialities. When speed-work is reduced, the potential possibilities of anaerobic conditions - which have been increased by training - are rapidly reduced. Hence sprinters and middle-distance runners must seek their improvement in "speed-endurance" early, during the period of general physical preparation (during conditioning in winter). In their special training (to develop special or specific endurance), - long endurance runs should be used only to the extent that might be necessary to maintain the desired level of general endurance -- but not to an extent that it will have a deleterious effect on the speed work.

Dr. Hollmann also points out the danger of overdoing continuous running training on sprinters and middle-distance runners: "Through too extended endurance run training, the protective tissue in the musculature which is imbedded between the single bundles of muscles in weakened. And in the last analysis, that is the factor to which the muscle fibers, so to speak, are attached. It is actually an element of the muscle itself. When this element of the muscle is weakened, it is theoretically possible that the susceptibility of the muscle to injury is increased. This contingency can be combatted by muscle-strength training. A muscle, like any other organ, is many-sided and the demands made upon it must also be many-sided."

For the speedster, continuous running training (runs of 3 to 5 kilometers in the woods) in the winter should precede sprint and tempo-run training (because endurance work and speed work are quite opposed to each other) and in the spring it should be limited to warm-up running. As for distance-runners, this stage of attaining general endurance (here essentially long runs in the woods) can be used in winter for a short time exclusively (perhaps from two to four weeks); then, however, general and special endurance work can be done together (since here interval training is closely related to continuous run training).

Combinations

As we can clearly see from the training schedules of world-class runners, their training consists of a favorable combination of the main training methods: (1) Sprint Training (muscle speed-strength); (2) Tempo-run (speed run) Training (muscle endurance or metabolism); (3) Interval Training (circulatory system); (4) Continuous Running Training (supplementary circulation and training for general endurance). The almost countless training methods of runners at all distances can be classified under these four headings. Even Swedish and Polish Fartlek or Speed-Play. This simplifies quite substantially the consideration of these training examples.

Thus there are basically only four main methods of training: two kinds of interrupted work (1) sprint training, (2) tempo-run (speed run) training (but here there is also a form of uninterrupted running, as shown above) and two kinds of non-interrupted work, (1) interval training, and (2) continuous running training. If one wanted to simplify the matter still more - or perhaps to summarize - the four methods could be compressed into two: (1) interrupted (sprint and one kind of tempo-run) on the one hand and (2) uninterrupted (a) interval, (b) another kind of tempo-run and (c) continuous. It is these few elements out of which the almost infinite number of variations of modern training have arisen. A coach who understands this will easily be able to reduce any training plan into its basic elements and at the same time derive great inspiration from the training schedules of famous runners.

Emphasis

These many combinations naturally have their own emphasis which make them applicable for individual distances or individual runners. We can distinguish these emphasis: (1) according to the nature of the race, i.e., according to the predominant physiological demands of a definite distance - where physical adaptation must be directed with emphasis in a definite direction, either in the direction of muscle-strength-speed development (primarily through sprint training) among runners of distances of 100 meters or in the direction of muscle-endurance in distances of 200 to 800 meters or primary emphasis on enlarging the heart, improving the performance of the circulatory system in runs of 1500 meters and up by stressing interval training. All other supplementary training methods are centered around this main point.

(2) Within these main directions, the emphasis will vary according to the time of the training period, that is, according to the season. At the beginning of winter endurance work is generally predominant. This means that the sprinter, in spite of his emphasis on sprint training as a whole, must bring other considerations to the forefront for the time being, tempo runs (speed or fast-pace repetitions) and continuous running supplemented by occasional sprinting. The middle-distance man will - within his tempo-run training - run longer distances (400 to 1000 meters) at appropriate pace, supplemented by continuous running, sprints and occasional interval training. The distance runner is already emphasizing interval training, even though not yet in concentrated form, with extensive supplementation by continuous running (from spring on) with occasional tempo-run training.

In the five winter months the emphasis of training and the schedule of supplementary work shifts from month to month, more and more in the direction of special training, the essence of which we have indicated under Number 1: distances shorter, speed increased.

(3) Placing of emphasis is further guided by the personality of the runner. Within the given framework emphasis must at all time be put on

correcting individual weaknesses, varying with each person. We must take into account condition (whether beginners, advanced, high-ranking performers or otherwise well-trained) as well as the available free time of every runner at any distance, all this so that we can get the most out of any given set of conditions.

All of these viewpoints (and more) must be taken into consideration by the coach or runner in the preparation of a training schedule for the determination of "optimal combinations" as well as emphasis of the most varied kind if any great success is to be attained. Although we can, at the present stage of sports-medicine research, precisely define the four main training methods and their particular physiological effects, and although the basic directions for the training at the various distances are clearly known to us, it is still up to the runner or coach to carry out the necessary combinations and emphasis, to control the effects constantly and to vary them according to particular needs. In training as well as in other fields, this distinguishes the artisan from the artist; the mechanic likes to follow a pattern and will lump everything together according to it while the artist among coaches will control his methods and proceed because he fully understands its meaning and its purpose. It is under such direction that highly gifted runners perform the miracles on the track which fill us again and again with amazement and renewed enthusiasm and inspiration. (The above is a synthesis of an article entitled, "Dauerlauftraining," by Toni Nett, which was published in the No. 2 issue of Die Lehre der Leichtathletik, dated January 12, 1960. It was translated from German by Ernie Westerhove and Phil Diamond, and is reprinted by permission of Toni Nett.)

Interval Training

by Professor Claude Smit,
Pretoria University, South Africa

The improvement in athletic attainments can be attributed to several factors. Improved equipment and facilities no doubt made their contribution in several fields of endeavour. It is also a well-known fact that the condition of an athletic track could affect the results. According to Prof. Dr. Carl Diem(1), the modern Olympic champion is physically better equipped and tends more and more towards the decathlon physique. He also voiced the opinion that the appearance in the sports arena of new races possessing more primitive reserves may, all things being equal, surpass the attainments of the older cultured nations. Although increased opportunity of competing on club, national, and international basis also acted as a stimulus, the phenomenal achievements in most forms of sport today must undoubtedly be ascribed to the improved methods of conditioning and training.

The time for the 400 meters has improved from 49.4 secs. in 1900 to 44.9 secs. in 1960. During the same period, the time for the 1500 meters improved from 4 mins. 6.2 secs. to 3 mins. 36 secs. Zatopek cut 50 seconds off the record for the 10,000 meters and in 1960 the Russian, Kutz, ran this event in 28 mins. 30.4 secs. These staggering times in the middle-, but especially in the long-distance races have been credited to the so-called Interval Training, or Travail par Intervalles also called Travail Fractionne or sometimes even referred to as The Fast-Slow Method. The principles of Interval Training today form the basis of all speed and endurance training. It is not only applied to athletics but, according to Mollet(2) together with weight training, now forms the basis of the training of champion swimmers, tennis and soccer players. In his paper, "The Significance of Physical Education in Human Health and Fitness", Dr. Wildor Hollmann has also stressed the importance of Interval Training for purposes of prophylaxis and rehabilitation in sports medicine(3).

The Evolution

The pioneer in this field was the Finnish coach, Lauri Pikhala, who, in 1920, already stressed the rhythm between work and rest in a method he called Tarrace Training, and whose principles were applied by the great Paovo Nurmi, Finland's legendary long-distance runner during the twenties. Mollet summarizes Nurmi's training methods as follows:

1. Development of the basic idea of rhythm through regulation not only of pace but of effort itself.
2. Systematic and specific training.
3. Dividing training into more numerous and shorter periods of time.
4. Expanding the ways which lead to the acquisition of good physical condition: life in the open air, good and abundant food, without excess; purification of the body through frequent 'Sauna' steam baths.

Towards the middle of 1930, Gosta Holmer, the Swedish national coach, who studied Nurmi's training method during his sojourn in Finland, decided to adapt these principles to Swedish conditions and thus produced the well-known 'fartlek' or speed-play method--a name said to be inspired by the way children play. Gundar Hagg and Andersson were products of this type of training and they broke several world records in a single season.

The Finnish training method was introduced to Germany by Gerschler who noticed the lack of sufficient speed work in Nurmi's method and consequently decided to increase speed without reducing endurance. Harbig, who served as guinea pig and ran 10 x 400 meters without stopping at one work-out, became 440-meters champion of the world. However, with the disappearance of Gerschler and Harbig from the sports arena with the advent of World War II, their teachings sank into oblivion only to be rediscovered when Zatopek appeared on the scene.

Zatopek, running as much as 60 x 400 meters at times in his training sessions, astonished the world with the intensity of his work-outs. In due course it became customary to speak of the Zatopek method which eventually became what is today known as Interval Training. Coaches experimented with this method and obtained excellent results, so much so that 80 per cent of all Olympic winners in 1936 and 1948, including four gold medalists of the 1952 Olympic Games, would have failed to make the grade in 1960.

It is not the object of this article to discuss the way in which the various leading coaches applied the principles of this method. The excellent chapter on Interval Training by Toni Nett(4), a leading German coach, could possibly serve as an example of how coaches approached this form of training. According to Nett there are five possible training stimuli:

1. Duration (distance of run).
2. Intensity (speed of run).
3. Number of stimuli (number of dashes and number of days).
4. Duration of recovery phase (length of pauses or intervals).
5. Nature of recovery phase (resting, walking or jogg ing).

He claims that hundreds of these conbinations are possible, but that they must be adapted to the physical and mental ability of the particular athlete. All five factors cannot be increased simultaneously. If one is intensified others must be slackened, e.g.:

Distance of Runs	Speed	Number of Runs	Length of Pause	Type of Pause
1. Same	Increased	Same	Same	lying down.
2. Same	increased	same	same	walk.
3. Shorter	increased	increased	same	walk.
4. Same	increased	same	shorter	walk.

Note--Zatopek's scheme according to this would read: same, same, increased, same, and jogging.

In endurance training experts suggested distances of 400 and 1,000 meters respectively for the 1,500 -and 5,000-meters races and shorter distances for speed training.

In this connection, Nett's most significant statement for the purpose of this article is that it is the trainer's task to discover the correct 'mixture' or combination of these factors for every individual athlete and for this the coach must possess the right 'nose', as he puts it. In other words, up to that time (1956) it was obviously largely a matter of trial and error.

Physiological Explanations

Empirically, Interval Training with its' characteristic rhythmical alternation between more and less work, has proved in practice that, in spite of its great output of work, stronger developmental stimuli with less fatigue are obtained than by means of the older form of continuous sustained effort. However, no scientific explanation was available as to why this is so. As late as 1957, Mies(5) still maintained that no satisfactory physiological explanation existed and that it is not known how to determine objectively the relationship of optimal duration of loading and recovery in Interval Training. The final break through was made by Hollmann in 1958 and subsequent elucidations are still based on his findings.

The three main factors to be considered when compiling an Interval Training schedule are:

1. The duration of work.
2. The duration of the recovery phase.
3. The work intensity.

Naturally, everything will depend upon the condition of the athlete or patient and his individual reaction. The higher the intensity of the work, the sooner exhaustion sets in and the less is the total amount of work done. In this connection, Nocker(6) quotes an experiment by Karrasch. A test person was given a load of 20 mkg/sec. on a cycle ergometer for the duration of 5 minutes, followed by a rest period of 7.5 minutes. After 10 minutes he was exhausted and had done a total of 12, 000 mkg. work; his pulse rate was 170/m. The same subject was then made to do the same amount of work for 2 minutes at a time with 3 minutes rest in between. Only after 24 minutes did exhaustion now set in, by which time he had completed a total of 28, 800 mkg. work. The pulse frequency was again 170/m. However, during the 3 minutes rest period the pulse rate did not return to its starting value, which, therefore, means that the renewed performance was imposed on muscles which had not recovered completely. Finally, when the working time was reduced to $\frac{1}{2}$ minute and the pause (or rest period) to $\frac{3}{4}$ minute, it was found that the pulse rate never rose above 100/m. Although the total amount of work done was again 28, 800 mkg., the difference was that the test person was not in any way exhausted and that after a few seconds the pulse rate had returned to its starting value.

According to Prof. Dr. Carl Diem the recovery must last only until the breathing and the heart are calm again and a feeling of freshness is felt. Immediately after that, the work (activity) must be resumed so that the athlete does not get unaccustomed to strenuous work, i.e. before he has completely recovered. Earlier, E.A. Muller and Lehmann(7) had already discovered the importance of pauses or intervals in Arbeitsphysiologie. In labor investigations in which the production and pulse rate were taken as criteria an optimum working time and the length of rest period had been established. The investigation revealed that short pauses are highly superior since the process of recovery takes place in the shape of an exponential curve so that the greatest part of the recovery takes place during the first two minutes or at most the first 2-3 minutes after the completion of the work. Lehmann therefore speaks of Lohnenden Pausen. Also investigations by Kossowskaja and Gratschewa on skin sensibility and skin temperatures revealed that the optimum pause should be of 2 to 3 minutes' duration. Metabolism during Interval Training was first investigated by Hollmann, Venrath, Schild, Bolt and Valantin(8). Loading was done by means of a cycle ergometer and turnmill ergometer. Two or more attempts were made on the turnmill ergometer with different loads for different durations, interspersed with varying periods of rest. The gross O_2 uptake the 'steady state' values, as well as the O_2 uptake during the recovery phase, were registered. In similar experiments on the cycle ergometer, the lactic and pyruvic acid levelsin the venous blood were determined. In another series of investigations every test person (subject) carried out a fixed mkg. work twice: first continuously and a second time interspersed with numerous pauses in which the load was either increased or only of minor intensity.

They found that in work of average intensity interrupted by short pauses (periods of rest), the gross O_2 uptake was less than in an equal mkg. work performed continuously. The prerequisite was that the duration of work, the intensity of work and the length of the rest pause were in relation to one another according to what was optimal for the test-person. It also proved that every test-person had an individual optimum which was independent of his condition of training.

The readings of the pyruvic and lactic acids in the venous blood indicated that the reaction of the lactic acid was quicker and more marked than that of pyruvic acid as had previously been established by Edwards and that both acids never reached the same levels during a second loading as during the first effort. On the contrary, they were often markedly lower. Hollmann's interpretation of the underlying physiological principles involved are briefly as follows: Fundamentally, every work which starts from rest is at first performed predominantly anaerobically. This is due to the delayed adjustment of the heart, circulation and respiration to the increased metabolic needs of the working or active musculature. On the average this adaptation lasts for approximately three minutes. Only after these three minutes will the active muscle have recovered sufficient oxygen as required by the particular workin question, i.e. if the work intensity is not too high. The favorable function of Interval Training is the result of the following physiological facts.

During the loading phase the reserve capillaries in the musculature are opened, the heart beat (pulse frequency) and the heart stroke volume as well as the minute volume of ventilation are increased. Then the activity is stopped and the recovery phase sets in. The main part of the recovery falls within the 1-2 minutes of recovery during which, on the average, 60-80 per cent of the recovery takes place according to the intensity and duration of the work. The higher the intensity, the longer the duration of the recovery. The duration of the work, on the other hand, is not so important for the duration of the recovery. When, for example, 70 per cent of the recovery has been completed and the new loading is resumed, the heart, circulation and respiration are then still adapted to the work, i.e. the heart beat (pulse frequency) is still high, the stroke volume still increased and the reserve capillaries are still open. Consequently, the new work (second load) can be resumed aerobically almost immediately. What is more, the lactic acid level in the arterial blood remains relatively low, which means the fatigue will be little and the athlete will be able to master a large dosage of work in a relatively short time, whereas had the work been continuous, the athlete would have been compelled to cease after a few minutes owing to exhaustion. For the required training effect, however, the total amount of work done plays an important role. Equally important are the numerous stimuli required by Interval Training in comparison to other forms of training. The steady work uptake and the repeated stoppage of work, i.e. the continuous alternating loading and unloading, stimulates the organism in higher adaptations, thereby forcing the organism to optimal development. This may best be illustrated by the development of the heart as this organ is the most accessible to modern research methods. The numerous stimuli to which the heart is subjected in a brief period of time result in a strong development of the heart in a much shorter time than is possible in any other method of training.

The physiological explanation for this is that during the loading phase the systolic pressure increases, whereas the diastolic pressure remains almost unchanged or, at most, shows only a slight drop. Simultaneously, the heart frequency increases steeply, only to drop sharply after a few seconds at the conclusion of the work, while the blood-pressure amplitude remains relatively high. The significance of this is that, during the recovery phase the heart functions with a very large stroke volume, thereby rendering dilatation stimuli on the walls of the heart. Thus it is possible to increase the heart volume from 200 to 300 ml. in a matter of 3 to 4 weeks. At the same time this results in a strong stimulus for the development of capillaries in the skeletal musculature.

In this way, the athlete attains all the advantages also for competitive running as needed in continuous work, i.e., he will have a well capillarized musculature, which is a prerequisite for endurance and a strong performance heart. In addition, favorable changes have taken place in the enzyme system.

It is interesting to note that Hollmann's results and explanations are substantiated by the Reindell's investigations in connection with the heart and Interval Training. He established that in the course of training according to principles of Interval Training lasting not even a full two months, the heart volume was increased by more than 100 c.cm., a result which until then normally took several months and even years to achieve. Reindell explains this as follows: the vigorously pumping heart is outwitted (as it were) by the short pause, and induced to transport the full volume of blood through the still open peripheral arteries, thus retaining the stimulus on the heart while the skeletal musculature is recovering. In this way, too, the cardiac muscle receives more training than in the continuous form of endurance training.

Practical Application

How can this theoretical knowledge be applied in practice? As has been stated, not only must three factors be taken into consideration, but they must be favorably attuned to one another. According to Hoffman this should be as follows:

1. Duration of effort.--This phase should be relatively short and not longer than 30 seconds.

2. Intensity of effort.--The stimulus must be strong enough and yet not too fierce, approximately 80 per cent of the athlete's maximum performance.

3. Duration of Pause.--As the dilatation effect on the heart takes place in the first part of the pause, immediately after the effort (loading), the pause should not be too long. It is recommended that it should never be less than 30 seconds and not more than 90 seconds.

Let us take a practical example: An athlete normally runs the 220 yards in 24 secs. This then constitutes his maximum performance. For training purposes he should therefore take 20 per cent longer than 24 seconds, i.e. 30 seconds. The number of times the 220 yards should be run will naturally depend on the athlete's condition, but usually the number of sprints vary from 10 to 20 with rest periods of 90 seconds after each. Then a longer rest period is introduced until the athlete is well rested. After that the whole series of 10, 12, 15 or 20 x 220 yards spurts are again repeated as above. On the whole, the series is repeated about five times during one training session. Thus we get:

30 secs. (effort) plus 90 secs.(pause) = 2 minutes
30 secs. x 2 =30 minutes
30 secs. x 5 (series) =150 minutes

Training session lasts 2½ hours

In the summer or athletic season, 'stars' or leading athletes should repeat the aforementioned training session at least four times per week. In addition, the athlete runs his particular race or distance at least twice a week. During the winter months, i.e. the off-season, weight training should be stressed.

If the athlete adheres to this scheme, then, according to Hollmann's investigations, he will never reach a higher level of lactic acid in the arterial blood than 70 mg. %, and, when an effort (load) is performed for 10 seconds the lactic-acid level will be only 30 mg. %.

In Germany all this is established clinically by a sports doctor, or, to quote Mollet's formula: athlete plus coach plus athlete physician plus laboratory equal success. Hollmann suggests a method that has as yet not been published. He recommends that the load chosen must be such that, immediately at the conclusion of the effort, the pulse frequency must be approximately 160 p/m and the rest interval or pause must last until the pulse frequency is between 110 to 120 p/m.

The pulse frequency or heart beats can easily be measured by placing the palm of the right hand on the chest over the heart area and counting the heart beats for 10 seconds, using the second hand of an ordinary wrist watch. Then multiply the number of heart beats by 6 which then gives the number of heart beats per minute. This scheme, however, is suitable only for men between the ages of 20 to 40. Should the scheme be applied to older persons, the starting pulse for men of 40 to 50 years should be 150 p/m and for men of 50 to 60 years only 140 p/m.

(This article was synopsized from the Vol. 15, No. 4, September, 1962 issue of "Vigor" magazine, and is reprinted by permission of the author.)

1) Diem, Prof. Dr. Carl.--"Intervall und Lockerheit". Jahrbuch des Sports, 1955-56. Wilhelm Limpert-Verlag, Frankfurt-am-Main, 1955.

2) Mollet, Major Raoul.--"Interval Training" in How They Train, by Fred Wilt. Published by "Track & Field News", Inc., P.O. Box 296, Los Altos, California, U.S.A., 1959.

3) Hollmann, Dr. Med. Wildor.--"The Significance of Physical Education in Human Health and Fitness", a paper read at the National Fitness Conference held in Pretoria from December 12-14, 1961. See Vigor, June, 1962 (Vol. 15, No. 3), page 8.

4) Nett, Toni.--Training des Kruz-, Mittel- und Langstreckenlafers. Wilhelm Limpert-Verlag, Frankfurt-am-Main, 1956.

5) Mies, Heinz.--"Fragen des Intervalltrainings". Festschrift zum 10 Jahrigen Bestehen der Sporthochschule, Koln. Wilhelm Limpert-Verlag, Frankfurt-am-Main.

6) Nocker, J.--"Grundriss der Biologie der Korperubungen". Sportverlag, 1955. Berlin.

7) Lehmann, Prof. G.--Muskelarbeit und Muskelermudung in Theorie und Praxis. Agf. Heft 56 (1955).

Muller, E.A.--"Regulation der Pulzfrequenz in der Hererholungs Phase nach Mudungderarbeit." Internat. Z.Angew. in Physiol. Einschl. Arbeitsphysiol. 16 (1955).

8) Hollmann, Dr. Med. W.--"Der Arbeits- und Trainingseinfluss auf Kreislauf und Atmung." Dr. Dietrich Steinkopf Verlag, Darmstadt, 1959.

Blood Test as a Guide to Training

by Major Kalevi Rompotti

Endurance of high order, unyielding physical and mental tenacity, and "guts are the secrets of success for the middle and long distance runner. But upon what does this psycho-physical endurance ultimately depend?

Endurance is partly a question of nature, partly a question of skill and ability to relax, and also a question of nutrition. Particularly from a physiological standpoint, endurance is a question of the body's ability to absorb oxygen. In athletic performances of longer duration, when the musculature has to work continuously at high tension, the ability of the organism to secure oxygen for the muscle tissues has a decisive effect on the working ability and endurance of the muscles. Vital capacity, or the amount of air we can get into our lungs, is thus by no means the only deciding factor. What matters is the extent to which the blood is able to absorb oxygen from the air in the lungs.

The body's capability of oxygen absorption also affects mental endurance, and depends upon the size and strength of the heart (minute volume and speed of circulation), the extensiveness of the network of capillary blood vessels, and above all upon the quality and the amount of blood.

Gothe described blood as "An entirely wonderful sap." A person weighing 70 kg has a total of about 5 liters of blood (approximately 5 quarts). Blood has the following composition: Plasma (50 - 60% of the whole blood volume). The platelets (250,000 per cu. mm. of blood). The erythrocytes or red corpuscles (40 - 50% of blood volume. 4½ to 5½ million per cu. mm. of blood.) The leukocytes or white corpuscles (5,000 - 9,000 per cu. mm. of blood, composed of 2 - 5% eosinophils, 0.5% basophils, 65 - 75% neutrophils, 20 - 25% lymphocytes, and 3 - 8% monocytes). Plasma is 90% water, 7 - 9% proteins, 0.9% inorganic salts, nonprotein nitrogenous bodies, nonnitrogenous bodies, blood gases, and special transport substances (enzymes, antibodies, and hormones).

The most important part of the blood with respect to capability of oxygen take-up constitutes the red corpuscles (Er) and its iron containing, red colored substance, hemoglobin (Hb), which lends the color to blood. The iron in hemoglobin readily combines with oxygen. Blood carries oxygen in the hemoglobin from the lungs to the muscle tissues.

It is clear that the more hemoglobin, i.e. iron, the red corpuscles contain (the redder the blood is) the more oxygen it will be able to carry from the lungs to the muscles. The more there are of these red corpuscles, i.e. the more blood the runner possesses, the larger the Hb surface which is available to combine with oxygen in the lungs and to deliver oxygen to the muscles. From the point of view of endurance it is therefore of

primary importance to the runner that he possess as much blood as possible with as much iron in his blood as possible.

The hemoglobin content of the blood is measured in grams per 100 cubic centimeters, and "normal" human blood contained 14 to 16 grams of hemoglobin per 100 cc. The hemoglobin content of blood may also be described by percentage (some definite figure between 14 and 16 grams per 100 cc of blood is regarded as 100% - a figure which certainly must vary with altitude, environment, etc.) In Finland, 15.5 grams of hemoglobin per 100 cc of blood is considered 100%. Thus we consider 1.5 grams equal to 10%, 11 grams equal to 70%, etc. (14 grams is equal to 100% for women as 15.5 grams is equal to 100% hemoglobin content for men.)

The middle and long distance runner is hardly in top condition unless the hemoglobin content of his blood is 15-16 grams per 100cc of blood (about 97 - 103%).

Obviously the blood picture and particularly the Hb and Er values are of great importance to athletic performances. If these values are high, the amount of Hb at least approximately 14.5 grams (93-94%), and the number of Er at least 4.7 million, the runner may train at maximum intensity. But if these values are average, Hb 13.0 - 14.0 grams (83 - 90%) and Er about 4.2 - 4.5 millions, he should train with caution. If these values are low, Hb 12.5 grams (80%) and Er 4 millions or below, he may do only very light training, or perhaps even rest and take medication prescribed by the sports-physician (iron and liver) until the blood values have increased favorably. If during training the blood values suddenly drop, it is a sign of too hard training.

It is noteworthy in connection with measured top values for blood that the following values were measured on the young Finnish skiier Mantyranta prior to the 1960 Squaw Valley Winter Olympic Games: Hb 18 grams (116-117%), and Er 6.5 millions. (He wom a relay gold medal.) On the Jamaican quarter-miler Herb McKenley, who once ran 440 yards in a world record 46.0, Er was measured while he was in top form at 6.8 millions. These represent maximum values. If the blood values exceed the above figures it is a sign of possible ill-health, the blood becomes too thick and sticky", thus decreasing its mobility.

If the amount of Hb is proportionately smaller as compared to the number of red corpuscles, it is wise for the sports physican to prescribe medication containing iron. If, on the other hand, the number of red corpuscles is proportionately smaller, the sports physician may prescribe either liver extracts or vitamin B12, either in liquid form, injections, or tablets.

In the past an index value called "I" was calculated as the ratio between the percent Hb and the Er value in order to ascertain which deficiency, Hb or Er, was proportionately greater. Nowadays a more accurate method is used to determine the average volume of red corpuscles (the Hematocrit value, volume of red corpuscles/number of red corpuscles). Normally the average volume of red corpuscles is 85-95 cu. mm. If the value obtained is lower than the normal figure it is a question of iron deficiency. If the value obtained is higher than normal it is a question of Er shortage.

Thus today one can hardly consider training of a higher order without cooperation with the sports physician. There is a definite advantage in following the blood picture. The Finnish sports physicians have found that if the athlete starts hard training, the blood and iron requirement of the organism increases. The result will be after a few weeks the plasma clearly increases, i.e. the volume of blood increases. This means, of course, a "thinning of the blood", i.e. the relative amount of Hb in the blood decreases. Later the Hb and red corpuscles begin to increase. When an equilibrium of blood composition in this respect thas been reached again the athlete is close to top condition. The time required to reach this equilibrium, starting at the date the hard training began, will vary according to individual difference but normally takes three to four months. Therefore, when after three to six weeks of hard training a decrease in Hb is found, this may be regarded as a normal phenomenon and need not cause alarm, provided the drop does not exceed $1\frac{1}{2}$ grams (10%). On the contrary, it seems advantageous to train so hard that it will influence the increase of blood plasma, causing a slight but temporary decrease in the relative amount of Hb. The plasma increase is a favorable sign because this is just what stimulates the formation of new Hb and new red corpuscles in the bone marrow.

At this early stage of training it is particularly advantageous to take such substances as iron, vitamin B12, and liver, as the bone marrow needs building material for the formation of red corpuscles. If the Hb drop exceeds 1½ grams (10%) the workouts have obviously been too severe.

Long duration training of the right kind may increase the amount of blood by 20%, or from 5 to 6 liters for example. Thus in final analysis we observe that the proper volume and intensity of hard training is the most important factor for increase in the capacity of oxygen take-up, resulting in increased endurance and tenacity. During hard training it seems desirable to check the variations in amounts of Eosinophils, because a steep drop in Eosinophils indicates overtraining or overcondition. If the number of white corpuscles exceeds 9000, it means infection somewhere in the organism and before training is continued the sports physician will seek to explain this increase in white cell count.

Following the blood values of athletes is essential to modern training. The importance of blood tests, naturally, should not be overrated, inasmuch as plenty of research in this area is still needed. But blood test results have already become a means to guide the coach at critical workout stages when it is otherwise difficult to determine if workouts should be increased or decreased in intensity. As a matter of fact, I consider it absolutely necessary that blood tests be given athletes preparing for important competition for a period of at least six months, and a minimum of once per month during this half year.

Biography

Kalevi Rompotti is chief coach of all military forces in Finland. A former international caliber middle distance runner, he was a Fullbright scholar at Stanford University in 1956. Rompotti is well known to European readers as one of the top coaches of that continent.

Physiological Fundamentals of Training Methods

by Dr. H. Roskamm, Prof. Dr. H. Reindell, and Dr. J. Keul (West Germany)

The historical development of training methods began with the utilization of practical experience alone and led to a pre-determined, scientifically founded training schedule. The value of this development has found marked expression by the fact that the German National Olympic Committee has created a commission for the scientific and methodical advancement of athletics (at the top performance level). Through the members of this commission sports-medical findings are to be made the basis for the training preparations of the elite of German athletes. The question arises, of course, whether there are positive results of physiological studies, from which decisive advantages may be expected in the utilization and "dosing" of particular training methods.

The application of a particular training method will always depend on the expected training results which, in turn, depend on the special demands of the particular branch of athletics and the individual constitution of the athlete.

The training result or aim may be considered as the improvement of the fundamentals of athletic ability, such as (1) Technique; (2) Strength; (3) Speed; (4) Locally-limited muscular endurance; (5) General endurance or staying power of the total-organism; (6) Tactics. These fundamentals are in their extent determined by natural tendencies, yet are capable of improvement through exercise within constitutionally set limits.

The Technique

The conception "technique" circumscribes the flow or sequence of motion (kinetics) of an athletic exercise. The technique is good if the motions are rational. This requires - first - maximum utilization of the laws of mechanics and - second - that the elements of the complete flow of motion are harmonically attuned to the style-induced mechanism of motion of the individual athlete.

The application of the laws of mechanics must be founded on the laws of Biomechanics and the laws of motion of man and beast. (Donskoi, USSR)

The length of stride in relation to speed is especially important in the economy of running. Högberg and Christensen - using a treadmill - have defined the most favorable length of stride through measurements of oxygen consumption. They found that rigid relations exist between running speed and length of stride. With increased speed greater length of stride is more ecnomical. There was a striking harmony between the actual length of stride of our best runners and the results obtained through their experiments. Consideration must, of course, be given to the physical height of the athlete. Only Nurmi's length of stride in his 1500m runs was found to have been too great in relation to his speed; his stride in these being from 7' 5" to 7' 7", while a length of from 6'3" to 6'11" would have been more advantageous for his pace. Thus, while his style was elegant, it was unecnonomical. The experiments have shown that the long stride at slow speed can be uneconomical. Münchinger proves this with his findings that the center of gravity in the moment of the forward "jump" is being lifted too sharply, and that the necessary hip and-shoulder counterthrust consumes too much energy. Münchinger further points out that the possibility of a runner competing at various distances with success, or shifting his specialty from one distance to another, depends largely on his ability to relate his length of stride to the altered requirements of speed. A runner will achieve his best results at distances with speed norms which are related to a length of stride most nearly that of his own.

An advantageous technique will not only increase the economy of motion but, in conjunction therewith, diminish the possibilities of damage or injury.

Apprentices being instructed in certain mechanical operations, working at them for 15 minutes followed by a pause of 15 minutes reached a given degree of proficiency in 14 days. Others, undergoing the same instructions on the customary 8-hour basis, needed two months to reach the same degree of proficiency (acc'dg to Graf). These experiements suggested a similar "interval" training for athletic progress. It must be pointed out, however, that such an "interval-like" practicing has nothing to do with that discussed below and whose effect is bound to the relation between short exertions and short pauses.

Strength

The strength of a muscle stands in close relation to the area of its cross section. An increase of strength is only possible with an increase in area of this cross section (thickness). Nöcker found that 1 square cm (3/8" x 3/8") of muscle will lift from 6 to 10 Kilograms (13-22 lbs.), regardless of the trained or untrained status of its bearer. The main stimulus for muscular increase lies in the tension acceleration in the muscular structure.

A characteristic example pertaining to the dosing of tension-stimuli is given in the story of Milo of Croton. According to Greek tradition he could carry a four year old bull simply because he had carried him every day since he was a small calf. This old story already points to two principles of strength-training: (1) To increase training stimuli with increased ability. (2) To apply substantially maximum stimuli in training.

Exhaustive studies into the frequency, amount and duration of training stimuli have been conducted by Müller and Hettinger. They came to the surprising conclusion that a single daily isometric contraction of a certain muscle with more than 1/3 of its maximum capacity is sufficient to create the desired training effect. An increase in strength (of that particular muscle) of 3% per week will be the result. This cannot be exceded by any other training method. If, however, this contraction is exercised with a frequency of less than once daily, the effect is correspondingly diminished. No increase of strength was noted where there was a lapse of 2 weeks between exercises. Rarick and Larsen were able to substantially confirm the findings of Hettinger and Müller.

It is, of course, difficult to accept these results, since they seem to contradict everyday experiences. It must be considered, however, that the actual employment of the muscles in a weight training session lasting one to two hours amounts to only two to six minutes. The average duration of an exercise was 3.3 secs, 3.48 secs, 4.12 secs for lift, snatch and press respectively. (Murray and Karpovich).

Other scientists arrived at different results. Friedebold and his associates noted the same increase in strength with training stimuli amounting to 2/3 of maximum, but also noted a smaller increase in the mechanical performance, the product of strength and holding power (the extended "hold" in weight lifting) compared with that achieved with maximum stimuli or power.

De Lorne, Rasch and Morehouse, Mateef and Hansen came to the conclusion that the maximum stimulus load will produce the best training effect.

Salter (in 1953), using 30 maximum daily contractions, found an increase of 52 to 88% in isometric muscular strength. It matters little whether 2 or 15 contractions per minute were performed. Nor was the effect different when isotonic contractions were used. Asa (in 1958) found that 20 isometric contractions per day produced better results than a single contraction per day.

Darus' and Salter's experiments (1955) showed an 18 to 46% increase in isometric muscle power when 30 maximum stimuli daily were applied.

Bonde Peterson (1960), using both male and female trial objects, found no ascertainable effect after one single daily isometric contraction of the elbow with application of maximum strength, holding the contraction for 5 minutes. When 10 daily contractions were accomplished, a training effect was noted although less than that found by Müller and Hettinger (1953). 15 minutes of heavy bicycle-ergometer work excuted by the men, however, led to an increase of isometric muscle strength of 23%. Bonde Petersen explains the different results obtained by researchers thus: (1) Hettinger and Müller as well as Darus and Salter used for their training and tests the same exercises and dynamo-meters. The possibility exists that the increase in strength was, to an extent, at least, brought about by an increase in dexterity, or imporved technique. (2) The varied muscles are trainable with different effect. (3) The fluctuating area of muscle power is relatively large.

Müller, Hettinger and Asa are of opinion that better training results may be obtained with isometric contractions. Rasch and Morehouse (1957) obtained a greater effect with isotonic contractions. Important are in this connection the findings of Fenn and associates (1931) according to which the development of muscular tension decreases, the greater the rapidity of the movement involved. For this reason it is held that there is hardly any increase in the muscular tension of sprinters, since the short bursts of speed do not offer sufficient growth-stimulus for the leg muscles. The only benefit in this direction may be derived from the emphasis placed upon the starts and initial accelerations in these races.

Of fundamental importance are also the results arrrived at by Müller and Hettinger concerning the atrophy of muscular power. An arm in a plaster cast may lose up to 36% of its strength in a week. After resumption of normal activities this lost strength will be restored within the same period. A single, short, daily exertion at 1/5 of maximum potential is just sufficient to prevent atrophy.

It is interesting to note that the training-constancy stands in close relation to the length of time during which the strength increase was accomplished. Quickly gained strength diminishes rapidly after termination of training, while slowly attained strength will maintain itself for a relatively long time. A training at intervals of 2 weeks is said to maintain a once established higher level of strength for more than a year.

In recapitulation the following may serve as a guide in the dosing of strength training: since there is no concurrence (by researchers) in the degree of intensity of the exertion, maximum stimuli in training are recommended. Even A. E. Müller pleads this latter method despite the results he was able to obtain with stimuli of just above 1/3 of maximum. This, especially, since it is hard to pin down a precise percentage and in view of the fact that there is an automatic increase in muscular strength in line with increased training effect, in short, "progressive training". All researchers are in agreement as to the advantages of daily training. In those forms of athletics where strength training is merely an adjunct to other work (as is the case in running), strength training every second day should be sufficient.

Speed

This is understood to mean the maximum speed with which a certain exercise may be accomplished in a given time. This speed is to a large extent a natural propensity. If a certain movement in athletics is accelerated through practise and training, it is for these reasons: (1) Through a better coördination of the elements of motion, the entire movement (technique) will become more rational and faster. (2) Increased muscular power may be an important factor. Thus the speed in a sprint race depends much on the ability of acceleration after the start through muscular power.

Speed can be increased by improving technique and strength. There is a widespread opinion that the speed of contraction if impeded by excessive muscular growth (Hypertrophy). Zorbas and Karpovich were able to prove the contrary to be true. Weight lifters possessed greater rotation-speed of the arms than ordinary persons.

Locally limited Muscular Endurance

When a muscle is subjected to extended stimuli its contraction becomes weaker and the frequency slower. The latent pause between stimulus and beginning of contraction becomes longer (according to Grandjean). This is muscular fatigue, the mechanism of which Gradjean describes thus: When the exertion of a muscle is driven to the point where the energy expenditure exceeds the recovery process in the tissues, chemical changes take place indicating a reduction of adenosin-triphosphoric Acid, Phosphocreatine, and Glycogen content, as well as an increase in Urea, Carbonic Acid and Lactic Acid.

These chemical changes stimulate certain nervous receptors of the muscle, sending afferent impulses to the brain, where we perceive this muscle fatigue in the form of general fatigue, often manifested in pain. The afferent impulses also induce a check on those centers of the central nervous system which controls the motor direction or steering of physical motions, causing a reduction in numbers and frequency of discharges of motor neuron.

When in the course of athletic exercise larger groups or areas of muscle are under strain, the effort-maximum will be limited by the capacity of the central mechanism. Muscular endurance is dependent upon and limited by the maximum capacity of the heart. This point will not be approached if only smaller muscle areas are under strain for a prolonged period, or a short though maximum effort occurs. In these cases the work capacity is limited simply by the local endurance capacity of the muscle involved.

It may be assumed that the local muscle endurance is in part limited by the existing capillarization of the muscle structure which, according to studies by Vannetti and Pfister, by Petren, Sjostrand and Sylen, by Hollmann and Venrath, may be improved through training. Mention must also be made of conversions of biochemical nature, manifested in an enlargement of energy sources, such as Creatin-phosphoric acid (Palladin & Ferdmann), Glycogen (Embden & Habs) and Potassium (Nöcker). In addition to this greater energy reserve the possibility exists that the trained body may exploit this increased store in an even greater measure. Nöcker & Associates showed that the trained muscle, under exhaustive strain and considerably reduced Potassium content, was better capable of contraction than the untrained muscle. It thus follows that the biochemical conversions in the trained muscle produce not only a greater energy reserve, but allow this to be exploited to a fuller extent. Better capillarization and the biochemical changes mentioned are the prime requisites for increased muscular endurance.

The rise of lactic acid concentration in the blood is less pronounced in trained than in untrained persons under the same conditions (Robinson & Harmon and others). This applies not only to an equal load, but also to an equal degree of effort - same pulse frequence. Lactic acid concentration takes place at a pulse frequence of 120 in untrained persons, at 140 in trained people, where the production of the acid is less pronounced.

The endurance capacity in a short maximum effort, requiring the consumption of a large amount of oxygen, depends on the degree of oxygen-deficiency a man can allow himself to reach. The maximum oxygen-deficiency a well trained athlete can endure amounts to 15-20 Liter (the greatest oxygen=deficiency ever reported, 228 L, was registered by Krest=ownikow after a 10,000m run). A deficiency of 2.5 L produces an accumulation of lactic acid in the blood. (Karpovich). This may reach 3 mg % per second (Hill). Since the maximum tolerance is approximately 130 mg %, it would follow that a man should be able to run - without breathing! - for 43 seconds. (Karpovich). Robinson and Harmon found that the average lactic acid concentration in nine men, tested after a run at maximum speed during a 6-months training period, increased by 38%. Since there was no increase in alkaline reserves during this training, the increased formation of lactic acid caused a reduction of the alkaline reserve.

Yet many factors involving local muscular endurance need to be clarified. Recent studies, however, have contributed considerably to the problem of its trainability: Petersen, Graudal, Hansen and Hvid have been able to show that the increase in muscular endurance is closely related to the number of daily stimuli. After a training of six weeks the endurance in dynamic muscle effort could be increased seven and eight-fold, when the number of isotonic contractions was set at 50 per day with 60% of maximum load. At 150 such contractions the endurance was increased 150-fold over the original ability. At the beginning of training the average result with 2/3 maximum weight was 16 lifts (just off the floor); after the training 843 lifts.

In another experiment where isometric contractions were used, the static endurance could be increased 10-fold. The dynamic endurance increase (41%) was, however, insignificant. The importance of these findings lies in the fact that they show, 1. That improvement of muscular endurance rather than muscular strength depends on the number of repetitions of an exercise and, 2. That dynamic work will only increase dynamic endurance, static work only static endurance. This indicates that in exercises where local endurance is of prime importance (gymnastics, boxing), the endurance training should be made up of the same exercises that are characteristic of the sport.

General Endurance of the Total Organism

In every exercise of more than one minute duration the general or over-all endurance (or stamina) plays a decisive role. In exercises of up to 30 minutes duration this is influenced and limited by the capacity of the heart. Decisive for the work capacity of the heart is its size. (Reindell & Associates). It is thus not surprising that an enlargement of the heart could be observed where the nature of the sport called for increased endurance efforts. Enlarged hearts - under strain - can favorably affect their pulse-volume (Reindell et al), thus enhancing the volume of heart capacity.

In training for organic stamina or endurance, in this case of the heart, two methods may be used: 1. Extended efforts, 2. Interval training.

Karvonen, using a tread mill, noticed increased ability or performance only when (in a run of 30 minutes, accomplished daily for four weeks) the pulse frequence was above 135 during the effort. While both methods will produce an enlargement of the heart, practical experience has shown that interval training requires less time and - in addition - enhances the ability for sudden bursts of speed and the final kick. Hollmann first probed the aspects of metabolism in interval training. The distinct efficiency of interval training with regard to heart volume could be ascertained through the extended studies of Reindell and Roskamm.

Increased absorption of oxygen during the recovery pauses in interval training on the bicycle-ergometer and the increased blood pressure amplitude at low average arterial blood pressure were the pertinent points leading up (in 1958) to an understanding of the increased pulse-volume during the recovery pauses of interval training. This constitutes the main stimulus for heart enlargement, which is the prerequisite for increased efficiency in interval training, and becomes readily and noticeably evident. Exceptional cases showed such evidence after only two to three weeks of interval training (Reindell, Roskamm and Gerschler).

In contrast with out results and those of other authors (Klotschkow and Wassilieva; Mies) the maximum oxygen intake was established by Christensen to occur during the periods of effort rather than between intervals. He declined to ascribe special stimulating benefits to the pauses of interval training. To clarify this divergence of results, recent research by Van Goor and Mosterd proved the correctness of our (Reid ell, Roskamm & Gerschler) above stated results beyond question.

Studies made by Mellerowicz, Meller and Müller (1961) as well as those by Meidorn and Mellerowicz (1961) do not - in our opinion - argue against the importance of the effect of the recovery pauses in interval training on heart and circulation, since the 3-minute-maximum-effort on the bicycle-ergometer employed cannot be considered a conclusive test of cardiac ability or capacity.

In actual practice, the following principles, based on physiological fundamentals, may be applied in the dosing of interval training: (Reindell, Roskamm and Gerschler): (1) Duration of recovery pauses 45 to 90 seconds. (2) Duration of separate running efforts one minute maximum. (3) Intensity of separate runs fast enough to cause a pulse frequence of 120 to 130 per minute at the end of the recovery pause.

In athletic exercises of long duration, such as a marathon run, the adaptive or utilization processes of the metabolism and the hormonal system assume particular importance. Decisive is the continuous supplementation of carbohydrate. Schönholzer coined the phrase "the ski runner starves on his course." Cortical Hormones are indispensable for the functional metabolism of the muscle, where their influence in the phosphoryl processes is paramount. According to Schönholzer it may be considered proven that mental and physical efforts or strains lead to a more or less distinct rise of corticoid or its metabolites in the urine. The fact that the corresponding plasma values tend to drop at the same time, indicates increased periphic consumption.

The occasion of hypertrophy of the adrenal cortex through training (according to Beznak, Verzar, Hort) indicates a tendency of the organism to advance the necessary safety factor in line with the highest possible demands of effort.

Tactics

Here we shall delineate the physiological aspects of tactics for the various running distances. The exponential (rather than linear) rise in energy consumption at increased running speeds (Henry), which is founded in the inefficiency of the anaerobic metabolism (Christensen), is of considerable tactical importance, since every change in speed is associated with a loss of energy and time (Münchinger). Every acceleration of pace, in the course of the race or towards its termination, is uneconomical from the physiological point of view. This is especially true for excessive opening speeds in middle and long distance running, for the comparatively slow adaptation between respiration and circulation at the beginning of any physical effort puts a great demand on the muscle metabolism. An even pace produces the best performance in middle and long distance races. Münchinger cites the following example in this connection: a 5,000m runner covered the distance in 15 minutes, passing the intermediate kilometers in 2:50, 2:55, 3:00, 3:05 and 3:10. The average deviation from an even pace was 3.3% With uniform speed his performance would have been 1.5% or 13.5 seconds better. This principle does not apply in sprint races run at maximum speed throughout. For longer races it is of greatest importance. Repeated training under competitive conditions as well as numerous actual competitions will school the athlete in the proper tactics.

The significance of the physiological fundamentals of the various training methods is in their practical application. The preceding physiological fundamentals provide important guide lines for practical training plans. 1. Training must at one and the same time improve the components Technique, Strength, Speed, Local muscle stamina, General organic stamina. 2. To attain these requisites for top performance daily training should be practised. 3. It should extend over the entire year in nearly identical intensity.

Technique and tactics can only be trained by using the respective competitive events for that purpose. They present special problems for every athletic event that can only be solved through the long experience of the coaches. For the components Strength, Local, and General stamina, general principles are applicable.

Series of short sprints (starts) provide optimum speed stimulus. Simultaneously they represent strength training. No particular increase in local muscle stamina and general organic stamina may be expected. Short and longer runs at racing pace provide optimum stimulus for local muscle stamina. Speed and strength training is involved in the shorter, endurance or stamina of the general organism in the longer runs. Interval runs are especially effective in training the general stamina. Speed, strength and local muscular stamina increases are parallel benefits.

In order to obtain improvement of general organic stamina two methods, as we can see, may be used: Interval training or long distance runs. The latter require more time per day and degree of effect than the former, to which must be added the simultaneous effects on speed, strength and local muscle stamina, as above mentioned. Thus interval training must be considered the most economical for this purpose.

For sprinters, middle and long distance runners the following program may be formulated: For sprinters, in order to increase strength, speed and local stamina, sprints and short runs (I and II). Middle distance runners must train for speed, strength and local muscle stamina. This will best be achieved through short and long paced runs (II and III). Since good organic stamina is also required, interval training - short runs and short recovery pauses - will be most beneficial. Long distance runners should prefer interval training as basic program with short and longer paced runs added for the optimum improvement of local muscle stamina. Marathon runners should - in addition - take an extended long distance run about twice a week, primarily to become accustomed to the special metabolic demands involved.

In those forms of sports, where the capacity of the leg muscles is of prime importance, interval training may be used to effect the requirements of speed, strength and endurance of theorganism. This latter through the effect ofincreased circulatory demands. Interval training is thus a good conditioner for all field games such as soccer, football, etc.

Summary

The fundamentals of athletic prowess are technique, strength, speed, local muscle stamina, general organic stamina and tactics.

The technique can be improved by daily training of the motions involved.

As we have seen, the studies concerning strength training have produced varied results. As long as no precise rules can be established it may be well to use a large number of repeated contractions with maximum effort.

The "trainable" components of speed can be increased by practicing the technique and through increased muscular strength.

Local muscle stamina or endurance will best be improved through very numerous repetitions of contractions with sub-maximum effort and in a form simulating competitive conditions.

To promote general organic stamina, long runs at constant (steady) speed, as well as interval training are in order. The advantages of interval training lie in the saving of time and in the bonus of speed, strength and local stamina improvement derived from it.

Tactics will be acquired in actual competition or in training races simulating competition.

The physiological fundamentals provide guide-lines for practical application but it remains the task of the coach touse these guides in the formulation of training in accordance with individual differences of the athletes.

Sports-medical research can only probe into the biological principles involved and offer their findings for practical training application.

(The above article was translated by Bernhard A. Schettkoe, American correspondent for "Leichtathletik," from the No. 27, June 3, 1962 and No. 28, July 10, 1962 issues of "Die Lehre der Leichtathletik," published in Berlin, Germany, and is reprinted by permission of Editor Toni Nett.)

Examination of Interval Training

by Toni Nett

An Investigation Into Its Effects

In running, we are dealing primarily with two kinds of muscles: (1) the skeletal muscles (e.g. the leg muscles) and (2)the heart muscle. In order to improve the specific function in short and middle distance running, the skeletal muscles must receive a strong "stress stimulus" but in the "endurance performer" the heart must undergo a powerful "expansion stimulus." The "stress stimulus" in the skeleton muscles is brought about by fast (perhaps all-out) running speed; the muscle must quickly contract to a high degree against great resistance (weight of the legs or the whole body). When in all-out running a powerful "stress stimulus" occurs, its effect is primarily on the "cross-section" of the musculature; the muscle becomes thicker, faster and stronger. At the same time the metabolism of the muscle (its storing up of energy, its alkali reserve) is strongly stimulated. If the running speed is somewhat reduced, the effect on the bulk of the muscle is similarly reduced but the metabolism is still powerfully stimulated (muscle endurance under strong oxygen debt). If the tempo speed is still further reduced, the effect on the musculature (cross-section) is almost nonexistent (insufficient stimulus) and the muscle metabolism is stimulated only to a lesser degree. On the other hand, there occurs a strong stimulus toward expansion of the heart muscle (through a strong "beat-volume" or "stroke-volume") immediately at the beginning of the recovery "pause", that is, when the runner slows down into a jog. Let's try to clarify this by using a comparison. (Usually such comparisons are of little value but it may help to make the principle of "heart adaptation" clear, or at least more generally comprehensible.)

Let's imagine that we have an ordinary rubber balloon, the kind you can buy at any fair, and that the balloon has a tiny opening at the bottom. If one were to blow it up with one's full lung-power, we would immediately have a gigantic sphere; the thin rubber wall would be tremendously stretched and would attain perhaps twice the size of a human head. In the first 30 seconds, therefore, there would be a strong "expansion stimulus" affecting the walls of the balloon after which it would slowly subside as the air escaped slowly through the tiny hole. The balloon would collapse as the "expansion stimulus" decreased and finally disappeared.

The effect of "Interval Training" on the heart muscle is very similar. The run (exertion) before the interval - say 200 meters in 32 seconds - is basically no different from the deep inhalation before the violent inflation of the balloon. The heart fills up suddenly, strongly, rhythmically, immediately upon the completion of the run, that is, at the beginning of the jog, whereupon a very strong "expansion stimulus" is exerted upon the walls of the heart. This lasts about 30 seconds (depending upon the runner's condition), then subsides slowly and within another 30 seconds dies away entirely. Through the many repetitions of the "expansion stimulus" (and the concommitant pumping of blood) during the individual "pauses" of a day's workout, these strong rhythmic suffusions of the heart muscle will gradually bring about heart adaptation. The heart cavities increase in size, are enabled to take in more blood and make it possible in running to pump more oxygen into the runner's working muscles. The oxygen supply during the run is thereby substantially improved, a favorable factor in endurance performance.

The tempo (speed) of the run has a decisive effect on the number of heart beats per minute. Thus all-out sprints, with maximum speed-strength exertion, will bring about a rate of well over 200 heart beats per minute. Likewise "tempo-runs" or pace-runs will produce over 200 per minute. But it has been discovered by sports-medicine researchers, principally Dr. Reindell and his colleagues, that the quick, strong suffusion of the heart muscle (strong, efficient pumping or extravasion of blood from the heart) at the beginning of the "pause" will not occur if the rate of the heart beat is too high. There is no building up of a strong "beat-volume" so that the stimulus for the enlargement of the heart muscle is lacking. It is due to this fact that sprinters have relatively small hearts and that middle-distance runners are also far below the endurance-performers in heart size. They are therefore significantly poorer in adaptation for endurance performance (supplying oxygen during the run) but of course this is not essential to their type of event.

Thus one might say here that the greater the "stress-stimulus" on the musculature, the less the "expansion stimulus" on the heart muscle". In such a case the heart muscle reacts not with increased "beat volume" but rather with an increase in frequency, in the number of beats.

After this introduction, let us turn to the scientific substantiation from the field of sports-medicine. Out of considerations of clarity and the available space, we shall confine ourselves to a few important explanations which are necessary for the further understanding of the matter. Thorough investigations were carried on in Germany by Professors Mies and Nocker, by Drs. Hollman, Mellerowicz, Metzner and others. The considerations most important, however, were presented by Dr. Reindell and his associates (Rosskam, among others) since they concentrated especially on heart adaptation. First, a summary of their work by the researchers themselves:

> "(1) The immediate "motion-stimulus" of the muscles, as is clearly evident in sprinters, leads to a hypertrophy (muscle cross-section enlargement) of the leg musculature but not to enlargement of the heart.
> (2) Since no relationship can be determined between sprinting activity and heart size, it can be concluded that the adaptation processes of the circulatory system - as evidenced in relative heart size - are not necessary for the sprinter. - -
> (3) Endurance performances, which exercise little growth stimulus on the skeletal muscles, do, on the other hand, lead to absolute and relative enlargement of the heart.
> (4) Endurance performance---in contrast to sprinting---is dependent upon the size of the heart."

Extensive investigations carried on for a period of years, both prone with a bicycle-ergometer and then continued in similar form on the sports field, produced a basic agreement in results. Tests were carried out with various degrees of exertion and the characteristic behavior in all forms was carefully noted; oxygen intake during exertion and in the intervals; emission of carbonic acid, breath volume per minute, pulse frequency and oxygen pulse (relationship between oxygen intake and heart beat count). The results are noted in excerpt:

> "During exertion, breathing, first of all, shows an increase in frequency (number of breaths) but no significant enlarge-

ment of the breath volume (depth) can be observed. Immediately after the exertion (at the beginning of the rest pause), slow but deep breathing begins"---. This continual variation in the "types of breathing" has a favorable effect on the respiratory capacity.
"---Intake of oxygen during the short, half-minute exertion is small; immediately after the conclusion of the exertion the intake of oxygen increases and reaches its high point in the first half-minute after the exertion.---
The pulse frequency (number of heart beats) shows an average increase, up to 150 beats per minute during the short single runs; this increase will last until about 30 seconds into the beginning of the interval pause after which it subsides quite rapidly.
---In principle, all investigations agree that the percentage values of the oxygen intake are substantially higher in the first half-minute after the exertion than they are during the run itself but in the volume of breath per minute and in pulse frequency there are no important variations between the exertion and the first half-minute of the pause.

A comparative consideration of the ventilatory and circulatory systems shows the following typical condition:---
In the first half of the pause the oxygen intake is higher than it is during the brief exertion. In spite of this increase, there is no further increase of the pulse frequency. Because of this, the oxygen pulse reaches its highest point in the first two half-minutes after the exertion. It is substantially greater during the recovery interval than it is during the run. Breathing becomes deeper and slower, the breath-equivalence (the breath volume per minute divided by the oxygen intake) undergoes an essential change. As an expression of increased breath-economy, it reaches its lowest point during the recovery period. Since oxygen-pulse and breath-equivalence furnish a measuring stick for economy of the circulatory and respiratory systems, it appears that economy is greatest not during the exertion but

in the recovery intervals. In spite of the heightened performance of the circulatory system, the pressure load during the interval is no greater than it is at rest. Recently Mies has also found that in interval running there is a further increase of oxygen intake and oxygen pulse during the pauses."

The contradictory behavior (increase of oxygen intake while the number of heart-beats remains constant or decreases) in the first part of the pause indicates that a greater volume of blood is being pumped into the circulation with fewer heart-beats. This can only occur with a greater expansion or extent of diffusion (beat-volume) of the heart. It is made possible by the fact that the blood pressure in the periphery of the body here remains relatively low. This great stretching of the heart-cavity muscle exemplifies the specific adaptation stimulus. The pumping capacity of the heart increases and the oxygen pulse rises, that is to say, with every heart beat a larger volume of blood can be pumped into circulation.

"It appears from this that---above all in the recovery phase through the great beat-volume, an especially optimal stimulus to improve the performance of the heart is generated. The increase in beat-volume during the recovery phase presents an effective stimulus to enlarging the heart (increase in pumping capacity). From experience with the adaptation of the heart to pressure and volume stress, we know that it is just this volume stress which is the essential stimulus to heart enlargement. It appears, therefore, that the chief stimulus for the adaptation processes of the heart occurs not during the actual exertions but during the respective rest intervals (pauses). The pause must not last too long. If the pause is substantially lengthened, there occurs a backing up of the blood from the arterial into the venous system, the result being that the conditions for an optimal increase in beat-volume during and immediately after the next exertion are no longer present.

So it is the pause which is of the greatest importance to the adaptation of the circulatory system to endurance performance. The single repeat runs are only preparatory conditions for the stimulus value of the pauses.

Dosage

In measurements on the athletic field---it appeared that training produced very good results when the individual runs were so calculated that the pulse frequency at the end of the pause amounted to 120 to 140 per minute" (during the run itself approximately 150-180). "Likewise in investigations using the bicycle-ergometer, it appeared that especially good economy in respiration and circulation was achieved - that is, an especially high stimulus-value of the pause - when the pulse frequency at the end of the pause came to 120 to 140 beats per minute. And again, heart catheter investigation among athletes proved that the beat-volume, reckoned by the Fick principle, reaches its maximum not under extreme stress, but when the pulse frequency is about 130 per minute." (Maximum = greatest expansion-stimulus on the heart walls)--- (Here we have the extreme limit of the effectiveness of Interval Training on the heart. The tempo must not be so high as to push the pulse count over 150 to 180 beats per minute!.). "From this we deduce the following practical basic principles:

(1) Duration of the pauses, 45-90 seconds.
(2) Duration of the individual exertion (run) one minute at most.
(3) Intensity of the individual exertion should be such as to produce a pulse frequency of 120 to 140 at the end of the pause.

Conditions (1) and (2) may be varied according to the characteristics of the individual events. But it is only Number 3 which permits the intensity of the workout to be adapted to the capacity of theindividual athlete. Likewise in the determination of the number of repetitions during a workout, a coach can be guided by the pulse frequency. If in the course of the daily workout the pulse at the end of the pause, as compared with 120 to 140 at the beginning of the workout, is substantially increased, the workout must be terminated.---

Through comparative pulse controls in the laboratory and in interval training on the track it was determined that the intensity and duration of the single effort would correspond to a stimulus-strength brought about by running 200 meters in 32 seconds.---"

There can be no doubt of the fact that "Interval Training" is an ideal training method for the adaptation of the heart for endurance performances; no other method can accomplish this purpose with such high efficiency. We also see that the outstanding distance runners rightly place their greatest emphasis on "Interval Training", 100 or 200 meter runs, for the most part in 15 or 32 seconds respectively, with very short pauses of under one minute, repeated some twenty-odd times (implemented by endurance runs and occasional tempo runs or speed runs).

"Interval Work" is not "Interval Training"

In the confusion which has arisen in coaching in the last few years, two concepts are often used interchangeably, namely, "Interval Work" and "Interval Training". What does "interval" mean? Unfortunately it is a word of many meanings. The idea of "interval" stems first of all from the basic principles of music theory and means "distance between", "intervening space", or "distance from one tone to another". It also means "space" or "span of time" or "time between one event and another". In medicine for example, "interval" indicates the quiet period between two attacks (e.g., in the mentally ill).

For some time the term "interval" has been familiar in work physiology as "tasks with interruptions" or with "creative" or "rewarding" pauses in which the pauses have the function of "recovery".

The term "interval work" was taken over by sports and here likewise meant "training with many interruptions" with many interspersed "recovery pauses". They saw its effect, first of all, in the skeletal muscles and the nervous system; during the recovery pauses the muscle was supposed to relax again to a great extent from its tension, be partially relieved from over-acidity, the nervous system to calm down from its excitation. These recovery pauses make possible - as they soon found out - a larger number (repetitions) of thoroughgoing "muscle stresses" (transverse section effect), a higher metabolism, a more effective schooling of the nerves (coordination in the process of learning technical skills) without greater fatigue. Uninterrupted work of equal intensity, on the other hand, was much more fatiguing and on the whole was not as effective. The possibility of increasing the work load and with it, increased training effect on the muscles and nerves with minimum fatigue was the essence and purpose of "interval work" with its interruptions or recovery pauses.

"Interval Work" is therefore used successfully in sprint training and speed work, in conditioning, in the schooling of nerve coordination (the learning process). Here the interval, the recovery pause, can also consist of a simple change in the type of work; then parts of the nervous system or of groups of muscles which had been working could recover while other parts are called into play (alternation in demands). In every case, however, the sense and purpose of interval work is "recovery" in some form after exertion in muscles and nerves.

The effect of "rewarding pauses" on the heart was for a long time unknown. Here, as far as I know, Prof. Reindell and his associates were the first to bring light into the darkness. After practical experience (especially Zatopek) made training runs continuous by jogging during the interval, that is, not interrupting the run but merely slowing it down, they investigated the behavior of the heart muscle and found that it did not partake of the "recovery pause". On the contrary, it was at this moment that the heart reached its highest specific stimulus (expansion stimulus through increased beat-volume) providing the preceding run had not been too fast (see above). This discovery was something entirely new and different and did not coincide with the old concept of "interval work".

So Prof. Reindell called this kind of workout "Interval Training with stimulating pauses" because the real training of the heart occurs during the intervals.

We must therefore distinguish more precisely between "interval work" which is concerned with the training of the muscle and nerve apparatus - with recovery intervals - and "interval training" which affects principally the heart muscle - with stimulus intervals - where there is indeed an interval, but no pause!

The juxtaposition of two similar terms with exactly opposite meanings I consider unfortunate since it continually leads to misunderstandings in discussions and articles. Almost no one distinguishes the meanings from one another; they are usually confused either from carelessness or ignorance. We should therefore perhaps designate "interval work", that is, training of the muscles and nerves with recovery pauses, as "Interrupted work" and on the other hand, call only the training of the heart (for the purpose of enlarging it) "Interval Training".

Interval training is heart training and indeed, a quite definite kind of heart training (endurance running is another kind) in which there are no recovery pauses but in which, through a sudden slowing down of the speed (jogging) in the intervals, the training of the heart takes place. The creation of a "beneficial beat-volume" in the interval produces the stimulus for "heart enlargement" or "increase in pumping space". Interval training is a constant alternation between mild metabolism effect during the training run and strong heart expansion for the preceding metabolism must - as we have seen - not be too high or it will eliminate the heart-expansion-effect because the beneficial beat-volume will not be present.

This is the reason why the middle-distance runner must put his emphasis on speed work (high metabolism) since he does not need an enlarged heart, just metabolically well-adapted muscles. The distance runner, on the other hand, must concentrate on interval training since he needs - above all - a large efficient heart.

According to this, sprint training, speed training and conditioning training can not be interval training because the preceding strong exertion does not permit the favorable beat-volume in the subsequent interval. The effect is limited to the musculature (strength, metabolism). Here the heart does not react interval with increase of the beat-volume, but in an increase in the number of beats; this does not permit the specific stimulus on the form of the heart (the expansion stimulus). Hence the heart remains small.

On the other hand, this will also illustrate the limitations of interval training; its effect is principally on the heart. The preceding muscle-metabolism-effect is inadequate and does not produce satisfactory adaptation for runs of 100 to 800 meters. On the contrary, the strong metabolism produced in speed-work (and even more so in sprint training) obviates the effect on heart enlargement. So speed work is limited to adaptation of muscle metabolism; the heart does not become sufficiently enlarged but the musculature, upon contraction of a large oxygen debt, gains greatly in endurance. Speed training therefore remains the specific method of training for metabolic adaptation of the musculature for high oxygen debt while interval training is the specific means for expanding the heart and hence for endurance performance (distance running).

Differences Between Tempo Training and Interval Training

In practical application, tempo training has much in common with interval training - for the most part short distances, similar or perhaps equal short pauses (because in tempo training a part of the hyper-acidity is purposely retained) so that at first glance both training methods might seem to be identical. The basic difference, however, lies in the variation of speed (tempo) which leads to the difference in effects as mentioned above. The one affects the muscles, the other the heart. As a consequence of the varied speeds employed, other indications of differences become evident: in interval training the slower pace (smaller oxygen debt, less acidity) permits a larger number of repetitions of the training run (and of stimulus intervals). In the faster pace of tempo training so many repetitions are neither possible nor advisable. Here it is not the quantity that matters, it is the quality.

There are also other immediately apparent differences: tempo training, in contrast to interval training, does not limit itself to short distances of 100 to 200 (or at most 400 meters. In interval training this limitation makes sense since its object is to allow as many stimulus intervals as possible to affect the heart muscle. Tempo training does not have to take this into account since its effects do not take place during the recovery interval but in the running itself. In this connection tempo training can and should bring in another aspect of training, namely, the duration of the exertion (longer runs up to 1000 meters and even more) at a relatively fast tempo to simulate race problems and to offer the opportunity to become accustomed to racing exertion and rhythm.

When over-enthusiastic advocates of interval training as a universal panacea for the development of heart and metabolism also speak of great successes in training for 800 meters, something just doesn't jive, in my opinion. Perhaps one might not be entirely clear about the difference between tempo training and interval training and might think that if one runs repeat 200's in say, 25 to 28 seconds with short pauses in between (as in I.T.) that this is also interval training. This pace, however, does not permit - as we have seen - any specific effect upon the heart because of the absence of increase in the beat-volume during the interval. Hence its effect on the metabolism adaptation of the heart muscle remains limited. But the effects of this tempo running are exactly the right ones! The successes are to be attributed to the fact that it is tempo running, not interval training.

Playing it Safe

Fanatical proponents of interval training might question the findings of the metabolism specialists and bio-chemists (e.g., Prof. Nocker and Jakowiew of the USSR) according to which a faster tempo is necessary for muscle adaptation than that necessary for heart adaptation (enlargement). In sprint training (increasing the muscle diameter by very strong stress-stimulus) the necessity for fast tempo is incontrovertible; no one questions it. In muscle metabolism both theory (science) and practice (the training of the world's best runners) testify to the validity of the research of the aforementioned scientists, that is, the necessity for a faster tempo.

In any case, those using tempo training for middle distance running aren't missing anything. They are playing it perfectly safe since this method of training, intensively carried out, has long since proved its high metabolism effect (muscle endurance under high oxygen debt) while with interval training, this still remains to be proved. "Whether interval training over short distances will also provide optimal stimulation for adaptation processes of the metabolism, the hormone system as well as the circulatory system, or whether supplementary training is necessary for optimal adaptation of this system - can at this point not be definitely determined." (Prof. Reindell)

It appears from practical considerations, that this supplementary training is already present in tempo training and should be used appropriately. And even if one could prove that the effects of interval training carry over into the metabolism - although everything points against it - we would only have a simplification (along with far greater monotony) of training and not a qualitative improvement because the strong metabolic effect of tempo training appears to have already been proved by scientific research and we are already using supplementary training methods in practice.

Dangers of Interval Training

In conclusion it must be pointed out that exaggeration of interval training is not without danger to the heart! Only a few years ago Prof. Reindell had no concern about this. At that time there was a well-known saying: "The danger lies not in too much training but in too little". For the most part, this precept is still valid today because it is the demand for high performance without adequate adaptation of the organism which presents the greatest danger. But now even Prof. Reindell has some reservations above the unlimited use of interval training because presumably several cases of heart injuries in recent times have been attributed, with some plausibility, to over-emphasized interval training. I shall quote literally what Prof. Reindell, in full awaredness of his responsibility, said to me a short time ago: "Interval training shows itself more and more to be a powerful means of stimulating the heart. It is therefore pure nonsense when I hear that some runners nowadays will do 50 to 100 hundred meter runs in their interval training." Readings of the pulse frequency should be carefully taken after a certain number of repetitions so that no injury from over-exertion might occur. Anything in this world can be overdone! So even this method of interval training, so beneficially effective in the development of endurance performance, can cause harm when used recklessly. Human common sense can never be replaced by a dead training schedule. So even in interval training, use moderation and common sense.

(The above is a synthesis of an article entitled, "Interval training," by Toni Nett, which was published in the No. 1 issue of Die Lehre der Leichtathletik, dated January 5, 1960. It was translated by Phil Diamond and Ernie Westerhove, and is reprinted by permission of Editor Toni Nett.)

Athlete and Adaptation to Stress

by Forbes Carlile, Australia

The training of athletes for strenuous physical activity today is much an art and less a science. We lack too many basic facts about the effects of muscular exercise on the human organism even for the most modern training regimes to be called scientific. Personal judgment, opinion, authority and sheer enthusiasm continue to play nearly as important a part in "producing" the champion, as in the earliest days of modern competitive running when Walter George of England, as far back as 1888, ran the mile in 4 minutes $12\frac{3}{4}$ seconds.

The modern textbook on coaching methods tells next to nothing of a scientific nature of how to train the body - functions for speed and endurance. What solid facts are there to enable us to do little more than guess why one athlete makes his record time while another, working to exactly the same training program may fail to perform even near his best? As Professor A.V. Hill says[1] in his article in the Encyclopaedia Britannica, "there is very little physiological knowledge about the changes which come over the body in physical training".

The guiding lights for many coaches have been the methods used by the reigning champion and the most successful trainers. Occasionally with imitation, real progress seems to have been made. For instance it is now generally accepted that an athlete for maximum possible performance must train for hours rather than minutes a day, and the "fast-slow" training principles first used by the Swedish runners in the 1930's is now widely and successfully practiced in many sports. But whether the improvement in standards is due to new methods or greater world-wide interest and participation, one can do little more than guess. Methods of training have not yet been evaluated scientifically.

It is not difficult to find the reason for the lack of knowledge about training, for the human body is a complex organism with what seems countless known physiological, psychological and social factors, acting and interacting. It is difficult and time consuming to make well-controlled experiments, holding enough variable factors constant, in order to come to many definite conclusions. Since modern civilized society holds the opinion that to strive for athletic honors is a worthy goal for some of its members, there is good reason for the scientist being curious about basic principles governing strenuous physical performances. There will have to be observation and experiment with the whole athlete directly in his particular specialized sphere of physical performance, if there is going to be real progress in solving the problem of how to train an athlete to perform his best.

While he should be aware of our general lack of insight into training mechanisms, he will make a poor coach who has no basic philosophy to guide his teaching. The purpose of this paper is to propose the acceptance of the General Adaptation Syndrome theory of Hans Selye as a scientific basic philosophy to guide the coach. Whether he believes that the more training the athlete does the better the eventual performance will be, or that it is not so much a question of how much but how the training is done, the present author suggests that the Selye "Stress" concept will provide the framework of a sound theory for future scientific observation and research in training.

The author suggests that a more general understanding of the Stress and Adaptation energy concept will prevent the waste of much athletic talent and hence add in some measure to the sum total of human happiness.

The Selye hypothesis of the General Adaptation Syndrome has important implications in the field of medicine, but it would appear to the present author that a knowledge of the G.A.S. and its implications will result in the gain of considerable insight to the coach who stresses his charges with physical exercise.

The stress concept

It has been accepted for some time that internal and external bodily stress plays an important part in determining the health of man. Long before Selye commenced to document with sound experimental evidence, it was widely realized that assaults by physical violence, microbes and disease, climatic conditions and nervous tension constitute the common human stresses. As Stewart Wolf,[2] a famous New York psychiatrist, has pointed out, nervous strain represented by threats and conflicts, real or imaginary, conscious or unconscious, constitute a large portion of the stress to which man is continually exposed.

There is now a considerable body of evidence showing the closs relationship between bodily stress and disease, and general malfunction of the bodily processes. Many biological mechanisms are involved in the stress response.

Many workers have contributed to this Stress concept, particularly in regard to the effect of the emotions on bodily disease, but Selye[3], experimenting mainly with rats, rabbits and guinea pigs, has been able to throw considerable light on definite reproducible effects of a wide variety of stresses on the animal organism. His research has taught us something of the mechanism of physical and mental stress by which bodily changes are brought about. Selye spotlighted the anterior pituitary and adrenal endocrine glands as playing parts in what he called the General Adaptation Syndrome. He emphasized the role of the hormones but many of Selye's critics believe that the over-emphasized the differential effect of hormones in the stress response. In this paper we shall concern ourselves with Selye's proposition about which there is very little argument, the General Adaptation Syndrome.

The general adaptation syndrome

Selye has shown that such stressing agents as infections, poisons, trauma from burns or mechanical damage, heat cold, starvation and muscular fatigue as well as having their own quite definite specific actions on parts of the organism have invariably, generalized and stereotyped non-specific effects on the body, superimposed upon all the specific effects.

The outstanding effects of prolonged stress which Selye reported (5, 6, 7) were:--(1) Enlargement of the adrenal cortex and cellular changes there indicative of increased glandular activity. (II) General atrophy of the lymph glands with concomitant changes in the blood cell count, particularly in respect of eosimophils and lymphocytes. (III) Erosions and ulcers in the gastro-intestinal tract.

These changes and others are characteristic of what Selye names the General Adaptation Syndrome (the G.A.S.).

Under the influence of various stressing agents, including muscular exertion which can be an important stressor, the body changes in such a way as to adapt itself. According to Selye this adaptation can be differentiated into three states:- (i) The Alarm Reaction. (ii) The State of Resistance. (iii) The Stage of Exhaustion.

The alarm reaction is sub-divided into two stages, shock and counter-shock. Shock represents the organism's initial response to a sudden exposure to stimuli to which the organism is either quantitatively or qualitatively not adapted. For example, an animal may be in a state of training for muscular exercise. Running on a treadmill for five minutes may cause a very mild G.A.S. while the untrained litter mate may show a marked response on stopping. But provided the stress is severe enough even if trained to withstand it, the animal will show some alarm reaction changes.

The changes of shock include diminished blood pressure, loss of muscle tone, a sustained very high heart rate and gastro-intestinal ulceration if the stress is very severe. However, with mild stresses, and exercise usually only acts as a mild stress, the main signs are merely transient high heart rate and some chemical and cellular changes in the constitution of the blood.

As Selye pointed out, muscular exercise as a stress gives a minimum of shock and a maximum of counter-shock. Exercise causing very little tissue damage precipitates an almost pure G.A.S. response.

In the stage of counter-shock the physiological changes of shock become generally reversed, e.g., blood pressure rises above normal, and soon it seems that the adaptive mechanisms in the body are proceeding at a greater rate than the destructive processes. Adaptation may be defined as being a state of the organism characterised by an increased resistance to stress through previous exposure to stress.

During the increased rate of adaptive processes of counter-shock the organism becomes active, shows evidence of increased psychic stimulation, and there are noticed activities indicating a sense of well being. Physiological changes including lymph gland atrophy and a lowered eosinophil cell blood count occur.

Resistance to all stress, including the stress which precipitated the reaction, is low during shock but during counter-shock resistance to all stresses is increased. However, the protection, called cross-resistance, of the counter-shock reaction is temporary. If the precipitating stress is continued, more or less unchanged, the animal goes into what Selye calls the Stage of Resistance when there is increased resistance only for that stress, and decreased resistance for all other stresses. The stage of resistance may be defined as the sum of all the non-specific reactions brought about by prolonged stimuli to which the organism has acquired adaptation.

In the stage of resistance the organism will continue to resist the original stressing agent but the animal becomes more vulnerable to other stresses which in addition to the original stress if severe enough, may each be capable of producing an Alarm Reaction super-imposed physiologically on the Resistance reactions.

The final stage of the G.A.S. is the Stage of Exhaustion, which represents the non-specific reactions resulting from prolonged overexposure to which adaptation has been developed but can no longer be maintained.

During the Exhaustion Stage, resistance to all stressing agents is lowered and any stress will precipitate a violent reaction of prolonged shock and death.

The passage of the animal from one stage into another is usually a gradual one and it is not always easy when specific effects of the particular stressing agent are evident, to recognize the stage. There seems little doubt, both experimentally and in practice, that resistance to all stresses decreases gradually as the Exhaustion Stage is approached.

Selye pointed out many times in his papers that we know practically nothing about the physiological changes occurring as the animal progresses from a state of resistance towards exhaustion. We know even less about human responses.

By way of general illustration of the G.A.S. response to cold as a stressing agent it may be of interest to re-tell Selye's story[8] of what happened to mice when taken from mild room temperature and placed in a freezing chamber.

When taken from the room at about 70 degrees F. and placed in an environment at close to freezing point the mice at first became prostrated with shock. They then started to run about and carry on their normal activities, at first appearing over-active (the counter-shock phase) and then apparently passing into the State of Resistance when it was difficult to tell the difference between them and mice living under normal conditions.

After some hours, one by one the mice began to succumb, becoming sluggish in their activity and finally dying in shock.

Those that have observed athletes during training will by now be able to discern that the Selye "cap" fits in many places. The present author suggests that the athlete when trained hard almost invariably shows many responses of the G.A.S.

Selye postulated that the animal organism (including man) has a finite, limited adaptation energy. But as Selye points out this concept is an abstraction insofar as we do not yet know the exact nature of Adaptation Energy. All we can say at present is that the body responds as though it has such a limited supply. The facts advanced by Selye, and the author's own observations on himself and other athletes who have been in severe training, supports the concept that stress effects are summated to draw on the limited adaptation energy.

When everything seems to be nearly equal some individuals can always be observed to be able to stand distinctly more training than others and continue to show improvement. Whatever may be the reason for this, whether it is because of hereditary constitutional differences or in the store of adaptation energy, the fact remains that only the naive coach would dispense a rigid system of written training instructions. Bitter experience has shown many times that what is one athlete's training "meat" might well be another's poison. An individual's Adaptation energy must be one of the first considerations.

Bibliography

1. Hill: A.V., Muscles and Muscular Exercise, Encyclopaedia Britannica, 11th Edition.
2. Wolf: S. (1950) Res. Publ. Ass. Nerv. Ment. Disease. Vol. 29, p.1090
3. Selye: H. (1950) Stress, Acta Inc. Medical Publishers, Montreal, Canada.
4. Loeb: R.F. Fremont-Smith: F. (1950) Res. Publ. Ass. Nerv. Ment. Disease. Vol. 29, p.p. 1088-1089
5. Selye: H. (1936) The Alarm Reaction. Canad. M.A.J. 34: 706.
6. Selye: H. (1936) A syndrome produced by diverse nocuous agents. Nature 138: 32.
7. Selye: H. (1937) Studies on Adaptation. Endocrinology 21: 169.
8. Selye: H. (1952) The Story of Stress. Acta Inc., Medical Publishers, Montreal, Canada.

Part II Application of the stress concept to training

The particular aim of training is to stimulate specific adaptation of the body by continuously repeating physical exercise of a specialized nature. Harmful effects of exercise stress becomes a more likely condition nowadays that rewards for sporting success are many, and high training mileage has become almost an obsession with many athletes and coaches.

Selye's concept that the body has a finite quantity of Adaptation energy and that stresses should be summated when considering their effects on the organism, he has stated to be his most important ideal gained from his many observations on stress research.

It was stated in Par I (Track Technique No. 5) that an important result of chronic exposure of the organism to a particular stress is to increase the resistance to that stress but to reduce the non-specific resistance to other stresses. The athlete may withstand a relatively great load of a particular exercise for which he has been trained, but more easily succumbs to other stressing agents such as chills and bacterial infection than the normal healthy person. This is not an uncommon observation.

Any stress, muscular exercise or otherwise, whether major or minor, according to Selye draws on the bank of adaptation energy, but the stresses for which the individual is less well adapted will draw the greatest debit and be most likely to hasten exhaustion reactions.

Stresses on the athlete

There are two important practical questions, firstly, what are the main stresses which may make a demand on an athlete's adaptation and, secondly, what signs and symptoms are indicative of a failing store of adaptation common to many athletes:

Muscular exercise; dietary inadequacy; climatic conditions, heat and cold; bacterial infections and disease; emotional conflict and unrest; insufficient rest and sleep; and miscellaneous stress - everyday wear and tear of living.

There is space only to comment briefly on this list and to mention some implications.

Even when everything seems ideal for an athlete's training it is fairly common knowledge that it is possible to overload the athlete with too much or too intense training. It is not proposed to go into training schedules here, but the general practice should always be to increase gradually the training load, giving the body time to make its changes of adaptation. Starting into a too severe training program with more enthusiasm than wisdom is a common cause of failure. Training should be increased gradually, not only in the one season but year by year.

Here is a very important lesson of the G.A.S. (the General Adaptation Syndrome). Exercise causes an Alarm Reaction with an emphasis on the countershock stage, and during this stage the individual may be mislead by his feelings of well-being even though his general powers of adaptation will be low and he may be fast traveling on the road to the Exhaustion Stage.

In order to have developed a high specific adaption for exercise it may be presumed a normal occurrence for the athlete to be at least in the early stage of resistance. Should he have passed too far into this stage, specific and general adaptation will be nearing their limits. A not particularly severe stress such as a race or time trial may then represent the last straw to his load.

The diet which may be completely satisfactory for the normal relatively inactive person may not contain the necessary quantity of nutrients, particularly vitamins for very strenuous training. There seems fairly good evidence (1 and 2) that Vitamin C and some of the Vitamin B Complex series fall in this group. Moreover, it is conceivable that there exist personal idiosyncrasies, some individuals needing considerably more of some chemicals than other for optimum function of their living processes.

It is interesting the Selye's rats made greater adaptation when on a high protein diet. Another point which may be overlooked by athletes is that food which may be easily handled by the digestive system of the normal person may constitute a stress to the athlete. A fat-rich or too bulky diet may be considered as falling into this category.

High temperature and high humidity often represent important stresses for nearly all athletes except the swimmer. When the body is generating heat at a high rate during exercise, to lose heat becomes a problem, and increased body temperature can become a severe stress. To the long distance runner or rower who must train on cold nights and also the swimmer practicing in outdoor pools, cold can take a severe toll on the athlete.

Bacterial infection and disease may be thought of as calling on a great deal of adaptation energy precipitating the G.A.S. Added to the physical exertion of training, disease might well be expected to precipitate early exhaustion. Such is found to be the case in practice. It is an ill-advised athlete who trains or races when ill.

Of interest is Selye's most controversial theory of the diseases of adaptation. Many diseases, he says, those which are not caused by any known pathogen, are caused more or less directly by stress. Such diseases as rheumatoid conditions, chronic high blood pressure and gastric ulcers he calls the stress diseases. It is certainly a well established fact that many conditions including psychotic and neurotic mental states, in fact most illnesses, may be precipitated by stressful conditions. Selye believes that the mechanism involved in his so-called Diseases of Adaptation is mainly a "derailment" of the body's hormone responses. Most psychosomatic research workers consider that this may, at most, be only one of a number of biological mechanism involved.

There is, however, nearly complete agreement that the sick person must have as many bodily stresses as possible reduced to a minimum for his speediest recovery. The athlete in order to produce his top performance similarly is found to require much rest and should keep warm and eat mainly easy-to-digest foods. Paradoxically, the athlete and the sick person require much the same type of treatment. Both require to save their adaptation energy.

Only a psychologically well adjusted and happy person will have a minimum of psychic unrest. Mental stress probably causes some body effects which acting through the nerve centers of the hypothalamus in some way (as yet uncertain) influence the anterior pituitary gland. The anterior pituitary in turn secretes the hormone A.C.T.H. which transported through the blood stream stimulates glandular activity in the adrenal cortex. The fact that emotional upset can affect the body and is associated with many types of physiological malfunction and disease certainly suggests strongly that the emotionally well balanced athlete with a good temperament and who has the personality factors generally associated with a "good sport" has an important advantage over the unhappy, restless individual who is kept busy dealing with battles not only in his competition but within himself.

Insufficient rest and sleep may be another stress decreasing adaptation energy and hindering maximum specific adaptation for muscular exercise. An athlete may be habitually getting insufficient rest and blame poor performance on everything except this fundamental restorative need. The athlete requires more rest than the non-athlete, but as far as the author is aware scientific information concerning the optimum sleep requirement during strenuous training does not exist.

Under the heading of miscellaneous stress, many and various factors could be discussed. For instance, smoking and drinking to excess may be stresses fairly well carried by the otherwise relatively non-stressed person, but to the athlete such indulgences will probably be at an adaptation cost he cannot afford. The everyday wear and tear of living involving the athlete's occupation, his traveling to work his hobbies, studies, and not least his social obligations, are all performed at the cost of some energy of adaptation. Serious consideration of these activities must be given by all concerned in preparing an athlete. These everyday stresses, outside of training itself are of utmost importance and should be first considered when planning a schedule and observing reactions to training.

References

1. F. Bicknell and F. Prescott - (1945). The Vitamins in Medicine. London, Heinemann.
2. The Nutrition of Athletes. A Symposium. The Brit. J. Nut. 2: 3. 1938.

Part III

When the sum total of stresses acting on an individual are such that the body is driven to show reactions of the stage of exhaustion, a few responses have been reported for humans.

The author's observations on athletes in severe training for a variety of sports have confirmed Selye's hypothesis that whether a person is ill from disease or stressed by other means such as exercise he tends to show common reactions. A short list of the more usual signs and symptoms of failing adaptation includes the following:

Chronic loss of body weight.

Joint and muscle pain not attributable to a particular local injury.

Chronically occurring intestinal upsets.

Swollen lymph glands (tonsils and inguinal glands).

Blocked nose and one-day cold (thinitis).

Skin rashes such as hives (uticaria).

Psychic unrest, irritability, insomnia, general fatigue often referred to as staleness.

General muscular tenseness.

Loss of weight in the training athlete, whether accompanied, or not, by poor appetite, may be considered as representing the general increased catabolism (destructive processes) of the body tissues which Selye says is characteristic of an advanced G.A.S. response. Some coaches and trainers of animals place considerable faith in the use of this sign as a guide. When visiting the Payne Whitney Gymnasium at the Yale University, the author saw the 1952 American Swimming Team candidates under coach R. Kiphuth carefully recording their stripped weights on a chart. This was a daily practice.

Joint pains have for some time been recognized as a common symptom of various disease states. Such symptoms in the athlete in terms of the G.A.S. would be interpreted as representing a highly stressed state. The author had some personal experience in this regard. Months after training had commenced and a fairly good specific adaptation to running long distances was demonstrated by improving time-trial performances, joint and muscle pains became a regular occurrence. When these general pains (combined with other symptoms such as extreme irritability) were disregarded, and training load maintained, there was a culmination in breakdown after a marathon race. The chief sign of the physiological breakdown was acute renal failure.

Swollen lymph glands, both the tonsils and in the groin area, and urticarial rashes (hives) have been noticed many times by the author both in himself and in other individuals in hard training. Almost immediate relief has always followed when stresses, including muscular exercise, have been removed.

Sleeplessness and nervious irritability are classical signs of the condition widely known as staleness. It is the author's belief that staleness may best be understood in terms of the G.A.S. that the individual has approached the stage of exhaustion. The similar condition characterized by lowered performance covered by the phrase "burnt out" may involve exhaustion reactions of the G.A.S. but it seems possible that organic structural changes brought about by maturation and other causes are of importance, because whereas rest will restore completely most individuals, the so-called "burnt out" athlete never reaches his previous performance level. It appears to the author to be a sweeping over-simplification to say that staleness "is only a state of mind", although, no doubt nervous factors are involved.

It may be reasonable to suggest that other signs of an advanced G.A.S. will be observed and reported in the future, not only in experimental animals but in humans. In humans who are training strenuously, their G.A.S. signs will usually be uncomplicated by the specific effects of disease. This makes the study of the athlete of general scientific interest. Signs and symptoms acting as signposts that adaptation is running out, may be applied to all kinds of stress states, not necessarily peculiar to the athlete. It is important to detect the less obvious physiological signs, such as small changes in the blood. These signs may warn us to take appropriate action, which invariably involves rest.

Just as a lighting of the stress load relieves the exhausted experimental animal, so rest has been found to restore the jaded, stale athlete. But how much rest the over-trained athlete needs, or whether there should be a complete rest from training, are a matter of judgment - decisions which will remain in the category of coaching "art" until we have gained more insight resulting from integration of scientific observation and experiment with the athlete.

The challenge for the physiologist is the determination and measurement of the amount of general and specific adaptations, or putting the question in a more direct way, to find reliable predictive tests of how long an individual would be expected to resist a given stress. Practically nothing has been done in this field of research.

The author has observed what he regards as straws in the wind. For instance in several athletes (including himself) who appeared to be in good general health, a condition which would generally be regarded as staleness occurred. Haemoglobinuria was often found immediately after training. Two of such athletes, members of the 1952 Australian Olympic team, acting on advice took heed of this sign, eased off their training, and went on to register personal records and reach Olympic finals. The haemoglobinuria did not occur later when these runners who were fairly well rested again trained strenuously. In other athletes the author has observed considerable changes from the normal count of blood eosinophils when they were obviously in a state of chronic fatigue. The blood eosinophil cell count showed very high peaks extending over a period of a week or more. No allergy or other illness could be detected. It looked very much like a stress effect.

There might well be expected to be many changes in addition to those already observed, which will act as indicators of the stress effect and whisper their warning while adaptation is high and potential performance level remains good.

Even in our present state of knowledge the astute coach can often observe and act on the warning signs and symptoms before he drives the athlete to exhaustion. Some of the changes mentioned above occur relatively early and prompt action by the coach in assessing the total stress load, and lightening it, can often save the situation. More than performance is at stake. The athlete's health may be in jeopardy.

Other practical considerations

The disarming state of affairs in an individual who is being slowly drained of his adaptation energy is firstly that changes are very small and and sometimes masked by the specific effects of a stress so that there may be an insidious movement towards exhaustion; and secondly, whenever an alarm reaction is caused, there occurs during countershock the feeling of temporary general well-being which may commence in the athlete an hour or less after a race or training session. The author learned this lesson by bitter experience, when steadily driving himself towards exhaustion for the 26-mile race. Feeling of chronic fatigue and joint pains were usually alleviated by training runs. Finally there occurred acute renal failure. Since this time (1950) Hans Selye frequently has reported renal failure as occurring when his chronically stressed animals reached the exhaustion stage of the G.A.S.

As has been suggested above, most athletes in training may be considered as being in a relatively early stage of resistance. Physiologically little or no difference to the normal untrained individual can be found. As the athlete moves along in the resistance stage, for a time increasing his specific adaptation and potential maximum performance, gradually the risk of straining increases as his general adaptation and finally his specific adaptation commence to be lost at a rapidly increasing rate. There is often a very thin line between training and straining. Vigilance and careful handling of the athlete are essential if good performance is not to be obtained as from a lucky-dip. Championship class performance is no guarantee that an athlete has reached his full potential. The athlete, even though he is winning and even breaking records, may still have a greater potential awaiting full development.

Training of an athlete is a great responsibility because two of his very important personal attributes are being used - the athlete's time and his powers of adaptation to life stresses. Training him may be likened to bending a green twig. The body may eventually mould itself to the force of continuously imposed physical exercise, but a little too much and the body, like the twig, may show signs of strain. More stress and the breaking point may be reached.

Rhythm has been named a characteristic of life. There is a time for strenuous activity and a time for resting. The rigidity of a too definite program of training may easily drive the athlete to exhaustion. The coach whose mind is obsessed by the idea that distance covered is all important, may for a while seem to get successful results with the use of his whip. But some of his pupils will invariably fall by the wayside as they reach the limit of their adaptation credit. The coach may be compared to the violinist feeling for the right note. He must proceed directly and definitely, at the same time listening carefully for the note he is producing. If his string has slackened slightly he must adjust his technique to meet the contingencies of the moment. The sensitive trainer with a background of scientific knowledge and with experience must feel his way carefully. He will not be too rigid a task master.

There were two holders of world swimming records. Both were in the final period of their training for the Helsinki Olympic Games in 1952. Both had been training consistently and hard, up to six miles a day and recording close to their best times. Then their times started to fall off. One swimmer believed he should train harder for as he said "did not slower speed show the need for more training"; the other swimmer eased off and swam slowly when he trained. He spent most of his time in bed. The wrongly advised, energetic one, by a long way failed to come up to his previous standard but the "lazy" one, who had developed a sound basic philosophy on the subject of training, won his Olympic race in record time. Their story well illustrates an application of the General Adaptation Syndrome.

Conclusions

Coaching athletes will become more scientific as our knowledge becomes greater and better organized, but the art will continue to lie in recognizing individual idiosyncrasies and blending the training exercise with enough rest to give the optimum amounts of specific adaptation and adaptation energy.

The coach can make contributions to training science by observing the athlete carefully. By noting those changes which may prove useful objective measures of the state of stress, the coach can hope to make possible a fairly close prediction of adaptation potential of the organism.

No matter what modifications and extensions are eventually made to the Hans Selye concept, the author suggests that the General Adaptation Syndrome theory in its present form is of great value to the coach who is seeking a sound scientific bases about which to organize his observations.

As Selye has said, "our facts must be correct; our teories need not be if they help us discover important new facts."

Physiological Basis of Training for Running

by Toni Nett
(Editor of "Die Lehre der Leichtathletik," published in Berlin, Germany)

No discipline of athletics is as controversial in its doctrine as that of running. If one reads the literature of professional periodicals throughout the world, one will find as many coaches and runners as there are opinions and methods. Even since the discovery of the physiological special effects of the so-called "Interval-training" in the last 10 years, there has not by any means been peace. On the contrary, much confusion is noted in all countries about wherein the real effect of this new method lies, what its limitations are, what type of runners should use this method Not infrequently one hears serious advice still recommending sprinters to indulge in an intensive "interval-training". And indeed this counsel is often obeyed. And then they are astonished at the fact that despite innumerable repetitions their performance does not improve. Here it would be better to say because of these innumerable repetitions. Thus confusion is in general widespread indeed.

Amidst the multiplicity of methods and opinions the physiology of work can give us the firmest premises. A coach who is not in a position to watch over the physiological effects of his method, must nowadays be regarded as a danger for his men, both as regards health and performance. Thus nothing is more important for a running coach than to obtain this information. This article is meant as a small contribution, and has been written with the least possible scientific jargon so as to enable it to be generally understood.

Oxygen Debt

We have to make a sharp distinction between two types of track distances: distances coverable only with the greatest possible "oxygen debt", and distances in which success depends on the "capacity for intake of oxygen" during the running. Thus "oxygen debt" and "oxygen intake capacity" are the two factors limiting performance. Listen to a physiologist, Professor Dr. R. Herbst, explaining this more exactly and scientifically:

"If in the carrying out of a certain task in a given time-unit a body needs a certain quantity of oxygen, the oxygen requirement reaches its maximum from the very start of the task. This does not, however, apply to the actual absorption of oxygen. As breathing and heart-action, through whose functioning the oxygen has first to be brought to our working muscles, only gradually grow stronger and accustom themselves to the given working conditions, oxygen absorption begins only gradually with the commencement of the work and attains maximum oxygen requirements only after some time. Thus the body suffers an "oxygen debt", which must be made up for after the completion of the task in the period of recovery."

It goes without saying that this oxygen debt becomes all the greater at the beginning of an activity, the greater the task, although breathing and heart activity strive to adapt themselves to the working conditions in direct ratio to the size of the task.

Above a certain size of task, however, the oxygen intake cannot catch up with the demand for oxygen, i. e. the output is so great that the per minute demand for oxygen exceeds the maximum intake capacity. Thus the oxygen debt constantly grows as a result until it reaches a maximum, where further work is impossible and the exercise has to be suspended. According to a calculation made by Hill an athletically built person can afford an oxygen debt of 15-20 liters, i. e. during an exercise he can, through the alkali reserve of the blood and tissue, bind so many acid metabolism products that in order to get rid of them oxydatively (burn them up) 15-20 liters of oxygen are needed. Thus if we take a bodily weight of 70 kg (154 lbs.) we get the same amount of lactic acid concentration in the tissues as Hill found in the isolated muscle after complete exhaustion through electric stimuli.

The factors which condition and limit our performance in individual branches of sport are, of course, varied. Over the shortest distance (100m) oxygen debt and intake don't play a vital role. This distance can be run without breathing. The effort thus expended is not large enough to produce an unbearable oxygen debt. What limits speed, apart from mental strain, is the rapidity with which the muscles can be contracted and relaxed, in other words the viscosity in the individual muscle-fiber, whose size conditions the internal friction of the muscles.

If the distance in increased, there comes into play, beside the viscosity (muscle-friction), as a second factor the maximum oxygen debt of which the body is capable. The same speed with which 100m are run can be maintained over 200m and 250m. Then however the exercise must be stopped because of total exhaustion. As in the few seconds of a 200m sprint only a few breaths can be drawn-the body thus receiving only a little oxygen for the oxydative elimination (burning up) of the acid metabolism products, a maximum oxygen debt is incurred. The oxygen requirement of a 200m runner is estimated to be 20 liters, the oxygen absorption in the same time is not much more than 1 liter, the oxygen debt being thus some 19 liters. The ability to run 2-300m at maximum speed is thus dependent on the alkali reserve (i.e. on the ability to eliminate adequately the acid metabolism products produced during the task.)

On the other hand maximum capacity for oxygen intake is of supreme importance for long distance runners. In sustained effort a steady state between dissimilation and assimilation processes must be arrived at: no more acid metabolism products must be produced by the effort than can be simultaneously eliminated oxydatively. The oxygen requirement (caused by the speed of running) must not therefore be greater than the simultaneous oxygen intake capacity. For a trained person the maximum absorption capacity is 4 to 4.6 liters per minute.

DEBT

Now the question arises. What determines maximum absorption capacity? Not maximum ventilation (breathing) capacity. In no sport does the volume breathed in per minute reach the extreme breathing capacity, i.e., that volume of breath which can be brought in by conscious excessive ventilation. If during increasing effort one measures the size of oxygen absorption and breathing, it will be found that the oxygen intake capacity soon reaches the extreme limit of maximum oxygen absorption capacity, whereas breathing volume increases further all the time.

The greater the effort, the less effective becomes the exploitation of the oxygen breathed in. In strenuous performances only a quarter to a fifth of the oxygen thus brought in is passed on into the blood in the given unit of time and thence to the working muscles. Thus the main factor in the limitation of oxygen absorption capacity is simply the size of the blood stream, the maximum output per minute of the heart. Sustained efforts are therefore achieved

DEBT

predominantly by performance of the heart.

Professor Dr. J. Nocker is in complete agreement and puts it as follows: "The oxygen debt is of decisive importance for short distances. It is recovered again after the completion of the task. The fundamental significance of this fact is that without this ability, no kind of heavy physical work can be done. A 100m sprinter needs about 8-10 liters of oxygen for his sprints. During the sprint the oxygen absorption is so small that for practical purposes it can be neglected. The sprinter runs 95% of his race by doing without oxygen and by using oxygen stored in the blood. In an 800m race the oxygen used up at maximum exertion is 27 liters. If the race lasts 2 minutes, then 18 liters oxygen debt faces 9 liters oxygen absorption during the racing time (a proportion of 2/3 to 1/3). Comparing the two factors, in this case the oxygen debt is twice as important as the oxygen intake."

The proportions are different in long-distance running. Here too the runner at first produces an oxygen debt. He is, however, forced to organize his speed so that, looking ahead, his expenditure of effort is no more than he can bring oxygen into his muscles via the bloodstream. Thus oxygen supply and energy output are balanced. Only in the final sprint does the long distance runner make use again of the last remnants of the maximum possible oxygen debt.

Heightened Hypertrophy Not Needed in Endurance Performance

At this point it must be made clear that an increase in muscle diameter (hypertrophy) is not necessary for the long distance runner, but rather impedes him. Professor Nocker puts it this way:

"Heightened hypertrophy means increased muscular development and increased muscular strength. This is a training method very important for sprinters and field athletes as well as for all exercises, where strength is required, and high intensity of work in a very short unit of time. For middle and long distance runners hypertrophy is not necessarily desirable as what matters here in the first place is the indefatigability of the muscle. This tirelessness of the muscle is purely a problem of muscular metabolism.

"For example I can hypertrophy the muscular system without moving it (static or holding work), i.e., through pure strain against unyielding resistance. I cannot however, influence the metabolism, without burdening the muscle beyond a certain threshold of stimulation (in movement) and this I achieve by running a distance at higher intensity in order to set up a stimulus in the muscular system which leads to acidization of the muscle, to its losing potassium.

"I can thus summarize: slow "interval training", running 200m in 30 to 34 sec., according to the state of training and performance, primarily develops the circulation (increases heart capacity-increases oxygen intake capacity during the race). The faster runs serve as muscle-metabolism training (especially repetitions of 200m in 26-29 seconds), particularly if the recovery intervals are kept short (about 45-50 seconds). In order to achieve a hypertrophy of the muscle, I need an even higher intensity, i.e., preferably the short distances at 90% of maximum performance. Now this does not mean running longer training distances for metabolism training. It is also very possible to train at 300m, 400m, 800m or 1000m distances. However, I am of the opinion that the shorter distances achieve the better results. Thus I have no objections to the somewhat longer training distances. They may even serve the purpose of conditioning one to these distances and improving co-ordination. But from the purely physiological point of view, I would like to emphasize that they are not absolutely necessary."

An expert has here outlined clearly the effectiveness of "sprint workouts" (muscle-speed improvement), "tempo-running workouts" (improvement of muscle metabolism, through building-up potassium reserve through frequent excess oxydization and energy-storing) for middle-distance runners, and "interval-training" (expansion of heart capacity for the purpose of getting greater oxygen supply during the race) for the long distance runner. It has also been made clear that interval training is not a panacea for all distances, but that it only serves to improve sustained effort through markedly superior blood and thus oxygen supply during the race. Thus slow interval training as "circulation-training" for 100 and 200m runners is totally out of the question, except perhaps at the start of winter training. One can too, without committing an error, count it out completely for the 400m runner. Its effect only starts with the 800m runner, as here the performance depends one-third upon the absorption of oxygen during the race. Nevertheless even in the 800m two-thirds of performance still involves oxygen loss. Thus here we get a very clear hint as to training emphasis: 2/3 sprint and tempo training, only 1/3 interval training each week. Only for 1500m should training become half and half. Thus the real significance of interval training only really begins at 1500m, and only with the long distance runner will the main emphasis be on interval training: for effectiveness of heart capacity enlargement it cannot be touched by any other method.

A clear distinction must be made between performances dependent on muscular elasticity and those dependent on muscular stamina. The muscular stamina is a function of muscle-metabolism which depends primarily on the increase in the alkali reserve and in the storage of energy ("potassium-battery"-Nocker). It is used mostly for distances from 200-800m, but it is still most important even at 1500m, as world class performances today are run at very high speeds. The development of muscular stamina through sprint-training is therefore a specific goal of training in middle-distance running.

On the other hand the development of muscular elasticity is dependent on the cross section diameter of the muscle (thickness and length), on the muscle-fiber structure and also, very essentially, on the co-ordination of muscle and nerve. The aim of sprint training is therefore to enlarge the diameter of the muscle and improve muscle nerve performance; it thus differs sharply from the aims of middle distance training and even more from long distance training. The latter depends first of all on efficient circulation (increasing heart capacity or capillarization of the muscular system). An increase in the diameter of the muscle, according to the well-known Muller-Hettinger investigations, is brought about by the "growth of internal tension"; the muscle has to be repeatedly tensed to the limit. This is what really stimulates the thickening of the muscular fiber. Also practice at middle speeds, is not conducive to the increase of tension required: what the muscle needs is a so-called subliminal stimulus. This in sprint training speed is the "specific stimulus" for improvement of muscular elasticity and therefore of the performance. It is the same in all kinds of sport which depend upon maximum production of elasticity (in a minimum time, even in athletic "weight training").

Dr. E. Van Aaken has voiced doubts as to the advisability of fast speed in training. He believes that a speed leading to excess acidization of the muscle could have damaging effects. There is no doubt that this high tempo is very uneconomical indeed, from a psychological point of view, but in the more than 60 years of sprint training at high and maximum speeds there is no evidence that this is harmful to adults. The gaining of muscle elasticity is unthinkable without a high, uneconomical speed, as it is only through great speed that the required amount of "inner tension" of the muscle can be achieved, since only this allows it to cross the "stimulus" threshold.

However, Dr. Van Aaken is correct in his view that working muscles without oxygen in sprint training should be preceded by a lengthy period of working with oxygen (aerobic working). This technique can be observed in all the world-class sprinters. In practice this means that in winter even the sprinter should go on lengthy runs (up to 3-5 km) at varied speeds or at a comfortable trot, in order to consolidate his "general staying-powers", in order to "run-in" or recondition the whole organism with the greatest of care, as one does a new car fresh from the factory.

Only this guarantees a solid basis for the later "speed-work". It is even possible that this holds not only for each individual training year but also for the overall development of the sprinter from his youth. In order not to get "burnt-out" later on through the exceptionally exacting demands of sprinting (working without oxygen), the racing in younger days ought probably to take place more with oxygen being supplied by the organism. This too, agreed Professor Reindell and Dr. Van Aaken, has a good "dampening effect" on the youthful organism and counteracts "neurosis" in youngsters.

Investigating the processes of muscle-conditions Muller and Hettinger took a cross-section of a static task (holding a weight) and found that the first training effect made itself felt a 30% of the maximum strength of the particular muscle; and that the effectiveness of the training could not be increased even after the tension between 45 and 60% had been passed. Against these results justified doubts were soon raised by men on the job, since in sport results observed on static work can't be gaily transplanted to dynamic (moving) work. Over the last few decades the general experience has been that increase in muscle strength can best be obtained by employing stronger stimula and with greater loading, even up to 90 and 100%.

Muller and Hettinger found in their investigations that with a 100% overload the endurance of the muscle was increased and the weight could be supported longer. Of course, the increasing of the diameter even here remained at least the same as with the lesser loading from 45-60%. Muller and Hettinger therefore found themselves advising in practice to work on loadings up to 100% as this, through increased stamina, would lead to improved muscle-performance. This stamina originates in its turn, as in "sprint-training", from the reaction to the excess acidization of the muscle which led to increase in the alkali-reserve and energy-storing. Thus from practice we obtain no reason for giving up our habitual methods of gaining muscle elasticity, methods which internationally are based on experience with very high speeds and very heavy loading.

Don't Overdo Strengthening Work

Likewise the sprinter's "strengthening work" (working up "condition") should not be overdone; because probably, as a result of the high "oxygen debt", the muscle capillarization can't be developed to the same degree. "The importance of stamina-exercises lies in improving muscle-capillarization. However, this is precisely wherein lies the purely negative aspect of pure strengthening training. When strong-man types show biceps and muscles which, through their own development, almost stand in their own way, then these people are naturally capable of fantastic feats of strength but they have no stamina owing to defective capillarization. (Dr. Hollmann) One should add: " . . . and on account of defective circulation-adjustment."

Professor Nocker is of the same opinion: "The following is to be said about the suitability of strengthening training (separate conditioning with weights, etc.). The danger of strengthening is more or less a question of the athlete's constitution. If I have a sprinter who has natural strength, it would be stupid to worry him with strengthening exercises. On the other hand one has to worry about those sprinters who do not have enough strength, whose muscles are as yet under-developed, who need strengthening exercises. With these men Nature has to be corrected. Strengthening training must thus be applied individually."

Speed--a Collaborative Effort of Muscles and Nerves

As has already been observed above, training to increase "absolute speed", which in the year's planning starts in earnest about Spring, aims above all at improving the co-ordination of the muscles and the movement-nerves. "Speed-training is a compromise between the two extremes of strengthening training and stamina training. Influencing the muscles is here not so apparent as in other forms of training, since in speed-training improving the functioning of the nervous system is the most important thing if we want to improve performance: the stimulation-performance speeds up. However, the essential thing is a markedly improved co-ordination of improvement, i.e., a top level working together of the individual muscles, whereby the speed is likewise increased" (Prof. (Nocker).

The mastering of fast sprinting is thus essentially dependent on the co-ordinating of the leg muscles during the fastest possible running movements. This co-ordination depends on the ability of the central nervous system (cortex) to cut out all superfluous, braking, friction-causing movements of those muscles that do not directly bear on the motion.

Co-ordinating the fastest possible economical running movement is a great achievement on the part of the central nervous system. It is not attainable overnight but requires quite long periods of time. Tiring during speed and co-ordination performances (sprinting, gymnastics, etc.) is not only a result of local causes, i.e. "over-acidization of the muscle", but is primarily concerned with the cortex, since the integration of the working muscles, by fitting together those muscles especially needed for a particular movement while simultaneously eliminating definite disturbing, hindering muscles (this must occur if maximum possible speeds are sought) causes "strain" in even the otherwise extremely capable brain. It is thus tiring of the nerves rather than tiring of the muscles, because in a way the "switchboard" operator (in the brain) can't make the connections quickly enough. Then the movements turn awkward and uneconomical again, until the fatigue has been overcome.

In a top class sprinter we admire the fluency of his running movements, his relaxation despite tension, the lack of fuss in his moving. These are all brought about by the major brain which can achieve perfect co-ordination of the muscular system at the very highest speeds without "misfiring". The bad sprinter runs too clumsily, spasmodically, with obvious over-exertion in the given unit of time. Using motoring language, you could say "he has his hand-brake on"; many muscles which in fact should not be brought in, which should be relaxing, are used and tensed also. This movement is unco-ordinated, unharmonious and uneconomical.

Learning economical sprinting movements, a good running style, in other words, is the outcome of the same learning process as learning any other sequence of movements in which co-ordination is the prime factor. These are the 3 steps.

1. Irradiation (first rough arranging of motions).
2. Concentration (first progressive isolation of those muscles that cause motion from those that hinder motion.)
3. Automatization (the master step, where isolation and thus co-ordination or movement skill has been attained.)

This learning is only achieved by thousands of repetitions, so that the nerves can be properly "conditioned".

It is a major goal of sprint-training, by means of suitable selection of training methods and above all the right training distances, to develop not only the elasticity of the muscle (diameter), but also the co-ordinating ability of the cortex; in order that the internal friction of the muscular system is lessened in motion and so that the elasticity thus attained can develop to the individual maximum speed with the least internal friction.

In sprinting, as elsewhere, the life history of this "learning-process" is characterized by the good old principles: "From the slow to the maximum speed" (degree of speed in co-ordination); "from the easy to the difficult" (size of load"; and "from a little to a lot" (amount of work).

If these principles are observed in the general development of the sprinter and in the development of the year's training from Autumn to the beginning of the "preservation of form" period (full racing season) both ("elasticity" & "absolute speed") will be increased. Running 60m at maximum speed suffices to increase or preserve the diameter of the muscle; the somewhat longer distances serve, with lessened speed, to improve running style (co-ordination), and raise the level of "muscle metabolism performance" (alkali reserve, energy storage). This improves "speed stamina", which often plays a decisive role for the 100m sprinter after about 70m, and above all for the 200m runner. "Absolute speed" alone only takes the sprinter 70m, then the role of "relative speed" ("speed-stamina") begins.

Tempo-training

What is tempo-training? In "tempo training" distances mainly between 100 and 1000m are repeated several times at high speed. Depending on the chosen speed one trots or walks during the recovery pauses. For example: if for a training distance of 200m a speed of 26 to 28 seconds is chosen, well-trained runners can maintain a trot for 45-60 seconds during the short recovery pauses which are of equal length, just as in "interval training" (where a distance of 200m usually is covered in 32 sec.). If however, especially in summer, one approaches the best time for 200m, one then walks in the recovery pauses which accordinly become longer. Here too the recovery pauses are intentionally kept short for the most part, as the aim is to maintain the excess acidization of the muscles to a certain extent. (see below). It is the same with longer training distances of 300 to 1000m. The speed chosen in "tempo running" decides (by the degree of excess acidization) whether one trots in the recovery pauses, or walks, as well as determining the duration of the recovery pauses (which depends of course on the individual's condition or fitness).

Where does the Effectiveness of "Tempo-training" Lie?

The specific effect of "tempo-training" is created in the tempo run itself: the high speed is the real stimulus on the muscular system, or more exactly on the muscle-metabolism. In "interval training", with its necessarily lower speed, (e.g. 200m in 32 seconds), the slow pace itself if merely the pre-condition which triggers off the active stimulus in the recovery interval, (i.e. in the pause), as the reaction in the recovery pause leads to a markedly greater heart capacity. "This large heart capacity results in the heart itself becoming bigger . . . Thus the conditioning of the heart and the circulation is brought about in interval-training mainly in the recovery pauses." (Prof. Reindell). This presupposes that the speed of the preceding run has not caused a heart-beat of more than 180-190 per minute! Thus in this case the low speed is the direct prerequisite of effectiveness in the recovery "interval" or "pause". For these reasons too the term "interval-training" came into existence, receiving a totally different meaning from that used hitherto. Previously all work with recovery pauses had been called "interval training". Today we speak of "interval training" only when the effect is created in the recovery pause i. e. the "interval". But because of the relatively low speed of the run itself there is not a sufficiently great effect on the muscles.

Thus by choosing one's own training speed one can dictate whether the training should affect the heart or the muscles; at slow speeds (e.g. 200m in 32 seconds) it is clearly the heart and the circulation that are effected and the effect is transferred to the recovery pause. At high speeds, however, (resulting in a very high heart-beat) the training mainly affects the muscular system and the stimulus takes effect during the run itself, the recovery pause being valuable only as "period of respite". These are the basic differences between "tempo training" and "interval training.

Middle Distances and Muscle Distances

Distances up to 800m are above all "muscle-distances" and not "circulation-distances" because here, the running performance depends on the ability to incur a very high oxygen debt whereas from 1500m on at the earliest (and I personally would rather include this in the muscle-distances) the performance depends upon the oxygen supplied during the race. Thus the sprinter and the middle-distance runner need a healthy heart, though not necessarily a large one, since here it is not possible to supply enough oxygen during the actual race however much one were to enlarge the heart by "interval training". It would be a complete waste of time.

Middle-distance running is a "function of muscular stamina", involving a high oxygen debt.'

How Does "The Training of Muscular Stamina" with its Oxygen Debt Function?

Running is a continuous sequence of muscular contractions. For this purpose the muscle needs energy.' This it gets from "metabolism" so that it doesn't get tired prematurely or indeed at all. As long as the body has sufficient energy, it can move and the runner can run.

Thus muscular energy is the most important factor in running. To acquire and store this energy is the main function of metabolism; food (carbohydrates, proteins, fat-carbon compounds) is built up, broken down and converted by the consumption of oxygen, resulting in the generation of energy. In active movement the heart, ciruclation and respiration play only a subordinate part: they are the servants of metabolism. "Only the muscle would come within the technologist's definition of a motor: an apparatus designed to convert a supply of chemical energy into mechanical energy (movement)." (Prof. Lehmann).

Thus metabolism affects ultimately the muscular system itself.

We possess a store-house which absorbs energy produced in metabolism by breaking down food in order to put it at our disposal again under certain conditions. The whole of the energy which is stored in our organism by the phosphorus compounds is termed "phosphate energy". This energy is not transmitted directly but goes via the so-called "potassium reservoir." (Prof. Nocker)

Thus in order to understand how to choose the right training technique (i. e. whether "tempo" or "interval"), it is vital to know the different ways of producing and storing energy in the two methods.

There are two ways in which matter breaks down depending on which speed is chosen: the so-called "aerobic" way, involving the supply of oxygen, the "anaerobic" way (or the production of energy without oxygen). "The energy for performances of short duration (at high speed) is derived predominantly from anaerobic processes, whereas in performances of longer duration (at low speed) the main role is played by energy obtained by the breaking down process which is accomplished by the consumption of oxygen. In anaerobic work, acids, especially lactic acid, are produced in the process of metabolism. This acid "environment" is very unfavorable to the activity of the muscular cell and, if sufficiently concentrated, has a paralyzing effect." (Prof. Nocker). At lower speeds there is either no lactic acid at all or at any rate the increase of it is negligible; the end products here are rather carbonic acid and water ("citric acid cycle"). Thus by choosing the running speed one can determine the way in which energy is to be produced, viz. either large quantities of lactic acid are created which leads to a very violent reaction on the muscles, or else the lactic acid is eliminated or kept down to a minimum (i.e. is harmless), so that the muscle "tires" either not at all or only to a slight degree.

The Creation of an Oxygen Debt

The first road towards the production of energy, "the conversion into lactic acid", is taken when the supply of oxygen is not large enough, as in the case of heavy muscular work. This way has great practical significance insofar as it enables the organism to generate more energy without using up oxygen. By forming lactic acid the muscle incurs an "oxygen debt" which is repaid later on . . . the greater the intensity of the work (the higher the speed) the more the level of lactic acid in the blood rises . . .

The normal method of producing energy, however, is oxydation (combusion causing oxygen to be consumed), and thus even in the presence of oxygen the pyruvic acid is not converted into acid but is broken down in the citric acid cycle, where the final combustion takes place, producing carbon dioxide and water. This is more economical if only because in oxydation about 30 times as much energy is released as is the case in the conversion of sugar into lactic acid. On the other hand the anaerobal way (without oxygen) has the advantage that it can mobilize energy more quickly, an advantage which easily retrieves the balance when the muscle is suddenly put under a great strain (at very high speed) so as to exceed the oxygen supply available at that particular moment. It must be realized that the amount of oxygen that can be brought to the muscle is limited and also that a certain time elapses before it becomes completely effective. Without the ability to produce energy by the anaerobal (oxygenless) method, performance would be extraordinarily limited. . ." (Prof. Nocker)

Muscle Conditioning During Metabolism

The two different ways of producing energy now means that the organism can be conditioned in different ways. This is of supreme importance for our choice of training-method, especially for the runner of distances from 200m to 800m, and is extremely important even for the 1500m runner.

" . . . The trained muscle learns how to work with a potential at which the untrained muscle would stop work. It is however essential that the stimuli (speeds) are strong enough above the "steady state" (the state of equilibrium between the oxygen supply and oxygen consumption)that lead to the emptying of thepotassium battery and constitute a sufficient stimulus so that during the resting-phase a re-charge is made possible which exceeds the original potential. On the basis of this and other investigations we have come to the conclusion that the development of the processes of conditioning in the muscular system generally requires the time to be longer and the stimuli to be in greater doses (higher speeds) than is necessary for the process of conditioning the circulation (heart, blood vessels). In training we often experience a discrepancy between the training-condition of the muscles and that of the circulation. Thus runners often explain to us that they had enough breath left, but that in the last burst they lacked the strength. (Instead of "strength", muscle-energy or staying power or sprinting stamina would be more apt in this case). Here stronger stimuli must be applied so as to force the lagging conditioning of the muscles to catch up. Thus next to stamina (interval training), which is directed first and foremost at the conditioning of the ciruclation, I recommend days with faster runs." (Nocker)

"This tempo training develops in the trained muscular system an increase in the content of matter in reserve, creative-phosphoric acid, adenosin-phosphoric acid, muscle coloring matter and potassium and phosphorus. Furthermore the stock of glycogen (stored starch) is doubled. Added to this is the fact that the trained muscle makes more economic use of this energy producing matter. Thus the untrained muscle only converts 4/5ths of the lactic acid formed to glycogen again whereas the trained muscle converts 6/7ths. Further the potassium content of the trained muscle is markedly higher. The increase in potassium in the trained muscle implies to a certain extent an increased charging of the "potassium battery". This view is supported by analyses of muscles directly following exhausting work. Whereas in the skeletal muscle of untrained animals when resting the potassium content was 603mg%, it had sunk to an average of 533mg% in those animals which had been loaded to the point of exhaustion. This difference is statistically exact and means that the more exhausting the work the lower the potassium content. With sodium it is just the opposite. In the course of this research a further difference was found in the reaction of trained and untrained animals whenplaced under strain. Whereas with exhausting work the untrained muscle reduced from 603mg% to 533mg%, the trained muscle showed a value of 635mg% when resting, which after exhausting work had sunk to 461mg%.This means that after absolutely exhausting work the potassium content is considerably lower in the trained muscles than in the untrained muscle. We believe that from this we can infer that the muscle's increased capacity for prolonged effort is closely connected with these changes. The trained muscle has both a higher starting-potential and also a lower finishing potential. It can therefore make more thorough use of its reserves. These findings are of fundamental importance because we know from previous research of our own that lack of potassium goes hand in hand with a loss of energy and that there is a close connection between the degree of fatigue and the potassium content of the muscle. If the potassium content sinks below a certain level, the muscle stops its activities." This also shows how important it is to charge the potassium battery by means of tempo training.

Higher Speed is Necessary

Prof. Dr. Jakowlew (USSR) also points to this need for greater speed in this matter of the metabolistic conditioning of the muscles through sprint training: "It must be observed that strains caused by short, repeated and very intensive speeds favor the accumulation of reduction proteins in the muscles and improve the ability of the muscles to mobilize chemical energy quickly and to convert it into the mechanical energy of muscular contraction. Results in experiments with animals have shown that the phospho-creatine content in the muscles increases in proportion to the extent to which the speed factor determines the training. Simultaneously this also improves the ability of the brain tissue to continuously maintain the responses of its inner "environment", while forming large quantities of acid products in the organism. In other words these strains create the biochemical prerequisites of the dynamic strength which is so important to sprinters and middle-distance runners.

Blood and its Respiratory Function

"Tempo-training" is not only more effective in increasing the store of energy, but also obtains its special significance from the processes of energy consumption.

The presence of large quantities of alkalis is of decisive

importance for energy consumption with a high "oxygen debt", for these are the antagonists of the great quantities of acids present (carbonic and lactic acid). They are the best friend of the middle - distance runner and of his performance - whereas the acids are to a certain extent his enemies as they paralyze or "poison" his leg muscles. Thus the alkalis have to neutralize the acids.

"To keep the environment in the blood slightly alkaline (ph 7.3 - pH indicates the Hydrogen-Ion value) is a task vital to the smooth working of the physiological processes in the blood. Certain substances in the blood can neutralize the acid products. These substances are called alkalis (blood buffers), one of the most important of which is sodium bicarbonate . . . The totality of the substances present in the blood that are able to combine with acids is called the alkali reserve." (Prof. Nocker). It is the specific duty of this alkali reserve to keep the blood's reserves constant.

Now, if a high alkali reserve is important for runners at all distances it is the decisive factor for the 200-800m runner. It also has a very great effect on the performance of the 1500m runner. In these distances run at high speed huge quantities of lactic acid enter the blood, which is not the case at the lower speeds over long distances. In long distances it is hardly necessary to combine with anything but carbonic acid as these distances are run with supply and consumption of oxygen more or less in a state of equilibrium ("citric acid cycle"). For the 200m distance however, an oxygen intake of only 5% is possible; for the 400m stretch, 17%; at 800m, 34%; in other words the 200m race must be paid for with an oxygen debt of 95%, the 400m, with 83%, and the 800 with 66%. It is hardly possible to demonstrate the difference in the physiological processes more clearly. . . "Speed, not distance, kills." This old time saying describes these man killing distances with complete accuracy; this is why they call for a different type of training.' Every runner at these distances whose muscular system has not been protected against the high quantities of lactic acid by an abundant supply of alkalis produced by "tempo-training" has shot his bolt after a very short distance. He crosses the line, if at all, among the "also rans. . ."

Sharp sprints even enable the runner to stand values below 7.3%. "According to our own researches as well as those in America, it is possible to accustom oneself by training to a high blood content of acid. Thus according to American experiments athletes trained in this way can even endure a percentage value of 6.9; i. e. a blood acidization which in normal medical practice would be regarded as being almost incompatible with life." (Dr. Hollmann).

Prof. Nocker too points to this fact: "In tempo-training short distances are run in quick succession at high speed. In so doing the muscle gets accustomed to anaerobal (oxygenless) work, and learns gradually to overcome without significant after-effects the state of over acidization which appears in all sprint work, and above all, the constant repetition of the stimulus makes the rest pause considerably shorter."

Tempo-training Essential for Middle Distance Runners

The runners of distance from 200m to 880m and in great measure also the 1500m runners should therefore not make the fatal error of using "interval training" with its low speed, because they would then forfeit the specific benefits of the conditioning of the muscle-metabolism. The effect of "interval training" is to increase heart-capacity and is thus important for those distances where oxygen is supplied during the race. If a middle distance runner places most emphasis on "interval training" he is then training for longer distances and not for his own. Such runners wonder why their sprinting stamina does not improve despite countless repetitions of 200m runs in 32 seconds, and despite their short recovery pauses, and why they always fade out in the last third of their middle distance race. The reason should be clear by now: the muscular metabolism wasn't sufficiently conditioned by "tempo-training" (insufficient storage of energy and alkali reserve); they "tired" too quickly because the high quantities of acids could not be neutralized.

"Interval-training" No Universal Panacea

It is well-known that the over-zealous champions who claim "interval-training" is the one and only road to success say that it has as many as 3 effects.

1. Increase in muscle diameter (improvement of muscle elasticity).
2. The effect on muscle metabolism.
3. The conditioning of circulation.

The excellent effect on circulation has been demonstrated. But it has not been proved at all that the other two claims are true. Neither does the practice of the world's best athletes suggest any corroboration.

It is, for example, maintained that in "interval-training" the "lack of oxygen" which arises stimulates the increase of the diameter of the muscles. However, in the first place, in "interval-training" the lack of oxygen is considerably smaller (than elsewhere) on account of the speed, which is far too slow, and, in the second place the muscle-physiologists Muller/Hettinger of the Max Planck Institute came to the express conclusion in their experiments, that as far as the increase in the diameter of the muscle is concerned, the sole responsible factor is the "inner tension" of the muscle. By constricting the blood vessels they could observe that the flow of blood (the lack of oxygen and its supply) is of no importance here at all. And because of the low speed in "interval-training" there is not even enough "inner tension" created, so that the training method is totally useless for increasing the diameter of the muscles (elasticity). As we showed above by referring to the researches of authoritative bio-chemists and metabolist-phsiologists, the low speed in "interval-training" is not adequate to the task of conditioning the muscles in metabolism, as here the acidization is intentionally kept low so that the specific conditioning factor in the formation of the alkali reserve is either not produced at all or, if it is, then only insufficiently. The effectiveness of interval-training is in fact limited to the circulation. That is the reason why sprinters, middle-distance and long distance runners cannot train with one method only (i.e. "interval-training") but that each has to consider in advance what results he wants to achieve: muscle elasticity (diameter and nervous system) improves with "sprint training", muscle metabolism with "tempo-training" and the circulation improves mainly with "interval-training"(and long distance running).

I wish to stress this because I am very often asked about it by confused trainers and athletes. Everywhere today one comes across disappointed runners who regard "interval-training" - which has spread like a fashionable disease - as the miracle method for all distances. In general the specific limited effect of "interval-training" has not been understood. And in fact "interval-training" is a miracle method - if it is used in the right place, namely, in the first instance for distances over 5000m, and secondly for distances above 1500m.

The middle-distance runner is warned against placing too much stress on "interval-training" in the sense used above. We find on the contrary that of the world's best runners, the long distance runners, besides their "interval-training", which indeed is most heavily stressed, also go in for "tempo-training" in order to increase the metabolistic conditioning of the leg muscles. None of the best sprinters in the world, or 400m runners, and only a few 800m runners ever use "interval-training" more than occasionally. They become good not despite but because of this absence of "interval-training". "Tempo-training" is used over all distances as the specific means by which to condition muscle-metabolism. "Interval-training" - as has already been stated - is limited to conditioning for "long-distance performances" and to supplying oxygen during the race itself. "Interval-training" is limited to expanding the heart - although here it is immeasurably superior to all other training techniques.

In order to forestall misunderstandings it must be stated in conclusion that one cannot start "tempo-training" at full effect in the winter. For here as elsewhere the well-known principles of strain are valid: "From a small strain to a big one" or "from a little to a lot". Therefore "general stamina" (i.e. by more or perhaps longer training distances at a lower speed) is to be acquired here too and on this foundation it will be easier to bear the greater speed needed to acquire the "specific stamina" (fewer but essentially sharper sprints at or below racing speed) which should be emphasized from March onwards.

(The above article is a synthesis of a translation from the No. 46, November 17, 1959; No. 47, November 24, 1959; and No. 49, December 12, 1959 issues of "Die Lehre der Leichtathletik," and is reprinted by permission of Toni Nett.)

The following graph represents the various components of running training, and their effects upon the conditioning process.

Legend: I = Strength. II = Speed. III = Local muscular strength. IV = General stamina.

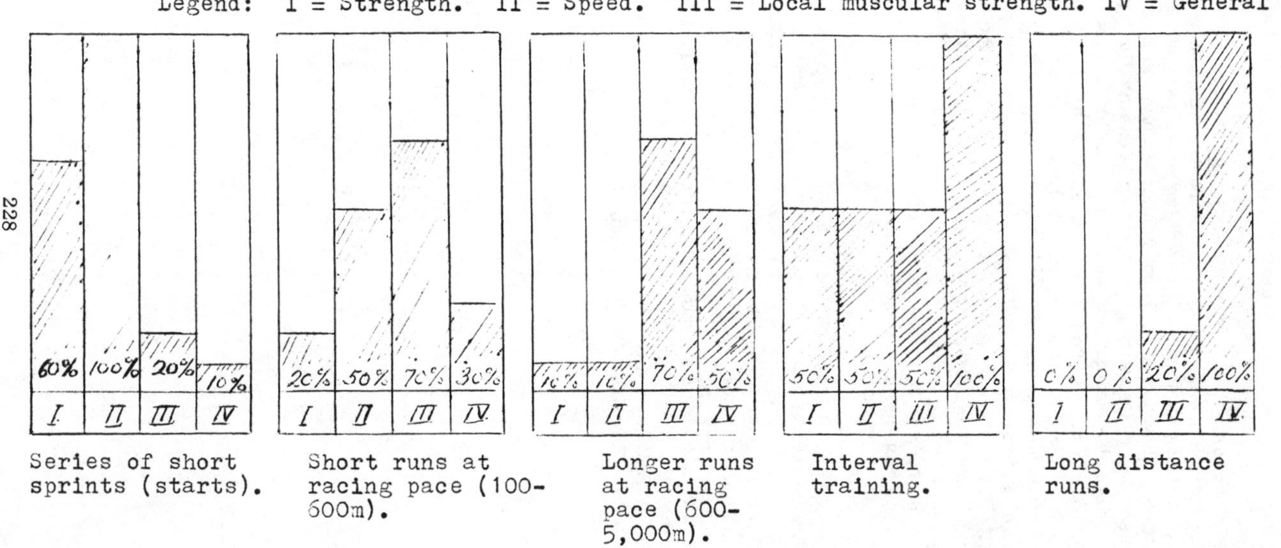

Series of short sprints (starts).

Short runs at racing pace (100-600m).

Longer runs at racing pace (600-5,000m).

Interval training.

Long distance runs.

Complex Training

by Toni Nett

(This article was translated and synthesized by Gerry Wichert from the No. 14, April 7, 1964 issue of "Die Lehre der Leichtathletik," published in Berlin, Germany. Here Nett seeks to place various training procedures in proper perspective, and points out that the truth lies in the mixture of training techniques used when seeking the optimum training method.)

The Complex Training-A Mixture of Several Methods

The era of the exclusive use of interval training is past. Years ago, interval training a'la Zatopek, then further development through Prof. Reindell and Woldemar Gerschler (short distance interval training 100-200 meter) was supposed to be "the method" to replace all others. This seemed to be a brilliant thought of great simplicity, hence the spreading enthusiasm was understandable. But now we have to admit that our enthusiasm was exaggerated and the results did not match our expectations.

Interval training, (short distances 100-200 meter) was very monotonous, and did not replace fully the other traditional methods (speed running, sprint training, long distance running, etc.) It was just one of several methods. Even Prof. Reindell admitted in previous years that he had fully recognized, at that time, the importance of speed running over great distances, and the increase of strength through running in the hills. Thus a while ago in Freiburg, interval training changed into a "complex training" (a mixture of short, fast reps., speed play over long distance, sprint training and long distance running) although, for the development of the specific endurance the fast, short interval training is preferred to the slow "marathon" type training, but, I would like to point out, that even at Freiburg, Germany, there exists only one kind of mixture for the "endurance men". Prof. Reindell said at Duisburg: "The various goals to be achieved demand a complex training. With one training method only, we are not able to tone up all biological functions necessary in running." Prof. Nocker has stated: "To develop general endurance, (including the multiplication of the capillary vessels) you have to do "endurance work." This may be accomplished by long distance running, speed play, and interval training. Many coaches and former first class runners who took part in the discussions at Duisburg, opinionated that now the "optimum mixture" of different methods is the modern training trend, in short the complex training.

Interval Training-Only Specific Means of Training

Today interval training is no longer universally the all important and "only" training method. It is merely one of many methods, but, it will continuue to exist. It was a valuable addition to the number of training methods already known. Enthusiastic to have found the "jewel of wisdom"- the shot went over the target. Today we use interval training for specific purposes. For example, there is no better method than interval training to enlarge the heart in the shortest possible time, but, this has its misgivings too- "easy come, easy go". The effect is not as stable, as the enlarging process of the heart by means of time consuming long distance running. There is no doubt though that in certain cases, (to overcome accidental loss of training time, before big meets or championships) a quick method to enlarge the heart (raising of endurance level) is needed. Nevertheless, this is not without danger to the heart itself, if the repetitions are not planned carefully. This is especially applicable to interval training using high numbers of repetitions over distances of 100 meters (16-14 sec.) and 200 meters (33-30 secs.) with extremely short recovery periods 45-60 seconds.

Short or Long Distance Interval Training?

Short distance interval training (as the only method used for the longer middle distances and long distances) is past history.
Today we universally use a mixture of:

A. Long distance running.
B. Long distance interval training. (400-600 meter stretches with incomplete recovery intervals.
C. Speed running. (Distances of 100-200 meter in high speed, with complete, or 2/3 complete recovery periods, also running in the hills, and deep sand.
D. Sprint training.
E. Complex Speed Play.

Recently made scientific experiments have shown that long distance interval training produces better results in terms of general endurance than short interval training. Prof. Reindell mentioned in his lecture the experiments of the Swedish Scientist Astrand: "Astrand found that interval training with longer periods of stress (3 minutes duration) will cause a better progress in endurance development than short periods ($\frac{1}{2}$ minute duration)." Dr. Hollmann mentioned in his lecture the results of experiment with rats. The increase of swimming endurance was greatest after interval training with 3 minute duration periods of stress, followed by the results of the 2 minute duration periods, followed again by those with 1 minute periods. It is impossible to compare scientific experiments with animals, and human athletes, but, in the development of general endurance it is remarkable that the, short-distanct interval training (100-200 meter) has almost disappeared, to be replaced by distances of 400-600 meter. To reiterate: the short distance interval training is generally on the way out, although, the long distance interval training continues to thrive as a method of developing general endurance.

Advantages and Disadvantages of Interval Training

To pick only a few of the focal points of the discussions past and present for example, Prof. Reindell "interval training used as endurance training is time saving. Furthermore it is a stimulus for muscle groups, and a certain stimulant for concentration of energy delivering substances, but, we can never have an interval training to increase strength without sprint training, up-hill running, and speed running." Prof. Nocker "All methods will help to achieve the goal. (Long distance, speed-play, and interval training. The interval training is time saving, with a high stimulus, but, has the disadvantage that the achieved condition may not be long lasting. (We will need a very fine and exact training dosage.) The time consuming long distance running achieves the same results, but the effect is stable, a solid foundation to build on for the other methods; such as; speed-running interval sprints, and uphill running. Perhaps the mystery of the success of Lydiard lies here?"

Critical Thoughts -Do We Use More Time For Long Distance ("Marathon") Training?

Sport physicians say: "Interval training is time saving." If it is true, it would be a deciding factor in amateur sports. Lydiard expressed a different opinion in his lecture: "Some coaches prefer to reach condition (endurance) through interval training in a short time, instead of slowly, through marathon training. This is wrong. We can create an interesting marathon training, and most important the athlete will achieve a stable form. We need only 1-2 hours on 6 days per week, and Saturdays 3 hours of running. This amount of time is needed for all athletes who would like to reach the top level. This goes for all track and field events and their different training methods."

Lydiard's Method: (Marathon training) The first four months of the year for his first-class runners:
100 meter average speed of 20-22 secs.
1000 meter-3:20-3:40 min.
1 mile-5:15-6:00 min.

Monday	10 miles-54-60 minutes duration.
Tuesday	15 miles-1:20 - 1:30 hours duration.
Wednesday	12 miles-1:04-1:10 hours duration.
Thursday	18 miles-1:37 -1:47 hours duration.
Friday	10 miles-54-60 minute duration.
Saturday	20-26 miles, slower speed. 1 mile in 7:00 min. Total time 2:30 to 3:00
Sunday	15 miles-1:20-1:30 hours duration.

This authentic explanation destroys the myth that New Zealand runners train 8 hours per day. Tulloh and the English runners do not run more than 1-2 hours per day either. We will have to separate, whether "Time Saving" means physiological adaption, or the time spent for the daily workouts. With regard to "time saving" in daily workouts; the objections of sport physicians do not seem valid in view of the facts. Short- or long distance interval training demands the same duration of workouts as any other form of training. For instance Prof. Reindell mentioned 2-3 hours daily for the complex training, or the interval training.

In the remaining month of the year New Zealand runners do not increase the duration of their daily workouts, the training is just more complex. The workouts include hill-running in the second part of the year, interval sprints, and speed running in the third part of the year, but, no additional time is needed for the once daily training unit. The objection that New Zealand training demands too much time, and is for "professionals" only, is not correct.

Specific Application

The purpose of "complex training" is to incorporate an optimum mixture of training methods and means of application in specific form.

A. The first stage of training: For better development of the vascular and capillary system, and economy of the organism. The slow long-distance running at steady pace, thus in metabolism balance.

B. The second stage: To enlarge the heart, long distance interval training, with short incomplete recovery intervals. Also the high speed long distance continuous runs (pulse not below 135 and not above 160). Thus, for the increase of general endurance, use both the slow and the faster long distance runs, interval training over longer distance (400-600 meters), and speed play.

C. The third stage: To increase speed, endurance, (medical term: local muscle endurance) speed runs, interval speed runs, interval sprints, running in the hills, mud and sand.

I agree with Lydiard's observation that, "The training of middle and long distance runners is like a jig saw puzzle. The coach has to know each part such as long distance running, interval training, speed runs, sprint training, and speed-play, but must fit them into the proper place. To put the puzzle together is the great art of coaching." The advantages and disadvantages are discussed all over the world, but, it is important that all methods have a place and a time in the yearly training program in proper specific dosage.

Training for 8-14 Year Old Boys

by Fred Wilt

Boys 8-12 years of age can benefit from training providing their workouts are voluntary, although this age group seldom has the interest for formal or regular training. Some 13-14 year olds with determination and singularity of purpose may use a carefully planned training program to advantage.

Children's physical education classes in American schools tend to minimize formal discipline, and emphasize team games, particularly those involving running. Basketball and other games which require many short, fast bursts of running and a minimum of inactivity are especially valuable in developing the youthful runner. Other activities of special value are various "tag" type games (where one runs to touch another), short shuttle relays, single-file follow-the-leader running at an easy speed where the runner behind sprints to the front in continually changing the lead, and hikes at "Boy Scout" pace (run 50 paces, walk 50 paces). One useful exercise involves group running round a track or play area, guided by instructions of the teacher at the center of the oval given by blowing a whistle. The whistle may be blown once each 15 seconds, and the runners alternately jog, sprint, and walk on successive blasts of the whistle.

Teams are seldom composed of runners in the 8-12 year age group. Their only formal competitive racing is the occasional relay or short sprint race in gymnasium or playground physical education classes. Their training should be regarded primarily from the viewpoint of general physical development in conjunction with other games. A daily workout program for 8-12 year olds is neither recommended nor opposed, and seldom found in actual practice. Workouts in this age group should come when the opportunity and inclination arises, preferably in the nature of play rather than formal training. Certainly the stopwatch is unnecessary here. The training distances should be short, and the speed of running should be generally "fast" but always in accordance with personal inclination and individual differences. Training distances need not be accurately marked on a track, but rather may be stepped off in approximate distances on playground or other suitable surface for running. The recovery between repetitions of fast running should be mere walking for a period according to personal inclination. This training should lend itself to the pleasant atmosphere of the group recreational situation.

For those who train with any degree of regularity, the equipment necessary is described under the chapter entitled, "Training Tips and Points to Ponder." Those who train only intermittently during the course of other games and play need not necessarily bother with special equipment.

The form used by athletes 8-14 years of age is no different from that described in the chapter entitled, "Fundamental Movements in Running." Youngsters may well have superior running form to adults, since they tend to run naturally and without preconceived notions of ideal form.

The warmup prior to workout for 8-10 year olds need be only 440 yards of gentle jogging or shacking, preferably no faster than 5 minutes. The 11-12 year old may jog 880 yards in approximately 7-8 minutes as a warmup. The 13-14 year old should jog at a speed of 3 minutes per 440 yards for 3/4 mile immediately preceeding training.

Boys between 8-12 years of age will seldom understand the purpose of a warmdown after training, and perhaps any recommendation in this regard will be ignored. However, for those who are interested, a warmdown of 440 yards jogging in 4-5 minutes will be sufficient. Boys age 13-14 should use a warmdown of 440 yards jogging in 3-4 minutes.

The following specific activities are recommended for the running training of boys 8-12 years of age during any formal workouts they may be given. The speed of these training runs should tend to be "fast," but always in accordance with personal inclination and individual difference. These are but a few of the infinite number of different workout routines which could be enumerated.

(a) Repetitions of fast running from 30 to 220 yards.
(b) Repetitions of skipping up to 110 yards.
(c) Repetitions of hopping on one leg.
(d) Repetitions of hopping on both legs simultaneously.
(e) Acceleration runs of 75 yards each. This means jog 25 yards, stride faster for 25 yards, and sprint 75 yards.

Specific Workouts for 8-10 Year Old Boys - to be used when the occasion arises for formal training. (They need not necessarily be taken in this order.)

WORKOUT I (age 8-10). (a) Warmup (Jog 440 y.) (b) 6-10 x 30-50 y. Walk 15-30 seconds after each. (c) Jog 440 y in 4-5 minutes.

WORKOUT II (age 8-10). (a) Warmup (Jog 440y). (b) 4 x 30-50 y. Walk 15-30 seconds after each. (c) Skip 110 y. Walk 1 minute. (d) Hop 30 y on right leg. Walk 15-30 sec. (e) Hop 30 y on left leg. Walk 15-30 sec. (f) 4 x 75 y acceleration runs. (g) Jog 440 y in 4-5 min.

WORKOUT III (Age 8-10). (a) Warmup (jog 440y). (b) 3 x 50y. Walk 30 sec. after each. (c) Skip 110y. (d) Hop 30 y on both legs. (e) 3 x 50 y. Walk 30 seconds after each. (f) Skip 110y. (g) 3 x 75y acceleration runs. Walk 30 sec. after each. (h) Jog 440 y in 4-5 minutes.

WORKOUT IV (Age 8-10). (a) Warmup (jog 440). (b) Hop 30 y on right leg. Walk 30 sec. (c) Hop 30 y on left leg. Walk 30 sec. (d) Skip 110 y. (e) 4 x 30 y. Walk 15-30 sec. after each. (f) Hop 30 y on both legs. (g) 6 x 75 yards acceleration runs. Walk 30 sec. after each.

WORKOUT V (Age 8-10). (a) Warmup (jog 440). (b) 4 x 30y. Walk 15-30 sec. after each. (c) Skip 110 y. (d) 2 x 50 y. Walk 30 sec. after each. (e) 4 x 75 y acceleration runs. Walk 30 sec. after each. (f) Jog 440 y in 4-5 min.

WORKOUT VI (Age 8-10). (a) Warmup (jog 440 y). (b) 2 x 75 y acceleration runs. Walk 30 sec. after each. (c) Hop 30 y on right leg. Walk 30 sec. (d) Hop 30 y on left leg. Walk 30 sec. (e) 6 x 30 y. Walk 15-30 sec. after each. (f) Skip 110 y. (g) 2 x 75 y acceleration runs. Walk 30 sec. after each. (h) Jog 440 in 4-5 min.

Specific Workouts for 11-12 Year Old Boys - to be used when the occasion arises for formal training. (They need not necessarily be taken in this order.)

WORKOUT I (Age 11-12). (a) Warmup (jog 880 y). (b) 8-12 x 60 y. Walk 15-30 sec. after each. (c) Jog 440 y in 4-5 min.

WORKOUT II (Age 11-12). (a) Warmup (jog 880). (b) 3 x 110 y. Walk 1 min. after each. (c) 2 x (skip 110 y). Walk 1 min. after each. (d) 4 x 75 y acceleration runs. Walk 30 sec. after each. (e) Hop 50 y on right leg. Walk 30 sec. (f) Hop 50 y on left leg. Walk 30 sec. (g) 3 x 110 y. Walk 1 min. after each. (h) Jog 440 y in 4-5 min.

WORKOUT III (Age 11-12). (a) Warmup (jog 880 y). (b) Hop 50 y on both legs. Walk 2-3 min. (c) 2 x 220 y. Walk 1-2 min. after each. (d) Hop 50 y on both legs. Walk 2-3 min. (e) 4 x 75 y acceleration runs. Walk 30 sec. after each. (f) Skip 110 y. Walk 2-3 min. (g) 2 x 220 y. Walk 1-2 min. after each. (h) Jog 440 y.

WORKOUT IV (Age 11-12). (a) Warmup (jog 880 y). (b) 2 x 75 y acceleration runs. Walk 30 sec. after each. (c) 2 x 110 y. Walk 1 min. after each. (d) 2 x 220 y. Walk 1-2 min. after each. (e) 2 x 110 y. Walk 1 min. after each. (f) 2 x 75 acceleration runs. Walk 30 sec. after each. (g) Jog 440 y in 4-5 min.

WORKOUT V (Age 11-12) (a) Warmup (jog 880 y). (b) 4 x 440 y in 80-90 sec. each, depending upon ability. Walk 3-5 min. after each. (c) 2-4 x 75 y acceleration runs. Walk 30 seconds after each. (d) Jog 440 y in 4-5 min.

WORKOUT VI (Age 11-12). (a) Warmup (jog 880y). (b) 2 x 880 y in 2:45-3:00, depending upon ability. Walk 5 min. after each. (c) 3-6 x 75 y acceleration runs. Walk 30 sec. after each. (d) Jog 440 in 4-5 min.

WORKOUT VII (Age 11-12). (a) Warmup (jog 880 y). (b) Run 3/4 to 1 mile at speed of 3 minutes each 440 y. Walk 5 minutes. (c) Hop 50 y on right leg. (d) Hop 50 y on left leg. (e) Hop 50 y on both legs. (f) 4 x 75 y acceleration runs. Walk 30 sec. after each. (g) Jog 440 y in 4-5 min.

Specific Workouts for 13-14 Year Old Boys. Unless otherwise specified, the speed of each of these training runs should be "fast," but in accordance with individual difference and personal inclination. These workouts need not necessarily be followed in this order. Stronger and more mature 13-14 year olds may well profit from the use of training recommended for 15-18 year old runners. 120 y acceleration runs for this age group means jog 40 y, stride 40 y, and sprint 40 y. Other than in the case of the particularly gifted youth, this training program is designed to account for the workout needs for racing at any distance this age group might encounter.

WORKOUT I (Age 13-14). (a) Warmup (jog 3/4 mile). (b) 3 x 60 y. Walk 15-30 sec. after each. (c) 3 x 120 y acceleration sprints. Walk 1 min. after each. (d) 2 x 220 y. Jog 220 y after each. Then walk 5 min. (e) 3 x 120 y acceleration sprints. Walk 1 min. after each. (f) 3 x 60 y. Walk 15-30 sec. after each. (g) Jog 440 y in 3-4 min.

WORKOUT II (Age 13-14). (a) Warmup (jog 3/4 mile). (b) 2 x 220y Jog 220 y after each. Then walk 2-3 min. (c) 440 y at what feels $\frac{1}{2}$ to $\frac{3}{4}$ best effort. Walk 3-5 min. (d) 2 x 110 y. Jog 110 y after each. Then walk 1-2 min. (e) 440y at what feels $\frac{1}{2}$ to $\frac{3}{4}$ best effort. Walk 3-5. (f) 2 x 120 y acceleration sprints. Walk 1 min. after each. (g) Jog 440 y in 3-4 min.

WORKOUT III (Age 13-14). (a) Warmup (jog 3/4 mile). (b) 4 x 220 y. Jog 220 y after each. Walk 5 min. (c) 4 x 110 y. Jog 110 y after each. (d) 4 x 120 y acceleration sprints. Walk 1 min. after each. (e) Jog 440 y in 3-4 min.

WORKOUT IV (Age 13-14). (a) Warmup (jog 3/4 mile). (b) 2 x 880 y in 80-90 sec. per 440, depending upon ability. Walk 5 min. after each. (c) 6 x 60 y. Walk 30 sec. after each. (d) Jog 440 y in 3-4 min.

WORKOUT V (Age 13-14). (a) Warmup (jog 3/4 mile). (b) 3-4 x (60 y/walk 30 sec./; 110 y/walk 1 min./; 120 y acceleration sprint/walk 1 min./; 220 y/walk 2-3 min.). (c) Jog 440 y in 3-4 min.

WORKOUT VI (Age 13-14). (a) Warmup (jog 3/4 mile). (b) 4 x 440 y in 75-80 sec., according to ability. Jog 440 after each. (c) 3 x 60 y. Walk 15-30 sec. after each. (d) 3 x 120 y acceleration sprints. Walk 1 min. after each. (e) Jog 440 y in 3-4 min.

WORKOUT VII (Age 13-14). (a) Warmup (jog $\frac{3}{4}$ mile). (b) 2 x 1 mile in 90 sec. per 440y, or 6:00 each. Walk 10 min. after each. (c) 4 x 120y acceleration sprints. Walk 1 min. after each. (d) Jog 440y in 3-4 min.

Fundamental Movements in Running

by Fred Wilt

1. Form is individual. By reason of individual physical makeup, no two athletes ever run in exactly the same way. Each athlete differs from every other at least to a minute extent in height, weight, bone structure, length and size of muscles, point of muscle origin and insertion, strength, flexibility, and posture, in addition to personality and numerous other features. Good form, therefore, can be described only in general terms. Even though the movement of all runners share certain basic mechanical principles, it is an error of the highest magnitude to copy the running form of another.

2. Body angle (lean) at uniform speed is nearly erect. The combination of internal muscular force exerted against the resistance of the ground and the external force of gravity plus wind resistance results in the running progression. At uniform speed the body angle tends toward the perpendicular, although a very slight forward lean may be necessary against wind resistance.

When the rate of acceleration is greatest, the forward lean of the trunk must be at its greatest. Thus a sprinter has a tremendous forward lean at the start of his race. From the instant the sprinter starts to the point where he reaches top speed, his rate of acceleration is gradually diminishing even though his speed is increasing. His degree of forward lean becomes less and less as he approaches top speed. At top speed, if the athlete were running in a vacumm with no wind resistance, there would be no body lean at all. Even on a calm day, however, a sprinter running at some 22 miles per hour creates his own wind resistance, requiring a very small forward lean.

The body angle is therefore dependent upon the drive of the legs and to a lesser extent wind resistance. In general, the greater the force exerted by the legs, the more lean is required in order to balance the leg drive.

No exact body lean can be specified to suit every runner, although it is correct to recommend that the body angle at uniform speed tends to be nearly erect. However, there is an illusion of forward trunk lean when the driving leg is fully extended (fig.1.8). A more accurate picture of lean may be had by viewing the runner in mid-stride (fig.3,6).

3. Leg action. The action of each leg may be divided into recovery, supporting, and driving phases.

The recovery phase starts the instant the rear or driving leg leaves the ground (fig.1) and ends when the same leg has moved forward and again contacted the ground beneath the athlete's center of gravity (fig.6). As the foot leaves the ground behind the body at the beginning of the recovery phase, the leg flexes at the ankle, knee, and hip joints, the lower leg folds up toward the upper leg, and the heel rises toward the hip. The faster the running speed, the greater is the tendency of the heel to "kick-up" toward the hip from behind.

This "kick-up" behind in the recovery phase is not a fault. It shortens the lever of the leg, permitting it to swing forward more quickly. This action involves a mechanical principle beyond dispute. The weight of a rotating body multiplied by the length of its moment arm squared is the moment of inertia. The greater the moment of inertia the more difficult it is for a given force applied to overcome it. The rising up of the heel toward the buttock in a natural movement reduces the length of the moment

arm, thus reducing the moment of inertia, and permits the leg lever to swing forward faster for the next stride.

The forward movement of the leg in the recovery phase may be compared to a pendulum action, although it results primarily from muscular force.

As the leg continues forward in the recovery phase, the height to which the knee is lifted depends upon the running speed. It is lifted highest in sprinting and least in jogging. The limit of the forward swing of the recovery leg coincides with the completion of the rear leg drive (fig. 1, 4, 8). After reaching the limit of its forward swing in front of the body, the upper leg is reversed in direction and the foot moves first forward and then downward. The leading leg should never be stretched forward in an exaggerated effort to achieve a longer stride. Increased stride length must always result from greater effort exerted by the rear leg during the driving phase. A runner cannot pull or "claw" himself forward by placing his front leg on the ground ahead of his center of gravity.

The recovery phase is completed as the leading foot sweeps downward (giving the appearance of a backward movement) in a "stroking" action and makes contact with the ground directly under the body's center of gravity.

The recovery phase takes longer than the driving phase. Sprinters are in contact with the ground little more than 40% of the time. The legs recover simultaneously when both feet are off the ground approximately half the time for each stride in middle-distance running.

The supporting phase begins with the landing of the forward foot beneath the body's center of gravity. The knee is bent as the outer border of the ball of this foot first makes contact with the ground. Immediately thereafter the heel comes to the ground naturally, with no effort being made to prevent it from grounding. This applies to sprinting as well as middle and long-distance running (fig. 3, 6). In this position, with the foot flat on the ground bearing the full weight of the body and the knee bent, the athlete moves smoothly forward so that leg thrust may be applied behind the center of gravity.

It has been suggested that the leading foot is grounded slightly in front of the center of gravity; the distance in front diminishing with an increase in speed. Regardless, there is a momentary period of support at the landing when the runner's center of gravity must move ahead of the foot to again be driven forward. The supporting phase ends when the center of gravity has passed forward of the foot in contact with the ground. The end of the supporting phase marks the beginning of the driving phase.

In the driving phase the body is propelled forward by the thrust of the leg in contact with the ground, exerting force behind the center of gravity. As the body progresses forward, the heel is lifted, the knee extends, and finally the ankle and toe extend well behind the body as the driving phase is concluded.

The runner may have the feeling of pushing the ground away from behind him during the driving phase. Throughout the drive, the leg functions as a third class lever, summating the forces of extension by the knee, ankle, and toes in that order. These extensions conclude with the driving leg relatively straight (fig. 8) and the foot well behind the body as the driving phase ends when the toe breaks contact with the ground.

Athletes should run in a straight line, preferably with the inner borders of the feet falling approximately along a straight line.

The line of force of the leg through the hip is "off-center" from the body's center of gravity, resulting in what is known as an "eccentric thrust." Thus, for example, the eccentric thrust of the right leg during the driving phase acting through the right hip, coupled with the forward lifting of the left leg in the recovery phase, causes the hips to rotate clockwise in a horizontal plane. This thrust also lifts the body no more than necessary to counteract the pull of gravity on each stride, and projects the body forward. Newton's third law of motion specifies that for every action there must be an equal and opposite reaction. The reaction to the forward projection of the body is absorbed by the ground. However, the reaction to the twisting actions caused by the leg thrust are absorbed by the upper body. Thus as the hips move clockwise in a horizontal plane, the upper body (arms, trunk, and shoulders) move counter-clockwise in the same plane.

4. Arm and shoulder action. The upper body (arms, trunk, and shoulders) absorb reaction to the eccentric leg drive, moving in opposition to the leg action. Thus the right arm and shoulder move forward (and backward) with the left leg, and the left arm and shoulder move backward (and forward) with the right leg.

In middle-distance running wherein cadence may be approximately 3½ strides per second, there is sufficient time to allow the trunk and shoulders to absorb much of the reaction to the twisting movements created by the eccentric thrust of the legs. This permits a somewhat mild arm action and flowing shoulder-twist noted in middle -distance running, resulting in conservation of energy.

In top-class sprinting, the cadence is 4½ strides per second, and sometimes as much as 5 strides per second. The shoulders cannot twist and untwist quickly enough to absorb the reaction to such frequent and powerful leg thrust. Therefore, in sprinting the shoulders are kept steady, and the reaction to the eccentric thrust of the legs is absorbed by the forceful and more tiring (but faster) arm action.

The upper arms move relatively straight backward and forward in running. However, the lower arms move in a slight cross-body direction in front, but do not cross an imaginary vertical plane bisecting the body into right and left halves.

In sprinting the arms tend to move more forward and backward with less cross-body motion, with the hands swinging no higher than shoulder height in front and no more than about a foot behind the hipline. The elbows tend to be bent at approximately 90 degrees. This bend increases as the hands swing in front of the body, and decreases as the hand passes the hip-line to the rear.

The lower arms may be carried slightly lower in middle-distance running, using more cross-body motion in front than in sprinting.

In both sprinting and middle-distance running the hands are carried in a relaxed "cupped" position.

The arms "follow" the legs and play a counter-balancing role in absorbing reaction to the eccentric thrust of the leg drive. However, since action and reaction are interchangeable, a fast and powerful arm action may be used in sprinting to speed-up the leg action.

5. Stride length is directly proportional to speed. The faster the speed, the longer the stride. The slower the speed, the shorter the stride. It is shortest in jogging and longest in sprinting. However, it is doubtful if a runner's sprinting stride length is longer than his stride length when running at his best 440 yards speed.

The stride length of sprinters vary between 7 and $8\frac{1}{2}$ feet (84 and 102 inches). A runner's stride length at middle-distance cadence is usually about twice the length of his normal walking step. The sprinter's stride is obviously the fastest, but the least economical in terms of effort required. Two naturally "short" middle-distance strides will carry the runner farther than one long stride with the two shorter strides requiring considerably less energy. Runners in races longer than sprints, wherein economy of energy is a paramount consideration, use a natural stride, not exaggerated, not long, not short, but of a length in keeping with maximum economy of effort for the running speed required.

Cadence times stride length equals running speed. Top recorded sprint speed is 36 feet per second. As the runner reaches top speed, he has less and less time in which to apply leg thrust during the driving phase. Sprinters usually require 43 to 45 strides to sprint 100 yards, and 47 to 49 strides to sprint 100 meters. It requires about 1000 strides to run a mile.

Both understriding and overstriding are faults. Each runner has his own optimum stride length at any given speed, depending upon leg length, muscle strength, and joint flexibility.

6. Head position. The head should be aligned naturally with the trunk, with the eyes focused a few yards ahead. In middle-distance running the head may sometimes turn somewhat from side to side without upsetting body balance. Throwing back the head at the finish tends to shorten the stride and straighten the trunk.

7. Breathing is essential and involuntary. Breathe in and out through both the nose and mouth.

8. Economy of effort means avoidance of unnecessary movements which tend to inhibit or impede forward progression. Physiologically speaking, even pace running is most economical, although level pace running does not always feel like level energy output.

Fortunately it is not necessary to think of the above details when running. Athletes who run naturally and without artificially imposed motion (such as overstriding and "toe-running" or attempting to prevent the heel from touching the ground) find their best and most economical form by much running at a variety of speeds over various distances and surfaces.

The "complete" coach should be familiar with the fundamental movements of running. However, he should be cautious in risking the possibility of confusing runners with these details, since there is much truth in this ancient rhyme:

The centipede was happy quite
    Until a toad in fun,
Said, "Pray, which leg goes after which?"
That worked her mind to such a pitch,
She lay distracted in a ditch,
    Considering how to run.

References

1. Alford, J.W. Ll., "Middle Distance Running and Steeplechasing." London: Amateur Athletic Association, 1960, pages 9-16.

2. Broom. Eric, "Sprint Questions and Answers," "Track Technique," September, 1962, No. 9, page 285.

3. Chapman, H.A.L., "Forward Lean in Sprinting," "Track Technique," September, 1961, No. 5, page 133.

4. Dyson, Geoffrey H. G., "The Mechanics of Athletics." London: The University of London Press, Ltd., 1962, pages 97-111.

5. Hopper, Bernard J., "Rotation, A Vital Factor In Athletic Technique," "Track Technique," December, 1962, No. 10, page 306.

6. Jewkes, Ronald A., "Middle Distance Running," "Track Technique," June, 1962, No. 8, page 232.

7. Wilt, Fred, "How They Train." Los Altos:"Track and Field News, 1959, pages 106-107."

Mechanical Analysis of the Running Movement

by Fred Housden
(British AAA Honorary Senior Coach)

In this article an attempt is made to analyze the action of running from a consideration of the forces exerted by and those exerted on the runner. As many coaches may have only a rudimentary acquaintance with the principles of mechanics, it is necessary to state the principles and deductions that will be used.

A. Most forces acting on an athlete will produce both a verticle and a horizontal effect. These two effects are independent of each other and can be considered separately. Their combined effect will be at an angle to horizontal and vertical, and this resultant force can be found in a simple way. Taking a force, which has a horizontal component of 2 units and a vertical component of 3 units, draw a rectangle with a horizontal side 2 units long and a vertical side 3 units long: the diagonal, approximately 3.61 units, will be the measure of the actual force and will give the direction in which it acts, approximately $56\frac{1}{2}$ degrees with the horizontal.

B. To increase an athlete's speed in a given direction a force must be exerted on the athlete in that direction and must be greater than the forces opposing motion.

C. If the direction of action of a force, acting on an athlete, passes through the athlete's center of gravity (CG), the effect may be a change in the athlete's speed. If it does not pass through the CG, there may still be a change in speed but there will also be initiated a rotation of the athlete round the CG. The latter type of force is often referred to as "eccentric thrust."

D. The force of gravity acts continuously vertically downwards.

(The letters A, B, C, and D in brackets hereafter are used to remind the reader when the above principles are being applied.)

The force which makes possible the movement of running is the reaction of the ground to the thrust exerted by the athlete's foot. These two forces are equal in size but act in opposite directions. Since the force of gravity acts continuously (D), it is not possible for an athlete to run keeping his CG at any definite level. While both feet are off the ground, the athlete's CG will have a downward acceleration, causing an upward speed to change to a downward speed. To compensate for this situation the athlete's CG must have an upward acceleration during part, if not all, of the period of time during which a foot is in contact with the ground. Actually, while an athlete is running at a steady speed, the movement of the CG is a series of risings and fallings exactly repeated for every stride taken. During the driving phase of each stride the athlete's arms and the thigh of the leading leg are raised, causing a rise of the CG in the athlete's body; during the period of no contact with the ground the arms and thigh are lowered, causing a drop of the CG in the body. Consequently, the up and down movement of the athlete's head will not be as great as the actual up and down movement of the CG. In other words the arm and leg action will influence the vertical movement of the athlete's trunk.

The vertical component of the ground thrust varies and unless actual measurements are taken it is not possible to say how large it is at any given time. However, it is reasonable to assume that it is large when the athlete's hips are not far from the vertical through the foot, and that it is small just before ground contact is broken. From this assumption it follows that the resultant thrust from the ground starts almost, if not actually, vertical and gradually deviates more and more towards the horizontal. It is possible to estimate the average vertical component of thrust. This depends on the comparison of the period of time of foot contact with that of no contact. From an analysis of films of a number of sprinters, running at maximum or near maximum speed, including David Sime and Peter Radford, it was found that, the period of contact being taken as 1, the period of no contact varied between 1.3 and 1.5. This means that while the athlete has foot contact with the ground he has in one unit of time to counteract the effect of gravity acting during 1.3 to 1.5 units of time, requiring a support thrust of 1.3 to 1.5 times his weight. In addition to this he has to annul the effect of gravity (D). Hence, during foot contact the sprinter is providing an average support of 2.3 to 2.5 times his own weight. This is an average; so at times he must provide a considerably greater vertical force. When and how he takes this big strain would make an interesting subject for research.

Although an athlete is far from being a "rigid body", one must assume that only forces acting externally on the athlete can affect the speed of the CG in space. These external forces are:

1. The force of gravity which acts continually in a downward vertical direction. (D)

2. The reaction of the ground which is equal to and acts in an opposite direction to the thrust of the athlete's foot.

3. The resistance of the air, which usually opposes forward motion, depends on the strength and direction of the wind, and increases rapidly with the speed of the athlete since it varies as the square of the relative speed of the athlete.

The numerous forces, which operate internal to the athlete's body, are all in the nature of "action and reaction." As an example, the force causing the thigh of the rear leg to rotate about the hip are balanced by equal forces acting in opposite directions on the hip-girdle and trying to rotate it the opposite way. These internal forces cannot assist directly in the propulsion of the athlete forward, but, by positioning the various parts of the body, they can ensure that the thrust on the ground reaches its possible maximum.

The effectiveness of the drive obtained from each leg will depend on the size of the average horizontal component and the time during which this average force operates. At the start of a sprint race this component is larger, as the period of ground contact is longer. In a 200m heat at the Melbourne Olympic Games in 1956, Thane Baker left his blocks with the time of foot contact with the ground twice as great as the time of no contact. It was only on his ninth stride that the time of no contact was equal to that of contact. Thereafter, as stated previously, these times would reach a ratio between 1.3:1 and 1.5:1. The faster the hips are moving the less easily can the legs increase this speed, because the extensions of knees and ankles have to be so rapid. Eventually, the athlete arrives at maximum speed, when the additional speed obtained during foot contact with the ground is just equal to the speed lost during the period of no contact.

An analysis of motion-films shows that the foot makes contact with the ground almost directly below the hips, the foot moving vertically, or very nearly so, at the instant before contact. The horizontal component of thrust is most probably nil at contact, increasing to a maximum value for a short time and then diminishing to zero as contact is lost. The stronger this horizontal component the smaller the angle of inclination to the horizontal of the actual drive from the ground will be, requiring a low position of the CG to prevent rotation backwards (C). Consequently, the athlete keeps his CG low at the start of a sprint, when this horizontal component is large, by using a marked forward lean of his trunk: gradually raises his shoulders as the speed increases and the horizontal component decreases; and runs with an almost upright trunk when his speed has reached its maximum. Again, when an athlete wishes to pass another competitor in a race, he must increase his speed (accelerate). It is necessary for him to lower his CG before he can accelerate, and he will only catch his opponent unawares if he increases his body lean suddenly. The line of action of the drive from the ground through the left leg will pass to the left of but at the same level as the CG, setting up a rotation of the trunk about its long axis: and this rotation will continue until the right foot meets the ground and a rotation in the opposite direction is set up. To run fast with a trunk twisting first one way and then the other is impossible, so the arms take up this twist automatically-the more vigorous the drive, the more vigorously the arms should work. This is very noticable at the start of a sprint race when the arms move fast through a wide range in order to keep the athlete in balance. As the sprinter builds up speed the thrust from the ground diminishes and consequently, although the arm action is still vigorous, the arms move through a shorter range. The distance runner takes fewer strides in each second compared to the sprinter, and runs comfortably with a certain amount of rotation of the shoulders, his arm action being far less vigorous.

To get some idea of the direction of the resultant thrust obtained from the ground, one would most probably be right in assuming that the vertical component, which has to arrest the downward movement of the athlete's CG and start it on its upward journey again, would start large, possibly increase slightly and then decrease to zero. At the same time the horizontal component would build up to a maximum from zero and then decrease. This leads to the belief that the line of action of the thrust will follow the movement of the CG forward and always pass it at CG level (or very nearly so) and slightly to one side. Only experiment can show the variation of the size of this thrust during the extension of the leg. How much is due to knee flexion, how much is due to ankle flexion, and when should these movements take place for maximum efficiency. Personally, I feel quite sure that most of the drive has taken place before the leg is in the position of full extension - a position shown in so many diagrams to illustrate the effective drive an athlete is obtaining.

It is not always realized how the rear leg can assist the drive obtained through the other leg. The foot leaves the ground with the leg at almost full extension. The leg fold up and in the case of the sprinter the heel approaches very near to the buttocks, this action most probably being a muscular reaction to the vigorous straightening of the leg. It is at this point that the other foot makes ground contact, and it is now that the rear leg should be brought forward rapidly. This acceleration is produced by the hip pulling strongly on the leg, and an equal force is transmitted down the other leg to produce an equal reaction from the ground. The acceleration must be forward, resulting in an equal forward reaction from the ground. The athlete must make the effort to pull his leg through fast as soon as the foot of the other leg makes ground contact, i.e. to give it great acceleration. It is the acceleration which calls for the additional drive from the ground, and it will only do so if there is ground contact. If the rear leg is brought forward too soon, its increased speed will be obtained by robbing the body of some of its speed. A strong downwards and backwards movement of the arm is necessary to obtain this great acceleration, which will be indicated by high thigh lift to the front. As the upward movement of the thigh is halted, some of its upward speed is transferred to the rest of the athlete, assisting the upward movement of the trunk.

Character and Running

by Brian Mitchell

(British AAA Honorary Senior Coach Brian Mitchell is a graduate of University College, Oxford, and head of the English Department at Faversham Grammar School, Kent, England.)

"For a purpose is, in the first place, a principle of limitation. It determines the end for which, and therefore the limits within which, an activity is to be carried on. It divides what is worth doing from what is not, and settles the scale upon which what is worth doing ought to be done. It is, in the second place, a principle of unity, because it supplies a common end to which efforts can be directed... It is, in the third place, a principle of apportionment or distribution."
R. H. Tawney - "The Acquisitive Society"

I - Theory

Since a known English athlete once said that what was wanted in coaching was less theorizing drivel, it is necessary first to state the function of theory, and see where it touches fact. For many, implicitly or explicitly, share a distinct, if not a positive dislike of theory, and have not noticed that it may, like a telescope, help us to see more, and more clearly.

Theory puts untamed facts in a cage; it ropes them together and allows the onlooker to view them more steadily. Instead of accepting one fact alongside another, and refusing to notice that there may be a discrepancy, the theorizer moves aside that fact which has been misinterpreted. If it is a fact that a cross-country runner can be successful and do all of his training on the road, and also a fact that another can be successful and never run on the road, then these two facts must be put together, with others, and made to disclose their importance. If it turns out, in the full analysis, that the road-running athlete relied too much on the apparently proven success of his method, then the "fact" which he exemplified must go, in favor of another. If the "fact" of his activity casts light on the "fact" of another method, then something of both may be kept. The point is, that the process of scrutinizing what men do, is the process known as "theorizing", and its value lies in the results to which it leads. These results comprise clearer understanding. "Theories without facts are worthless; facts without theories are blind." My task in this chapter is, to assemble some observable facts about the cross-country runner's attitude to his sport, and to try to construct some theories out of these facts.

I would say, to begin with, that observation, experience and that which comes to us by way of our senses, our imagination or our intelligence (where that is directed to the understanding of somebody else's experience, as in reading another man's book) are the only valid data in an investigation such as this. What I have seen, been next to, done myself, or been told about; this is the stuff which can be truly called "fact". How this stuff is linked, and what the implications of it all are; that is the "theory".

If the theories are, finally, weak, it will be because the information is in too short supply, or because I have not understood it, or because assumptions are made that really are not true. For example, I assume the existence of a quality called "will-power." I cannot analyze it, or say where it rests, nor can I find a philosopher or a physiologist who can do so for me. But I have worked on the assumption which the novelist William Golding hints at, in "Free Fall", when he says that free will is like the taste of potatoes. You know that potatoes have a taste, but how can you describe it? Similarly, we know that, in some athletes, as in some men who climb the Eiger in winter, there is a faculty which we label "will-power". Where, in the bone, nerves, muscles, blood, or anywhere, is it to be found? It would be as fruitful to search for the physical hammock of consciousness; not finding it, would we deny the difference between ourselves and stones? Not being able to describe or trace will-power, shall we necessarily dismiss it? Or use some other words? Surely, again, observation, experience and intelligence lead us to notice the fact of selfcontrol, refusal to succumb, desire to conquer, and purpose. I have used the assumption that these qualities evince the existence of the general quality called "will-power". And, even if no such thing as will-power exists, it is possible to see something going on in ourselves and others. I can look at my own feet, and lift them when the mind is heavy and the slope steep.

Thus, the attempt is to throw light on the characteristics of distinguished runners, and in particular on those characteristics which are found among the cross-country fraternity. There are many observable facts, and one tentative theory might embrace these. The practical purpose served by such an attempt is to show aspiring athletes what kind of mental equipment they need.

II - The General Situation

One of the attractions of sport, not only of athletics, and of any deliberate activity, is that there comes, whether mildly or rigorously, a moment of truth. There is a point at which a man subjects himself to an examination, and the examination tests his present ability. It is difficult to dodge conclusions such as those that thrust themselves at you when you find yourself in an examination room, given a strictly limited amount of time in which to do a clearly defined piece of work, for which, in the nature of things, you are not totally prepared. It is impossible and pointless, for an athlete who has set himself to run seven miles, to refuse to admit the degree of failure involved; a watch or some other men will be the means of an absolutely categorical statement. That someone else has covered the distance in less time, is a blunt comment. The question at issue is, what happened in all the days that led up to the day of the race, and what will happen next? How did you prepare yourself for failure, and what do you consequently intend to do?

Looking back and forth involves reason, intelligence, imagination, and these are faculties which might easily be under-rated. An athlete, or his coach, needs them badly. It is necessary to understand what has happened, is happening and will happen. Part, at least, of the psychology of competitive running covers that area where reason and brain are used. The athlete, but more often actually the coach, needs to understand what he must do, proper coaching necessitates no shouting, self-advertisement or other kinds of dramatization, but rather, and primarily, the fullest possible body of knowledge, the widest possible imaginative vision, and the desire to offer the lot to the athlete. For, at all stages of his continuing effort, the athlete has got to know what is happening. How do I start? What should I do now? What went wrong? What next? These are the regular questions that puzzle the athlete. They are answered only as a result of intelligence, and perception. The athlete who says, as so many do, that he never knows what he is going to do in a certain training session is, in the strictest sense, a fool.

All that the athlete does, then, must be purposeful, aimed at a particular end which he has clearly in view. If this is so, he will find what needs to be done, what obstacles there are, and what kind of person he must be if he is to reach the day of his examination in workable condition. One thing is certain. The very high level of physical fitness and mental alertness required is not obtained passively. It cannot be piped into a man by way of television, and nobody can be massaged into a 28-minute six miles. There is a demand for continual action.

III - What satisfaction?

It is inevitable that the roots of a desire to run and more so to compete, lie too deep for general speculation. A detailed biography would reveal some of the incentives which a particular man carries with him; anthropology would distinguish what in the background informs character. The nature of the satisfaction derived from competitive running must be, in part, composed of purely animal pleasure at movement and sensation, as a child loves to swing up and down, or a tired man welcomes his bed. But, such satisfaction will lie in training, rather than in the hectic and uncomfortable business of racing. And it is a fact that most athletes, by taking up the sport, commit themselves to racing, at whatever level.

Leaving aside the obvious satisfaction incidential (though none the less important for that) to the sport, such as the social side of the club life, team participation, travel, which are powerful enough to maintain a man's interest for a lifetime, the question of purpose persists. Whatever he may say, the serious athlete does not run cross-country purely for his health. In any case, I am not here concerned to examine the kind of athlete who ticks gently over, surrounded by dozens of other far more important things than his running. It is the one who tackles the activity as if it were meaningful, that interests.

The reason for undertaking a few years, or even a few months, of extreme and punishing physical activity, must lie embedded in the very nature of a man, and possibly of men generally. As Robert Browning wrote - "Incentives come from the soul's self." This analysis will be too elaborate for some people, but objection will not establish untruth. One man looks for gold, one man does not, one is not interested, one does not believe in its existence; none will alter the fact of its being there. One man strives for some end, others see neither an end nor any point in striving; that does not deny the validity of the claim that there is an end. When an athlete conceives a notion to test himself, to run up against a difficult task, to see how well he can perform a certain activity, then he is showing that he has something of the artist in him, because he is unusually discontented with his prevaliling condition and he seeks to understand how deep his resources are. It is not important that few men do actually test themselves, nor does it matter that there are hundreds of ways of doing so. What does matter is, that action, achievement can never be futile. More obviously, find intellectual accomplishment such as scientists advance or moral wisdom relayed to others, helps mankind. But so, too, does the slightest of efforts, by raising its performer to a higher degree of self-respect and pride, or by persuading him that he still has a long way to go, lift at the same time some part of his audience onto that new level of awareness. That is what we mean by saying we are "impressed"; and that is one function of art. It seems to me that all athletes have some faint and instinctive understanding that this is one reward which the sport has to offer. The athlete will compete for such satisfaction. Satisfaction is the opposite of discontent. Discontent may be removed by action. The athlete acts, and even those who watch him are, in a way acting. That is why they enjoy what he is doing.

If, then, cross-country running happens to be an activity which appeals to a man, it does so because it offers him at least a partial, or a promise of, satisfaction. The many social benefits which gather around participation in the sport add to this satisfaction and possibly smother it. But, if the final test, the race, is to be really meaningful, the athlete must see it as a test and not as a social occasion. The social occasion comes afterwards. What the athlete is really working for is the resolution of a little private battle

Principle and practice: Look steadily, clearly and deliberately at what you are trying to do. See the race as a severe test of your present ability. Admit its importance to you. Do not dodge the lesson it teaches. Respect your own efforts and your own little bit of success.

IV - Environment and the Athlete

Although the activity of running, and particularly of cross-country and long-distance road running, is a rigorously personal affair, it should be clear that every individual who takes up the sport is very much influenced by a background which is, in large measure, common to him and his opponents. For example, in Britain, there is now a style of living which is different from anything we have known before, and which is likely to touch quite firmly most of our athletes; a man may live in the industrial north of England or in the uniquely suburban areas of the south, yet common influences are at work. This is not to say that the influences are always and in detail the same, but rather that the tempo of life, the difficulties or lack of difficulties, the routine, the likes and dislikes of the people are noticeably often of the same general quality. The working day is about eight hours, two days in seven are usually free from the demands of earning a living, the mass of people do not go short of food, the armchair and the television set have their positions prominently in the living room near the fire, everybody is exhorted to buy certain things, go to certain places for their holidays and use their free time in particular ways. And many put up umbrellas when it rains, particularly at the older universities. All of this must, inevitably, affect and partly condition those who take a notion to run, and run hard.

The nature of present-day industrial society is such, that it must color a man's outlook, make it difficult for him to search out any absolute standards of value, remove from him a physical toughness and resilience which many of his ancestors would have been forced to acquire, and place him a few steps away from that kind of temperament which is the possession of the gifted athlete. That we still have gifted athletes among us is often a surprise to me. I see, week after week, adolescent boys who will take a bus (streetcar?) rather than a walk, and who will applaud the cigarette advertisements and the horseless disc-jockeys, rather than what little call of the wild is left. This is hardly their fault. Their attitudes, and thus their actions, result from the particular society which has bred them; it is a society directed in many ways by popular songsters, castrated troubadours, worshippers at the shrine of the new car. So it is very difficult for the athlete to appear, and when he has appeared it is still difficult for him to shed some of the urban skin and face the country on a cold, wet day.

Each athlete should become aware of those limitations which have been thrust upon him so that he can set about breaking them up where necessary. I am not suggesting a back-to-the-cave-or-the-Kalahari-desert movement, for I accept neither the logic nor the morality of that, but there is an area of a modern man's character which has been taught, by his environment, not to like hard exercise. A potential athlete cannot allow this aspect of society, or this area of his own disposition, to dominate him. It would prevent him from training in the winter. Some parts of what is glibly called "progress" must be warded off. Luckily, due to particular family influences, to that continuity of interest in sport which a structure such as the British system of clubs preserves, and finally to a subtle stubbornness in human nature which is made necessary still by all forms of destruction and all contact, however distant, with the need for most people to earn their own living and at least strive for something - because of these elements of life, not everything in modern life is accepted happily by everybody. If the strongest tendencies were wholeheartedly accepted, there would be no cross-country running.

V - ". . . back to my sole self"

It is of crucial importance to remember that the great bulk of discussion of about human activities is concerned with factors outside the particular individual. Influences, advice, comment or help of any kind are aimed at a person, and the problem of achievement, and the difficulties of it, is really, finally a problem for one person inside one body and not more than partly reachable from outside. It is the "person", the "self," "the throng and stack of being" of which the poet Hopkins writes that is important. And this is a very complex and dark sport indeed -

"Nothing else in nature comes near this unspeakable stress of pitch, distinctiveness, and selving, this selfbeing of my own. Nothing explains it or resembles it, except so far as this, that other men to themselves have the same feeling. But this only multiplies the phenomena to be explained so far as the cases are like and do resemble. But to me there is no resemblance: searching nature I taste self but at one tankard, that of my own being."

Hence, it is difficult to coach, other than at the level of schemes of physical exercise, shouting with stop-watches, bits of superficial advice stemming from a lack of thought; hence, too, it is rare to come across an athlete who will not settle for mere instructions but seeks to find out for and about himself, and seeks help only from somebody else when he is convinced that other person wishes to understand as deeply as he himself does. There is an element in Percy Cerutty (with whom the newspapers and most of the fickle public and athletes have had their temporary fun) among the incoherence and armwaving, that touches this rock-bottom meaningfulness. It is there, at the center of an athlete's character, that the best work can be done.

While launching a few hypotheses as preliminaries to writing this chapter, I had correspondence with an athlete who has had the minimum of external success, but who nevertheless exemplifies the solitary and essentially personal nature of an activity such as distance-running. Out of a difficult childhood and physical illness comes a personality with an edge to it, and from this grows what we call will-power (denied by some cloistered philosophers, but not denied in the annals of actual tangible effort). The man looks out on the world but also looks in at himself, and this is not just sick musing, because it issues forth in action. He tests his own strength by walking and running very long distances, and by lasting out in an open lifeboat after his ship is torpedoed. He takes deep pleasure in the activity of running, doing things merely to prove to himself that he has it in him to do them. It is at this level that the true athlete works. Even the athletic failure knows in his heart that there is such a level, and every coach with a glimmer of perception has fished at this depth though not knowing what bait to use in order to hand up what is down there.

A man, and particularly one who, like an athlete, is bent on achieving something, will get maturity, optimism, even a religious sense, out of his experiences and endeavors, of what ever order; and out of a relationship with that area of th world which is not purely social (and, therefore, inevitably shallow), the area with which the poet, playwright, novelist and priest is concerned, he will get a practical strength which will take him through difficult times and uncomfortable physical conditions, one of which may be a cross-country race, but particularly the months prior to it. He must look at himself and his life to find that pride which is a sin but also a virtue. It will make him a better athlete if he has an enormous incentive. This testing oneself is the biggest incentive of the lot.

It will be said that a lot of shallow, unintelligent and plainly unpleasant people succeed at running, and thereby make nonsense of any claim that one has to search for any sort of depth of character. Indeed, there are athletes who have not the intelligence to know what they are doing; they need help in planning their work, but they may have the best of built-in incentives to succeed and their lack of brain does not signify lack of character (by which I mean, at its most primitive level, the light in a man's eyes; and, at its most developed, the prophet). "Shallow" in the sense of there being nothing to look for, or applied to a person who will not look, I grant as a crippling handicap, but not a complete denial, because there can be depth when certain present restrictions are removed, and there will be particular reasons why a person will not search in his own cupboards. Moreover, it is doubtful whether any of these apparently destructive characteristics would be found to any significant degree in the people whose names stand right at the top of the lists, or whether they exist where they do exist without compensation.

The practical outcome of this concern with, and perhaps search for, an identity, is the that the athlete should be persuaded to take himself seriously (never solemnly - there is a gap between the two as big as the biggest puritan). He must see what amount of will-power he has got, taste the depth of pleasure in his chosen activity, combat the influences which he has examined and found wanting, never let his passion for his sport prevent him from seeing that it is, after all, one activity among many and that a fast seven miler is not as valuable as a Beethoven symphony. The seven miles takes in part of what the symphony totally covers.

VI - The Race

"All actions arise from a condition of mind". G. K. Chesterton

When an athlete deliberately has limited the number of his activities, distributed his energies and intentions so that there is some kind of unity in what he does, then he looks to the time and place at which his efforts can be tested. This testing is the race. It is carried out against the clear criteria of other men and the watch. Herein lies much of its attraction, both for athletes and spectators. There is almost pure competition, a minor struggle of physical and mental powers. It is for this moment that the genuine athlete prepares himself. Fortunately, he can have dozens of such moments, and many chances to reform himself. Always, he should keep in mind his objective and, particularly, should he know which races matter, for so much carefully nurtured strength is regularly spent on ones that do not.

It is absolutely necessary to be fully award of what you intend to do in a race long before the race starts. Herb Elliot has written of this and acted upon it. The extraordinary man in any field of activity is clear-sighted and knows what lies behind the dictum, "make up your mind." Consider how imperfectly any job will be done by a man who has not thought about it. How much less perfect will be the achievement when the activity to be undertaken involves not just understanding and imagination, but resolution too. All activities call for some degree of resolution, but where the physical discomfort is likely to be extreme, then the necessity for a special condition of mind is so much greater. The runner knows exactly what to expect by way of discomfort, but it pays him to have concluded before the race that he will not surrender to this discomfort. Thus, he can be his own best prompter when he remembers what he said he would do.

Again, this quality of resolution, determination, will-power, is evidenced. At the moment when he races, the athlete's resolve will be of a particular order, made so by all the factors of inheritance and environment, and, I think, by his own level of consciousness, imagination and vision, whereby he may stand apart from the necessarily powerful internal and external influences. Not only is the power in him an immediate and present one, but it is also a potential one, for he may see its limitations and wish to copy other men in whom it exists in a more perfected form. He gets plenty of opportunity for this. His level of resolve can be tested time and again in the rigorous conditions of the race.

Fundamentally, racing is in no way a struggle against one's opponents, but rather against oneself. Opponents help. Timetrials are the toughest possible test. Every training session is of the nature of a time-trial, because there is a challenge at every point where discomfort sets in; every race provides the external stimulus of opponents and audience, both aids to will-power. It is an exceptional individual indeed who can get a surge of adrenalin purely from the reserve tank of his own character. If he can do it, if his intentions are that firm, he will be by so much the more accomplished athlete. Then the addition of antagonists and shouters will be useful but not imperative. He will be in such a frame of mind as to render all external aid superfluous.

It is, incidentally, vital to remember that races upset the large majority of athletes. "Nerves" before the start; confidence in oneself; wish at a certain stage of the race to give in; these are factors which are not the possession of just a few unfortunate people. The best athletes do not let their fear of the race put them off, do not lack confidence, are prepared not to give way when the moment comes. It is always salutary to recall that Chataway, after he had beaten Kuts over 5,000 of the most crucifying meters seen at London's White City, commented on the existence of a point in that race at which he was momentarily tempted to give way. Having got past that point, he beat Kuts in the last few strides. Strangely, most runners will see a man go past them, not close with him, yet go on to complete the distance; the strength to cover the full distance is there, and often to come back in the later stages, but the swift resolve to chase a man may be lacking. This is not, of course, to forget that intelligence must be used to judge pace and to assess whether it would be foolish to go after your opponent. Understanding and determination here stem from proper physical conditioning, and this will very largely control the vital moves. Still, it was hardly thought that Chataway's physical condition surpasses that of Kuts.

Concerning that condition so vaguely called "nerves", when a man feels physically weak before a race; when he might back out if given the chance; when there is a very real kind of fear in him; this state of mind does, at least, illustrate the existence of imagination and its physical manifestation . Just as, in the dentist's waiting room, we can see in our mind's eye what is going to happen, and we do not altogether like it, so the athlete runs his race before he runs it, and is upset by the doubt and the discomfort. The same symptoms will arise when a time-trial is carried out. Why not in an ordinary run, and why not once the race is on? In a sense, too, it is better to be in the dentist's chair than in his waiting-room, and easier to have a single filling than a mouthful of extractions. First, the athlete is subjecting himself to an amount of discomfort and it is as well to recognize this, for it cannot be avoided; once you accept that it cannot be avoided, then it becomes a shade less frightening. Second, the more deliberate, comprehensive and thorough your training has been, the less worried will you be by the race or trial. Third, as a training run is known to be not drastically important, so should the race be known to be of no final consequence, but just a part of life and hardly reckoned to be out of universal consequence; therefore, the intelligent, imaginative, fairly well-balanced athlete will take the race for what it is really worth, treat it as fun, and not treat it any less seriously for that. Zatopek had this are perfected; men like Bannister perhaps have too much imagination and keep away from the races. Finally, and practically, it is of great value to pretend the race has actually started before it does. Knowing that, once the first few hundred yards are covered, you will feel better, it pays, in warming up, to run those first few hundred yards and get them over. The act of taking hold of the nerves and muscles quietens them. Nevertheless, there cannot be a quick and quack remedy for the fear of an overpowering situation, and the solution to a difficulty here lies much further back down the training path, where it is part of the fullest possible training routine. The necessary effects of extreme effort must be conquered many times.

Thus, the athlete's outlook matters considerably. He comes to the race knowing fully what he intends to do, what is involved, and what it is all worth. He can only fail himself, and only he can know the degree of failure.

VII - Cross-country in particular

(a) Training

It is perhaps time to emphasize that "we run because we like it, through the broad, bright land," and that the cross-country runner knows this particularly well. The man who runs primarily on the track seems to me to have his own patented blinkers, and will have missed much of the sheer pleasure of running. Ideally, an athlete can train over the country throughout the year, at least twice a week, and race over it in the proper season. He will certainly benefit mentally and physically. If he can taste the essential pleasure of movement when it takes place away from concrete and chronium, he will get a kind of vigor which is valuable in itself. If he can remember that, while he runs, some live in iron lungs and some who could take exercise prefer cigarettes and feeble comments, then his pleasure will be complete and his fortune good.

In winter, wherever cross-country is a sport of importance even to a few people, weather conditions will be bad for most of the time, and training will have to go on. There is no reason at all why the weather should prevent a man from running in Britain or in most of Europe; in Scandinavia and possibly in North America, it may present a problem, but often the weakness is in the attitude of the athlete and not in the surface of the snow. The past winter (1962-3) in Britain has been severe, with deep snow for the best part of two months, but this has not prevented the serious athlete from training and racing; hundreds of schoolboys have kept at it, though hundreds, of course, gave way. The attitude of the true athlete should be one of indifference. Fog will stop him on occasions, and extreme cold will persuade him to wear the proper clothes; fundamentally, he is not affected by weather.

It follows that the athlete will understand the necessity for regularity in training. This must be virtually an unbreakable rule. The violinist, Yehudi Menuhin, has said, "You cannot build, unless you build every day," and this holds good for every intellectual, artistic and physical pursuit. There must be persistency. Without constant activity and reaching out, nothing, in athletics certainly, will be achieved. But there is room, too, for intelligence, reason, understanding and imagination. Often we see a man losing his form, and the more he loses it, the harder he tries, and the more he loses it. Regularity does not only imply a constant level of effort. Often, a constant effort in terms of the number of runs will necessitate a fluctuating degree of severity.

If, in training, the cross-country man compels himself to overcome obstacles, to attack relentlessly the task which he has set and which he should fully understand, then some of this decisive strength which he has practised in his training will carry over into his racing. It is certainly no guarantee that he will race hard and up to his capacity, but it is a central part of his preparation. What is omitted in training is not likely suddenly to appear in a race. What is included in training is sure to help. Disciplined practice of resistance to fatigue makes fatigue more bearable.

(b) Racing.

The cross-country race is, inevitably, long and exhausting. That it is often too long and too exhausting for many who take it on, is obvious; the finishing "funnel" offers too many examples of the inability or unwillingness of men to prepare themselves properly for extreme exertion. The gradual loss of form during the prolonged season, or the observable and seemingly deliberate stupidity of those many athletes who have reached some sort of worthwhile level of performance only to beat themselves down by continual and dramatic efforts which reason would object to if reason got a look in, show that it is, at least, advisable to make an intelligent study of the race and its effects. In Britain, at the moment, there are several men who have had international honors but not kept their places at the top because they have not cared to see that it is often more intelligent not to race. Preparation is more profitable than reparation.

If intelligence must be used in preparing for competition and in allowing yourself a certain number only of hard races, then intelligence can also be used in deploying effort in the actual, particular race. While there is little point in attempting detailed plans of any race (because the unknown factors of opponents' condition and intentions, and of your own immediate condition, make this much of a guessing game) and because it is a surer procedure to wait until you are under way before you decide what you can, and will, do, there is yet some value in judging your starting pace, spreading your effort, knowing how to tackle the hills (except on the continent of Europe) and knowing when to strike out for home. A preview of the course, too, has its value, and the runner must always know what sort of surface and contour to expect. Finally, though, it is his physical condition and his intention to do well that will take the athlete through, and no amount of crafty study on the morning of the race is going to affect this.

If, as is reasonable, many cross-country races are to be used as part of the training routine and not as important or decisive efforts, then it is as well to know beforehand just how the race is going to be used. If it is a two-lap course, the second lap can be run hard; to avoid the complete exhaustion of a resolute exertion, only the second part of a race need be taken seriously. Or you may decide to allow a certain weaker opponent to get so far ahead before setting off to catch him; or you may take a steady pace until a particular mark on the course, and go hard from there. Thus, the training run is deliberate, but something of a race.

An athlete must, at all costs, avoid developing what may be called "local pride". By this, I mean that fatal attachment to victory in small club runs or slow races. In Britain, before Christmas, very many athletes get used to a certain racing tempo which possibly takes them to the front of local championships, and these men clearly forget what is happening elsewhere. Then, from January to March, they suffer a series of shocks, in county, area and national championships, where they meet runners who have achieved a kind of racing pace which kills off those whose "local pride" has kept them at a particular level. The athlete must never stop looking at what some ideal best runner is doing. He must always remember that somewhere there is a runner, and most probably a group of runners, who can beat him easily. He must remember always that he is, at every moment, running too slowly.

Wisely, also, the cross-country runner and distance runner will see that it is quite ridiculous and arbitrary to race, or feel that there is a need to race, on every seventh day. It happens that seven is a magic number, still with us after many centuries and likely to stay. But the conscious athlete will need to forego any reliance on magic or ritual, placing his faith in intelligence and understanding rather than in that text which says, "And he raced on the seventh day." There is an absolute need to govern the number of days that pass between races, and not to let them govern you. It is a constant surprise to me, that only a few athletes will see and accept this. To the extent that an ambitious runner lives in a country where athletics is not highly organized, he has the advantage. In Britain, athletes feel some mystic compulsion to go and race on the seventh day. If they are primarily cross-country runners, they are like those people who must eat because it is five o'clock. Eat when you are hungry and ready for it.

VIII - And the last shall be first

In summary, what kind of a man will win? Who is he, who limits, unifies and distributes his efforts in training, so that he may dominate the race? Who has the character to do?

There is no formula, and many of us would revolt at the notion that there could be. For myself, I detest both the idea of the autocratic coach and the egotistic athlete. I hate to think that one man can dragoon a few others and construct them after his own image. European history has too many examples of this, on a very large scale, to make it attractive. Conversely, I do not applaud that extreme individualism which exhibits a loud mouth and an ignorance of famine relief. There must be still a healthy mind in a healthy body. The athlete must know that, be he ever so great, within one year of his success, few will recall his name. That is reasonable, since, what he does should be primarily of importance to himself and not so much to others; though a few may draw inspiration from what one man accomplishes and this is how a lot of teaching gets done.

Here, then, is the clue. The athlete must, if he is worth anything at all, discover an integrity and a modesty that will allow him to keep his sport in perspective, and to pursue it for his own satisfaction. He is something of an artist, and the best artists are not in popular journalism, popular music or the chain libraries. They cannot be, because integrity and lack of concern for public applause implies a silent, solitary effort which accepts whatever applause comes but is not greatly moved by it. And the true artist has at least two qualities which the accomplished athlete will strive for. First, he is never, at any stage, satisfied; always, he knows that he has missed perfection. (At some point, he will read the poetry of Robert Browning). Therefore, he drives harder than his neighbor. Second, and I think of supreme importance, he is, without all the arrogant connotations of the word "egotistical", carrying out his activities for himself, not for the crowd, or the club, or even the national flag. The crowd, the club, even the nation, will benefit, but mostly the solitary artist draws sustenance from his own efforts, in so far as he does not mind at all what the crowd says or does. Of course, he listens to them and they are an ever-present potential influence, but, finally, he goes about his own business. The outstanding athletes have known this instinctively.

If the athlete who is habitually last intends to be first, that is all that matters. Some men will never be first actually and visibly; a one-legged high-jumper will not get over seven feet. But that is to measure as the world does. If a man intends to be first, and knows absolutely the meaning of that word "intends" and does not just "say" that he is going to be first, or "wish" that he could be, then he will be like Ernest Hemingway's old man and the sea. That, really, is the psychology of the athlete. The rest is special detail and particular knowledge.

Language of Training

Training terminology involves a specialized area of knowledge often confronted with a problem of precision in meaning. This review of selected basic terms is made for the purpose of establishing a more precise understanding of the language used in the study and discussion of training.

Athletics is a term used in the USA to refer to all sports such as football, swimming, boxing baseball, track and field, cross-country, basketball, wrestling, etc. However, in most countries other than the USA the term "athletics" refers specifically to track and field, and to no other sport. In most non-English speaking countries the term "light athletics" refers specifically to track and field athletics.

The International Amateur Athletic Federation (IAAF), whose official address is 4 Great Winchester Street, London E.C.2, England (telephone LOndon Wall 2291, telegraphic address "Marathon," London) was founded in 1912 to formulate a code of rules and regulations for competition and a common amateur definition acceptable throughout the world, and to establish an authentic register of world and olympic records. Today the objectives of the IAAF as outlined by Rule 2 of the IAAF constitution are: (1) The establishment of friendly and loyal co-operation between all members for the benefit of amateur athletics throughout the world. (2) To compile rules and regulations governing international competitions for men and women in amateur athletics. (3) To ensure that all contests between members of the Federation shall be held under the laws and the rules for competition of the Federation. (4) To affiliate national governing associations and federations. (5) To decide any dispute that may arise between members if called upon to do so. (6) To co-operate with the Organizing Committees of the Olympic Games in carrying through the organization of the athletic competitions and as delegated by the International Olympic Committee to supervise and control all the technical arrangements. (7) To frame regulations for the establishment of World, Olympic, and Continental amateur records in athletics. The membership of the IAAF is comprised of the duly elected national governing associations or federations of countries, in control of amateur track and field athletics, cross country running and walking, which agree to abide by the rules and regulations of the IAAF. Only one member for each country can be affiliated with the IAAF, and the jurisdiction of the members of the IAAF shall be limited to the political boundaries of the country they represent.

An amateur is described by the IAAF rules relating to eligibility of athletes to compete as one who competes for the love of sport and as a means of recreation, without motive of securing any material gain from such competition. These rules make ineligible for IAAF competition any person who since reaching 16 years of age has competed in any sport for pecuniary reward; has competed knowingly against those ineligible under IAAF rules; has ever received any pecuniary consideration for teaching, training, or coaching in any sport (physical education teachers may teach physical education for pay but not coach for pay); has at any time been financially interested in any track and field event in which he has entered; writes, lectures, or broadcasts for payment upon any track or field event or competition without prior permission of his national governing body; sells or pawns any of his prizes; receives any compensation for using the goods or apparatus of any firm, manufacturer, or agent, or allows his name or his static or moving picture to be used as a means of advertising or recommending the goods of any firm, manufacturer, or agent; competes in a foreign country in competition not recognized by the governing body of such country; accepts directly or indirectly any money or other consideration for expenses or loss of earnings, other than what is permitted under IAAF rules (usually only actual cost for travel, meals, lodging, and $2 or 14 shillings 6 pence sterling daily out-of-pocket expenses).

The rules governing competitive cross-country racing are described in Rule 33 of the IAAF rules of competition. These rules provide: (1) The race shall be run on a bona fide cross-country course properly marked. (2) The course must be marked preferably with red flags on the left and white flags on the right which must be visible from a distance of 140 yards (125 meters). In all other respects the rules governing track competitions shall prevail. (3) When laying out the course very high obstacles should be avoided, so should deep ditches, and dangerous ascents or decents, thick undergrowth and in general any obstacles which would constitute a difficulty beyond the aim of competition. (4) The distance for women shall not be greater than 3,000 meters or 2 miles.

IAAF rule 32 governs the **scoring of team races** such as cross-country. Under this rule, the method of scoring shall be optional and may be any one of the following: (1) By scoring the least number of points, according to the positions in which the scoring members of a team finish. The finishing positions of the non-scoring members of a team shall be scored in computing the scores of other teams, but when a team fails to finish the requisite number to score, it shall be eliminated; or (2) By scoring the least number of points, according to the scoring positions in which the scoring members of a team finish. The positions of the non-scoring members of a team whether it finishes all its members or not shall be scored in computing the scores of other teams; or (3) By scoring the least number of points according to the positions in which the scoring members of a team finish. The finishing positions of the non-scoring members of a team and the members of a team which fails to finish the requisite number to score, shall be elminated; or (4) By scoring the lowest aggregate of the times recorded by the scoring members. If two or more competitors tie for any place the points for the places concerned shall be aggregated and divided equally among the competitors so tying. In case of a tie on points, the team whose last scoring member finished nearest to first place shall be the winning team.

Training involves a series of physical activities deliberately planned and carried out and a mental attitude deliberately cultivated for the purpose of increasing efficiency in running and racing. Increased efficiency in running involves production of maximum muscular energy with a minimum of effort. To the dedicated athlete intent upon achieving the maximum of his competitive potential, training is prone to become a way of life. Not only does he devote the maximum available time to physical activity (short of the point of diminishing returns), but also governs his personal life aside from physical activity in regard to sleep, food, and social activities according to the best interests of training. Like many other forms of human endeavor, training has its own special difficulties in the moral domain. The athlete must guard against an attitude of mind so concerned with training that more important issues of life such as religion, family, study, employment, etc. become only a boring interlude of what has become a major pre-occupation and business of life. The maximum amount of time and effort any athlete should devote to training will always remain a personal decision involving individual values and circumstances of life. In the torrid swirl of modern competition wherein many athletes make training and racing a major pre-occupation, it is well to keep competitive success in perspective and not forget that the game is still the game, not the end of the world.

The warmup means preliminary exercise as physical and mental preparation for strenuous exertion. In the case of the runner, this "limbering-up" involves about 15 minutes of activity, progressively including shacking, jogging, striding, calisthenics, and acceleration running to sprint speed, interspersed by moments of walking. One of the major purposes of the warmup is psychological preparation for exertion. Some of the physiological adjustments which occur during warmup include: (1) body temperature rises slightly, (2) arterioles supplying the muscles dialate, (3) muscle temperature increases, (4) muscle viscosity decreases, (5) stroke volume of the heart increases, (6) heart rate increases, (7) blood pressure rises, (8) pulmonary and bronchial blood-flow increases, (9) respiration becomes deeper and faster, (10) splanchnic circulation diminishes, (11) the processes of digestion and absorption slow down, (12) glycogen stores in the liver are converted to gluclose and passed into the general circulation, and (13) vasodialation of the skin.

The warmdown is exercise gradually diminishing in intensity following severe exertion, for the purpose of facilitating return of the circulatory system and bodily functions to a resting or pre-exercise state. After intense running the body's circulatory adjustments have flooded the leg muscles with blood. If all exercise stops suddenly, stagnation of the blood (stasis) occurs, excess tissue fluid is not removed rapidly from the muscles, and stiffness is likely to occur. Following severe exertion, the athlete should keep his muscles active, slowly decreasing the rate of effort, until the circulatory adaptations to exercise have had time to become reversed. As a practical matter, after intense running following competetion or a workout, the runner should jog, then shack, and finally walk, for a total of 5-10 minutes.

Workout is a term often used interchangably with training. Strictly speaking, a workout refers to the physical activities which take place during one specific session (of training). As an example, a runner might plan a year round training program calling for one workout each day. His weekly training program might specify that each Wednesday his workout include 60 x 150 yards.

Technique is the method of performing the mechanical details of an art. With regard to running, technique is essential movement obeying the mechanical principles involved in this activity. Style is the interpretation of technique in accordance with personal characteristics of the athlete. Thus technique provides the general framework of essential motion obeying mechanical principles, while style refers to adaptation of technique according to individual differences of the athlete.

A pedestrian is a person traveling by foot, while the seldom used term "pedestrianism" refers to footracing in general, whether it be walking or running.

Walking is defined by IAAF rule 45 as progression by steps so taken that unbroken contact with the ground is maintained. This rule further specifies that the advancing foot of the walker must make contact with the ground before the rear foot leaves the ground, and that during the period of each step, in which a foot is on the ground, the leg shall be straightened (not bent at the knee) at least for one moment.

Walking involves pushing the body out of balance, while it is supported over one leg and then bringing the swinging (driving) leg forward in time to prevent the body from falling. This process is repeated with each step by an increasing force until the desired walking speed is attained. The leg action in walking may be divided into (a) the swinging phase, (b) the supporting phase, and (c) the double supporting phase. The entire period one leg covers the swinging and supporting phases is called the "double step".

The swinging phase in walking starts at the instant the toes of the rear leg leave the ground, and ends as the heel of this leg touches the ground in front of the body.

The instant the heel touches the ground in front of the body in walking marks the beginning of the supporting or propulsory phase. The supporting phase ends at the instant the large toe leaves the ground behind the body.

The double supporting phase of walking falls between the swinging phase and supporting phase, when both feet are in contact with the ground. The double supporting phase almost disappears if walking is performed at maximum velocity, when the walking movement borders on the mechanics of running.

In walking the heel always makes contact with the ground first in front of the body, and the supporting phase is always longer than the swinging phase. In ordinary walking wherein steps are approximately 32 inches, an increase in the cadence to 190 steps per minute (more than 3 steps per second) always results in running. Race walking involves a different style, whereby the cadence may be increased to as many as 220 steps per minute (about 4 steps per second) and step length is increased to 47-51 inches.

The speed of walking varies between the stroller's gait of approximately 3 miles per hour (5 minutes per 440 yards), to the road race of 7 miles per hour, and the track event in which 8 miles per hour can be exceeded.

Velocity in walking is limited by the step length which is determined by the possible distance between the feet while both are on the ground, and by the time necessary for the leg to complete its swing. This time cannot be less than half of the swinging time of a physical pendulum which has the length and weight of the leg.

The run is a type of locomotion wherein there exists no theoretical limit of velocity on such mechanical grounds as found in walking. The major objective of running is to increase the speed of progression. This is done by causing the body to float in the air with each step for a short time, during which period the step is made longer than the span of the legs would otherwise permit. This is a period of "double float" during which time both feet are off the ground. In contrast to walking with its double supporting phase, there is never a phase of double support in running, but rather the swinging of the rear leg begins before the front leg swing has ended and thus before the front leg contacts the ground. The swinging time in running is <u>always</u> longer than the supporting time. Average steps made in running are twice as long as walking steps, and in ordinary running the vertical movements (up and down) are less than they are in the walk. In running the legs are more bent when they make contact with the ground than in walking, and most runners make contact with the ball of the foot first as the leading foot comes to the ground. Generally speaking, the slower the running speed, the shorter the step, and the faster the run the longer the step.

Shack is a term familiar to English athletics, but seldom used in the USA. Shacking means very slow running at a speed of perhaps 5 minutes per 440 yards, landing flat-footed with possibly a slight jarring action. The head travels parallel to the ground, the upper body remains relaxed and perpendicular, the steps are quite short, and the arms hand loosely by the sides. Although the speed of shacking may on occasion be as slow as walking, contact is broken with the ground at each step, and there is no period of double support as in walking.

To jog or **jogging** means running at a speed of 2 to 3 minutes per 440 yards, or 8 to 12 minutes per mile. The steps are very short in jogging (the slower the speed, the shorter the step), the arms may or may not hang down to the sides or be dropped from time to time for greater relaxation, the body remains perpendicular, and foot-plant tends toward flat-footed running. The form used in jogging as opposed to form used when running at a faster pace differs only in intensity, as jogging involves a generally quieter running action. Jogging is usually part of the warmup activity of the runner, and is generally used during the recovery period after fast runs in interval training.

The stride is the distance covered in one step at any speed during running.

Striding is a rather ambiguous term used to vaguely indicate any running speed between jogging (2-3 minutes per 440 yards) and sprinting (absolute maximum speed).

To sprint means to run at full speed. Sprinting is running at maximum possible speed. Since sprinting involves running at maximum speed, there can be no such phenomenon as an "easy sprint." In good sprinting, the cadence is $4\frac{1}{2}$ steps per second, or approximately 45 steps in a 100 yards sprint race.

Fartlek is a Swedish word which means "speed play" or "play of speed." It is a form of training featuring informal fast-slow running popularized by Gosta Holmer, former National Coach of Sweden. Fartlek involves great quantities of running at a variety of speeds, preferably (though not necessarily) over natural surfaces such as grass, woods, or golf courses.

Although there are infinite varieties of fartlek, a typical example might be: Without benefit of stop watch timing, run in the wood, on a golf course, beach, road, or track. Jog 10-15 minutes at a speedof 8-10 minutes per mile, covering $1\frac{1}{2}$-2 miles, as a warmup. Perform 5-10 minutes of vigorous calisthenics. Run at a fast, steady, continuous speed for 4-6 minutes, covering $\frac{3}{4}$ to $1\frac{1}{4}$ miles. Walk 3-5 minutes. Jog about 1 mile in 8 minutes, taking 4-6 x 75-110 yards sprints enroute. Sprint uphill 150-200 yards if a hill is available. If no hill is available, run 660 yards at near maximum speed at the moment. Jog 1 mile, taking very short, fast 5-10 yard rushes or bursts of speed enroute. Walk 10 minutes. Then, on a track, road, or other level area where one can achieve good speed, run 2-4 x 440 yards at racing speed, jogging 440 yards after each. These 440's should be timed with a stop-watch if possible. Jog 1 mile in about 10 minutes to complete the workout.

Holmer's original description of Fartlek training involved running both in the woods and pace running on the track daily. The track running included 440, 660, 880, and 1100 yards fast, followed by appropriate recovery periods, and repeated an adequate number of times, on various days according to plan. Fartlek training done correctly is tough, demanding, and most effective. Innumerable combinations of various distances and speeds can be incl-uded in the woods running. The Fartlek as practiced by many runners today has often degenerated into indiscriminate jogging, or a long, slow run off the track, totally devoid of speed, and bears little relationship to the very excellent type of training advocated by Holmer.

Interval-training (interval-running) is a form of training featuring formal fast-slow running. It involves 5 variable factors including: (1) the distance of the training runs, (2) the number of repetitions of the training distance, (3) the speed of the training runs, (4) the duration of recovery period after each training run, and (5) the type of activity (walking or jogging) during the recovery period after each training run. Interval-running involves repeatedly running a specific distance at a pre-determined speed, resting a specific period of time following each fast run. A workout of 10 repetitions of 440 yards in 65 seconds each, jogging 440 yards in 2½ minutes after each for recovery, would be an example of interval-running. Different individuals attach different nomenclature to the work phase (fast run) and the rest phase (slow run or walk) in interval-training, but this is of little significance. Some refer to the repetitions of fast running as the interval, while others refer to the recovery period as the interval. Interval-training is usually done on the track, with the fast repetitions of the training runs timed with a stop-watch. This need not necessarily be the case, as interval-training might well be done off the track over unmarked surfaces without benefit of stop watch timing.

Repetition-running is a refinement in interval-training which has been described by Franz Stampfl as running a given distance at a pre-determined speed a specified number of times with complete rest after each such fast run. In actual practice repetition-running differs from interval-running in terms of the length of the run, and the degree of recovery after each fast run. Repetition-running is concerned with running comparatively longer distances (such as 880 yards to 1¼ miles) with relatively complete recovery (often by walking) after each. Interval-running involves running relatively short distances (110 to 440 yards) at fast pace (near racing speed or faster) with a recovery something less than complete after each. The recovery in interval-running usually involves jogging a distance equal to the fast run in a speed 2 to 3 times as long as required to complete the fast run. Repet-ition-running is more exhausting than interval-running, and continues to become more so as the fast runs approach the final racing distance. For this reason, repetition-running over longer distances should be at considerably less than racing speed. When repetition-running reaches racing speed, the length of the fast runs should not exceed more than half of the actual racing distance.

Weight-training means lifting weights to develop physical strength. Strength is gained by giving muscles more work to perform than they are normally required to do. The harder muscles are worked, the greater the power they develop. It was once generally believed that athletes in endurance events such as running should lift light weights, using a high number of repet-itions. Current opinion indicates runners gain more benefit from weight-training by lifting heavy weights, as it produces greater strength. Essential features of weight-training are: (1) use of heavy weights and (by necessity) few repetitions, (2) using a near maximum number of repetitions of which the athlete is capable at the moment, and (3) as the strength of the athlete increases, the weight to be lifted must also be increased.

In lifting there are two types of muscular contraction, "isotonic" and "isometric." In an isotonic contraction, the muscle contracts so that the two ends approach one another, the muscle works concentrically, and shortens and thickens. If a weight in the hand is lifted toward the shoulders by bending the elbow, the muscles which flex the forearm are working isotonically to move a constant weight. If the weight is lowered through the same path, with the same muscles "paying out" against the force of gravity, the muscles are working eccentrically, the ends are being drawn apart, and the muscles become longer and less bulky. If the forearm supports the weight parallel to the ground with the elbow bent at a 90 degree angle, the muscles are under tension although there is no movement, and the muscles are working isometrically or statically. If the muscles are made to work against an external force greater than themselves, which straighten the arm, they perform a negative contraction. Simply stated, an isotonic contraction is one which causes an object to be moved, while an isometric contraction is one against an object which cannot be moved. Semi-isotonic exercises are lifts where weight is kept in certain positions for a limited time before the lift is continued. In semi-isometric exercises the weight is lifted to a certain height where its movement is stopped by an immovable object (such as bars or pegs) and the lifter continues by applying isometric pressure.

Circuit training consists of performing a number of exercises, usually 6 to 8, which require the use of all the major muscle groups of the body. The athlete proceeds from exercise to exercise, performing a predetermined number of repetitions of each. He goes round this circuit three times, requiring about 15 minutes. As he becomes stronger, he increases both the number of repetitions and the quality of each exercise. However, the number of circuits remains at three. Circuit training, which is a form of strength training, should be done at the end of a normal workout. This type of training isusually done indoors, as it enables large numbers of athletes to train simultaneously thus encouraging efficient utilization of facilities. A circuit might consist of: (1) stepping on and off a bench about 20 inches high, (2) squats with weights held in the hands, (3) jumping off and on a bench with weights held in each hand, (4) sit-ups with weight held behind the neck, (5) push-ups, (6) chinning a bar, and (7) dips on parallel bars.

Over-distance is a term used in running training which means running continuously for a distance beyond the athlete's racing distance. For example, over-distance for the miler might be 1¼, 1½, 2 or 3 miles, or farther.

Under-distance is a term used in running training which means running less than racing distance. For example, under-distance for the miler would be anything less than one mile (110, 220, 440, 880, or 1320 yards).

Contact refers to effective striking distance or the relative distance between runners during competitve racing. If one runner is close enough to another to catch and pass him, he is in contact. If the distance that separates them is so great that it precludes the probability of the runner behind catching and passing the runner in front, then contact has been broken.

Physics is the science that deals with matter and energy that do not involve change in composition or with action of different forms of energy on matter. Mechanics is the branch of physics which deals with the interrelations of force, matter, and motion. Since human motion obeys the laws of all motion, body mechanics or biomechanics is the application of physical laws to the human body at rest or in motion. Energy is the ability or capacity to do work, or that which puts force into operation to produce motion, which in turn produces work. Kinetic energy is the energy of motion or the energy of an object by virtue of its motion. Potential energy is the energy of position or the energy of an object by virtue of its position. Inertia is a body's resistance to change in movement. Mass is the amount of material of which an object is made. The mass of an object is a measure of its inertia, or its resistance to change of motion. When mass is acted upon by gravity, it is possible to measure the force it exerts toward the center of the earth, which is its weight. Force is push or pull, or the effect of one body on another. Force varies directly with the square of the velocity. Acceleration is the rate of change of velocity. Force equals mass times acceleration. Momentum is mass times velocity and is the measure of the quantity of motion possessed by a body. Center of gravity refers to the point where gravity acts, or a center of mass or weight from which the body could be suspended in perfect balance in any position. In an erect position, with arms to sides, a man's center of gravity will average 57% of his height. This point is about 1 inch below the navel, roughly midway between belly and the back. A woman's center of gravity in the same position is roughly 55% of her height.

Velocity is the rate of change of position in a given direction. Having magnitude and direction, velocity is a vector quantity, and the term should be used when referring to motion which is in a linear or in a curved direction.

Speed is the term used in referring to irregular motion. If a runner is negotiating a winding cross-country course at a constant speed of one mile each five minutes, his velocity in any one direction is continually changing due to the constant change of direction.

Physical endurance or stamina is the ability of muscles to continue working at high efficiency over a prolonged period. This is the property usually associated with the slender muscles of the long-distance runner or the worker with spare build who performs the same light task hundreds of times daily without fatigue. Physiologically, the general physical endurance of an athlete is an expression of circulatory and respiratory efficiency in both the central mechanism and in the muscles locally, and it results from the ability to elminate waste products with sufficient rapidity to prevent the onset of fatigue. This quality is also known as circulatory-respiratory endurance, the ability to sustain exercise of medium intensity involving the whole body which demands compensatory adjustments in the circulatory and respiratory systems. Stamina, physical endurance, or circulatory-respiratory endurance depends mainly upon training the capillary beds in the muscles and lungs, and conditioning the heart and blood vessels so that a larger circulatory-respiratory function will develop.

Strength is the athlete's capacity to exert muscular force against resistance, involving these mechanical and physiological factors which determine force in any particular movement: (a) size and number of muscles activated, (b) number of muscle fibers involved, (c) muscle groups co-ordination, (d) muscle condition, and (e) lever action involved.

Muscular endurance is local endurance representing the capacity for continuous performance of relatively heavy localized activity such as sawing wood or working a pump-handle. Only small demands may be made on respiration and circulation before local exhaustion begins. Among the qualities upon which muscular endurance depends are (to a large extent) strength, muscle tissue viscosity, and efficiency of blood supply in the muscles used.

Work in athletics implies the overcoming of resistance. In the scientific sense, a force (push or pull) must move an object through some distance. Therefore, Work = Force x Distance. Dill defined moderate work as that amount of activity which uses energy at a rate of three times or less that of the basal metabolic rate (basal metabolic rate is the energy expenditure at complete rest). In hard work the energy used ranges between three and eight times the basal metabolic rate. An average metabolic rate of about eight times the basal rate is as much as can be maintained for eight hours. In moderate and hard work, only minor blood changes occur, lactic acid concentration and alkaline reserve are apparently unchanged, and the heart rate, respiratory volume, and circulation rate remain in linear relationship with the metabolic rate, thus a "steady state" is maintained. In maximal work, wherein energy above eight times basal metabolic rate is expended, the performer enters the "over load" zone in which a steady state can not be maintained, and breakdown (necessitating reduction of work and recovery) is not far away.

Power means rate of work or horsepower. Power = force x velocity. One horsepower = 33,000 foot pounds per minute or 550 foot pounds per second. Power is apparent in the ability of an athlete to propel his body through space. Power development demands fast, explosive movements against resistance, usually involving the entire body to maximum effect. A top-class sprinter may develop 14 horsepower in a hundred yards dash. The athlete's efficiency in running is affected by his capacity to develop power.

The overload principle states that increases in muscular hypertrophy, strength, and endurance result from an increase in intensity of work performed in a given unit of time. The work may be intensified by raising the cadence (as in running faster) or by increasing the resistance against which the muscles contract (as in lifting heavier weights). Whether the exercise is isotonic or isometric does not appear to be of significance. The overload principle provides the rational for all progressive resistance exercise programs. The essence of progressive resistance exercise is that the total work done by muscles in a given time in regular exercise periods must be increased progressively. Progressive resistance exercise (progressive loading) may be achieved either by increasing the resistance which the muscles are required to overcome, or increasing the number of repetitions against the same resistance in a work interval of equal duration.

The "aktivitatshypertrophie" theory was formulated by Roux in 1905. His student, Lange, in 1917 postualted that only when a muscle was required to perform work of an intensity beyond the usual, would it respond with growth. This was the first clear enunciation of what has become the most basic principle in exercise physiology, the overload theory. The first experimental demonstration in support of this theory was presented by Petow and Siebert in 1925 when they showed that hypertrophy followed only when work of greater intensity than usual was required of a muscle. An increase in the duration of work without an increase in intensity was without effect.

Flexibility and suppleness refer to the range and ease of movement which may be produced in the articular joints (joints so formed as to permit motion between the parts) of the body.

Second wind is a phenomenon of concern to the beginner and the novice, but seldom experienced by the well-trained or veteran runner. A feeling of breathlessness is sometimes experienced just after the start of a race, which is associated with a feeling of distress. If the running is continued, this distress disappears and may be replaced by a sense of relief. When this change occurs one has experienced the so-called "second wind." The physiological basis of second wind is not entirely clear, and it may not be entirely a respiratory adjustment. The second wind may involve both physiological and psychological adjustments to the stress of suddent exertion. It apparently comes more easily and quickly when the body is warm. Since well-trained runners seldom experience the second-wind, it appears that the adjustments associated with this phenomenon are brought about during the warmup and prior to the start of intense running in the case of these athletes.

Stress means any condition, generally environmental, which places an unusual burden upon the organism. Stress may be any painful, infectious, adverse, or deleterious force or various abnormal state that tends to disturb the body's normal physiologic equilibrium (homeostasis).

Conditioned reflex or response is a response to stimulus originally inadequate to elicit it. The conditioned reflex, trained reflex, or behavior reflex is one that is gradually developed in the body by training and association through the frequent repetition of a definite stimulus.

Hypertrophy means increase in size of individual muscle fibers and the muscle as a whole caused by repeated use, which, in turn, increases the strength of the muscle. Only when a muscle is overloaded does it respond by undergoing hypertrophy.

Coordination is the functioning of groups of muscles in proper interrelationships and sequences. It is the harmonious working together of muscles or groups of muscles in a complex action or series of complicated movements. Skeletal muscles are found in groups with specific functions to carry out such as flexion and extension, external and internal rotation, abduction and adduction. For example, in bending the elbow several muscle groups are involved. The agonists or prime movers give power for flexion. The antagonists contribute to smooth movements by maintaining tone yet relaxing and giving way to movement of the flexor group. Other groups of muscles hold the arm and shoulder in a suitable position for action and are called fixation muscles. The synergists are muscles which assist the prime movers (agonists) and reduce unwanted or unnecessary movement. Activity of these opposing muscle groups is coordinated in relation to the degree of tension exerted.

Fatigue is a condition in which the performance of a certain amount of work meets with increased difficulties and is carried out with a decreasing effect. There is a subjective feeling of locomotor inhibition which eventually leads to complete muscular impotence. With the onset of fatigue, greater and greater will power is required to perform a specific task, and the precision of the locomotor act gradually decreases. All systems of the body fall victim to fatigue, not merely the locomotor function alone. Biochemically, fatigue means the accumulation of lactic acid in the muscles which has reached the point of seriously impeding muscular contractility. Lactic acid removal from the muscle by the blood stream is inadequate. Thus it is obvious increased or accelerated circulation retards fatigue. The accumulation of lactic acid in the muscle may reach a level of 10-15 times the normal resting value. Moderate exercise gradually increases the level of lactic acid in the blood, which is met by an appropriate increase of oxygen intake during and after exercise. In violent exercise the accumulation of lactic acid is much more rapid, and thus the circulation becomes more inadequate to carry off the surplus lactic acid, regardless of increased oxygen intake by rapid respiration. Complete fatigue is the state in which a muscle has lost its power to contract. Incomplete fatigue is a state of lessened irritability and contractility. Complete muscle fatigue seldom occurs in the human body, but can be induced in an excised muscle. By common usage, fatigue signifies a sensation of tiredness or a psychic state. From a theoretical viewpoint, either or both of two causes may produce acute muscle fatigue. One cause is exhaustion of the ATP supply. The other is accumulation of waste or "fatigue substances" such as lactic acid, this being the more important factor in the human body since the available energy materials are rarely depleted. Fatigue substances accumulate in muscles whenever circulation and respiration prove inadequate for their removal. Recovery from fatigue involves simply rest, relaxation, and the reestablishment of mormal blood circulation in the muscle. From a practical viewpoint, increasing fatigue is accompanied by increased pain, agony, distress, torture and suffering. Fatigue, the athlete's constant training and racing companion and ever-present obstacle to competitive success, is not without its psychological effect, as to feel fatigued does not necessarily mean fatigue has set in to the extent of necessitating slowing the pace or stopping. Through training the runner constantly seeks to develop a physical and mental tolerance, callousness, and contempt toward fatigue which will enable him to persevere and drive himself on at increased effort, even in the face of excruciating agony resulting from fatigue.

Tension means putting something on the stretch. Muscle tension is the normal conditon of muscles that are in a state of moderate contraction which gives them tone. Emotional tension refers to anxiety, fearfulness, apprehension, fright, excessive concern, worry, and/or frustration.

Relaxation is the return of muscles and ligaments to their normal level of tonus after a period of contraction. By popular athletic usage, relaxation implies reduction, lessening, or slackening of either muscular or nervous tension or both.

Rest means repose after exertion or ease after work or effort. It implies freedom from anything that tires, troubles, disturbs, or pains.

Recovery in an athletic sense implies restitution, restoration, or return to a relatively normal resting state following exercise, as in returning to a normal rate of respiration by resting after intense physical effort.

Sleep is a physiologic state of relative unconsciousness and inaction of the voluntary muscles, the need for which recurs periodically. It is a period of regeneration of the higher nervous system and of muscular tissue, the nutritive and metabolic processes continuing. Sleep is a state of natural unconsciousness of surroundings, during which the human mechanism rests, recovers, and renews itself.

Physical fitness is the development of the body to a state or condition which permits the performance of a given amount of physical work, when desired, with a minimum of physical effort. The efficiency of physical effort depends upon the mutual development of the muscular, respiratory, and circulatory systems integrated and coordinated by the activity of the central nervous system.

The cell is the smallest unit of life. When a large number of similar cells are found together they are known as a tissue. A group of tissues working together to do a special task forms a mass known as an organ (such as the heart or brain). A group of organs working together to do a complicated job for sustaining life in the body is called a system. Thus cells form tissues, tissures form organs, organs form systems, and systems form the human body. In general, it is possible to group the organs of the human body into nine major systems: (1) The skeletal system, which includes the 206 bones of the body and the connective tissues that hold them together. (2) The muscle system, comprised of about 620 muscles which move the arms, legs, feet, hands, fingers, head, and trunk of the body in addition to pushing food through the body and circulating blood through the heart. (3) The nervous system. (4) The digestive system, which breaks up food so it may be absorbed to supply energy for life itself. (5) The respiratory system, which inhales air into the body from which it extracts oxygen, and extracts carbon dioxide to be exhaled from the body. (6) The circulatory system. (7) The lymphatic system, consisting of lymph fluid, lymph vessels, and lymph glands. (8) The endocrine system, producing hormones from the endocrine glands which circulate through the body via blood vessels and act as messengers to the different systems, regulating their activities to satisfy the body's needs from moment to moment. (9) The reproductive system.

The respiratory system consists of the nose, pharynx, larynx, trachea, bronchi, and lungs. This system introduces oxygen from the air into contact with hemoglobin of red blood cells and removes carbon dioxide and water.

The digestive system consists of the alimentary canal and the accessory glands such as salivary glands, the pancreas, and the liver. The main functions of the digestive system are to receive, digest, and absorb food, and elminate some wastes.

There are six kinds of **chemical compounds** regarded as foods: (1) proteins, (2) carbohydrates, (3) fats, (4) vitamins, (5) minerals (inorganic salts), and (6) water. The body uses these foods in the following ways: (a) they are burned as fuel to supply heat and energy, (b) body tissues are built from them (repair or growth), (c) new compounds are built, such as hormones and other secretions, and (d) they are used to maintain an internal environment favorable to normal cell activity. The oxidation or burning of absorbed foods is called catabolism, while the building of body tissues is called anabolism. Catabolism changes foods into simpler compounds, while anabolism utilizes foods to form more complex compounds such as tissue proteins and glandular secretions.

The three major foodstuffs or nutrient compounds of the body are porteins, carbohydrates, and fats.

Proteins are formed of sulfur (S), phosphorus (P), Carbon (C), oxygen (O), hydrogen (H), and nitrogen (N). Proteins are built into simple compounds called amino acids and used for growth and repair of protoplasm.

Carbohydrates are formed of carbon, hydrogen, and oxygen, and release energy quickly. Common examples of carbohydrates are (a) starches ($C_6H_{10}O_5$), (b) sugars, including simple-glucose, fructose, and galactose ($C_6H_{12}O_6$); double-sucrose, lactose, and maltose ($C_{12}H_{22}O_{11}$), and (c) cellulose, found in cell walls.

Fats are composed of carbon, hydrogen, and oxygen. Energy is released when fats are burned with oxygen or oxidized.

Nutrient elements of the body are: (1) Iron (Fe), which is part of hemoglobin in red blood cells, and is found in liver and vegetables, (2) Magnesium (Mg), part of chlorophyll in green plants, (3) Calcium (Ca), which builds bones and teeth, and is found in milk, vegetables, and meat, (4) Iodine (I), which is a part of thyroxin secreted by the thyroid gland and is found in sea food and iodized salt, (5) Trace elements, which are needed in only minute quantities and consist of copper (Cu), zinc (Zn), cobalt (Co), and fluorine (F) which reduces tooth decay. These minerals in addition to Sodium, Potassium, and Phosphorus are considered important to the nutrition and function of the human body. Those most likely to be deficient in the American diet are calcium, iron, and iodine.

For distance events, a **diet** of 100 grams of protein, 700 grams of carbohydrate, and 150 grams of fat has been recommended, in addition to adequate vitamins and minerals daily. A daily diet for speed events has been recommended consisting of 210 grams of protein (mostly meat), 350 to 400 grams of carbohydrate, and 100 to 130 grams of fat. These figures represent the order of magnitude only.

The excretory system consists of the urinary organs (kidneys, ureters, bladder, urethra), the respiratory system, the digestive system, and the skin. The main function of the excretory system is elimination of waste products that result from cell activity.

The calorie is the commonly used term to express food values, and is defined as the amount of heat required to raise the temperature of one kilogram of water (about one quart) one degree Centigrade. One gram of ingested protein or carbohydrates yields on the average 4.1 calories of heat. One gram of fat produces about 9.3 Calories of heat.

The daily Calorie requiresments for adults range from 2000 (resting) and 3,000 (light work) to 4,000 (heavy work). A study of 28 athletes at the 1948 Olympic Games revealed a caloric intake ranging from 2,113 to 4,739 daily, with an average of 3,350 daily.

Vitamins are organic chemical substances essential to normal metabolic functioning of humans. Only very small amounts are needed, but lack of necessary vitamins results in a vitamin-deficiency disease (avitaminosis) such as scurvy, beriberi, rickets, and pellagra. When different vitamins were discovered they were named by letters of the alphabet. So many have now been discovered it is more practical to give them chemical names. Some of the vitamins necessary for good health are: A (carotene), B_1 (thiamin), B_2 (riboflavin), B_6 (pyridoxin), C (ascorbic acid), D (calciferol), E (alpha tocopherol), and K (naptha-quinone).

The nervous system. Each kind of tissue is made up of its own paticular kind of cells. Nerve tissue is made up of nerve cells. A man is born with all the nerve cells he will ever have. If a nerve cell is damaged, the nerve will not (like bone, muscle, or skin) produce a new cell to take its place. This does not mean that once a nerve has been cut it is forever destroyed. Repair of a divided nerve may take place by the nerve fibers which still retain connection with their cells growing until they reach their original destination. Each nerve cell is composed of a cell body from which stem branches, or fibers. On one side are a number of short, twiglike branches called dendrites. On the other side is a long branch know as the axon. The nerves connect all the parts of the body with the brain or with the spinal cord. The outer endings of the nerves are equipped with sensitive receptors which pick up impulses and send them to the main part of the nerve cell to be transmitted to the brain. The brain receives and indentifies the information. If action is necessary, the brain decides what action to take, and then sends out messages over the nerve to the muscles to carry it out. Nerves that carry messages from sense organs or skin to the brain are sensory or afferent nerves. Those which carry messages from the brain to muscles or glands are called motor or efferent nerves. The body can move because of the manner in which bones are joined. Muscles move the bones. Nerves carry the messages which tell the muscles when, where, and how to move. The bundle or nerves in the backbone makes up the spinal cord. Sometimes messages transmitted by the sensory (afferent) nerves are so simple they need not go all the way to the brain for a decision. Such messages merely travel via the sensory nerves to the spinal cord, where a connector nerve picks up the message and transmits it to a motor nerve which in turn causes a muscle or muscles to contract accordingly. Such a movement is called a reflex action, and the connector nerve is known as an associative neuron. In addition to the activities of the nerves described above, and to reflexes, there is a special nervous system to handle activities in the body which take place automatically, such as the muscular action involved in breathing and digestion. The nerves that work automatically are different from the other nerves, since the muscles they control are mostly the smooth, or involuntary muscles. Messages are sent from one nerve to another by electrical means.

The central nervous system consists of the brain, the spinal cord, and their interconnections. It can be regarded as the central office, with numerous switchboards, of the body's communications system, which directs, coordinates, and controls the activities of the rest of the body. Whatever we consciously feel to do is the concern of the central nervous system. Also resident here are our unconscious thoughts, feelings, and conflicts. The body functions such as breathing and digesting food, by which we live but which are rarely aware of and do not consciously direct, are also controlled by the central nervous system. These automatic functions are directed by the autonomic nervous system.

The peripheral nervous system operates at the outside end, or periphery of the total nervous system, and connects with the central nervous system, bringing sensations to the central nervous system and taking orders from it. The peripheral nervous system consists of 12 pairs of cranial nerves, such as auditory (hearing), optic (sight), olfactory (smell), etc., and 31 pairs of spinal nerves which conduct the sensory impulse and the motor impulse. At the far, or outside end of the nerve trunks are end plates or end organs, capable of picking up stimuli (heat, cold, pressure, sound, etc.) and of delivering orders for action to the glands, muscles, and other cells to which they are attached. The end organs that pick up sensations or stimuli are called receptors, and those that deliver orders are known as effectors.

The autonomic nervous system is a part of the central nervous system. Its key units include a series of ganglia strung along the spinal column outside its bony structure. The autonomic nervous system has several names. It is also called the vegetative nervous system because it controls man's most elementary functions. Since it responds to the stress of feelings and emotions, one part of it is designated as the sympathetic nervous system, and another part (usually antagonistic) the parasympathetic nervous system. The autonomic nervous system innervates all smooth muscle tissue in the body, the heart, and the glands. Both sympathetic and parasympathetic fibers go to most of these organs. The sympathetic nervous system speeds up the heart beat and slows digestion, while the parasympathetic nervous system slows heartbeat and speeds digestion. Most of the innumerable reflex acts by which the body functions are controlled by the autonomic nervous system, at the level of the spinal cord and the ganglia outside it. They do not come to the conscious attention of the brain, although the brain may not be completely unaware of what is going on. It is the intensity of stimulus that normally determines if a particular event rises to the level of consciousness.

The human heart is a four-chambered muscular organ, shaped and sized somewhat like a man's clenched fist, located behind the breast bone, just above the diaphram, with its apex pointed to the left. It is enclosed in a double-walled sac, called the pericardium. A central partition divides the heart into a right and left half, but no blood can pass directly through this partition from one side to the other. Each side of the heart has two chambers, the auricle above and ventricle below, with a connecting passage and valve in between. Thus the human heart is a living, four-chambered pump that circulates blood throughout the body, by means of its strong rhythmic beat. Each heartbeat starts with a contraction of both auricles and ends with a contraction of both ventricles. The auricles or atria are thin walled, not very muscular chambers which receive blood from the viens. The ventricles are thick-walled, muscular chambers which send blood out to the arteries. The right ventricle pumps blood to the lungs and through the pulmonary circulation. The left ventricle, which is the largest and most muscular chamber, pumps blood to the body through the systemic circulation. Valves regulate a one-way flow of the blood. Systole is the pulling together or contracting of the muscles of the heart chamber. Diastole is the opening or relaxing of the muscles of a heart chamber. Blood pressure is the forcing of blood against the artery walls, and is measured with a sphygmomanometer at the brachial artery just above the elbow. The reading is normally 120/80 or 120 for systole and 80 for diastole.

The normal resting **heart beats** 72 times per minute, which adds up to about 100,000 times a day, or 40 million times per year. Although heart rates over 300 beats per minute have been reported in healthy men during exercise, it is well known that training reduces both the resting heart rate, and the heart rate during exercise. This is due in part to an increase in stroke volume of the heart resulting from training. (Stroke volume is the volume of blood ejected by each ventricle of the heart during a single systole.) It is not unusual for a well trained athlete to have a resting heart rate well below 50 beats per minute.

Stroke volume (systolic discharge) is the volume of blood pumped into the aorta by each contraction of the left ventricle of the heart. The stronger the heartbeat, the larger the systolic discharge or stroke volume, and vice versa.

Morning pulse rate (or basal pulse rate) is a simple test used by athletes as an indication of physical condition. It involves merely counting the pulse rate each morning before getting out of bed, and prior to any exercise whatever. Count the pulse rate before rising for a full minute with a watch or clock having a second hand. Record this figure daily in the training diary. Soon a pattern will be established which will vary only slightly from day to day. However, a rise of about 10 beats or more per minute from the established pattern for no explainable reason may indicate the athlete is off-color physically to some degree, and consideration may well be given to easing the training.

The Sino-atrial (auricular) node (Sinus node) (S-A Node) is the "pace-maker" of the heart; the specialized tissue from which arise the electrical impulses that initiate contractions of the heart.

Cardiovascular system. Cardio refers to the heart, and vascular refers to the blood vessels. Cardiovascular therefore refers to the heart and the blood vessels associated with the heart.

Blood is the fluid that circulates through the heart, arteries, capillaries, and veins, carrying nutriment and oxygen to the body tissues. Blood in the arteries is bright red in color; blood in the veins is much darker, sometimes a brownish red. The adult human body contains 5 to 6 quarts of blood, weighing about 7 to 8 pounds, and accounting for about 5% of the body weight. Blood transfers oxygen and carbon dioxide between the lungs and the body cells, carries from the digestive system the food that cells need and gets rid of their waste products via the organs of excretion, conveys hormones, helps regular body temperature, and fights off infection. Blood consists of a pale yellow liquid, the plasma, containing the microscopically visible formed elements; the erythrocytes, or red blood corpuscles; the leukocytes, or white blood corpuscles; and the thrombocytes, or blood platelets.

Hemoglobin (symbol Hb) is the red respiratory protein of erythrocytes (red cells) in blood. It consists of about 6% heme (heme is an iron compound of protoporphyrin) and 94% globin (globin is a protein). Hb in the red cells of the blood transports oxygen from the lungs to the tissues, and this oxygenated form of Hb is known as oxyhemoglobin. The oxygen is readily released in the tissues, where Hb becomes reduced hemoglobin. Reduced hemoglobin combines with the carbon dioxide in the tissues resulting from cell respiration, and hemoglobin carbamate is thus formed. Hemoglobin carbamate (a compound of Hb and CO_2) is the principal form in which carbon dioxide from the tissues is transported in the blood to the lungs. In the lungs carbon dioxide is released and exhaled. The Hb then combines with oxygen in the lungs, forming oxyhemoglobin, and the cycle continues. Authorities differ slightly in what is regarded as the "normal" Hb content of blood. In adults 100 cubic centimeters of normal blood contain on the average between 11.5 grams and 19 grams of Hb. In adult males the average is 14 to 18 grams of Hb per 100 cc of blood, while in adult females 100 cc of normal blood may contain 11.5 to 16 grams of Hb.

Blood sugar refers to the glucose (monosaccharide or simple sugar) which is dissolved in the plasma of the blood and delivered to the cells in the body to supply them with energy. It is one of the most important foods. The blood sugar level normally varies from 80 to 100 milligrams per 100 cubic centimeters of blood.

Glucose is a simple sugar having the formula $C_6H_{12}O_6$; the form in which carbohydrate is transported in the blood and metabolyzed in the tissues. Glycogen is the form in which carbohydrate is stored in the body; a complex animal starch molecule built up of large numbers of glucose molecules. Glycogenesis is the formation of glycogen from simple sugar or lactic acid. Glycolysis is the anaerobic breakdown of glucose to lactic acid.

The circulatory system or vascular system consists of the heart, the blood vessels and blood, and the lymphatic vessels and lympth. The circulatory system transports various substances to and from the body cells, protects the body against invading microorganisms, and helps regulate the heat of the body. Since the body is composed of billions of cells living together as a unified community, each cell cannot secure its own food, dispose of its own wastes, etc., and must therefore have their foot and oxygen brought to them and their wastes collected. The system which provides this all-important transportation function is the circulatory system. Actually, two system are involved in the circulatory system, a greater and a lesser. The greater system is the circulation throughout the entire body (systemic circulation). The lesser system is the circulation through the lungs (pulmonary circulation). Blood is pumped by the heart through an elastic system of blood vessels. The blood vessels form a continuous closed system made up of three main divisions. The arterial system carries the blood via the arteries from the heart to a vast network of minute vessels, the capillaries. Oxygen, nutrient, and other materials pass through the thin walled capillary system into the tissue fluid or lympth which bathes every cell of the body. From the tissue fluid these substances pass into the cells. Some of the fluid portion of the blood, the plasma (which has the same composition as lympth), passes through the capillary walls to form tissue fluids. Excess tissue fluids (lumph) is returned to the blood stream through a system of lymphatic vessels. From the capillaries the blood is collected and returned to the heart in the veins (venous system).

Vasomotor System. The arterioles and venules are composed chiefly of involuntary muscular fibers that constricts when excited. The muscle fibers are arranged in a circular pattern and when innervated either contract to halt the blood flow into the capillary bed or relax and allow to blood to flow through into the capillaries. The musculature of these vessels are supplies with nerve fibers that are either excitatory and contract the muscle fibers or are inhibitory and relax the muscle fibers.

Those which cause contraction are called vasoconstrictors; those which inhabit or cause the muscles to relax are called vasodilators. Both groups are collectively called the vasomotor system.

The lymphatic system consists of lymphatic capillaries, the lymphatic vessels, the lymph nodes or glands, and lymph. Lymph is the fluid, outside the blood vessels, in which the cells and tissues of the body are constantly bathed. It is much like the fluid part of the blood (blood plasma), except that it is the part that has oozed through thin walls of the smallest blood vessels. In the lymph are dissolved proteins, fats, sugar, and other substances brought by the blood stream, which the cells need for their life processes. Also in the lymph are the waste products given off by the cells, such as urea, uric acid, and large numbers of white blood cells called lymphocytes. In exchanges which take place between tissues and blood stream all the products of exchange must pass through the tissue fluid (lymph) which bathes the cells. A continuous interchange of fluid occurs between the tissues and the blood stream, some fluid leaving the blood at the arteriolar end of the capillary and fluid returning to the blood at the venous end of the capillary. The lymphatic vessels return some of the tissue fluid or lymph to the general circulation. The lymphatic capillaries are thin-walled tubes which, like blood capillaries, are composed of a single layer of cells. Lymphatic capillaries differ from blood capillaries in that they end blindly and their caliber is slightly greater than that of the blood capillaries. Lymph flows from lymph capillaries in all parts of the body into the lymphatic vessels. These lymphatic vessels are like veins in structure but the walls are thinner and valves are more numerous. They join together into larger and larger lymphatic vessels, which eventually lead into a large vessel, called the thoracic duct. This duct empties into one of the large veins near the heart. At intervals along the lymph channels are situated oval masses of lymphoid tissue called lymph nodes or lymph glands. The large ones, called lymph glands, are found in the neck, groin, and armpits. The lymph nodes and glands are masses of lymphoid tissue whose function is to produce lymphocytes (white blood cells) and act as filters to remove impurities and microbes from the lymph stream. The most important function of the lymphatic system is the removal of protein from the tissue spaces. Most of the fluid leaving the arterial capillaries flows among the cells and returns to the venous capillaries. About one tenth of the returning substance is of such large molecular weight, such as the protein, that it cannot enter the venous capillaries. Since there does not seem to be a limiting factor in the porosity of the lymphatic capillaries they offer no resistance to the flow of fluid protein. The only limiting factor to the size of the foreign particle that can be moved by the lymphatic capillary is the size of the lymphatic capillary themselves. Without this essential function we would probably die within 24 hours.

The endocrine system is composed of the glands of internal secretion. Practically all bodily activities are regulated and controlled in part by the endocrine, or ductless glands, so called because their secretions (hormones) do not pass through tubes or ducts but pour out directly into the blood stream. The seven important endocrines are the pituitary, thyroid, parathroids, thymus, adrenals, islet cells of the pancreas, and gonads. The secretions of the endocrine glands are taken up directly by the blood stream in contrast to the exocrine glands which empty their secretions into ducts. The endocrine system and the nervous system share in the control of all the activities of the body tissues. Generally speaking, the nervous system controls the more rapid responses of the body to changes in the outside world or external environment which require immediate response if the organism is to survive. The endocrine system more frequently controls the slower changes or adaptations. of the body to its environment. The adrenals, a pair of endocrine glands shaped something like Brazil nuts, sit astride each kidney. Each adrenal consists of the outer shell or cortex, and the core or medulla. The medulla, which produces adrenalin, or epinephrine, known as the emergency hormone, is connected directly with the automatic nervous system. In times of emotional stress or danger, extra adrenalin is released into the blood stream, where it quickens the heartbeat, increases the energy-yielding sugar in the blood, slows up or stops digestion, directs blood into the large muscles, dilates the pupils of the eye, may cause the hair to stand on end, and generally prepares the body for fight or flight. The adrenal cortex produces different hormones, including cortin and cortisone.

Muscles are the flesh of the body, and make up about 40% of the total body weight. A man is born with all the muscle fibers he will ever have. The function of muscles is to move themselves and other parts of the body. It is in the joints of the body that movement of the bones take place. Muscle tissue has the special ability to shorten itself, causing the bone on which it pulls to move. Muscle tissue covers the body in sheets and bands that lie between the skin and the skeleton. Most muscles extend from one bone to another. When two bones are connected by muscle and one of the bones is held still, if the muscle between them contracts and shortens, the other bone must move. The point where the muscle is fastened to the unmoving bone is known as the origin of the muscle. The point where the muscle is fastened to the bone that is to be moved is called the insertion. Sometimes the muscle is not attached directly to the bone, but to a tough, non-stretchable cord known as a tendon, which is in turn attached to the bone. Muscles do not push; they can only pull. Each muscle is separate, controlled by a special nerve or set of nerves that connect it with the spinal cord and the brain. No muscle acts alone. There is generally the following coordinated set of actions: (1) the signaled muscle contracts; (2) the muscle or muscles opposing it (its antagonist) relaxes; and (3) adjoining muscles spontaneously contract to increase the efficiency of the contracting muscle. There are three types of muscle in the human body: (1) voluntary or striped (striated) muscle, which is the bulk of the skeletal muscle; (2) involuntary or smooth muscle, such as that making up the muscular layers of the intestines, blood vessels, and bladder; and (3) the heart (cardiac) muscle, which is striated but involuntary. Voluntary (striped or striated) muscle is made up of a series of parallel fibers bound together in bundles by a sheath of firm connective tissue. There are many such bundles of fibers in a single muscle. The sheath of firm connective tissue is rich in blood vessels and nerves which must supply the fibers. These muscles fibers have transverse striations or lines which may permit their contractions and elongations. Surrounding each fiber is a sheath, known as the sarcolemma. The sarcolemma is a continuous tube from the termination of one muscle fiber on to the next. This tubular structure (sarcolemma) will facilitate the contraction and relaxation of the fiber within it in the same way as will the connective tissue sheath of the bundles which envelop the muscles. When muscle fibers contract, the chemical events that take place leave certain waste products, especially carbon dioxide and lactic acid. When the amount of exercise or number of contractions a muscle performs exceed a certain limit, the lactic acid cannot be removed as fast as it is formed. This affects the nerve endings of the muscle. Muscular fatigue occurs when lactic acid accumulates in the muscle and spills over into the blood stream.

Homeostatis refers to the state of equilibrium in the living body with respect to various functions and to the chemical composition of the fluids and tissues, e.g., temperature, heart rate, blood pressure, water content, blood sugar, etc. It is also known as the process through which such bodily equilibrium is maintained.

A ligament ia a band or sheet of fibrous tissue connecting two or more bones, carilages, or other structures, or serving as support for fasciae or muscles. Simply stated, ligaments hold bones together.

A tendon is a fibrous cord or band of variable length serving to connect a fusiform muscle with its bony attachment. It may unite with the muscle at its extremity or may run along the side or in the center of the muscle for a longer or shorter distance, receiving the muscular fibers along its lateral border. Tendons (or sinews) are white glistening cords or bands which serve to attach the muscles to the bones.

The all-or-none law provides that if a stimulus is applied to a single muscle fiber which is strong enough to produce a response, the muscle fiber will give a maximal contraction, no matter what the strength of the stimulus. Not only muscle and nerve cells, but all cells are thought to react according to the all-or-none law. It is analogous to the trigger mechanism of a gun, as pulling the trigger either fires the gun or it does not, and pulling the trigger harder does not make the gun fire harder. However, tissues and organs, which are made up of cells, do not follow the all-or-none principle. Tissues and organs react with graded responses to graded stimuli. The answer to this apparent contradiction is explained by the fact that each muscle fiber obeys the all-or-none law but different muscle fibers have different thresholds to which they will respond to stimuli. If a weak stimulus is applied to a muscle, only those muscle fibers with very low thresholds will be activated.

As the strength of stimulus is increased, more fibers are brought into play, a phenomenon known as recruitment. The more fibers that are activated, the greater the whole muscle contraction.

The "staircase" phenomenon or treppe means if a number of stimuli of the same intensity be sent into the muscle after a quiescent period, the first few contractions of the series show a successive increase in amplitude. For example, if a muscle is stimulated at a rate of once or twice per second with constant or equal stimuli, it will respond with increasingly stronger twitch contractions, regardless of the quality of stimuli. But with repeated stimulation a landing or plateau is attained, after which the response to each stimulus is exactly the same. This "staircase" phenomenon indicates previous work in some way makes the muscle better able to do successive work. One explanation for this phenomenon is that chemicals and heat produced during contraction increase the muscle's irritability, although what mechanism is involved is not definitely known.

Adenosin triphosphate (ATP), adenosine diphosphate (ADP), adenosine monophosphate, phosphocreatine, glycogen, creatine, lactic acid, anaerobic (without oxygen) reaction, aerobic (with oxygen) reaction, and myosin are some of the terms used in explaining the **chemistry of muscle contraction.** Even though the chemistry of skeletal muscle contraction and energy exchanges in muscle metabolism are very complex and still not complegely understood, coaches and students of training nevertheless need at least an elementary and superficial familiarity with the processes which enable muscles to move the body through contraction. Although a clear understanding of advanced biochemistry is necessary to comprehend the more technical aspects of this topic, one over-simplified general description is presented here.

Muscle tissue contains glycogen (polysaccharide, a carbohydrate sometimes referred to as animal starch) and phosphates. Muscle tissue requires oxygen to live, and uses oxygen even at complete rest. The amount of oxygen used increases considerably when a muscle contracts. The muscle at rest produces carbon dioxide, the amount formed increasing proportionately as the muscle contracts in performing work.

Certain chemical changes in the constitution of the muscle take place during contraction. The phosphates change form, glycogen concentration diminishes, lactic acid ($C_3H_6O_3$; the end product of the anaerobic metabolism of glucose or glycogen) increases, and the turnover of oxygen and carbon dioxide is elevated.

Adenosine triphosphate (a condensation product of adenine, ribose, and 3 molecules of orthophosphoric acid), phosphocreatine (creatine phosphate, a compound of creatine with phosphoric acid), and glycogen are present in resting muscle. During muscular activity adenosine triphosphate (ATP), is converted to adenosine diphosphate (ADP), and ADP is converted to adenosine monophosphate. As each phosphate bond is lost (ATP to ADP to adenosine monophosphate) a tremendous amount of energy is liberated. This energy so liberated is used by the muscle to contract, serving to perform work. This breakdown of ATP requires no oxygen and is an anaerobic (without oxygen) reaction. Thus it is believed that the breakdown of ATP is the primary chemical reaction of muscular contraction, as this is the reaction which supplies energy. The other chemical reactions of muscular contraction are used to resynthesize (re-combine into a complex whole) the basic ATP.

During contraction the phosphocreatine in the muscle splits, to free creatine and to liberate the high energy phosphate bond, thus again releasing energy. However, this energy is not used directly for muscular contraction, but rather it is believed to be used to resynthesize ATP. This is an anaerobic (without oxygen) reaction.

By a complex chemical process during contraction the glycogen is the muscle is converted into lactic acid, and in this process of conversion energy is also released. This energy liberated by the conversion of glycogen in the muscle to lactic acid is believed used for the resynthesis of phosphocreatine. This is also an anaerobic reaction.

The above reactions may continue without oxygen in muscular contraction to the point where there is no ATP, very little glycogen, and high lactic acid concentration in the blood and muscles. In order for the muscle to recover, a part of the lactic acid must be oxidized (aerobic, with oxygen, reaction). The energy produced by the oxidation of approximately one-fifth of the lactic acid is used to reconvert the other four-fifths of the lactic acid to glycogen.

To reiterate, these are the primary reactions in muscular contraction, each of which produce energy; (a) ATP provides energy for contraction of the muscles, (b) phosphocreatine provides energy for resynthesis of ATP, (c) the conversion of glycogen to lactic acid provides energy for resynthesis of phosphocreatine, and (d) oxygen reacts with one-fifth of the lactic acid to provide energy for the reconversion of the other four-fifths of the lactic acid to glycogen.

So long as the supply of ATP remains adequate, the muscle can contract without oxygen. During severe exercise such as fast running, there is not time to oxidize all of the lactic acid formed. Consequently, lactic acid accumulates in the blood and muscles to the extent that eventually the activity must stop. After activity stops, breathing continues at a high rate, and the lactic acid is thereby oxidized. Thus during the period of rapid breathing after exercise the debt of oxygen accumulated during severe exercise is repaid.

Oxygen debt, therefore, is the amount of oxygen required in the post-exercise recovery period to reverse the anaerobic reactions of the exercise period. The oxygen debt is the difference between the oxygen requirement during exercise and oxygen intake during performance of the exercise. The deficit in oxygen intake during severe exercise represents a debt which is repaid during recovery.

A recent theory of the nature of oxygen debt indicates the rebuilding of ATP, ADP, and phosphate requires oxidative energy. Without adequate oxygen, ADP and phosphate accumulate, stimulating uptake of oxygen by cells. This depletion of ATP and accumulation of ADP and inorganic phosphate is presented as a basis of oxygen debt.

Lactic acid is a vertual poison to muscular economy, as an accumulation of more than a few tenths of one percent results in muscular pain and contraction of the muscles ceases. The accumulation of lactic acid in the blood and muscles is the most common limiting factor of muscular activity, as it is a direct poisoning rather than an interruption of the energy supply.

Lactic acid must eventually be oxidized, but during exercise it may be temporarily dealt with in other ways. There are buffers in the blood which are substances that can neutralize acids. These blood buffers (collectively known as the alkaline reserve) can neutralize great amounts of lactic acid during exercise. During recovery after exercise when sufficient oxygen is available the chmical reactions of buffering may be reversed. Proper training over an extended period of time will greatly increase the amount of blood buffers in the blood available to neutralize the acid effects of lactic acid during exercise, but eh ingestion of alkaline substances in an attempt to build up the alkaline reserve (blood buffers) has been proven impossible.

A well trained athlete may absorb 4 liters of oxygen per minute, and acquire an oxygen debt of about 15 liters. When the maximum oxygen debt is incurred, the activity must cease. In running the oxygen requirement increases as the square or cube of the running speed. Doubling running speed from a level requiring 4 liters of oxygen per minute will increase the oxygen requirement from 4 to 8 times. It has been estimated that a runner must sprint 50 to 55 seconds to accumulate a maximum oxygen debt. The factors setting the absolute maximum limit of oxygen debt have not been definitely established. Correct training is believed to increase the amount of oxygen debt which can be accumulated. This may be due to blood buffer (alkaline reserve) increase available for neutralizing lactic acid, to increase amount of ATP in the muscles, or greater ability to tolerate the pain of fatigue.

Approximately 12% of the total weight of skeletal muscle is myosin. This protein (myosin) is a very long molecule, although even in the resting state it is not completely elongated. When the muscle is relaxed the myosin molecule is partly folded. The myosin molecules during muscular contraction become much more folded. This folding of the myosin molecule is believed directly responsible for the shortening of the muscle during contraction. In the chemical process causing the myosin molecules to become folded, it is believed the ATP transformation plays a prominent role.

Runners usually train by alternately running fast and slow, or in other words following each fast run with a rest pause or recovery interval. The recovery intervals are equally as important as the fast repetitions of running to the training process, since the following are among the chemical changes in the muscles during rest: (a) ATP and phosphocreatine are resynthesized, (b) lactic acid is oxidized or resynthesized, (c) muscle glycogen stores are replenished, (d) liver glycogen stores are replenished, and (e) end products of the neutralizing action by the blood buffers undergo reverse chemical reactions, liberating lactic acid and other acids for oxidation or elimination.

Intense running often produces fatigue in the arms for no apparent reason, whereas it would be expected that the legs should be the site of fatigue. The locally produced lactic acid in the legs may be diffused by the blood into less active parts of the body, thus preventing the excessive build-up of acidity in the legs. This helps explain why fatigue may be felt in the arms when the legs are exercising vigorously.

Metabolism is the term applied to all chemical reactions which take place in living cells. This includes all of the chemical processes by which food is converted into either work or structure. Frequently, however, the term is confined to oxidations which are the ultimate source of biological energy. The energy which the body expends under conditions of complete rest is known as basal metabolism. The basal metabolic rate (B.M.R.) is the amount of heat produced in the waking state when the body is at complete rest, 12 to 18 hours after the last meal, in a comfortably warm environment.

An acid is a chemical substance which, in solution, releases hydrogen ions. Acids taste sour, turn blue litmus paper red, unite with bases to form salts, and in general have chemical properties opposed to those of alkalis. There are many acids present in the human body.

An alkali (or base) is the opposite of an acid, and turns red litmus paper blue. It neutralizes acids and forms salts with them.

Lactic acid is an organic acid having the formula $C_3H_6O_3$. It is the end product of the anaerobic (without oxygen) metabolism of glucose or glycogen. During exercise the contracting muscles produce lactic acid when their supply of oxygen is insufficient to meet the energy requirements. When lactic acid is thus poured into the blood in increased amounts during severe exercise, a dangerous rise in blood acidity is prevented by the action of blood buffers which neutralize the acid. Lactic acid is buffered by blood bicarbonate. Prolonged strenuous exercise may produce so much lactic acid that the bicarbonate buffer in the blood is greatly reduced in amount and blood acidity increases so rapidly that exhaustion may follow soon after.

Pyruvic acid (CH_3-CO-COOH) is an intermediate compound in the metabolism of carbohydrate. Once glucose is inside the cell, enzymes convert glucose to pyruvic acid by the process of glycolysis. At the completion of glycolysis two molecules of pyruvic acid will have been formed and the energy released from this formation will have been used to form three molecules of A.T.P.

The buffer prevents marked changes in the pH of a solution when acid or base (alkali) is added to it. (The term pH is a symbol for the hydrogen ion concentration of a solution, indicating the degree of acidity or alkalinity. An ion is an electrically charged atom or group of atoms.) Although acids continually pour into the blood from cell metabolism, the blood pH remains remarkably constant (slightly alkaline, ranging between pH 7.35 and 7.45), thanks to the action of the blood buffers. Lactic acid is buffered mainly by the bicarbonate buffer in the blood. Respiration and kidney excretion are also buffer devices. Training over an extended period will greatly increase the amount of blood buffers (collectively known as the alkaline reserve), although ingestion of alkaline substances in attempts to increase the alkaline reserve beyond regular physiological capacity has proven fruitless.

All of the body fluids are supplied with an acid base buffering system that prevents any excessive change in H - OH ion concentration. If, as in exercise, the H ion concentration changes measurably, the respiratory centers are stimulated to assist in the removal of the CO_2 which causes the H ion concentration to return toward normal. If the H ion concentration is such that the first mechanisms mentioned cannot properly control the H or OH ion concentration the most powerful of the acid base regulatory mechanism, the kidney, will readjust the hydrogen ion concentration.

The alkaline reserve is the amount of alkali (bases) in the blood available for neutralizing acids. This is primarily sodium bicarbonate.

Acid-base balance is the relative proportions of acid and alkali (H and OH ions) in the blood and tissues. When blood pH is normal (7.35 to 7.45) a state of acid-base balance is said to exist.

Capacity of the lungs. Tidal air designates the amount of air that flows in and out of the lungs with each quiet respiratory movement, the average figure for an adult male being 500 cubic centimeters (cc). Inspiratory reserve volume is the amount of air that can be breathed in over and above the tidal air by the deepest possible inspiration. This is estimated at about 1800 cc. Expiratory reserve volume is the amount of air that can be breathed out after a quiet expiration by the most forcible expiration. This is about 1800 cc. Residual air is the amount of air remaining in the lungs after the most powerful expiration. Estimated on the cadaver, it is about 1200 cc. Reserve air is the residual air plus the supplemental air in the lungs under conditons of normal breathing, approximately 3000 cc. When the thorax is opened, the lungs collapse, driving out the supplemental and residual air; but before the alveoli are entirely emptied, the small bronchi leading to them collapse and entrap a little air in the alveoli. Air trapped in this way is designated as minimal air.

Respiration refers to the gaseous exchange between the organism and its environment. The chemical features involved in this process are the absorption of oxygen and the elimination of carbon dioxide.

Internal respiration is the exchange of the respiratory gases within the internal environment.

All the cells are bathed with fluid and this area is known as the internal environment. Internal respiration is the exchange of respiratory gases between the tissue cells and the internal environment.

External respiration is the exchange of carbon dioxide and oxygen between the blood in the pulmonary capillaries and the air in the lungs.

Respiratory Quotient. The relative amounts of carbon and oxygen that are contained in the molecules of protein, fats and carbohydrates differ; therefore, the relative amounts of oxygen consumed and carbon dioxide produced during the metabolism of each type of food will vary. The ratio between carbon dioxide output to oxygen intake is known as the respiratory quotient or simply R.Q.

Adaptation in a training sense is the advantageous change in function or constitution of tissue, organ, system, or body to meet new conditions. Adaptation energy is the energy required in making the adaptation to meet new conditions.

The General Adaptation Syndrome theory by Dr. Hans Selye postulates that stressing agents, as well as having their own quite specific actions on parts of the organism, invariably have generalized and sterotyped non-specific effects on the body, superimposed upon all the specific effects. Prolonged stress results in certain physiological adjustments and changes by the body in adapting itself to the stressing agent. This adaptation of the body can be divided into three stages: 1. The alarm stage. Sodium and chloride levels in extracellular fluid fall, while potassium rises. Blood glucose falls. 2. Stage of resistance. The body fights back. Blood levels return to normal. More ACTH is released, and the body tries to combat factors causing stress. (ACTH is adrenocorticotrophic hormone, manufactured in the pituitary gland, which stimulates the adrenal gland to release the hormone cortisone.) 3. Stage of exhaustion. If the original stress is not removed, the adrenal gland becomes depleted of cholesterol, there is hemorrhage into the cortex, ACTH fails to be formed. Sodium and chloride and Glucose levels in the blood fall, potassium and phosphate levels rise, and death results from exhaustion.

One factor in the art of coaching lies in recognizing individual differences and applying proper volume and intensity of training with sufficient rest to produce the optimum amount of specific adaptation. Carlile suggests that the General Adaptation Syndrome Theory is of great value to the coach seeking a scientific basis upon which to organize his training observations.

Tetanus (or lockjaw) is an acute, infectious disease. When the germ invades the body, almost invariably through a puncture or laceration, it multiplies and produces a powerful poison (or toxin) that irritates and excites the nerves of the spinal cord. Symptoms may come on from 2 days or a month after infection, but usually within a week. All of them are muscle spasms or contractions, more or less violent, resulting from nerve irritability. Any wound that brings this germ into the body can bring about tetanus, a serious, often fatal disease. The deeper the wound the worse, because tetanus bacilli grow better without oxygen. The risk of getting tetanus today is not great because it is possible to immunize with tentanus toxoid. Tentanus bacillus is most frequently found in soil contaminated with horse, cattle, or human exrement. The bacillus lives and multiplies in the intestines of animals, with whom most people have little contact. Physicians give tetanus toxoid immediately when there is any risk that a wound may be infected with tetanus bacillus, as in the case of a spike wound.

A cramp is a painful spasm of a muscle, usually of the foot, calf, or thigh, due to an incoordinated muscular movement or to the muscle having been exposed to heat or cold. They may also be caused from dietary deficiencies, particularly of calcium, socium, vitamin B_1 and salt.

The "stitch" is a stabbing pain, usually on one side or the other, which may occur in the upper abdomen or sometimes in the lower thorax. It is usually induced by severe effort, although some public speakers have experienced stitch in anticipation of their performance, thus indicating the possibility of psychological origin. Severe pain from "stitch" may limit the athlete's performance and lead to cessation of physical effort. The exact cause of "stitch" is unknown, although the most likely cause is lack of oxygen in the diaphram - in which case relief may be had by bending calisthenics toward the affected side, with hand pressing in the region of the pain. Other possible causes may include severe exercise too soon after eating or drinking liquid, downhill running, gas in the stomach, and constipation.

Heat exhaustion (heat stroke) may occur in running middle and long distances in excessively hot and humid weather. Body temperature is kept within narrow limits (normal is about 98.6 degrees F, or 37 degrees C), fluctuating between 97.3 and 99.1 degrees F. In temperate climates radiation (and convection and conduction to a lesser extent) from the skin accounts for in excess of 60% of heat loss from the surface of the body. The remaining heat loss results from evaporation of perspiration (sweat) from the skin surface and respiratory tract. In hot weather the heat loss through radiation remains about the same. The additional heat must be lost by sweating. If water and salt loss through excessive sweating while running in hot weather are not replaced, dehydration results, sweat secreation stops, and the heat regulating mechanism fails. Severe physiological disturbances then occur, such as temperature rise to 105 degrees F or over, faintness, staggering gait, dizziness, headache, nausea, vomiting, purposeless movements, choking, muscle cramps, confusion, and convulsions. Treatment includes cooling the body with cool baths, ice packs, or rubs, and treatment for shock. Prevention includes ingestion of water during long distance running and acclimatization prior to competition if the athlete is performing where climatic conditions are warmer than those to which he is accustomed. The athlete should spend at least two weeks in the warmer competitive environment to allow acclimatization to take place prior to competition.

Adrenaline (epinephrine) is a hormone secreted by the medulla of the adrenal glands; two small endocrine glands, one located above each kidney. Adrenalin is secreted under conditions of emotional stress, excitement, or circumstances which demand special effort. When secreted into the blood stream under such conditions, adrenalin is responsible for the following "fight or flight" actions: It constricts smooth muscle of the skin, dialates the pupil of the eye to admit more light, constricts smooth muscle of the abdominal blood vessels and cutaneous blood vessels, dialates smooth muscle in blood vessels of the heart (coronaries) and of skeletal muscles, increases heart rate and cardiac output, raises blood pressure, relaxes smooth muscle in the wall of the bronchioles resulting in better supply of air to the alveoli, stimulates respiration, inhibits movements of the digestive tract, contracts sphincters of the gut, inhibits the wall of the urinary bladder, contracts ureters and sphincter of the urinary bladder, mobilizes muscle and liver glycogen and thereby increases blood sugar, stimulates metabolism, exerts a favorable effect on contracting skeletal muscle and thereby delays the onset of fatigue, and increases the coagulability of the blood. Under quiet resting conditions the blood contains very little adrenaline.

Bibliography

Abrahams, Harold, and Crump, Jack, "Athletics." London: The Nadrett Press, 1951.

The Achilles Club, "Modern Athletics." London: Oxford University Press, 1958, edited by H.A. Meyer.

Alford, J. W. Ll., "Middle Distance Running and Steeplechasing." London: Amateur Athletic Association, 1960.

Anthony, Catherine Parker, "Textbook of Anatomy and Physiology." St. Louis: The C. V. Mosby Company, fifth edition, 1959.

Bannister, Roger,"The Four Minute Mile." New York: Dodd, Mead, and Company, 1957.

Chapman, H.A.L., "Track and Field Athletics." London: W. Foulsham and Co., Ltd., 1961.

Diem, Carl, "Olympische Akademie." Frankfurt/M: Nationales Olympisches Komitee fur Deutschland, 1961.

Disley, Joh, "The Young Athlete's Companion." London: Souvenir Press, 1962.

Doherty, J. Kenneth, "Modern Track and Field." Englewood Cliffs: Prentice-Hall, Inc., second edition, 1963.

Duncan, K.S., "The Oxford Pocket Book of Athletic Training." London: Oxford University Press, 1948.

Dyson, Geoffrey H. G., "The Mechanics of Athletics." London: The University of London Press, Ltd., 1962.

Hall, D. M., "Dynamics of Group Action." Danville: The Interstate Printers and Publishers, Inc., 1957.

Johnson, Warren R., "Science and Medicine of Exercise and Sport." New York: Harper and Brothers Publishers, 1960.

Kimber, Diana Clifford, Gray, Carolyn E., Stackpole, Caroline E., and Leavell, Lutie C., "Anatomy and Physiology." New York: The MacMillan Company, fourteenth edition, 1961.

Klafs, Carl E., and Arnheim, Daniel D., "Modern Principles of Athletic Training." St. Louis: The C. V. Mosby Company, 1963.

Laugley, L. L., and Cheraskin, E., "The Physiology of Man." New York: McGraw-Hill Book Company, Inc., second edition, 1958.

LeMasurier, John, "Interval Running Plus Fartlek In Training Distance Runners," "Scholastic Coach," October, 1958, Vol. 38, No. 2, page 40.

Mills, A. R., "Middle-Distance Running." London: Phoenix Sports Books, 1961.

Morehouse, Laurence E., and Miller, Augustus T., "Physiology of Exercise." St. Louis: The C. V. Mosby Company, fourth edition, 1963.

Morehouse, Laurence E., and Rasch, Philip J., "Scientific Basis of Athletic Training." Philadelphia: W. B. Saunders Company, 1958.

Morgan, R.E., and Adamson, G.T., "Circuit Training." London: G. Bell and Sons, Ltd., second edition, 1961.

Natan, Alex, "Sport and Society." London: Bowes and Bowes, 1958.

Rasch, Philip J., and Burke, Roger K., "Kinesiology and Applied Anatomy." Philadelphia: Lea and Febiger, second edition, 1963.

Schneider, Edward C., "Physiology of Muscular Activity." Philadelphia: W. B. Saunders Company, 1940.

Smillie, I.S.,"Injuries of the Knee Joint." Baltimore: The Williams and Watkins Company, 1962.

Stampfl, Franz, "Franz Stampfl on Running." London: Herbert Jenkins, 1955.

Steindler, Arthur, "Kinesiology of the Human Body." Springfield: Charles C. Thomas, 1955.

Thorndike, Augustus, "Athletic Injuries." Philadelphia: Lea and Febiger, fifth edition, 1962.

Tisdall, R.M.N., and Sherie, Fenn, "The Young Athlete." London: Blackie and Son, Ltd., 1934.

Toomsalu, Ruddi, "Race Walking," "Track Technique," March, 1961, No. 3, page 80.

Twomey, J.J., "Christian Philosophy and Physical Education." Twickenham: St. Mary's College, 1958.

Webster, F.A.M., "The Science of Athletics." London: Nicholas Kaye, 1948.

Whitlock, Harold H., "Race Walking." London: Amateur Athletic Association, 1957.

Williams, J. G. P., "Sports Medicine." Baltimore: The Williams and Watkins Company, 1962.

Wilson, Mitchell, "The Human Body." New York: Golden Press, 1959.

Wilt, Fred, "How They Train." Los Altos: Track and Field News, 1959.